EDUCATION ON THE INTERNET

Jill Ellsworth

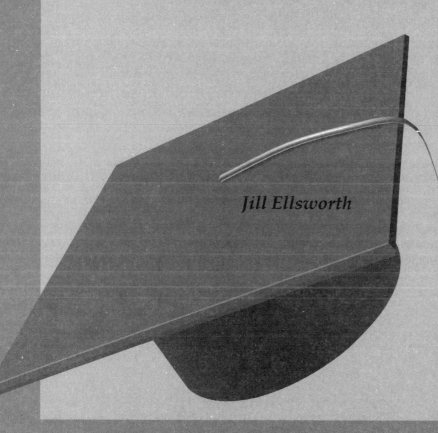

SAMS
PUBLISHING
201 West 103rd Street
Indianapolis, Indiana 46290

This book is for Matt.

Trademarks

Publisher
Richard K. Swadley

Acquisitions Manager
Stacy Hiquet

Managing Editor
Cindy Morrow

Acquisitions Editor
Mark Taber

Development Editor
Mark Taber

Production Editor
Jill D. Bond

Editorial Coordinator
Bill Whitmer

Editorial Assistants
Carol Ackerman
Sharon Cox
Lynette Quinn

Technical Reviewer
Billy Barron
Lay Wah Ooi

Marketing Manager
Gregg Bushyeager

Cover Designer
Tim Amrhein

Book Designer
Alyssa Yesh

**Director of Production
and Manufacturing**
Jeff Valler

Imprint Manager
Juli Cook

Manufacturing Coordinator
Paul Gilchrist

Production Analysts
Angela Bannon
Dennis Clay Hager
Mary Beth Wakefield

**Proofreading/Indexing
Coordinator**
Joelynn Gifford

Graphics Image Specialists
Jason Hand
Clint Lahen
Dennis Sheehan

Production
Katy Bodenmiller
Georgiana Briggs
Elaine Crabtree
Juli Cook
Casey Price
Brian-Kent Proffitt
Kim Scott
Susan Shepherd

Indexer
Chris Cleveland

OVERVIEW

CONTENTS

ACKNOWLEDGMENTS

A book like this never gets done alone. I am grateful for the assistance of many people, among them are the following:

Dave Kinnaman: Dave contributed Chapters 1-3 and Appendix B to this book. He showed grace and wit under stress. Dave is a systems analyst for a large state education agency, and moderates a statewide education newsgroup. His specialty is career and labor market information. You can reach him at kinnaman@world.std.com or kinnaman@tenet.edu. Nicely done, Dave.

Matt Ellsworth: Matt edited every line of every page, showing insight, clarity, and humor. He is a technical writer and Internet expert who can be reached at oakridge@world.std.com. Thanks Matt.

My Students: My students have shown me that teaching also is learning. They have made teaching a joy.

The Internet: I appreciate the thousands who have built the Internet and continue to voluntarily "give back to the Net." It's a wild world out there, and I am glad to be a part of it.

ABOUT THE AUTHOR

Jill H. Ellsworth, Ph.D. (je@world.std.com) is a university professor with research interests in distance education and computer-mediated learning. She is a consultant and frequent speaker concerning the Internet in education and business. As an active participant on the Internet, she is known for creating *Dr. E's Eclectic Compendium of Electronic Resources in Adult and Distance Education*. Additionally she is the author of the *Internet Business Book*, numerous articles and chapters in scholarly journals and books, and is an editor for three electronic journals. Ellsworth is a graduate of Michigan State University and Syracuse University.

INTRODUCTION

And gladly wolde he lerne, and gladly teche.

—Geoffrey Chaucer

The Internet is a huge, amazing, world-wide system of voluntarily interconnected networks with literally millions of documents, resources, databases and a variety of methods for communicating—it has become the best opportunity for improving education since the printing press started putting books in the hands of millions.

This opportunity is just starting to be tapped by educators; this book will show examples of what is currently being done in classrooms, and beyond those, give specific examples of opportunities for education as yet untapped.

The heart of this book, however, is the compilation of hundreds of specific Internet education resources, with descriptions and instructions on how to access each one. These are resources for K-12, undergraduates, graduates, distance learners, and for those learning on their own.

In this book you'll find answers to questions such as the following:

- Where can I find information on (*fill in almost any subject*)?

- How can the Internet be integrated into class projects and assignments?

- What can I do tomorrow with my students?

- How do I get on the Internet?

- How are college faculty and others using the Internet?

The Internet is a new medium, requiring new strategies and new learning. And it is where education increasingly is happening.

Following are some common myths:

- Some feel that the Internet is too hard to learn—it's not. Kids and adults from all corners of the world are using it easily. All it takes is a little time to open the door.

- Some feel that the Internet is too expensive—it isn't. You can get free accounts on some of the community Freenets, and commercial access can be obtained for as little as $5 to $10 a month.

■ Some think of the Internet as a huge BBS or a commercial service, such as CompuServe or AOL—it's not. The Internet is a voluntarily connected group of over 25,000 networks, with over 30,000,000 people currently connected world-wide. Also, the vast majority of the information and resources available on the Internet are free—the information has been offered voluntarily by tens of thousands of individuals and institutions in the Internet spirit of "giving back to the Net."

Current estimates are that the Internet, which has doubled in size in the last 9 months, will have 100 million people online by 1998. The Internet is not going away, its not a passing fad like pet rocks.

The Internet is changing daily, and this means that by the time this book reaches you, many new sites and resources will have been created. Some sites mentioned here will have faded into the sunset, others will have changed addresses or sites. The good news is that the Internet itself provides tools for finding new resources or locating old ones through strangely named search tools such as Veronica, Gopher, Archie, and WebQuery. This book is a launch pad—to reap all the benefits from the Internet you will need to keep up with it as it grows.

An active tradition of the Internet is that each individual will give back time, information and effort to the Net. A friend of mine, Dave Kinnaman (`kinnaman@tenet.edu`), says "information wants to be free," and the denizens of the Net of all ages help to make it so.

It is an exciting time to be in education. The Internet offers new opportunities for students and teachers alike to learn in interesting ways. This book is full of examples of how others are using the Internet in education. For K-12, you will find curriculum ideas and lesson plans; for higher education, you will find curriculum ideas, projects, and term paper ideas.

Who Should Read this Book?

This book is written for anyone interested in using the Internet to improve education—it covers all types of educational opportunities and resources on the Internet. It will be useful to K-12 personnel, college faculty and administrators, students, parents, and lifelong learners.

This book was written on the assumption that you are already a little familiar with the Internet, and have already gained some basic skills. If you have never used the Internet, start this book by going to Appendix A—here you will find a quick course in how to get access to the Internet, and how to use its most important tools. If you are already familiar with the Internet, just jump into Chapter 1 to start learning about incredible Internet resources for educators.

A Quick Look At How This Book Is Organized

The first section of the book covers K-12 education, with information on specific resources and how the Net is currently being used.

■ Chapter 1 discusses why it is important for K-12 people to use the Internet, K-12 projects, Internet classroom methods and lesson plans, practical help for teachers using the Internet, help in decoding the confusing buzzwords associated with the Net, and some examples of what schools are already doing on the Net.

■ Chapter 2 is focused on information related specifically to subject areas, such as language arts, history, health, science, and more.

■ Chapter 3 provides information to help you find your own way to the cutting edge of K-12 methods and information on the Internet.

Part II of this book is about the Internet and Higher Education, both at the graduate and undergraduate level. It also covers teaching, scholarships, libraries, and Internet resources.

■ Chapter 4 gives an overview of higher education and the Net, how the Internet is being used in academe, and how it affects faculty, students, and administrators.

■ Chapter 5 focuses on undergraduate education, with information and resources arranged by school and discipline. Many examples of current use are provided.

■ Chapter 6 deals with Internet sources relating to graduate education in business, law, medicine, library science, and research.

■ Chapter 7 discusses teaching and learning broadly, including Computer-Mediated Communication, learning styles, and strategies for using the Internet for teaching and advising.

■ Chapter 8 centers on scholarship, research, libraries and resources.

Part III focuses on distance learning and informal learning on your own. Information on strategies, guides, and lists for going off on your own are featured.

■ Chapter 9 discusses the growing phenomena of distance learning, and including delivered and supported via the Internet.

■ Chapter 10 will help you strike out to learn on your own. Many guides and sources of information on the Internet itself are discussed.

Finally, there are two appendices. Appendix A is a very interesting feature. It is an entire short course about the basic tools of the Internet, including e-mail, FTP, telnet, Gopher, and World Wide Web. It also provides tips on using the search tools, such as Veronica and Archie, and instructions on how to access the Internet. By no means exhaustive, it will, however, give the beginner a place to start, and will help the more experienced user brush up on skills, or check out a procedure. Appendix B covers ERIC and other resources.

How to Use this Book

Because this book addresses so many different facets of education on the Internet, different groups will want to use the book in different ways.

■ For K-12 Teachers

If you have used the Internet before, go directly to Chapter 1. Here you will find information on using the Internet with K-12 education, and then continue with Chapters 2 and 3 for even more examples. If you are new to the Internet, you first may want to go to Appendix A, follow some of the examples, and then go to Chapter 1. Have a look at Chapters 7 and 9 for ideas related to teaching as well.

■ For College and University Faculty

Depending upon your Internet skills, you first may want to go to Appendix A, or start with Chapter 4 for an overview of the Internet and higher education. You then may want to look at the discipline-oriented resources in Chapters 5 and 6 for ideas. If you are planning curricula and courses, you'll find Chapters 7, 8, and 9 useful.

■ For Parents

Parents will find Chapters 1-3 particularly useful in understanding what is going on in K-12 education and the Internet. (And, for a look ahead, Chapters 4 through 6 may prove useful, too.)

■ For Students

College students may want to go directly to Chapters 5 and 6 to get some ideas regarding how to use the Internet to complete assignments and for class projects. Chapter 10 will give you some ideas about where to get more information as well.

High school students may want to go to Chapters 2 and 3 for a quick look around at what others are doing. Chapter 1 also has a section for locating schools that are on the Internet.

- For the Lifelong Learner

  Anyone who wants to learn on their own should check out Chapter 10 for references and resources for independent learning. Also, the subject-specific resources found in Chapters 4 through 6 will be useful to many professionals, as well.

An Exceptional Opportunity

This is one of the most exciting times to be learning about the Internet. It is expanding and becoming more user-friendly. It is not just for gear-heads—it is for everyone. Explore, and use the Internet to help you to accomplish your personal and professional goals.

Knowledge is power... Let's go!

Conventions Used in This Book

The following typographic conventions are used in this book:

- Code lines, commands, statements, variables, and any text you see on the screen appears in a `computer` typeface.

- Anything that you type appears in a bold **`computer`** typeface.

- Placeholders in syntax descriptions appear in an *`italic computer`* typeface. Replace the placeholder with the actual filename, parameter, or whatever element it represents.

- *Italics* highlight technical terms when they first appear in the text, and are sometimes used to emphasize important points.

Within each chapter you will encounter several icons that help you pinpoint the current topic's direction. Their meaning should be clear when you see them used in the context of the book.

THE INTERNET IN ELEMENTARY, MIDDLE SCHOOL, AND HIGH SCHOOL

THE INTERNET AND THE CLASSROOM

Oh, the places you'll go.

Dr. Seuss

This chapter will *not* tell you *what to do tomorrow* in your classroom with the Internet, unless one of the examples just happens to fit your immediate needs.

Instead, this chapter first highlights two major ideas.

■ Why it's a *GREAT* idea for K-12 schools to use the Internet.

■ Ways to classify and group the many types of things you can do with the Internet.

These are intended to help you make clear objectives for your uses of the Internet, and to help you see the whole terrain, rather than the narrow path ahead. With clear intentions, and a broad view of the Net, you will be better prepared to learn, and to guide others' learning on the Internet.

Next, several sources of already existing lesson plans, project ideas and educational Internet methods are provided. One of the great strengths of the Net is that *anyone* is able to build on the good ideas already available in the Net, and thereby have more time to creatively adapt projects to exactly meet special, local, and personal needs.

This chapter also reviews some of the many efforts now available to assist teachers who are beginners on the Internet. You also will find what I call the *buzzword gibberish decoder* (BGD), which will help you find your way among many projects that have similar sounding names. Finally, there are some technical sources you can go to if you happen to be the type of person who wants to understand *why* the computers are hooked up to the network the way they are, and a small sample of K-12 schools already on the Net.

Tip: If you *do* need some quick ideas on what to do in class tomorrow, refer to Chapter 2. Choose a topic area you or your students would be interested in, and several resources will be at your fingertips!

So, here is what's ahead:

■ What's so good about the Internet as a place for learning?

■ All types of K-12 Projects on the Internet

■ Internet Classroom Methods, Projects, and Lesson Plans

■ Helps for teachers using the Internet

■ The Buzzword Gibberish Decoder (BGD)

■ Technical help for K-12 schools

■ Schools already on the Net

What's So Good about the Internet as a Place for Learning?

Why use the Internet in my home or classroom to enhance student learning? The Internet has resources in abundance, and provides methods for teaching children more than just facts.

Will this be a good way to help children prepare for the future? The Internet is becoming an integral part of life. It is used in education, business, and in leisure, and students will need to become familiar with the Internet to become prepared citizens.

The following sections discuss new ways to to think about education, and the educational values of the Internet.

The Internet and Learning

What *is* good about the Internet and learning? The first answer is that it is a powerful releaser of emotion, motivation, and engagement for students. Some students gravitate to the Net like nothing before in their lives. While the Net is unlikely to completely replace athletics and/or music lessons, for some students it is the best opportunity ever made available to them. These children soon realize that their rewards on the Internet will be in proportion to their investment in learning Net skills, and learn all the more for it.

Contacts around the world, in far away places, make any project more dynamic, and more interesting. Often, the Internet has the most current information available anywhere. Both teachers and students can be invigorated by the freshness and immediacy of the Net.

> **Note:** This is not intended to be a comprehensive review of all the good reasons why every school should be using the Internet. Rather, this will briefly list, in broad strokes, how the Net is being used to accomplish important educational goals, in some cases goals that *could not be achieved* without Internet access.

The next answer is that the Net *is* the future. It's probably less expensive than a high school sports program, and Internet fitness will stay with students for life, because these skills are intellectual, not physical. Keyboarding is only the surface. Kids learn to ask better questions, to make better arguments, and to present themselves more positively over the Net.

Beginning with e-mail, children concentrate harder to express themselves when sending a message to another country or state. They work on vocabulary and clarity as never before. When they know a student in Stockholm, or an engineer at NASA will be writing back, children recognize the difference between slang and formal language.

Speaking of formal language, learning computer languages, that is, learning to *program* computers, is a tremendous mathematical learning opportunity. Computer operation is based in math, and truly understanding computers requires some fairly sophisticated mathematical and scientific concepts. Kids who get hooked on the Net tend to excel in other areas of math and science.

The Internet is fast becoming the largest reservoir of knowledge ever known to this planet. Students quickly grow adept at finding and retrieving remote information, and then go on to develop more sophisticated search and retrieval strategies. They begin to really appreciate librarians for their access and retrieval skills, and no longer see them as magical *sources* of books and information.

Teachers are challenged to help determine how to deal with the masses of retrieved information. For students, this is the beginning of learning analysis, evaluation, and application. These writing, thinking, and knowledge skills are applicable in almost every curriculum area.

And many of the Net's best resources are human beings, not computers or databases! Old friends, new friends, experts of all types, colleagues, specialists, and fellows of stripe are on the Net, just waiting for you. Teacher isolation can become a thing of the past.

Time and Space Disappear

Old constraints of time and space are not relevant on the Net. In Net time, Australia is just as close as the state capital. E-mail arrives in minutes, and huge files can be copied in seconds.

Teachers can use e-mail to perform consultations without expecting to play telephone tag, and students can exchange several volleys with keypals before a surface mail letter would have made a one way trip. (Internauts—people who explore the Internet—often call surface mail "snail mail.")

Sending mail on a Listserv to hundreds of people is no more laborious than sending a single message—the Net does the extra work for you!

Learning on Your Own

Like a worldwide personal library, the Net encourages students, teachers, and parents to find and use new information. Internet tools enable anyone to find and retrieve almost instantly new information, data, images, and even software that is personally interesting. Sometimes the material is simply not available except on the Net. Students also can learn on the Net educational independence and intellectual autonomy.

Because the Net is more current and dynamic than any library could be, students and teachers learn that using the Net can save them time. (See Chapter 10 for more information regarding learning on your own.)

On the Internet, They Don't Know if You Are a Dog!

The Net is color-blind, and does not discriminate. Socially induced prejudices, such as appearance, gender, race, and behaviors can fade away, because students learn that they are judged solely on what they say and how they say it.

Hearing-impaired people actually may have an advantage on the Internet, because they are not distracted by outside noises.

In a popular *New Yorker* cartoon, two dogs are "talking" while one uses a computer. The pooch at the computer keyboard says to the other, "On the Internet, nobody knows you're a dog!"

It's true, class, race, ability, and disability are removed from consideration in Internet communication.

Are We All Adults Here?

Once a youngster has a sizable vocabulary and is articulate, there is little to keep him or her from conversing over the Net like an adult. Likewise, adults can masquerade as kids. This has recently been recognized as a security concern.

It now is widely acknowledged that safe telecomputing for kids must be taught *before* the keyboard and modem are freely available in an unsupervised environment. Local policies differ greatly, and general guidance is available in *RFC 1578*. Access information for *RFC 1578* is discussed later in this chapter.

There simply is no substitute for incorporating issues of ethics into the technology curriculum. Just as teachers recognize safety issues in laboratories and around machines and shop equipment, these issues, too, must be addressed around Net access. Establishing clear rules, and consequences for breaking them, is a school-wide or district-wide responsibility. It cannot be done effectively without parental involvement and support.

RFC 1578, the *Internet Q&A for K-12 schools* says "...schools need to exercise reasonable oversight while realizing that it is almost impossible to absolutely guarantee that students will not be able to access objectionable material."

All Types of K-12 Projects on the Internet

Now let's explore the many ways that students, parents, and teachers can use the Net to improve and enhance learning. There are dozens of ways people are now using the Internet for learning in schools, homes, and workplaces.

Following are the most fundamental methods. It may seem simplistic, but there are only a few options that are inherent in the machine-human combination:

Communication	*Net Tool*
Person-to-person	E-mail, IRC (chat)
Person-to-many	E-mail, Listserv, newsgroups
Many people-to-many people	E-mail, Listserv, newsgroups, IRC (chat), Moo and Muse
Person-to-computer	telnet, FTP, Gopher, WWW
Person-to-many computers	Veronica, Gopher, WWW
Computer-to-person	Personal news services, beeper services
Computer-to-many people	Custom news services
Computer-to-computer	Content indexing, updating, and Net monitoring

There are several ways to classify these Net tools with different combinations of students, teachers, and curriculum goals, as in the following:

Professional collaborations among educators

Students' collaborative investigations

Students' and teachers' access to scientific expertise

Students' and teachers' access to information (libraries, etc.)

Students' and teachers' access to computers and software

Collaborative development and delivery of instruction and materials

Teacher education and enhancement

Electronic publishing of students' products

And yet here is another practical method of organizing the options, from a different perspective:

Professional Activities

Research

Collaboration, sharing, exchange of information

Overcoming space and time to bring together groups with common goals

Around the school district or county

Around the region, country, or world

Information Access

Catalogs, databases, archives

News services

Software

Text-Based Virtual Reality

MUDs and Muses with defined content, such as the following:

Oregon Trail, Lewis and Clark

Small stream ecosystems

Discovery of planet Mars

French and American Revolutions

Congressional or Parliamentary actions

How these combinations manifest with various Internet tools is truly fascinating to behold. This section covers briefly the some basic Internet tools—e-mail, FTP, and telnet. This section also mentions two other useful Net tools—Gopher and World Wide Web. (Specific instructions for using these and many other tools are in Appendix A.)

E-Mail

E-mail (electronic mail) is the most common Net service. Many people who have e-mail cannot use most other Internet services, except through e-mail.

E-mail is something new and different from face-to-face talking. E-mail is like an answering machine with text rather than voice. You respond *when* you like, *if* you like, and delete the messages you don't care about. You can save the messages on a certain topic and find a good way of dealing with them as a group, rather than one by one.

Net enthusiasts can send and receive e-mail from anywhere. Home computers, portables, and laptops quickly are growing in popularity, and home modems are flying off the shelf, especially since fast error-correcting modems are now around $100 or less.

> **Note:** A modem is similar to a telephone for your computer. Modems speak a type of weird computer Esperanto, so that two computers with modems can communicate.

Message slips waiting for you tell about a telephone call you missed. With e-mail, however, you often will have already received e-mail from someone and responded, before you even get to the classroom to see the telephone message slip that says they called before they resorted to e-mail.

E-mail, through the magic of the Net, can expand from the communication between two people to communicating with many people. It then can expand to many people communicating with many people.

To send a single message to many people, after you've composed and tested the message so you know what it "looks" like when it arrives, you just add more names to the address space in your mail program.

Listserv Lists

The predominate method for most people to communicate with groups of others on the Net is by way of *Listserv lists*. A Listserv is an automated mailing list, kept on a computer. You put your own name on the list, and remove your name when you no longer want to receive mail from that list.

Most lists enable you to put your mail "on hold" when you go on vacation. Many lists also are stored as archives, so that you can search and read messages and exchanges that happened months or years ago.

Time acts differently on the Net—debates and discussions are preserved, as if suspended in time. Reading last year's discussion often feels as if it was currently happening. So much so that you might not be able to stop yourself from writing e-mail to those whom with you agree (or disagree!), even though the "real" discussion was recorded months ago.

When you add your name to a Listserv, you start getting mail from that computer mailing list. You alone choose the topics you're interested in, and you subscribe to only lists you want to explore.

> **Tip:** Shortly after you subscribe, you might want to also practice *unsubscribing* and *resubscribing*, so that you know how to do it, if you ever need to stop your mail. Save the instructions!

On most lists today, everyone on the list gets *every* e-mail message sent to the list. Some lists, however, don't allow e-mail to be distributed to the list members unless the person sending the mail is a subscribed member of the list. Some lists are private, so that you cannot add your name to the list without the approval of a *gatekeeper* (list moderator).

The following example is an exchange that took place on a list devoted to discussions of education, in which one member of the list asked the others to recommend middle school hypercard stacks (complex Macintosh data files).

```
To: Multiple recipients of list EDUFOO <EDUFOO@Nowhere.EDU>
Subject: Nifty Hypercard Stacks

John  said:

>I am teaching a middle school hypercard class this spring and would like

>to show my students some examples of student-created "cool" stacks.

Dear John,

I have recently done some training for teachers and downloaded quite a few
hypercard stacks to show them what is available out there. I cannot
guarantee that all of them were done by students, however I will give you
some names and places to get them.

1. Go to the University of Minnesota Gopher -> (then) Computer Information
-> The Apple Computer Higher Education gopher server -> Macintosh Freeware
and Shareware -> University of Michigan Macintosh Archive -> Hypercard
stacks.

Quite a few of these are nicely done. I have looked at bird anatomy (very
good, done by student at Yale); DNAteacher (good); fastball fractions
(shareware, good); whales (okay); and Internet tour (very good). There are
many, many more that I have not had time to download.

2. You might do a word search for a program called Hyper Frog SW. I do
not know where I got it from, but it was done by a high school student and
is very impressive.
```

```
3. Go to the Ecogopher at University of Virginia -> Education:  Ecogopher
Environmental Library -> KSC Kilburn Earth and Environmental Science
Information gopher -> Environmental Science -> Sense of Place. HQX.

This is a hypercard environmental newsletter produced by students at
Dartmouth. It is very nicely done. It is said to be published twice a
month and that you can subscribe to it, however I have only been able to
find one issue on-line (Jan, 1993). I have not yet tried to subscribe.
The address to subscribe is:  SOP@dartmouth.edu. This is for all inquiries
about back issues, submissions, subscription, etc.

4. Go to the University of Minnesota Gopher -> Computer Information -> The
Apple Computer Higher Education gopher server -> Macintosh Freeware and
Shareware -> Infomac -> Stanford University Info-Mac archive.

I have not "surfed" here much but have heard that they have some good stuff.

I hope this is helpful.
Sincerely,
Mary Jane
```

Notice that when Mary Jane responded to John's request, she only quoted a few lines from John's original message. This lets the reader know the context of the message, but does not "waste bandwidth" by resending the entire message back to everyone on the list.

Also, Mary Jane went out of her way to provide John with several excellent resources, exemplifying the Net cultural value of "giving back" to the Net community.

FTP—File Transfer Protocol

FTP is a way of requesting a file data or some software from a remote computer to send you a file, FTP transfers are usually made very quickly.

Until you know how to use FTP, you really can't say you're friendly with the Net. Sure, Gopher can bring home the bacon, too; however, not all FTP sites are set up for Gopher, and until you can FTP, you'll be missing out on a lot.

When you FTP, you first ask permission to visit the distant computer. If it's okay (not too busy, and so on), the remote computer lets you in and allows you to look around it's innards, asking what files are in each directory, copying files, and changing directories up and down at will.

If you know where to find the files you want, you can go right to them and transfer copies of them back to your computer. Otherwise, you can just snoop around and window-shop, looking for things that sound interesting.

Use mget

The mget (*many get*) command is more flexible than the regular get command, and easier to use. For example, mget allows you to ask for copies of all files that begin with a certain letter. It also will send you one file, if only one file matches your request.

```
mget Ch*
```

This instructs the computer to send you copies of all files (in the current folder or directory) that begin with the letters Ch. mget will ask you for confirmation for each file copied, so you may have to press **y** a few times. It's much easier, however, to press **y** (for yes) 10 times than it is to type 10 exact, case-sensitive 20-letter file names. UNIX file names are case-sensitive, and can be very long and complicated. Additionally, there are not yet strong Net conventions on UNIX file-naming. Use mget, it's easier!

Let's run through a couple examples of what you can get by way of FTP, and show you actual commands to do it yourself.

To start, get a document called Scott Yanoff's Special Internet Connections, which you can use to get information on a lot of intersting sites including telnet, the next Net tool you'll need.

At the Internet prompt, type **ftp**, and then type the exact address shown on the following line. Press Enter when finished.

```
%> ftp csd4.csd.uwm.edu
```

Very quickly, as the remote computer responds to your request to come for a visit, the screen will change:

```
Connected to csd4.csd.uwm.edu.
220 csd4.csd.uwm.edu FTP server (Version wu-2.1c(3) Fri Oct 29 13:50:21 CDT 1993)
ready.
Name:
```

Your next job is to state your business by identifying yourself (in Net jargon), as an *anonymous* FTP visitor. So you type **anonymous** and press Enter.

If the remote computer is not too busy, and is in a good humor today, it will signify acceptance of your visit by asking you to sign the register book as you enter, just for the records, of course.

```
331 Guest login ok, send your complete e-mail address as password.
Password:
```

Your next response, while a little confusing, is to enter your full Internet address.

The following is a typical response after you type in your password:

```
230-University of Wisconsin-Milwaukee FTP server
230-Local time is Wed Jul 27 22:04:14 1994
230-
230-If you have any unusual problems, please report them
230-via e-mail to help@uwm.edu.
230-
230-If you do have problems, please try using a dash (-) as the
230-first character of your password -- this will turn off the
230-continuation messages that may be confusing your ftp client.
230-
230-Please read the file Policy
230-  it was last modified on Mon Dec  6 08:06:40 1993 - 233 days ago
230 Guest login ok, access restrictions apply.
Remote system type is UNIX.
Using binary mode to transfer files.
ftp>
```

Tip: It's hard to fathom, but the remote computer knows *exactly* who you are and is keeping a record of the date and time you visited. If you don't give your real Internet address as a password, the remote computer *will* know you are fibbing, and may scold you.

You're now connected to a remote computer in Milwaukee!

Moving along, you need to change directories (or *folders* for you Macintosh users), because the file you want is not in the first (or top) directory; it's in a subdirectory. To get to the right directory, type **cd** (for CHANGE DIRECTORY) and then enter the name of the directory to which you want to change (in this case, **/pub**), and then press Enter.

```
ftp> cd /pub
```

The computer in Milwaukee responds with the following:

```
250-This directory contains public files for anonymous users.  Files may
250-be read, but not written (use "/incoming" for writing new files).
250-
250 CWD command successful.
ftp>
```

Now that you're in the correct directory, type **get**, press the space bar, enter the exact filenames as shown in the following example, and then press Enter. The file name inet.services.txt is not in a format that a DOS machine could use, so I have to give it a new name—yanoff.txt.

```
ftp> get inet.services.txt yanoff.txt
(original name)      (new name)
```

> **Note:** Why are two filenames are given? Because long UNIX filenames aren't accepted on DOS computers, and I want to ensure that you actually get something out of this first example. So, you first type the name of the file as it is on the remote computer, and then you type the new name with which you want the file to arrive.

Now you have a copy of the new file named yanoff.txt. It is full of great telnet sites, which you will want to explore in the next section. The Yanoff guide is not limited to educational resources, but you will find many interesting items in there.

You can shop around for more files, but for this example, there is another site to visit.

To tell the computer in Milwaukee that you're ready to leave, type **bye** and press Enter. When you are prompted if you're sure you want to leave, confirm by pressing **y**. No gratitude is necessary. Milwaukee did it's job, and you followed the rules, got your file, and you're out of there.

That's how FTP works. You visit a remote site, and bring back your goodies. How fast can you fill up a hard disk with this kind of free information and stuff? (Very fast!)

FTP Goals 2000 Documents

You can FTP *Goals 2000* documents directly from the U.S. Department of Education in Washington, D.C. The files also are available by Gopher and WWW, as shown in the following example. There also are folks to help (by e-mail) if you have trouble. These kind souls usually respond with solid help within 24 hours on weekdays.

```
FTP to  ftp.ed.gov  then change directories (cd) to /ED_wide/initiatives/goals
then get the file named  00-INDEX
```

Where to find it

Anonymous FTP

Site	`ftp.ed.gov`
Directory	`/ED_wide/initiatives/goals`
File	`00-INDEX`

> **Tip:** Almost all the directories at this site contain a file named `00-INDEX`. If the site administrators keep the file up to date, the `00-INDEX` files will tell you the names of all the other files in that directory, and sometimes a little bit about them. You usually should first look at the `00-INDEX` file, to save yourself from FTPing the wrong file by mistake.

You now have the main listing of all the directories on Goals 2000.

Now you can dig one step deeper, and look in the `/overview` subdirectory for `file7.txt`, which provides a nice summary of what Goals 2000 is all about. Go ahead and change directories and get the file named `file7.txt`.

> **Tip:** Although the access instructions will always give the complete directory name that you would use from the very top directory, in this example you aren't in the top directory. You only need to move one directory down, from the `/goals` directory to the `/overview` directory. To make it simpler, just type **cd /overview**.

Where to find it

Anonymous FTP

Site	`ftp.ed.gov`
Directory	`/ED_wide/initiatives/goals/overview`
Files	`file7.txt`
	`00-INDEX`

Now you have a nice summary of Goals 2000. To get an idea what else is in the /overview subdirectory, so that you can FTP back here in the future. You might also want to get the 00-INDEX file.

The U.S. Department of Education has many useful K-12 items in this location, so come back and visit again soon. Following is what you'll see:

```
Goals 2000 on the Internet

Date: Tue, 26 Apr 1994 19:19:31 -0700

Sender: kstubbs@inet.ed.gov (Keith Stubbs)


Subject: GOALS 2000 Legislation

              GOALS 2000 ON THE INTERNET

      The most comprehensive federal education legislation in
decades has hit the superhighway.

      The GOALS 2000: Educate America Act -- which President
Clinton signed into law on March 31, 1994 -- is now available via
Internet in the Education Department (ED) "online library."

      "This is part of our effort to improve customer service,"
said U.S. Secretary of Education Richard W. Riley. "We are going
to be stocking the shelves of our online library, in the months
ahead, with information that can help parents and teachers,
citizens and students transform their schools and reach the
National Education Goals."

      The library offers the full text of GOALS 2000, and also
fact sheets and other information on the Act, which is designed
to help America reach the National Education Goals and to move
every child toward achieving high academic standards.

      Other materials available in the department's online library
include the National Education Goals Panel 1993 annual report,
ED's "helping your child" series for parents, A Teachers Guide to
the U.S. Department of Education, various research reports and
education statistics compilations, as well as "pointers" to other
education resources on the Internet.

      The department's online library is currently maintained by
the Office of Educational Research and Improvement on its
Institutional Communications Network (INet).

      The library also includes:

      o     announcements of new publications and data sets;
      o     news releases;
      o     funding opportunities;
      o     event calendars;
      o     general information about the department;
```

o   searchable ED staff directory;
o   descriptions of ED programs;
o   directories of effective programs;
o   directory of education-related information centers;
o   research findings and syntheses;
o   full-text publications for teachers, parents, and
     researchers;
o   statistical tables, charts, and data sets;
o   pointers to public Internet resources at R&D
     centers, regional laboratories, ERIC Clearinghouses,
     and other ED-funded institutions.

Accessing the library requires certain software -- either a
Gopher client software or World Wide Web client software (such as
NCSA Mosaic or Lynx) -- or you must be able to "telnet" to a
public access client elsewhere.

If you are using a Gopher client, point it to:

                    gopher.ed.gov

or select "North America-->USA-->General-->U.S. Department of
Education" from "All/Other Gophers in the World." Follow the path
Department-wide Initiatives (Goals 2000...)-->Goals 2000 Initiative.

If you are using World Wide Web (WWW), point your WWW client
to our uniform resource locator (URL):

                    http://www.ed.gov/

and follow the link from our WWW server to our Gopher server.

Another way to access the library is by using file transfer
protocol (FTP). To do this, FTP to:

             ftp.ed.gov   (logon anonymous)

If you have difficulty accessing our services, please contact
us at one of the following addresses:

        inetmgr@inet.ed.gov
        gopheradm@inet.ed.gov
        wwwadmin@inet.ed.gov

Keith M. Stubbs   (voice) 202-219-1803
Director, Education Info. Resources Div.   (fax) 202-219-1817
US Dept of Education/OERI   Internet: kstubbs@inet.ed.gov
555 New Jersey Avenue, NW Rm 214c
Washington, DC 20208-5725

Telnet

Using *telnet*, you can access a remote computer, read files and data, and use the remote computer's other services.

A few telnet servers also enable you to e-mail files or *session output* to your e-mail address. So you see, telnet can expand beyond just reading information onscreen, or capturing the screen image in a file for later editing or printing.

Telnet is a lot like your local dial-up computer Bulletin Board Service (BBS). You use your computer to talk to another computer, about information and services the remote computer can provide for you.

Telnet also is a way you can use powerful Net access programs, such as Gopher, WWW, Veronica, Archie, WAIS, and others. If your local site can't, or won't, provide you with these services, you can telnet to a site that does have them, and use them there. It's a little slower, but you usually can accomplish the same goal.

You start a telnet session much the same way you start an FTP session. Type **telnet** followed by the address of the location you want to visit.

To be sure you are getting the format used for this particular example, using, here is how the first example is summarized in English:

```
telnet to the site  k12.ucs.umass.edu  and login as  guest
```

To get you started, following are some places to which you can telnet.

University of Massachusetts (*UMassK12*)

Where to find it

Site	k12.ucs.umass.edu
Login	guest

> **Tip:** Many telnet sites require you to register upon entry. This is really no big deal, except that you need to *remember your password* from one visit to the next, so you don't have to go through the new user question-answer routine every time you visit.

This is one of the best developed telnet sites of K-12 educators. The registration is simple, and DOS/Windows users can choose color ANSI graphics, which makes the screen easier to read and understand.

Note: Under item 13 of the UMassK-12 telnet site—Access other online services—you will find item 7 called Fun, Games and Sports. Sports scores and schedules are available here, 24 hours a day!

Try out a couple of the menu items, exit, and then move onto the next site.

Virginia's PEN (Public Education Network)

Where to find it

Site	vdoe386.vak12ed.edu
Login	guest
Password	guest

For more information

E-mail	Harold Cathern (hcathern@vdoe386.vak12ed.edu)
Surface mail	Virginia Department of Education
	101 North 14th Street, 22nd Floor
	Richmond VA 23219

This is a typical example of a statewide educational network. As a guest, you will not be allowed access to most of the areas that registered users may access. If you are in Virginia, however, you will want to register and try out this service.

Educators access Virginia's *PEN* via a local call to one of several sites across the state, or through a toll-free line if they are located in a remote area. PEN includes discussion groups, news reports, study skills guides, reference works, and curriculum resources.

A unique and exciting feature is the History Pavilion (under main Menu item Electronic Academical Village), where students and teachers can pose questions to designated historians who will respond *in the character* of key historical figures, such as Thomas Jefferson and James Madison!

FedWorld

Where to find it

Site	`fedworld.gov` or `192.239.92.201`
Login	`new`

For more information

| E-mail | Bob Bunge | `bob.bunge@fedworld.gov` |

You can access *FedWorld* over the Net in several ways, including FTP, telnet, and WWW. The FedWorld telnet site supports up to 50 simultaneous connections. White House documents available from this telnet site can be searched using keywords. You are required to register as a new user, so save your password, or you'll have to start all over again the next time you visit.

From the main menu, choose `Library of Files`. From the Library of Files menu, select a topic library, such as `W-house`. You then can choose option `F` to find files and then choose option `K` to search by keyword. Keywords are very general—such as security, world, order, economy, health care, crime, state names, executive, and so on.

All free files at this telnet site can be transferred using FTP from `ftp.fedworld.gov` (`192.239.92.205`). Conveniently, directories at the FTP site have the same names as the Libraries at the telnet site. Each FTP directory has a `directory_name.LST` file that lists a description of each file in that directory. They claim the list file is updated daily!

What Should a Teacher Try First in the Classroom?

As usual, that depends on your own comfort level, and on the equipment and support available. Watching adults learn can be quite helpful to kids, so you shouldn't necessarily wait until you're an expert to start using the Net in school. It can be very comforting to some youngsters to see an authority figure be just as frustrated with this new technology as they are.

The least expensive alternative starting place is e-mail. No color is required on the computer monitor screen, and practically all Internet service providers offer some type or variation of e-mail. And even the youngest children, perhaps even kindergartners, can learn many things from e-mail, such as the following:

- *Geography*—Mapping the locations of e-mail friends.
- *Language Arts*—What words do people use to describe themselves? How do formal and informal speech differ? What does it take to compose a letter? What happens if the keys aren't pressed in the "right" order?
- *Communication*—What parts of the message are vital to understanding it? What parts are required for it to be sent and received?
- *Cultural Diversity*—What holidays are celebrated by the remote person(s)? What are their favorite foods and what hobbies do they enjoy? How do they make a living? Who lives in their household?

As your learning audience becomes more experienced and more sophisticated, the whole Net opens to their keyboards. Teachers around the world are using this new information medium to foster learning in every conceivable curriculum area. Chapter 2 provides you with leads for a dozen different topical areas and examples of how teachers are incorporating the Net into every curriculum!

Classroom Methods and Lesson Plans

Teachers are interested in tried-and-true lesson plans, as long as they know they have the freedom to use them as they please. The nice thing about the Internet is that you can get good projects that already have been tried, and then make them even better by customizing them for your circumstances and needs.

Many sources for lessons plans and project ideas are already available on the Net. The following sections discuss a few, just to get you started.

AskERIC Database Of Lesson Plans

AskERIC has been collecting lesson plans for some time now, and as a consequence, their collection is extensive. Have a look!

Where to find it

Gopher	ericir.syr.edu
Telnet	ericir.syr.edu
Login	gopher

How Teachers Find Projects

In May 1994, Beverly Hunter asked three Listserv lists (Kidsphere, CoSN, and NII-Teach) where teachers find projects. The responses are categorized, summarized, and available by Gopher.

Where to find it

Gopher	`unix5.nysed.gov`
Directory	`K-12 Resources`
Gopher	`digital.cosn.org`
directory	`CoSN Activities/COSNDISC/CoSNDISC Topics`

The following is a sample from one of the responses:

```
*William Gathergood <wgatherg@magnus.acs.ohio-state.edu>

In the last two years, I have started five projects which involved over 1500
students in 28 countries. I started one called The Reynoldsburg Geography
Project. I listed the registration information on a local newsgroup in
Columbus, misc.education and Kidsphere. Within three days, I had 380
participants from 22 states and countries.

The key to finding projects is to understand how someone starting a project
gets the word out. I use List-servers and Newsgroups. Two Listservers I
use are Kidsphere and k/12.Euro-teach, the latter because most of my
projects are international.

The best general education newsgroup is misc.education. There are probably
a hundred thousand teachers around the globe who read that one. There are
other newsgroups which specialize in certain subjects.
```

The newsgroup `misc.education` is on Usenet. For information on how to access Usenet newsgroups, see Appendix A.

NASA Spacelink Lesson Plans

The *NASA Spacelink* site also doubles as a dial-up site, so some menus offer you the option of choosing a download protocol (such as Kermit, Xmodem, or Ymodem).

> **Tip:** Downloading over the Net is never as fast as FTP. First, FTP the document to your "holding area" on the host computer through which you access the Net. Then download it to your personal hard drive from your "holding area" on the host computer.

Where to find it

Telnet site	spacelink.msfc.nasa.gov or 192.149.89.61
login	newuser
password	newuser

Anonymous FTP

Site	spacelink.msfc.nasa.gov or 192.149.89.61
Password	guest
File	README
Modem	205/895-0028

Register and carefully read the instructions—it is menu-driven. The response sometimes is quite slow, so you may have to wait.

> **Tip:** Look for the default option in brackets near the cursor. [V] means "view."

The main NASA Spacelink menu looks like this:

```
1. Log Off NASA Spacelink
2. NASA Spacelink Overview
3. Current NASA News
4. Aeronautics
5. Space Exploration: Before the Shuttle
6. Space Exploration: The Shuttle and Beyond
7. NASA and its Centers
8. NASA Educational Services
9. Instructional Materials
10. Space Program Spinoffs/Technology Transfer
11. International Space Year (ISY)
```

Choose 9. Instructional Materials, and you will see the following:

```
Instructional Materials

0. Previous Menu
1. Main Menu
2. Living In Space Activities
3. Space Science Activities
4. Commercially Available Software for Aerospace Education
5. How to Obtain NASA Educational Publications
6. Astronomy Information
7. Very Lo-Res "Graphics"
8. Film/Video List
9. Careers in Aerospace
10. NASA Educational Fact Sheets
11. Computer Programs & Graphics
12. Key Dates (by Ralph Winrich)
13. Materials from Outside Organizations
14. 1990-1991 High School Debate Topic Information
15. Liftoff to Learning Series—Educational Videotapes
16. Miscellaneous Aeronautics Classroom Activities
17. Using Art to Teach Science
```

Select 2. Living In Space Activities and you will see

```
Living in Space

0..Previous Menu
1..Main Menu
2..Food Lesson Plans
3..Clothing Lesson Plans
4..Health Lesson Plans
5..Housing Lesson Plans
6..Communication Lesson Plans
7..Working Lesson Plans
8..Space Station Research & Design, 7-12
9.."Down on the Moon" Activity
```

Most of these options are groups of lesson plans. To check out one set of plans, select 2. Food Lesson Plans to display the following screen:

```
Living in Space
Food Lesson Plans

0..Previous Menu
1..Main Menu
2..Background, 1-3
3..Background, 4-6
4..Background, 7-12
5..Grades 1-3
6..Grades 4-6
7..Grades 7-8
8..Grades 9-12
```

These well-developed lesson plans have background information, objectives, vocabulary, motivation, activities, and experiments. As you can see, they are presented by grade levels in progression.

51 Reasons—FARNET Success Stories

In February, 1993, a call went out from *FARNET* (The Federation of American Research Networks) for the submission of success stories. Over 150 submissions were gathered from across the United States, and beyond. FARNET makes a selection of these stories available as a printed book, *51 Reasons: How We Use the Internet and What It Says About the Information Superhighway*. The book provides concrete examples of how the network is being used to further research, education, industry and manufacturing, the health services industry, and more.

In cooperation with The Coalition for Networked Information, FARNET makes the full collection of stories available on the Internet.

Where to find it

Anonymous FTP

Site	`ftp.cni.org`
Directory	`/CNI/documents/farnet`
Files	`stories-index`
	`README`

The stories are sorted alphabetically by the state from which they originated. The file names end with the two-letter postal abbreviation for that state. When you FTP to get them, all the stories for a particular state are within a directory just for that state. All 37 of these stories have K-12 educational themes.

Where to find it

Filename	Story Name
`story141.AL`	Alabama high school teachers use Internet via Alabama Supercomputer Authority
`story087.CO`	Project assesses Internet role in operations of an entire school district
`story130.IL`	Study on telecommunications use in teacher/student communication

Filename	Story Name
story121.IL	Collaborative Visualization (CoVis) project allows teachers to communicate
story119.IL	9th grader collaborates with researcher on lake-effect snow project
story112.IL	A constructivist introduction to Newton's Laws of Motion—NASA engineer and a 5th grader
story111.IL	How children use networks to make "giant leaps" in space
story110.IL	Pre-service teachers use PowerBooks and the network to communicate
story109.IL	Students study outer space while improving writing skills via network
story108.IL	Earth Day Treasure Hunt Project
story134.IN	Ball State U. assists local school to develop networked curriculum
story025.MA	SCANNING FOR GOLD III: Kidnet—networks in education
story024.MA	SCANNING FOR GOLD II: Creative Writing Groups and Peer Review of Articles
story028.MI	Interactive Communications & Simulations: The Arab-Israeli Conflict Simulation
story027.MI	Interactive Communications & Simulations: The [poetry] Guild
story026.MI	Interactive Communications & Simulations: The 1990's Earth Odysseys
story084.MN	International Arctic Project engages students in environmental awareness
story051.MS	FARNET Stories—Mississippi
story162.NE	Math teacher uses Internet to have students telecommute
story090.NE	KIDLINK provides forum for children to discuss global environment
story050.NJ	The Future is Present with my Students
story045.NJ	Public schools have access to wealth of shareware software via Internet
story046.NV	Nevada elementary school is tutored from Antarctica via Kidsnet and Ednet

Filename	*Story Name*
`story116.NY`	Exploring the World of the Internet
`story103.NY`	Bringing Supercomputers to High School Classrooms
`story101.NY`	Internet Collaboration Facilitates Innovative Science Collaboration
`story100.NY`	Supercomputers in the Classroom: Internet Catalyzes Curriculum Change
`story022.NY`	CyberPuppy's Storyware—"networked" authoring software for K-12 market
`story122.PA`	KIDSNET Mailing List
`story038.PA`	Geometry Software Story
`story073.RI`	Geogame, an on-line geography exercise by the FrEdMail Foundation
`story036.TX`	What is MathMagic?
`story043.VA`	Using Global Educational Networks: Topics from the Internet
`story042.VA`	Telecommunication Projects That Work... and Why!
`story031.VA`	Our Global Neighborhood—Telecommunications in the Classroom
`story207.VT`	Vermont: Telecommunications for Educational Reform
`story124.WV`	Mentoring Science Students via Electronic Mail

For more information

E-mail   Martha Stone-Martin (`stories@farnet.org`)

> **Tip:** If you are FTPing stories from two or more states, you can use the `cdup` FTP command after getting your first state, to move back to the `/farnet/` directory. Then, use the `cd` command to move to the next state directory from which you want to `get`.

The following are excerpts of two sample FARNET stories, just to give you an idea of what they are like:

```
Document:  50  —  story162.NE
Submitted by:  Cindy Carlson, Teacher
Department:  Math Department
Organization:  Kearney High School
     Address:  3610 Ave. 6
                      Kearney, NE    68847                USA
       Phone:  (308) 234-1720
      E-mail:  ccarlson@nde.unl.edu
```

The Story

I teach math at Kearney High School, Kearney, NE and I have been
using telecommunications, i.e.. Internet, quite extensively in my classes.
In particular, I have been using Internet in a class labeled Consumer
Math. This class is comprised of kids for whom the phrase
"students at risk" was coined. The main objective of telecomputing
in this class is to keep the students interested and to keep them in
attendance.

These students have been actively corresponding with other students
from across the US as well as from places as far away as Korea, Fin
land, Japan and Australia. Being a consumer class, incorporating
specific objectives of the course has been quite simple since everyone, no
matter where they are in the world, is a consumer.

Of course, dialog has not been just about simple price
comparisons and in some instances has become quite personal between
writers, but the interest of these students has grown tremendously.
Not only have they gained knowledge of other parts of the world but
their writing skills have improved and most importantly, they have
shown enthusiasm towards something good and worthwhile.

Since the beginning of second semester, I have not incorporated
telecomputing in my consumer math class. There are two main reasons
for this:

     1. My class doubled in size at semester and we do not have
     the facilities to accommodate that number of students in the
     telecomputing.

     2. It has become nearly impossible to access Internet within a
     reasonable time and at a reasonable time of the day. I do have
     access to a local number at Kearney, but because of the system
     set-up I do most of my work at home on my own PC and it is long-
     distance to utilize the Kearney number.

Occasionally, I present math problems taken from BBSs and data bases to
my accounting classes, but I hope to be able to telecommute again with my
consumer kids.

Following is another excerpt of a story:

```
Document:      33  —  story050.NJ
Submitted by:  Ferdi Serim, Computer Teacher
Department:  Upper Elementary School
Organization:  West Windsor/Plainsboro Regional Schools Street
      Address:  75 Grovers Mill Rd.
                    Plainsboro, NJ   08536          USA
        Phone:  (609) 799-0087      Fax:  (609) 520-1376
        E-mail:  wwp@tigger.jvnc.net


The Future is Present with my Students

In reflecting on my life as a teacher in the past year, the Internet played a
major role for me and my students. I strive to make my classroom a
place where children feel comfortable exploring, and through the Internet our
"playground" is truly global.

Communication is the key to everything we undertake, and I want the
children to know me as a lifelong learner who enjoys their progress and
is unafraid to learn new things before an audience. Knowing one's limits
requires defining boundaries of skill, understanding and imagination.

Transcending present limits happens when one becomes motivated,
excited by an idea or ability just out of reach, and becomes sufficiently
dedicated to disregard the discomfort of inevitable obstacles until they
become visible in the rear view mirror!


Highlights

By choosing the Internet as a focus for my Professional Improvement
Plan, unusual, innovative and special programs were inevitable. Among
these, Chernobyl, Eagle Excellence, Solar Sailing and Festival Artwork
stand out in my mind.

The Chernobyl exercise lasted only 36 hours, but it was profound. On
Monday at noon a message came in over the Internet stating that 40
students from the contaminated zone in Chernobyl would be visiting a
health spa in England for recuperation, and requested greetings. On
Tuesday morning, my first two classes discussed the implications for
these children, and used our word processing skills to craft "get well"
messages.
We received a reply from the two Russian teachers, who clearly were
amazed that US children knew and cared about the plight of their
students, and proceeded to answer the questions gleaned from our
messages. History, science and language arts blended to make a
personal sense of current events tangible to our students in a way
otherwise impossible and nearly unimaginable!

75 of our students have now gained the distinction of having their
original computer artwork on display in a worldwide gallery of
computer art on the Internet.

Solar Sailing captivated 3 sixth grade classes during the initial month of
school. Students designed and researched their own original Solar
Sailing spacecraft, established jobs and staffing, and joined in with over
```

50 schools to conduct a simulation on October 18 to celebrate Columbus's 500th anniversary. We had help from a NASA physicist, and real video footage from space to add to the realism.

I have used the Internet to make contact with Spanish speaking students and had some of our bilingual students write to keypals in Spanish. We have used graphics and Logowriter programs to speak in the universal language of images and mathematics for students who do not yet have sufficient command of English to work exclusively in that language. I have devised individual projects for special needs students to succeed in mainstreamed classes by pairing with other students in a mentor role, or using storymaking software to create success and pride in accomplishment, and opportunities to share these with entire classes. Individualization is the key to meeting diverse needs of students.

Working together, we all will ultimately reach the goal of extending similar opportunities (to those my students enjoyed) to learners everywhere of any age.

Internet Resource Directory (IRD) for Educators

The *Internet Resource Directory* (IRD) of resources was written and revised by educators. The "infusion ideas" volume includes some elaborately developed lesson plans. Several topic areas are covered, including archeology, art, chemistry, Earth Day, and foreign language telecomputing, among others. One of my favorites is *Bringing the History of Mathematics into the Mathematics Classroom* by Carol A. Waldron. It is appropriate and adaptable for grades seven through ten.

Where to find it

Anonymous FTP

Site	tcet.unt.edu
Directory	/pub/telecomputing-info/IRD
File	IRD-infusion-ideas.txt

While you're there, you might as well FTP the whole IRD set, so go ahead and get these files too:

Files	IRD-ftp-archives.txt
	IRD-listservs.txt
	IRD-telnet-sites.txt

As you might expect, these files contain Anonymous FTP Archives, Lists of Listservs, and selected telnet sites favored by K-12 educators.

Internet Reference Success Stories

Librarians in K-12 settings will want to obtain this wonderful sampler of what the Internet can do for librarians. In many cases, particularly for the smaller libraries, the Internet provides information that would otherwise be inaccessible. In some cases, currency or speed of retrieval makes the Internet the best resource to which to turn.

Where to find it

E-mail	Karen G. Schneider
	kgs@panix.com
	karens@queens.lib.ny.us

A couple of the listings might be of interest, even to non-librarians! Have a look. The following stories have been collected by Karen Schneider.

```
Brian Herman, Glenview Public Library, Illinois:

A high school student needed the geographical coordinates of
Glenville, Illinois for his math project. I used the Geographic
Name Server which I accessed through telnet to
martini.eecs.umich.edu 3000. I left the printout on the desk for
others to use, since we often get a barrage of calls on the same
topic when certain High School projects are assigned.


Rachel Cassel, Binghamton University, New York:

A patron was looking for the text of the UN Declaration of  Human
Rights in 1948. We did a Veronica search and located the full
text of the document at the gopher kragar.eff.org, path
/academic/civil-liberty/human-rights.un.

I've seen a problem instructors have given in classes on gopher
where they have students use Veronica to search for data to
compare the unemployment rates of  Detroit and Los Angeles.
```

Help for Teachers Using the Internet

Several groups have recently recognized that many teachers may need special services to become Internet-literate. Even *after* a classroom teacher overcomes all the hurdles of finding time and money for buying computers, getting a telephone line installed, connecting the modem, learning to use the communications software, and getting connected with access to the Internet, there *still* is a need to sort out the myriad of options for what to use in class *tomorrow*.

Well, maybe you're still just trying to get that phone line installed. Where can you seek help in making the argument that your classroom needs a phone line? Where can you find other teachers who can walk you through the decisions about which software to use on which projects? How do you keep up with new Net stuff without spending all night on the computer? Here are some projects that are designed to help K-12 teachers!

> **Tip:** After you get "smooth as silk" with this Internet stuff, don't forget that you were once a "clueless newbie" and didn't know FTP from telnet! Everybody has to start where they are, and if you can lend a helping hand, it will pay off in the long run!

NASA Knowbot Project

During the summer of 1994, NASA began recruiting grade 3 through 8 teachers in Texas to collaborate in designing "knowbot" technology for teachers to locate information on the Net. While this project now is in its infancy, NASA has had sustained successes with K-12 educators in areas of science and mathematics, and this project will be worth watching. Texas educators in grades 3 through 8 are invited to e-mail Wanda Jackson at wjackson@tenet.edu or voicemail at (512) 471-3241.

The GENII Project—University of Tasmania, Australia

GENII is a worldwide volunteer consortium of networked educators. GENII means Group Exploring the National Information Infrastructure. They say the Internet is the "precursor of the NII," and they have the foresight to name themselves for what the Net is becoming! GENII is intended to facilitate the training of classroom teachers in skills that are necessary to use the profusion of resources on the Internet, so that teachers can incorporate the Net into their classrooms.

GENII has the following goals:

1. Create a *VIRTUAL FACULTY.*

    The VIRTUAL FACULTY is intended to be a networked group of educators dedicated to "being there" for the K-12 teacher when they are ready to learn the new skills associated with accessing the Internet. This FACULTY will be an ongoing resource for teachers as they become more familiar with the workings of cyberspace and begin the process of introducing the tools/resources to the classroom.

2. Write the Curriculum.

The VIRTUAL FACULTY will research, write, and publish a manual that covers the following:

- Achieving Net access
- The how-to's of common Net protocols
- Resources/Pointers
- Lessons for integration into regular coursework
- Netiquette and acceptable use of the Internet

3. Develop a Pointer Repository.

The VIRTUAL FACULTY will establish pointers for the following:

- Net-training
- Technology implementation in schools/communities
- Subject-oriented resources
- School restructuring ideas, etc.
- GENII-generated online instructional materials

GENII's goal is to help organize access first by teaching the basic skills necessary to achieve a connection, and then providing an entry point into the Internet "jungle." Once inside, the Virtual Faculty will be there to be your friendly, knowledgeable guide.

Where to find it

E-mail	`kwallet@vdoe386.vak12ededu` or `kwallet@mwc.vak12ed.edu`
U.S. contact	Ms. Katherine B. Wallet
	Chairperson of the Science Department
	Courtland High School
	6701 Smithstation Road
	Spotsylvania, VA 22553
E-mail	`gduckett@deakin.oz.au`
Surface mail	George Duckett
	Deakin University, Burwood Campus
	Faculty of Education
	221 Burwood Highway
	Burwood, Victoria 3125
	Australia

Following is a list of other active members of the GENII Virtual Faculty Project:

Marty Gay, Port Townsend School District, Port Townsend, WA

   `martini@olympus.net`

Terry Lee Moore, Environmental Research Laboratories, Boulder, CO

   `tmoore@erl.noaa.gov`

Tice Deyoung, Department of Defense, ARPA, Virginia

   `deyoung@arpa.mil`

Leni Donlan, East Whittier City School District, Whittier, CA

   `ldonlan@netcom.com`

The Global Quest: The Internet in the Classroom—NASA

NASA (the National Aeronautics and Space Administration) is offering a great 12 minute video, entitled *The Global Quest: The Internet in the Classroom.* It features K-12 students and teachers. The video is a good short piece to show reluctant administrators and interested parents. High school and middle school teachers praised this video. The opening states that the video may be freely copied for educational use.

Where to find it

Voice	216-774-1051, ext. 293

Beginning Teacher Computer Network—Harvard University

The idea of the Beginning Teacher Computer Network at Harvard University School of Education started out primarily as a way to support brand new teachers, using e-mail. Teacher education faculty, student teachers, and supervising teachers can stay in close contact electronically. The University of Virginia's Teacher-LINK and the University of Kansas' UNITE work along similar lines.

These groups use electronic text communication to enable teacher training faculty, student teachers, and teachers in the field to improve teaching by staying in touch and solving problems together. Although the Harvard network is growing and adding new services (a CHAT room, and current education majors have recently been allowed on), these efforts generally are not yet open to all K-12 teachers. Rather, they support the graduates of particular universities.

The following section, and the GENII project mentioned previously, are the first steps toward dealing with these needs on a career-long basis for all teachers.

NOVAE>> GROUP>> Teachers Networking for the Future

This grassroots group is designed to keep teachers abreast of new developments in educational uses of the Net. It is by teachers, and for teachers, and free. They share articles and tips on many topics of interest to teachers:

- Internet lists, FAQs, Gophers, WWW, etc.
- Funding for Teacher Education and equipment
- Elementary (K-5) and Middle (6-8) School Projects
- Secondary (9-12) School Projects

The following are some excerpts from their announcement:

```
Date: Thu, 2 Jun 1994 05:44:48 -0600 (MDT)
From: Arthur Galus <c6460101@idptv.idbsu.edu>
Subject: NOVAE GROUP
        THE UNIVERSITY OF IDAHO PROUDLY HOSTS THE NOVAE>> GROUP>>


      _   _    _     |  _
    / \   / /  \ | /        NOVAE>> GROUP>>
   /   \ / / _ * _           Teachers Networking for the Future
  / /\ \/ /   / | \
 / / \  /    / |             Robin Powlus robin_p@server.greatlakes.k12.mi.us
/_/   \_/_____            Leni Donlan              afcleni@aol.com
    /_____/               Kathryn Amanda Cossi     kcossi@tenet.edu
   / /                       Bob Melchert    melchert@raven.csrv.uidaho.edu
  / / /___                   Bill Jacobson            wmjake@pen.k12.va.us
 / /___/ /                   Andy Wright      awright@ccantares.wcupa.edu
/_____/                   Arthur Galus       c6460101@idptv.idbsu.edu


Fellow Educator:
     Your most valuable asset is your time. How best to invest your
time often forces you to forego opportunities that, frankly, you may wish
you had time to enjoy. If you have found yourself with very little
time to explore the Internet and to learn of the opportunities opening
up for educators there, then perhaps NOVAE>> GROUP>> is the listserv
for you.
     Created by educators, NOVAE>> GROUP>> is a listserv that provides
timely news articles to classroom teachers who really don't have time
to drive the Information Highway. Weekly postings from teachers and
other educators just like yourself keep you abreast of the electronic
world pulsing around us all. Here are some comments from users who
have found NOVAE>> GROUP>> to be an important tool in their day to day
operations:
```

"Educators are better judges of content and process issues than computer folks (myself included) and we really benefit from your mining of resources that we may not know of."

"I am responsible for the K-12 computer activities in the Southern York County School District and enjoy your lists of interesting "finds". Keep them coming."

"Thank you for sending the information that you have so far. It has been very helpful to me and my staff."

"Myself and several members of the faculty at Bloomsburg Middle School are always interested in telecommunication project, information, and news about the Internet. Your messages are extremely valuable and helpful along these lines. THANKS!!"

"It's a BIG world out there but (you are) helping to make it more accessible. Helps to know other teachers and kids have the same cares, concerns and frustrations. We have been in contact with others we could never have met without the link and have done collaborative projects with students thousands of miles away!   Thanks you!"

"Since this is the first year for us, it has kept us informed about available resources on the Internet. We were also able to make international connections from the materials which were sent."

"We have distributed the information to the whole teaching staff. Some are excellent opportunities and others as information. Thanks for surfing the net to find this stuff... we don't have the time."

NOVAE>> GROUP>> selects articles to fit the following subject groups as they become available:

    Internet Information (includes lists, FAQs, and information on gophers, WWW, etc.)

    Funding/Teacher Education Information (includes grants, workshops, televised conferences, etc.)

    Elementary (K-5) and Middle (6-8) School Projects (all subjects as well as keypal information)

    Secondary (9-12) School Projects (math, science, social studies, etc.)

If you are interested in requesting our service for yourself or for your school, send us the following information and you will be added to the list.

    YOUR NAME
    YOUR COMPLETE E-MAIL ADDRESS

Send your request to Bob Melchert (melchert@raven.csrv.uidaho.edu) or Art Galus (c6460101@idptv.idbsu.edu).

PreSTO Listserv—Preservice and Student Teachers Online

Mississippi State University's College of Education offers the PreSTO discussion list as a forum to encourage collaboration among preservice and student teachers around the world. Faculty members are welcome, but are reminded that this is a *student* list!

Where to find it

E-mail	Listproc@ra.msstate.edu
Body	subscribe presto *YourFirstName YourLastName*

For more information

E-mail	Dr. Larry S. Anderson
	LSA1@Ra.MsState.Edu
Voice	601/325-2281

SuperQuest for Teachers—National Center for Supercomputing Applications

This is the newest variant of SuperQuest. SuperQuest now is an intensive three-week workshop in computational sciences and modeling (with discovery learning and exploration) for high school math and science teachers. National Science Foundation funding will allow a year-long follow-up on these master teachers. The first access point is about the project in general. The second access point is called the SuperQuest Daily Observer and is a day-by-day account of the teacher training workshop.

Where to find it

URL	http://www.ncsa.uiuc.edu/Edu/Superquest/sqt/index.html
URL	http://www.ncsa.uiuc.edu/Edu/SuperQuest/sqt/observer.html

National Center for Student Research—Mandeville, Louisiana

Mandeville Middle School is the site of the *National Center for Student Research*, which houses electronic journals and databases created and maintained by and for students. The Center stresses scientific methods and publishes reviewed abstracts of student research. They offer free program development and teacher training materials for those interested in a student research center approach to classroom instruction.

Where to find it

Telnet

Site	nptn.org
Login	visitor
Choose	The Science Center
Choose	National Student Research Center

For more information

E-mail	John I. Swang (nsrcmms@aol.com)

Buzzword Gibberish Decoder (BGD)

Unfortunately, a few words are just too popular on the Net, causing confusion and unnecessary complexity. While no one person knows *all* the uses that a particular word is now enduring, this section is designed to help you distinguish some very popular and/or cryptic names and acronyms.

This decoder will not provide details on more than a few entries, but rather this section is designed help you tell one project from another and recognize organizations as they evolve through new names. At least one method of contact is supplied for over three dozen entities.

A1

See *Academy One.*

Academy One

Part of the National Public Telecomputing Network (NPTN) and associated with the Freenets (see Chapter 3 for Freenet listings). Also related to the Middle School Network. This is a resource for primary and secondary school teachers, students, and administrators.

Where to find it

Telnet   `freenet-in-a.cwru.edu` or `129.22.8.75`.

BBS

Bulletin Board System, a local dial-up service available by modem. One way to access the Internet.

Electronic Schoolhouse

A portion of the America Online (AOL) service environment, only available to paid subscribers to America Online. For America Online subscription and price information, send a brief e-mail request to `info@aol.com` or call 800/827-6364.

Empire Internet Schoolhouse

Marion French's New York NYSERNet gopher site for K-12 educators. Also mentioned in Chapter 3.

Where to find it

Gopher   `nysernet.org 3000`

FidoNet

This worldwide system of over 15,000 BBSs has no headquarters. FidoNet enables you to log on to your personal account through a modem to use e-mail to and from the Internet (and sometimes FTP by e-mail). Local FidoNet BBSs generally are free to use, but e-mail users may incur per-message charges. K12Net is the

K-12 educational portion of FidoNet. FidoNet reaches places where direct Internet connection is not available. A computer, modem, and telephone connection to a local bulletin board are all you need. To find the telephone numbers of active bulletin boards in your region, call a local computer store or your public library.

FrEdMail

Free Educational Electronic Mail Network started in 1986. It grew to be the largest BBS-based education network, and now is called *Global SchoolNet* (also mentioned in this list). FrEdMail projects included "Acid Rain," in which students around the country collected rain samples, plotted national data, and shared research, conclusions, and essays on the causes and effects of acid rain; and "Experts Speak," in which one group of students assuming the personalities of historical figures was interviewed by another group of students to determine their assumed identities. The Global Grocery List project (mentioned later in this list), also was begun under FrEdMail auspices.

Global Change Network

This project is associated with TERC, and funded by NSF.

Where to find it

Gopher   hub.terc.edu.

Global Classroom

Associated with Global Classroom Youth Congress, the goal is to bring the voice of youth into cyberspace, particularly comments and recommendations from youth on the use of global networking and the Internet in schools.

Where to find it

E-mail   Seth J. Itzkan (GlobalCR@aol.com)

WWW URL   http://www.mit.edu:8001/afs/athena/user/a/w/awillis/
                www/GCYC/GlobalCR.html

Global Classroom List

A Listserv discussion list for international student e-mail debate.

Where to find it

E-mail　　　　Listserv@uriacc.bitnet with the message
　　　　　　　subscribe GC-L *YourFirstName YourLastName*

Global Grocery List

GGL, a "global grocery shopping spree," started as part of FrEdMail. This project has no timetable. You just collect your local grocery prices at your convenience, e-mail them to GGL central, and keep checking your mail box for the price lists of other participants. Prices from around the world can be used in math, science, social studies, health studies, and writing. They can be used to practice calculations, as an information basis on which to draw conclusions, and as a springboard for writing assignments.

Where to find it

E-mail　　　　dwarlick%ncsdpi.fred.org@cerf.net

Global Learning Corporation

Corporate home of World Classroom, a curriculum and information network for K-12 schools, brings together students to work on structured curriculum activities in science, social studies, language arts, foreign languages, and current events. WorldClassroom also provides a series of Guest Speakers who are experts from a variety of professions that are of interest to students and teachers.

Where to find it

Telnet　　　　global1.glc.dallas.tx.us or 198.140.162.1
Login　　　　demo3
Password　　　WORLDCLASS (all uppercase)
Voice　　　　1-800-866-4452

GlobalNetwork Academy

Also known as Globewide Network Academy (GNA, which also appears in this list), is associated with Diversity University (formerly known as USENET University). See *Globewide Network Academy*.

Global Quest

A free video on the educational potential of the Internet, prepared and available from NASA.

Where to find it

Voice   216/774-1051, ext. 293.

Global SCHLNet

A variant spelling of Global SchoolNet Foundation (formerly FrEdMail), a BBS network dedicated solely to K-12 education. Computer stores, the public library, education agencies, or computing centers at local colleges can provide information about available Bulletin Boards in your area.

Global Schoolhouse Project

This effort, funded by the NSF and other sponsors, has the motto "Linking Kids and Educators Around the World."

Where to find it

                janice@cnidr.org or gfitz@cerf.net
Voice   619/433-3413 or 619/931-5934.

Global SchoolNet Foundation

Formerly FrEdMail, this organization has an "ideas list" that connects you to over 150 electronic bulletin boards (called electronic mail centers) operated by individuals and institutions. Each bulletin board represents a "node" on the system and delivers Internet e-mail to many teachers and students. A mature, grassroots, inexpensive system, these nodes are located at universities, district and county education agencies, and local schools. They specialize in e-mail and collaborative projects. Their motto is "Linking Teachers and Students Around the World....We consistently publish the best curriculum-based collaborative learning projects via e-mail available on the net. Our volume is not high, but our quality is always consistent...We moderate the list and only top-notch projects get posted."

Where to find it

E-mail   Al Rogers at arogers@bonita.cerf.fred.org

Voice   619/475-4852

E-mail Request   fred@acme.fred.org (asking about the ideas list and
                  Global SchoolNet templates)

The following is a brief introduction to Global SchoolNet guidelines:

```
How to Design a Successful Project

Over the years, Global SchoolNet Foundation has evolved a number of
guidelines and principles which have led to many successful collaborative
projects involving hundreds of classrooms and thousands of students.
Like many aspects of successful teaching, we have found that planning
is the key to success.

The guidelines  presented below have been validated in numerous
highly successful classroom based projects on the FrEdMail Network.
These guidelines, along with the template for writing you own "Call
for Collaboration" will help guide you through a successful online
learning experience with your students.

1.  Design a project with specific goals, specific tasks, and
    specific outcomes. The more specific, the better;  the more
    closely aligned with traditional instructional objectives, the
    better. Avoid "sister school" and "pen pal" projects.

2.  Set specific beginning and ending dates for your project, and set
    precise deadlines for participant responses. Then, make a time
    line and provide lots of lead time to announce your project.
    Post your first call for collaboration at least six weeks before
    the starting date. Repeat your call again two weeks before the
    starting date.

3.  If possible try your project out with a close colleague first, on
    a small scale. This can help you troubleshoot and solve both
    technical problems as well as problems with the basic project
    design.

4.  Use the template at the end of this article to design your call
    for collaboration. Then post your call to
```

```
CALL-IDEAS@ACME.FRED.ORG and we'll forward it to our
international mailing lists for you. If you
provide us 6-8 weeks lead time, we'll re-post it for you again
two weeks before the project begins.

In your call for collaboration, be sure and include:
- Goals and objectives of the project
- grade levels desired
- how many responses you would like
- contact person
- Time line and deadlines
- Your location and complete contact information
- what you will do with the responses (The best projects provide
  some form of interaction; in any case, be sure you provide
  some form of "payback" to your contributors so they will have
  incentive to collaborate with you.)

Also, be sure your call includes examples of the kinds of
writing or data collection which students will submit. This is
important to the success of the project.
```

5. Find responsible students and train them to be part of your project. You're probably already doing this if you are using technology in the classroom. This will be a big time saver.

6. At the conclusion of the project, follow through on sharing the results of the project with all participants.

    - If you publish any student writing, send a hard copy to all who participated.
    - Have your students collaborate on writing up a summary of the project, describing it, what they did, what they learned, and what changes they would make in the project. Post that message on the network for all to see (not just the project participants).
    - Send a copy of this summary, along with project proceeds, to your principal, PTA president, superintendent, and board of education president.
    - Have your students send a thank-you message to all contributors.

Global Studies High School

This is a Listserv discussion list.

Where to find it

E-mail   Listserv@onondaga.bitnet with the message subscribe
                GLBL-HS *YourFirstName YourLastName*

Global Village News

This electronic newspaper is associated with K12Net and, therefore, part of FidoNet. This publishing project gives students of all ages a chance to produce and enjoy a worldwide educational newspaper.

Globewide Network Academy

Also known as Global Network Academy (GNA), this is associated with Diversity University Moo and affiliated with USENET University. This endeavor provides higher education via the Internet in a virtual campus setting. Age restrictions are not so important here as is readiness to learn.

Where to find it

WWW URL   `http://uu-gna.mit.edu:8001/uu-gna/index.html`

Help by e-mail `joe@astro.as.utexas.edu` or `gna-webmaster@sun.dsy.de`

GNA

See *Globewide Network Academy*.

I*EARN

The non-profit International Education and Resource Network, includes over 400 schools in 21 countries empowering teachers and young people (K-12) to work together in different parts of the world. Their motto is "Youth Making a Difference in the World Through Telecommunications." I*EARN uses video-speaker telephones (using regular telephone lines, slow-scan, black and white images), e-mail and online conferencing for exchanges to enable students to make a meaningful contribution to the health and welfare of people and the planet. They want to see students go beyond both simply being "pen-pals" and working on strictly "academic" work to use telecommunications in joint student projects designed to *make a difference in the world* as part of the educational process. I*EARN is associated with the Copen Family Fund.

A few examples of recent student projects include the following:

- *The Contemporary*—A news magazine
- *A Vision*—An award-winning literary journal

- *Planetary Notions*—An environmental newsletter
- *Liberty Bound*—A human rights newsletter
- *ICARUS*—An ozone measurement and newsletter
- *The People We Admire—Las Personas que Admiramos!"*—A bilingual study of cultural heroes
- Holocaust/Genocide Project & Newsletter
- Water pollution measurement
- Rainforest Project
- Support for children in Bosnia and Somalia
- Building wells for clean water in Nicaragua

Where to find it

E-mail	Ed Gragert iearn@copenfund.igc.apc.org
Voice	914/962-5864
Fax	914/962-6472

K12Net

This is an inexpensive, decentralized, grassroots method for schools to begin Internet use. K12Net has several curriculum-related conferences or "echo forums." It is based on the worldwide FidoNet organization of local dial-up BBSes. A growing network, K12Net provides estimable low-budget educational e-mail services to millions of teachers, students, and parents in metropolitan and rural areas throughout the planet, giving them the capability to meet and talk with each other on educational issues, and exchange information and share resources on a "global" scale.

Although direct connection to the Internet provides much *faster* communication (seconds or minutes), it costs far more than FidoNet's communication lags of hours and days. For K-12 educators with severely limited funding, K12Net and Global SchoolNet may be the only Internet e-mail options to seriously consider.

Where to find it

Fidonet	Helen Sternheim at 1:321/110
Internet e-mail	helen@k12.ucs.umass.edu

KIDS

This is the KIDS part of KidSphere.

Where to find it

E-mail   joinkids@pittvms.bitnet

Kidlink Lists

This is a large collection of related Listserv discussion lists focused on children aged 10-15, including the following:

List name	Topic	Listserv Address
KIDFORUM	Kidlink coordinators	@vm1.nodak.edu
KIDLEADR	Kidlink coordinators	@vm1.nodak.edu
KIDLEADRP	Portuguese Kidlink coordination	@vm1.nodak.edu
KIDLINK	Kidlink Project list	@vm1.nodak.edu
KIDPLAN	Kidlink planning	@vm1.nodak.edu
KIDPLAN2	Kidlink workgroup	@vm1.nodak.edu
KIDPROJ	Special kidlink projects	@vm1.nodak.edu
KIDLIT-L	Children's Literature discussion	@bingvmb.bitnet

An example Kidlink project (desert and desertification) is highlighted later, in Chapter 2.

Where to find it

E-mail   listserv@vm1.nodak.edu
Message   get kidlink master
              get kidlink general

Kidlink Gopher

This is a Gopher with projects aimed at 10 to 15 year olds.

Where to find it

Gopher   kids.ccit.duq.edu or 165.190.8.35

Kids Weathernet

This is an e-mail project for elementary classes to collect and share weather and climate data, coordinated at Manzano Day School in Albuquerque, New Mexico.

Where to find it

E-mail   Bill Wallace echo@bootes.unm.edu

KidsNet

See *KidSphere*.

KidSphere

KIDSPHERE (previously KidsNet) is a Listserv mailing list for grown-up's list associated with the KIDS list for kids.

Where to find it

E-mail   KidSphere-Request@vms.cis.pitt.edu

Middle School Network

Associated with Academy One and the National Public Telecomputing Network. This program is for middle school parents, educators, students.

Where to find it

E-mail   Herbert Vaughan

xx104@nptn.org or hvaughan@rs6000.baldwinw.edu

National Public Telecomputing Network (NPTN)

This is a non-profit organization which develops free, public-access, community computer systems in cities throughout the USA. This growing network is attempting to build an apparatus similar to the National Public Radio system. Although based on the Freenets, this project has grown beyond them, joining Ameritech in the Learning Village project which has government cooperation in Illinois, Indiana, Michigan, Ohio, and Wisconsin.

Where to find it

E-mail	Tom Grundner
	`tmg@nptn.org`
Voice	216/247-5800 or 216/368-2733
Fax	216/247-3328
E-mail	Linda Delzeit
	`linda@nptn.org`
Voice	714/527-5651
E-mail	`info@nptn.org`

Anonymous FTP

Site	`nptn.org directory /pub/nptn/nptn.info/` `basic.guide.txt`

National Student Research Center (NSRC)

This project wants "children around the world to become humanitarian and ecological 21st century citizens in an ultimately diverse and highly interdependent, science and technology based, global community." The project is coordinated at Mandeville Middle School in Mandeville, Louisiana. Project E-Journals and databases are housed in the NSRC's Electronic Library located in America Online's Electronic School House (AOL KEYWORD: ESH). Once in the Electronic School House, Apple users should select Project Libraries and Exchanges. PC and Mac users should select The Schoolhouse Project Libs icon in the lower right corner, and then highlight National Student Research Center for access to the Library. The e-journals and databases also are housed in the NSRC's Electronic Library located on the National Public Telecomputing Network. Telnet to nptn.org and sign on as VISITOR, and then select THE SCIENCE CENTER. For access to the E-Library, select National Student Research Center, and then select E-JOURNALS. Users then can highlight journals or databases for perusal before downloading.

NSRC products also are on the Technology Education Research Center's (TERC) Gopher nicknamed *The Hub*. Users should Gopher to `hub.terc.edu` to access The Hub or use the menu path `GOPHERS AROUND THE WORLD\NORTH AMERICA\USA\MASSACHUSETTS\THE HUB`. Once in, select `RESOURCES FOR MATH AND SCIENCE\EDUCATION`, and then select `SCIENCE`. To view e-journals and databases before downloading, select `NATIONAL STUDENT RESEARCH CENTER ELECTRONIC LIBRARY`.

NPTN

See *National Public Telecomputing Network* (associated with the Freenets and Academy One).

NSRC

See *National Student Research Center*.

NSF

The National Science Foundation, is a U.S. government education, research funding, and dissemination agency.

SCHL Net News Service

This is a news branch of Global SchoolNet. See *Global SchoolNet*.

Scholastic Network

This is a commercial educational publisher.

Where to find it

Gopher	`Scholastic.com 2003`
WWW URL	`http://Scholastic.com:2005/`
E-mail	Eadie Adamson
	`eadie@aol.com`
Voice	212/343-4940

School Renewal Network

The National Education Association (NEA) and IBM (International Business Machines Corporation) are backing this effort at school reform. This electronic network is intended to create a research base by a community of actively engaged practitioners and researchers.

Where to find it

Voice   Shari Castle at 202/822-7783

Schoolhouse

See *Electronic Schoolhouse*, *Empire Internet Schoolhouse*, *Global Schoolhouse*, and *Virtual Schoolhouse*.

TERC

The *Technology Education Research Center*, located in Cambridge, Massachusetts, is a center that provides valuable help to K-12 school people all over the Net. A special interest is curriculum projects involving telecomputing. Services include outreach, technical assistance, curriculum guides, and information dissemination. TERC a publishes a free newsletter called *Hands On!*.

Where to find it

Gopher   hub.terc.edu
E-mail   Ken Mayer ken_mayer@terc.edu
Voice   617/547-0430
Surface mail   Technology Education Research Center (TERC)
               2067 Massachusetts Avenue
               Cambridge, MA 02140

Virtual School of Natural Sciences (VSNS)

This is part of Globewide Network Academy. See *Globewide Network Academy*.

World Classroom

This is brought to you by Global Learning Corporation in Dallas, Texas. See *Global Learning Corporation*.

Youth Congress

See *Global Classroom*.

Technical Help for K-12 Schools

U.S. schools have a tremendous need for technology planning. Some of the more affluent schools are already on the Net, as you'll see at the end of this chapter. But what about schools (and districts) where not even one computer is networked to another? What about thousands of classrooms with no telephone connections? Vast numbers of schools in the U.S. still have only two telephone lines, often for a dozen or more adult workers to "share."

The task of K-12 technology planning, while daunting and financially challenging, is already begun for you. The following sections discuss some guides and well thought-out answers to your K-12 technology planning questions.

Building the Future: K-12 Network Technology Planning Guide

This comprehensive "final draft" guide addresses the latest in technical communications networking and will be the basis of network and school site infrastructure planning in California. It will assist in planning for the use of technology as an integral part of the education reform goals as required in *Goals 2000: Educate America Act* signed into Law, March 31, 1994. The guide is in Gopher form, so you can access it one chapter at a time only.

Where to find it

Gopher	`goldmine.cde.ca.gov` or `165.74.7.50`
Directory	California Dept. of Education-general information

For more information

E-mail	Carole Teach
	`cteach@goldmine.cde.ca.gov`
Voice	916-654-9662

National Center for Technology Planning

At Mississippi State University, graduate students have prepared technology planning aids which are available to FTP or by WWW.

Where to find it

Anonymous FTP

Site	`ftp.msstate.edu`
Directory	`/pub/archives/nctp`
Gopher	`gopher.msstate.edu`
Menu	`/Resources Maintained at MsState University/National Center for Technolgy Planning`

K-12 Internetworking Guidelines

This Internet Working Draft provides technical guidance to the K-12 educational community on school networking and connections to the Internet. It is too technical for new computer users, but has two very important points that anyone involved with schooling should be aware.

■ All schools should begin *now* to become ready for the approaching National Information Infrastructure (NII) by designing their network technology on a star-based pattern. No, this is not a science fiction story! It's practical down-to-earth advice from the best of the technical experts. A star pattern is based on a central computer, or server, with other computers connecting to it in a radiating pattern (as in a star or asterisk).

If each campus links individually and directly all its computers to a central on-campus server, then the various campus servers can be linked similarly to the district or county server. And the district servers will be linked to the regional or state server. Each computer serves the others below it in the hierarchy.

This star network "topology" is the preferred way to go, because it will be the most flexible design when the powerful new services, such as integrated voice, data, and video, of the NII arrive.

■ Network management and network support and training should be budgeted at the campus and district levels *from the start*. Adding funds for these vital services later will only increase their cost, and decrease user satisfaction and success. Sure, students will do much of this for free, but they will need new software, and everyone will need training.

If your school doesn't yet have a "star topology" computer network, then the technical people who are working on it should have this working draft.

Where to find it

Anonymous FTP for the East Coast

Site	`ds.internic.net` or `198.49.45.10`
Password	`guest`
Directory	`internet-drafts`
File	`draft-ietf-isn-k12-guide-01.txt`

Anonymous FTP for the West Coast

Site	`ftp.isi.edu` or `128.9.0.32`
Password	`guest`
Directory	`internet-drafts`
File	`draft-ietf-isn-k12-guide-01.txt`

Anonymous FTP for the Pacific Rim

Site	`munnari.oz.au` or `128.250.1.21`
Password	`guest`
Directory	`internet-drafts`
File	`draft-ietf-isn-k12-guide-01.txt`

Anonymous FTP for Europe

Site	`nic.nordu.net` or `192.36.148.17`
Password	`guest`
Directory	`internet-drafts`
File	`draft-ietf-isn-k12-guide-01.txt`

Internet Request for Comments (RFC) 1578, FYI #22

This document is designed to help you from the very beginning of getting the Net into your school. The real title on this easy to read document is *FYI on Questions and Answers—Answers to Commonly Asked "Primary and Secondary School Internet User" Questions.* You can expect to hear it called *RFC #1578*, or *FYI #22*, or simply "that neat Internet Q&A for K-12 schools."

It's author, Jennifer Sellers of NASA NREN (`sellers@quest.arc.nasa.gov`), organized *FYI #22* as a set of commonly asked questions, each followed by their answers.

This is one of the places to begin a search for answers to questions about how to do the following:

- Use the Internet in K-12 educational settings
- Find school support for an Internet connection
- Solve start-up and technical problems
- Deal with security, viruses, and ethics
- Arrange educational collaboration and projects
- Find the resources you need for a project

RFC 1578 (February 1994) also contains a detailed, seven page glossary that you can use to broaden your understanding of the intricacies of the Net.

Where to find it

Anonymous FTP for North America

Site	`ds.internic.net or 198.49.45.10`
Directory	`/fyi`
Filename	`fyi22.txt`

Anonymous FTP for the Pacific Rim

Site	`munnari.oc.au or 128.250.1.21`
Directory	`/fyi`
Filename	`fyi22.txt`

Anonymous FTP for Europe

Site	`nic.nordu.net or 192.36.148.17`
Directory	`/fyi`
Filename	`fyi22.txt`

K-12 Schools Already on the Net

Elementary, middle, junior high, and high schools (and school district offices!) are already on the Net, providing their communities, parents, students, and teachers with exciting new information opportunities. The following sections discuss a sample of Gopher and WWW sites operated on K-12 campuses. First up are elementary schools, followed by middle, junior high and high schools, and then followed by district offices.

Note: This is not intended to be a comprehensive list of K-12 sites. The site called Outpost at URL `http://k12.cnidr.org/janice_k12/k12menu.html` will help you with even more.

Glenview District 34 Schools' WWW Server

Glenview District 34 Schools, a K-8 district in Glenview, Illinois, has an interesting World Wide Web server. The seven schools of this suburb, north of Chicago, offer something unusual on the Internet—the online public access catalogs of its seven primary libraries. In addition, they offer access to the Glenview Public Library through the Web server as well.

In addition, the students of the John H. Springman Junior High have just created their own homepage by and for kids. They also are involved in a Global School House project, and will be contributing their findings in the area of disaster planning.

Where to find it

URL	`http://www.ncook.k12.il.us/dist34_home_page.html`
URL	`http://www.ncook.k12.il.us/sp/sp_home_page.html`

For more information

E-mail	John Mundt
	`mundtj@ncook.k12.il.us`
Voice	708/998-5007

Grand River Elementary School—Lansing, Michigan

The fifth grade class seems to be the ring-leaders here at this school Web site, but the rest of Grand River Elementary is close behind. This is a Web site where the kids have actually created the homepage themselves, and maintain the informtion with their teacher.

Where to find it

URL   `http://web.cal.msu.edu/JSRI/GR/BradClass.thumb.html`

For more information

E-mail   Brad Marshall

                   `grsch21@pilot.msu.edu`

Claremont High School—Claremont, California

This site includes links to academic resources for Claremont High School students, current research data and publications in knot theory, and access to their anonymous FTP site, along with descriptions of the school and its computing resources.

Students have created their own homepages. They expect some departments to add additional links to discipline-specific high school resources.

There also is a link to the Claremont Colleges' Library system. This WWW server also includes links to Pasadena's Jet Propulsion Lab, Harvey Mudd College's Web site, and Pitzer College's new WWW server for K-12 access.

Where to find it

URL   `http://www.cusd.claremont.edu`

For more information

E-mail   Robs John Muir

                   `rmuir@chs.cusd.claremont.edu`

Voice   909-624-9053

Monta Vista High School—Cupertino, California

Monta Vista High School has been exploring new ways that the Internet can be used in K-12 education. This server is part of their ongoing project integrating the Internet into a high school setting, both for their own benefit, and as an example for other schools showing how easily students can get involved.

Where to find it

URL   http://www.mvhs.edu/

For more information

E-mail   Mark Wang

               mwang@walrus.mvhs.edu

```
Mark Wang, Student ('95) * Monta Vista High, Cupertino, CA USA
"The union of the mathematician with the poet, fervor with measure, poison with
correctness, this is surely the ideal."
 William James

Internet: mwang@walrus.mvhs.edu  AOL: MarkWang1
WWW: http://www.mvhs.edu/~mwang   Disclaimer: I speak not for Monta Vista
```

Armadillo Gopher and Web Server

Donald Perkins of the Houston (Texas) School District has been on the cutting edge for a long time. He has just added a WWW interface to the renowned Armadillo Gopher. Although this is *the* site for Texas studies, Donald packs this site with links to educational resources worldwide.

Where to find it

URL   http://chico.rice.edu/armadillo

For more information

E-mail   Donald Perkins dperkins@tenet.edu

Princeton Regional Schools

Great student created WWW home pages and the school newspaper are just the start of this Web site. Here, you also will find administrative information about the district, New Jersey State Education Policy news, and much more.

Where to find it

URL   `http://www.prs.k12.nj.us`

Vocal Point—Boulder Valley School District

The district publishes a monthly online newspaper called *Vocal Point*, prepared by students. The first edition was released in June, 1994. Noah Horton, a 13-year-old at Centennial Middle School, designed and programmed the HTML (HyperText Markup Language) that creates your online newspaper while you read it.

To quote Jill Tucker, an information contact for the project, "By creating a newspaper using the networks as a key information source, the students are allowed to complete a cycle of information processing: hypothesize, retrieve, process, theorize, and produce."

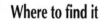

Where to find it

URL   `http://bvsd.k12.co.us/cent/Newspaper/Newspaper.html`

For more information

E-mail   Jill Tucker

              `jtucker@knightrider.com`

Voice   303/938-8427

From Here...

Next, in Chapter 2, you can look up Internet resources by areas of the K-12 curriculum, such as literature, biology, history health and more. Then after that, Chapter 3 has information on resource material in other curriculum areas.

INTERNET RESOURCES BY K-12 CURRICULAR AREA

Education is not the filling of a pail, but the lighting of a fire.

William Butler Yeats

The Internet contains enormous, growing quantities of information. Almost all of this useful information today is text-based, and the majority of it is in English. While these are the *current* circumstances, they are, as with the rest of the Internet, subject to rapid change.

The Internet is just full of information, and finding the right material to read is as important as dealing with it properly, once it is found. As discussed in Chapter 1, just finding materials soon might be much less of a problem for teachers and students. The real creativity in teaching is, and will continue to be, *what you do with the children and what they do together.*

This chapter assists you in finding the right resources to light the fire in a dozen broad curricular areas:

- Agricultural Education
- Business Education and Marketing
- Computer Science
- Counseling, Special Education, and Adventure Education
- English Language Arts, Literature, Speech, Poetry
- Fine Arts—Theater, Drama, Music, Dance
- Health, Nutrition, Family Planning, and Sex Education
- Journalism
- Mathematics, Algebra, Calculus, Geometry
- Sciences, Biology, Chemistry, Physics, Astronomy, and Earth Sciences
- Social Studies—History, Government, Civics, Economics
- World Languages

Note: These subject groupings are not intended to convey anything other than that the material is somewhat similar, and sometimes is found in close proximity in libraries and on the Net. The subject groupings are not exclusive or strict, either. Separating mathematical resources turns out to be difficult, because many science resources are intermixed with mathematical materials. Please be sure to check out related topics, such as math and science areas if you have interests in either!

Agricultural Education

These sources of information on *Agricultural Education* are only the tip of the iceberg. In the United States, most Land Grant universities have long been involved in delivery of agricultural information over the Net, and many of them are now providing materials appropriate or adaptable to K-12 educational needs. Gophers appear particularly popular in this field.

Not Just Cows—Wilfred Drew (Version 2.0, October 14, 1993)

Revised and expanded, *Not Just Cows* is an admirable and wise place to start looking for agricultural information on the Net. The rest of the title is *A Guide to Internet/Bitnet Resources in Agriculture and Related Sciences*.

Where to find it

Anonymous FTP

Site	`hydra.uwo.ca`
Directory	`/libsoft`
Files	`agguide.dos, agguide.wp`
Site	`ftp.sura.net`
Directory	`/pub/nic`
File	`agricultural.list`

For more information

E-mail	Bill Drew `drewwe@snymorva.cs.snymore.edu`
Voice	315/684-6055
Fax	315/684-6115

PEN Pages—Pennsylvania State University

Although some of the information on this server is specific to the Pennsylvania area, most of it is appropriate for any rural, agricultural region. This site is quite comprehensive, covering crop pricing and production, nutrition, family farm issues, and includes the *Horticultural Engineering Newsletter*.

Where to find it

Telnet

    Site   `psupen.psu.edu`

    Login   *your two-letter state abbreviation*

Advanced Technology Information Network

Another comprehensive source of agricultural information, this site in California's productive Central Valley, includes international trade information, weather data, health and safety details, and much more.

Where to find it

Telnet

    Site   `caticsuf.csufresno.edu`

    Login   `super`

GreenDisk Paperless Environmental Journal

This environmental information exchange scans hundreds of different sources on a wide range of topics; "everything from renewable energy to marine mammal protection to toxic waste disposal." Look here for a `magazines` directory that gives you issue-by-issue annotated contents listings of environmental magazines, with addresses for subscribing, and a `newsletters` directory that does the same for newsletters.

Where to find it

    Gopher   `info.umd.edu`

    Directory   `Education Resources/Academic Resources/Agriculture`
                 `Environmental Resources/Greendisk`

    Choose   `Using the GreenDisk, Order form`

For more information

    E-mail   `greendisk@igc.org` or `70760.2721@compuserve.com`

FDA Electronic Bulletin Board

Contains Food and Drug Administration information, including actions, congressional testimony, news releases, consumer information, information on AIDS, and information on veterinary medicine. This telnet site is very well-designed, once you get past the BBS registration.

Where to find it

Telnet

      Site   `fdabbs.fda.gov or 150.148.8.48`

      Login   `bbs`

For more information

      Voice   301/443-7318

GRIN—National Genetic Resources Program, NGRP-USDA-ARS

The *NGRP* Gopher server provides germplasm information about plants, animals, microbes, and insects within the National Genetic Resources Program of the U.S. Department of Agriculture's (USDA's) Agricultural Research Service (ARS). This also makes connections to other biological gopher servers.

Where to find it

      Gopher   `gopher.ars-grin.gov`

Agricultural Education

Veronica searches of all Gopherspace for `agricult* educat*`, `agricult*`, and `agricult* product*` turned up over 100 "hits." Here are the 13 most worth checking out for new and interesting agriculture information:

Where to find it

Gopher

ava.bcc.orst.edu

burrow.cl.msu.edu

econwpa.wustl.edu

gopher.awis.auburn.edu

gopher.fhcrc.org

gopher.metla.fi

gopher.stolaf.edu

gopher.tamu.edu

mudhoney.micro.umn.edu

services.dese.state.mo.us

seymour.md.gov

solar.rtd.utk.edu

swami.tamu.edu

AGINFO—University of Delaware Extension System Gopher

This is an exciting, new "experimental" UNIX Gopher server being set up at the University of Delaware for the College of Agricultural Sciences. Although the builders warn that this Gopher is "still under construction," you will see in Chapter 3 that Gophers require ongoing work to maintain, even after "construction" is done. This Gopher is already looking great.

Where to find it

Gopher   bluehen.ags.udel.edu

Following is what the Gopher's main menu looks like:

```
University of Delaware Extension System Gopher
1. About AGINFO
2. Search AGINFO <?>
3. Recent Additions to AGINFO
4. College of Agricultural Sciences - Information/
```

```
 5. College of Agricultural Sciences - Information (Hypertext) <HTML>
 6. University of Delaware Botanic Gardens (hypertext) <HTML>
 7. AGINFO Plant Database/
 8. New and Prospective Student Information/
 9. Information by Department/
10. Information By Topic/
11. Information by Type of Publication/
12. Cooperative Extension /
13. Personnel Directories/
14. Delaware Water Resources Information System/
15. Off-Campus Information Systems/
```

If you have a WWW browser, such as Mosaic, be sure to check out the lovely `Online Tour of the University of Delaware Botanical Gardens`.

Where to find it

URL	`http://bluehen.ags.udel.edu`

For more information

E-mail	Betsy Mackenzie
	`betsy@bluehen.ags.udel.edu`
Voice	302/831-2511
Fax	302/831-3651
Surface Mail	Betsy Mackenzie
	Department of Food and Resource Economics
	College of Agricultural Sciences
	University of Delaware
	Newark, Delaware 19717-1303

University of Wisconsin Extension System Gopher

This Gopher was recommended by the Dissemination Program Director at the National Center for Research in Vocational Education at the University of California at Berkeley as a good source of agricultural education resource materials. The recommendation was made on the Listserv discussion list VOCNET.

Where to find it

Gopher	`joe.uwex.edu`

U.S. Department of Agriculture Economic Research Service

This joint project of the Mann Library at Cornell University and the Economic Research Service of the U.S. Department of Agriculture contains more than 100 data sets. The data covers a very wide range of agricultural topics, including international and climate data. Many of the files are in Lotus 1-2-3 .WK1 format, so if you transfer them by FTP, be sure to type **bin** first to switch to binary mode.

Where to find it

Gopher   usda.mannlib.cornell.edu

Anonymous FTP

Site   usda.mannlib.cornell.edu

Directory   /usda

Agricultural Market News Service—U.S. Department of Agriculture

Here you can get commodity market reports that are updated daily. Send the following e-mail message, and follow the instructions returned to you by the Almanac server.

Where to find it

Almanac server

E-mail   almanac@oes.orst.edu

Body   send market-news catalog

Directory of Agricultural Professionals

U.S. Department of Agriculture Cooperative State Research Service's *Directory of Professional Workers in State Agricultural Experiment Stations and Other Cooperating Institutions* is over a hundred years old, so it didn't start out on the Net, but here it is now!

Where to find it

Anonymous FTP

Site	`eos.esusda.gov` or `192.73.224.111`
Directory	`pub/epubs-mg`
File	`hort-dir.zip`

For more information

Voice	202/720-8155
Fax	202/690-0289

Surface Mail Steven Robert Conn
US Department of Agriculture
14th & Independence Room 3328s
Washington, DC 20250-0900

Business Education and Marketing

In the following sections, you will find a number of Listserv discussion lists and Usenet Newsgroups about Business Education and Marketing, and a pair of business related Gophers. While they usually are considered to be for older age groups, certainly parents and business and marketing educators will be able to find fresh ideas to adapt to their lives and classrooms from these daily open discussions. Don't forget to look at Chapters 5 and 6 as well for business related information.

BUSETH-L—Business Ethics

This is a moderated Listserv list, so the moderator must "approve" your subscription. Send a note to the moderator rather than the usual `subscribe listname-l` `YourFirstName YourLastName` message.

Where to find it

E-mail	`UCSBILLB@ubvm.cc.buffalo.edu`
Moderator	William H. Baumer

E-EUROPE

The *Eastern European Business Network* is for those interested in doing business in Eastern Europe countries. It links businesses in Western Europe, Asia, and North America with businesses in Eastern Europe.

Where to find it

E-mail   `listserv@pucc.princeton.edu`

Body   `subscribe E-Europe` *`Your Name`*

ESBDC-L

Small business development centers communicate using this list.

Where to find it

E-mail   `LISTSERV@MUSIC.FERRIS.EDU`

Body   `subscribe ESBDC-L` *`Your Name`*

FLEXWORK

The *Flexible Work Environment* list discusses off-schedule, part-time, and other alternate working arrangements, such as telecommuting.

Where to find it

E-mail   `listserv@psuhmc.hmc.psu.edu`

Body   `subscribe flexwork` *`Your Name`*

INVEST-L

The topic here is student managed investment portfolios.

Where to find it

E-mail	`listserv@tcubvm.is.tcu.edu`
Body	`subscribe INVEST-L `*`Your Name`*

JAPAN

This discussion is about the Japanese economy and Japanese business systems. *Association of Japanese Business Studies* (AJBS) is an independent academic association devoted to research and discussion.

Where to find it

E-mail	`listserv@pucc.princeton.edu`
Body	`subscribe JAPAN `*`Your Name`*

Net Business and Marketing newsgroups

If you have access to Usenet Newsgroups, here are some you can look for.

```
alt.business.multi-level

bit.listserv.buslib-l

k12.ed.business

misc.invest

misc.invest.canada

misc.invest.funds

misc.invest.technical
```

Pacific Business Researchers Forum—PCBR-L

Pacific Business Researchers Forum discusses all business issues related to the Pacific nations.

Where to find it

E-mail	listserv@uhccvm.uhcc.hawaii.edu
Body	subscribe PCBR-L *Your Name*

FORUM—Real Estate Forum

Real Estate Forum is a discussion of matters of general interest to real estate researchers and students. Housing market analysis, announcements, research, and data needs are covered topics.

Where to find it

E-mail	listserv@utarlvm1.uta.edu
Body	subscribe RE-FORUM *Your Name*

RECMGMT

RECMGMT is a records management discussion group that shares information and ideas on this list about a variety of systems and platforms.

Where to find it

E-mail	listserv@suvm.acs.syr.edu
Body	subscribe RECMGMT *Your Name*

RISKNET

RISKNET discusses risk and insurance issues.

Where to find it

E-mail	listproc@mcfeeley.cc.utexas.edu
Body	subscribe RISKNET *Your Name*

SPACE-INVESTORS

This list discusses investment in space-related companies, and includes any space-related investment opportunities or any events affecting these potential investments.

Where to find it

E-mail	SPACE-INVESTORS-REQUEST@CS.CMU.EDU
Body	subscribe SPACE-INVESTORS *Your Name*

National Bureau of Economic Research

This Gopher operates out of Harvard University, and contains surveys of consumer finances and an indexed series of working papers on economics.

Where to find it

Gopher	nber.harvard.edu

Small Business Administration Industry Profiles

Here is a Gopher that contains the full text of many Small Business Administration government documents.

Where to find it

Gopher	umslvma.umsl.edu
Directory	Library/Government Information

Financial Web

The University of Texas maintains a WWW page for accessing all types of financial and economics WWW servers on the Net. This site is particularly complete.

Where to find it

URL   `http://riskweb.bus.utexas.edu/finweb.html`

Business Periodicals Online

The Gopher at the Internet Company includes, through their Electronic Newstand, the full text of articles from many business periodicals, including *Inc.*, *Business Week*, *The Economist*, and others.

Where to find it

Gopher   `gopher.internet.com`
Directory   `Electronic Newstand/Business Publications`

Computer Science

Students, parents, and teachers will find interesting new ways to think about computer science in this section. Several software archives are detailed, and Gophers and WWW sites also are identified.

Teaching students how to use computers is so much more important to *their* lives than it was to their teachers and parents; it is hard to overestimate the impact that good computer skills will have over the lifetime of today's students.

CICA: Center for Innovative Computer Applications

Indiana University at Bloomington's site holds a massive collection of *Microsoft Windows*-related free and shareware files. Many fonts, icons, games, sounds, drivers, utilities, and so on are available.

Where to find it

Anonymous FTP

    Site   `ftp.cica.indiana.edu` or `129.79.26.27`
    Directory   `pub/pc/win3`

EFF—Computers and Academic Freedom Archive

The *Electronic Frontier Foundation* operates this site containing First Amendment, privacy, and other weighty materials about high-technology legal entanglements over the Internet.

Where to find it

Anonymous FTP

Site   ftp.eff.org or 192.77.172.4

Usenet Computer Science Newsgroups

If you have access to Usenet Newsgroups, here are some to look for:

    alt.bbs

    comp.bbs.misc

    comp.compilers

    comp.edu

    comp.lang.apl

    comp.lang.lisp

    comp.lang.lisp.franz

    comp.lang.lisp.mcl

    comp.lang.lisp.x

    comp.lang.logo

    comp.org.fidonet

    comp.patents

    comp.research.japan

    comp.robotics

    info.academic-freedom

    k12.ed.comp.literacy

    news.software.anu-news

Trace Center: Disability and Computer Access Information

The *Trace Center* is part of the University of Wisconsin. The Trace Center is a Rehabilitation Engineering Research Center on Adapted Computers and Information Systems, and is funded through the National Institute on Disability and Rehabilitation Research, U.S. Department of Education. They specialize in communication by the non-speaking and physically disabled; the control mechanisms used to operate computers, communication aids, home environmental controls; and computer access—ways to make computers, electronic equipment, and information systems more accessible to people with disabilities.

Where to find it

Gopher   trace.waisman.wisc.edu

ISAAC or IKE (IBM Kiosk for Education)

This University of Washington site has grown far beyond a well-developed BBS-type telnet site, with generous help from IBM. Not coincidentally, it has a large amount of information about IBM computers and software. New users must register for full access. Remember your access code and password.

Where to find it

Telnet

     Site   isaac.engr.washington.edu or 128.95.32.61

For more information

     Voice   206/543-5604

MicroMUSE

This is an attempt to create an environment for experimentation and exploration. While some educators question the validity of this type of text-based fantasy, others see language learning and discovery occurring. There is little question that new forms of communication are required for future technology, and this is one forum for inventing new communication methods.

MicroMUSE provides a 24th century "science fantasy" environment in which students can learn new textual communication patterns. This environment is elaborate and can be consuming, so look out for possible cases in which students may become too involved in the fantasy.

Where to find it

Telnet

Site	michael.ai.mit.edu
Login	guest
Exit	/quit or QUIT (all caps)

World Window

World Window provides access to a menu system from which many other sites can be accessed. If you only want to become familiar with *one* telnet site, this may be the one to use. When prompted for a password, just press Enter to gain access to all publicly available services.

Where to find it

Telnet

Site	library.wustl.edu

Macintosh Software Archive

Stanford University has a large selection of Macintosh software on their Anonymous FTP site. It is worth a look around for all types of Mac software.

Where to find it

Anonymous FTP

Site	sumex-aim.stanford.edu
Directory	info-mac

Washington University Public Domain Archive

This public domain archive provides a large collection of freeware and shareware for sundry computer brands. The root directory contains the README file, which you should read first.

Where to find it

Anonymous FTP

Site	`wuarchive.wustl.edu`
Directory	`/info`
File	`arrangement`

The Ada Project—Women in Computing

The *Ada Project* is a Clearinghouse for information and resources relating to women in computing, and includes conferences, projects, discussion groups, organizations, fellowships, and grants.

Where to find it

URL	`http://www.cs.yale.edu/HTML/YALE/CS/HyPlans/tap/tap.html`

Computer-Mediated Communication Magazine

Computers are changing the way we communicate. Here is a magazine devoted to helping us understand these new forms of communication.

Several issues are available, starting with May 1994.

Where to find it

URLs	`http://www.rpi.edu/~decemj/cmc/mag/index.html`
	`http://www.rpi.edu/~decemj/cmc/mag/1994/jul/nets.html`

Clearinghouse of Subject Oriented Resource Guides

This collection of resources guides is ever growing, and contains several items on computer engineering, computer science research, computer software and hardware, computer mediated communication, and computer standards.

Where to find it

Gopher	una.hh.lib.umich.edu
Directory	inetdirsstacks

Computer Literacy Project

This Gopher houses much K-12 computer curriculum and computer literacy information.

Where to find it

Gopher	info.utas.edu.au
Directory	Departments/Education/Computer Literacy Project/Computer Literacy Survey/REPORTS
Gopher	gopher.dana.edu
Directory	K-12 Networking/ Computer Literacy Project (mirror from U. of Tasmania,Australia)/ Computer Literacy Survey/ REPORTS

You can obtain by FTP much of the same information.

Where to find it

Anonymous FTP

Site	ftp.dana.edu
Directories	educ
	educ/complit
Files	readme_r.pts
	index.txt
	abstract.txt

For more information

E-mail	Marcin Paprzycki
	paprzycki_m@gusher.pb.utexas.edu
E-mail	Tony Mitchell
	tmitchel@tigger.stcloud.msus.edu

Georgia College EduNet

This is a BBS containing a large collection of online resources for K-12 educators, including Internet directories and online texts, *CNN* and *Newsweek* Curriculum guides, a software evaluations library, Georgia's Quality Core Curriculum, a multimedia file exchange for Macintosh, Apple II, Apple IIgs, IBM, Amiga platforms, and so on. All new users must register.

Where to find it

Telnet

| Site | gcedunet.peachnet.edu |

National Center for Supercomputer Applications (NCSA)

The *Software Tools Group* (STG) at the National Center for Supercomputing Applications develops user-friendly data analysis and visualization software that is released into the public domain, that is, free and unrestricted. There is so much software here, it's best to begin with the README files to get a feel for it first, then explore!

Where to find it

Anonymous FTP

| Site | ftp.ncsa.uiuc.edu |
| Files | README.FIRST, README |

University of North Carolina Office for Information Technology

This provides information and software, including experimental computer applications, multimedia sound and pictures and movies, and graphic images files in various formats.

Where to find it

Anonymous FTP

Site	`sunsite.unc.edu`
Directories	`/pub/academic`
	`/pub/multimedia`

Macintosh Science and Technology Archive

This is the Naval Research Lab's public archive. It specializes in Macintosh computing and programming. This site also contains materials on biology, geology, physics, and chemistry.

Where to find it

Anonymous FTP

Site	`ra.nrl.navy.mil`
Directory	`/MacSciTech`
File	`_readme.txt`

Newton

Newton is an educational BBS sponsored by the Argonne National Laboratory Division of Educational Programs. All new users must register. Remember your password! The purpose of this BBS is to promote teacher and student networking and the exchange of ideas, classroom to classroom. This site is primarily aimed at teachers in science and math. All new users must register.

Where to find it

Telnet

Site	`newton.dep.anl.gov or 146.139.100.50`
Login	`bbs`
Password	(blank)

For more information

Voice	708/252-1794

CareerMosaic

This location contains in-depth information on several computer-related companies: Read-Rite, Symantec, U.S. West, National Semiconductor, Tandem Computer, Intuit, and so on.

Where to find it

URL   `http://www.careermosaic.com/cm/home.html`

For more information

E-mail   Mark Hornung

           `mhornung@pa.hodes.com`

Voice   415/813-8432

Fax   415/856-1181

Counseling, Special Education, and Adventure Education

K-12 counselors, special education teachers, and adventure education teachers are called on to do many things. This section is to provide several resources that can be useful in their work.

Because some of the resources in this section draw on college-level materials, parents and teachers will need to review this material to consider its use and application in the K-12 arena. Each item may be useful in the right context, with the proper preparation and supervision.

Cornucopia of Disability Information

This Gopher lives up to its name—it is a veritable cornucopia of great information on the legal, administrative, and technological aspects of people living and learning with all types of sensory, mobility, and learning disabilities.

Where to find it

Gopher   `val-dor.cc.buffalo.edu`

Sexual Harassment Bibliography

This is a beginning bibliography and some resources on sexual harassment.

Where to find it

Anonymous FTP

Site	`beech.cic.net or 192.131.22.5`
Directory	`/pub/ETEXT/pub/Politics/Feminism/GenderIssues/` `SexualHarassment`
Files	`sexual-harassment-bibliography.gz sexual-harassment-` `resources.gz`

Experiential Education Web Pages

The Association for Experiential Education (AEE) now has a WWW homepage housed at the Princeton University Outdoor Action Program. AEE is a not-for-profit, international membership organization. With members in over 20 countries, AEE's diverse membership consists of individuals and organizations with affiliations in education, recreation, outdoor adventure programming, mental health, youth service, physical education, management development training, corrections, programming for people with disabilities, and environmental education.

Where to find it

URL	`http://www.princeton.edu/~rcurtis/aee.html`

For more information

E-mail	Rick Curtis
	`rcurtis@ariel.princeton.edu`
Voice	609/258-3552

Big Computer Pals

Big Computer Pals is a Big Sister/Brother interaction across the network and aimed at the handicapped. There is no restriction on the type of handicap and has included sensory, mobility, educational, and emotional. The list `Bicompal@sjuvm.stjohns.edu` is a "personals" listing where people find big and little pals. Most of the interactions then are done through private mail.

This is a private list, so to join, you should contact Bob Zenhausern at one of the following locations:

Where to find it

E-mail	Bob Zenhausern
	`drz@sjuvm.stjohns.edu` or `72440.32@compuserve.com`
Voice	718/990-6447
Fax	718/380-3803

Plugged In is Looking for a Few Good Brains

Are you interested in helping a generation of young people learn about technology? *Plugged In* is a non-profit organization that designs and operates computer literacy projects for local community-based youth service providers in East Palo Alto, CA. Plugged In runs collaborative learning projects that use new technologies and provides training and technical support for staff at Boys and Girls Club facilities.

Plugged In is the "anchor" of proposal to establish a *National Youth Center Electronic Network*. This network would link Youth Centers that work with low-income children across the country, providing youth access to the Net and facilitating joint projects and the exchange of information. Plugged In now is looking for individuals who understand the technology, but also have a clear vision of how technology can benefit young people, particularly those from low-income families.

To get information on how you can participate in *Plugged In*, check out the WIRED Online archives:

Where to find it

WWW

URL	`http://www.wired.com/Info/plugged.in.html`

For more information

E-mail	Bart Decrim
	`PluggedIn@aol.com`

This Listserv posting details the Plugged In "curriculum" or program model, and gives specific details kids and parents would want to know before participating.

```
Date: Fri, 24 Jun 1994 11:43:00 -0700
From: Arthur R. McGee <amcgee@NETCOM.COM>
To: Multiple recipients of list COMMUNET <COMMUNET@uvmvm.umv.edu>
Subject: Plugged In (fwd)

...The National Youth Center Electronic Network Project is a demonstration designed
to help the leaders, staffs, and clients of community youth centers serving low-
income neighborhoods improve the lives and opportunities of children and community
members through the power of information technology and worldwide electronic
communications. The project will electronically link youth centers across the
country enabling these agencies to improve the development and delivery of youth
services and programs. In addition, use of electronic networks will introduce the
concept of electronic communications into low-income neighborhoods in meaningful
and useful ways, treating the youth center as an information superhighway point-of-
entry.
\...\

A Model for Collaborative Electronic Communications Projects:
The sites chosen to be pilots for this Project are New Haven,  Connecticut, and
East Palo Alto, California, two cities which share a myriad of problems and a
wealth of opportunities. Despite resources that include Yale University and
nationally recognized theaters and research hospitals, New Haven suffers from
rampant unemployment, a high school dropout rate hovering near fifty percent,
significant drug-related gang activity, and its status as one of the country's
poorest cities. East Palo Alto shares similar problems. For example, 87 percent of
its elementary school children qualify for free or reduced school meals and 80
percent of their families receive Aid to Families with Dependent Children (AFDC).
In 1992, the city's homicide rate surpassed those at New York, Los Angeles, and
Chicago. Like New Haven, East Palo Alto also has significant resources available
because of its proximity to Stanford University and Silicon Valley and a wealth of
local nonprofit organizations dedicated to serving its predominately poor popula-
tion.
\...\

The project will establish several models for the application of community-based
electronic networks and services. Leadership, Education, and Athletics in Partner-
ship (LEAP), a proven youth services delivery agency operating multiple youth
centers in the New Haven, Connecticut area, will serve as the lead project agency.
It will provide a model of the impact of electronic communications on service
delivery, education, and training in a community service delivery agency with
little previous exposure to electronic networks and applications. Plugged In, a
proven youth and family computer learning organization providing services at
multiple youth centers in the East Palo Alto, California area, will serve as a
facilitator of computer learning for the youth. The ability of Plugged In to
provide its youth with computer and electronic communications training via a
national youth center network will serve as a model for youth center outreach in an
electronic context.
The Morino Institute and its Community Technology Assistance Center will facilitate
the establishment and operation of the national youth center electronic network and
maintenance of a national youth center information repository. This effort will
```

serve as a model for electronic network providers to become active in providing
services to disadvantaged and low-income communities. The KRH Group will serve as
Project Facilitator.
\...\

Process:
The project will address these objectives by networking selected community youth
centers across the country and by developing local expertise to facilitate the use
of electronic communication technology. This pilot effort will take the following
steps:
1. Train youth center staff in the use of electronic communications and emerging
computer technologies.
2. Develop and implement curricula focused on electronic communications and
emerging computer technologies for use in youth centers serving low-income communities.

These curricula will address:
    a. electronic literacy, including technical skills;
    b. educational skills, including reading, writing, mathematics,
       and research;
    c. social skills, including group dynamics, self-esteem
       development, and expansion of the children's known world.
3. Build a repository of information about youth center programs,
curriculum models, drug abuse programs, counseling, intervention programs and
training courses, to be accessed and supported by youth center staff, clients, and
the community at large.
4. Establish a national network linking youth centers across the country to
facilitate both access to the repository and communication among youth center
staffs and clients.
5. Build community electronic leadership skills through the training and employment
of high-school-aged low-income youth in youth centers.
6. Sponsor an annual youth center networking conference at which youth center
staffs and clients will share programs, ideas, and experiences regarding the
application of networking technology in community youth centers.
\...\

Service Delivery Model:
LEAP operates educational and social development programming for 7 to 14 year-old
children in seven sites in Connecticut -- five in New Haven and one each in
Hartford and New London -- all serving low-income communities.
LEAP's educational model targets child literacy, and the organization is nationally
recognized for its development of educational curricula focused on low-income black
and Latino youth.
\...\

Facilitation Model:
Plugged In designs and operates computer literacy projects for local
community-based youth service providers in East Palo Alto. Serving over 300
children in its own facility and in neighborhood-based community youth centers,
Plugged In staff runs collaborative learning projects that use new technologies,
providing training and technical support for staff at Boys and Girls Club facilities in the area. Already implementing network based projects with many of its
children, Plugged In is uniquely positioned to expand these efforts and serve as

the model for introducing electronic communications technology to existing community youth centers.
\...\

Provider Model:
The Morino Institute will serve as the model for national network service providers
to offer technical assistance and support to community youth centers. Standard
'worldware' software (word processing, electronic mail, educational programs) will
be employed to facilitate youth center operations, to introduce electronic computer
communications into the youth centers, and to deliver services to the communities.
The Institute will link the centers electronically via the Internet to share the
resources, ideas, successes, and techniques that have been collected in an information repository. Through these links, center staffs and youth from low-income
neighborhoods can draw information about programs and activities that will be of
direct interest and application. The Institute will manage the network and provide
assistance in its operation and expansion.
\...\

Knowledge Base Model:
Through the efforts of the project partners and additional advisors,
significant expertise and knowledge will be collected. This knowledge will include
operations methodologies and implementation strategies developed by Plugged In;
curricula and service delivery materials created by LEAP; and funding, technical
assistance, and collaborative efforts identified by the Morino Institute. This
information will form the foundation for a repository of community youth center
knowledge.
\...\

Summary:
This project defines the public information network model for the community youth
center in terms which match the needs of a large segment of the American public.
The demonstration project also ensures that research in community networking is
problem-driven, dealing with real problems affecting real populations and providing
real outcomes. Those who are most directly affected by the outcomes will have daily
control over the design and operation of the electronic networks.
The model that emerges from this project addresses networking processes as much as
networking architecture. It includes community empowerment as much as community
information. It seeks community outcomes as much as community presence. If this
pilot demonstration effort is successful, additional community youth centers in
additional communities across the United States will be added to the model to
demonstrate scalability of infrastructure and impacts.

"One reads about the global community, but the Internet enables (students)
to walk the walk, not just talk the talk."
Anonymous -- The Internet in K-12 Education
Carnegie Mellon University

For even more information, contact director Bart Decrim at
PluggedIn@aol.com

English Language Arts—Literature, Speech, Poetry

One of the greatest advantages now available to students, that was completely unavailable only a generation ago, is the capability to perform full-text searches of documents with a simple word/text processor.

Once a student has a Shakespeare play on diskette, for example, the text can be searched for words or combinations of words. It's now much easier for a student to see characters develop by searching for that character's name. This enables the student to focus on one character's lines at a time, and to follow the play's progress from that character's point of view.

Symbolism can be explored by searching for `roots` rather than whole words, such as searching for `flor` and `flo` rather than `flower`. These powerful new tools are only now being grasped for their true worth.

Open Computing Facility—University of California at Berkeley

This archive contains many useful full-text documents, including works by Lewis Carroll, Monty Python, Shakespeare (with several subdirectories), E.E. Cummings, and many others. Choose your favorite!

Where to find it

Anonymous FTP

Site	`ocf.berkeley.edu`
Directories	`Library/Literature`
	`Library/Poetry`
	`Library/Shakespeare`
	`Library/Politics`

Project Gutenberg and Duncan Research Shareware

Project Gutenberg hopes to provide 10,000 books in e-text format by the year 2001. Everyone is invited to deposit electronic versions of non-copyrighted books with the Project. The project now has hundreds of texts appropriate for K-12 education. Lewis Carroll's *Alice*, and his *Snark Hunt* are shown simply to whet your appetite.

Where to find it

Gopher	`gopher.maricopa.edu`
Directory	`District Information/Virtual Library/Materials-Books/` `Digital Documents/Electronic Books`

Anonymous FTP

Site	`mrc.cso.uiuc.edu`
Directory	`pub/etext`
Files	`NEWUSER.GUT, INDEX100.GUT`

For more information

E-mail	Michael Hart
	`hart@vmd.cso.uiuc.edu`
Surface Mail	Project Gutenberg
	National Clearinghouse for Machine Readable Texts
	Illinois Benedictine College
	5700 College Road
	Lisle, Illinois 60532-0900

Gatekeeper

This site also contains files on a wide variety of subjects, from maps to computer games and recipes. There are numerous shareware and freeware programs. The *Federalist Papers* and *Paradise Lost* are here, too. Most of these files are compressed and require specific decompression programs to open them. If decompression is *not* something you're comfortable with, this site probably would not be too much fun.

Where to find it

Anonymous FTP

Site	`gatekeeper.dec.com`
Directories	`pub`
	`pub/data/gutenberg`
	`pub/data/shakespeare`

E-Text Archives of Speeches and Debates

Two particularly rich sources of full-text documents, containing both speeches and debates, are the *E-Text Archive* at the University of Michigan and the *CICNet, Inc.* site, also in Michigan. These archives are quite extensive. A sample of topics are free speech, hate speech, human rights and AIDS speeches, and political speeches released from the White House. Many of President Clinton's speeches are here, including speeches to the American Medical Association, the American Association of Retired Persons, and several other health care-related speeches.

Where to find it

Anonymous FTP

Site	`etext.archive.umich.edu` or `192.131.22.8`
Directory	`pub/Politics`
Site	`beech.cic.net` or `192.131.22.5`
Directory	`pub/ETEXT/pub/`
Directory	`pub/ETEXT/pub/Politics`

One Book List

The *One Book List* enables everyone to name just one book. You choose the reason why and the book, and make your statement about what the rest of the world should read.

Following is from the announcement by Paul Phillips, at InterNIC Information Services:

> "My proposal is this: one book. I would like for each of you to decide on a single book that you would most like for the world to read, and mail me the author and title. The book that, for you, was the most influential, or thought-provoking, or enjoyable, or moving, or philosophically powerful, or deep in some sense you cannot properly define, or any other criteria you wish to set."

Where to find it

WWW

    URL   `http://www.internic.net/~paulp/one-book.txt`

For more information

        `finger paulp@is.internic.net`

American Literature—AMLIT-L

This list is for the exchange of information among scholars and students of American Literature.

Where to find it

    E-mail   `listserv@mizzou1.missouri.edu`

    Body   `subscribe AMLIT-L `*`Your Name`*

AUSTEN-L

This is a moderated list for British fiction readers that chiefly discusses Jane Austen and her times. If you enjoy Jane Austen's novels and those of her contemporaries, such as Fanny Burney, Maria Edgeworth, and Mary Wollstonecraft, this is the list for you!

Where to find it

    E-mail   `listserv@vm1.mcgill.ca`

    Body   `subscribe AUSTEN-L `*`Your Name`*

CAMELOT

CAMELOT discusses the mythology and history surrounding King Arthur and the Knights of the Round Table and the Holy Grail—sometimes known as the

"Matter of Britain." All related subjects are covered, including re-enactment, literature, linguistics, archaeology, and mysticism.

Where to find it

E-mail	`camelot-request@castle.ed.ac.uk`
Body	`subscribe` *Your Name*

Kidlit-L

Want to find a new idea about children's literature in the classroom? *Kidlit-L* is a discussion group moderated by Prue Stelling that is focused on just that.

Where to find it

E-mail	`listserv@bingvmb.cc.binghampton.edu`
Body	`subscribe Kidlit-L` *Your Name*

Usenet Newsgroups on Literature, Speech, and Poetry

If you have access to Usenet newsgroups, the following list are some to look for.

```
alt.cyberpunk.chatsubo

alt.hypertext

alt.mythology

alt.postmodern

alt.prose

alt.prose.d

alt.pulp

alt.usage.english

bit.listserv.gutnberg

bit.listserv.literary

bit.listserv.mbu-l

bit.listserv.words-l
```

```
comp.edu.composition

misc.writing

rec.arts.int-fiction

rec.arts.poems

rec.arts.sf.misc
```

Project

Elementary Project

Using the Internet, locate electronic pen pals around North America and the world. Once pen pals have been located, use the pen pals to discuss local customs, dances, folklore, and so on. This project enables the children to meet others, learn about their own and other local customs, and to practice their writing skills.

Resources of Interest

1. Look at the *Fine Arts* section of this chapter, including the Usenet newsgroups.

2. Make contacts through these lists and Usenet Groups:

   ```
   k12.chat.elementary

   k12.chat.junior

   k12.chat.senior

   k12.chat.teacher

   Penpal-L discussion list at listserv@unccvm.uncc.edu

   Kidlink Kidlink Project list at listserv@ndsuvm1.vm1.nodak.edu
   ```

3. Try a WebQuery for related materials, such as the following one on folklore:

```
WebCrawler Search Results (p1 of 3)
WebCrawler Search Results
   Search results for the query "folklore":
   1000
http://sil.polytechnique.fr:5035/topics.html/Detente.html
   0656 The Temptation of Saint Anthony: Gluttony
   0323 Info Knoten
   0300 Astrotext
   0258 Summer Course
   0233 Sunderland
   0194 What Is A Banshee?
   0169 ftp://ftp.germany.eu.net/pub/books/big-dummys
guide/README
   0167 BUBL Information Service Web Server
```

```
0155 Mosaic Universidad de Guadalajara.
0154 Arts & Humanities
0148 Directories at FTP.LuTH.SE
0139 WPSU Playlist - May 1, 1994
0127 Richard Murray's personal W3 page
0122 Attractions in and around Bergen, Norway.
0114 Paul is dead?!?
```

Fine Arts—Theater, Drama, Music, Dance, Visual Arts

More and more sound and graphics files are turning up on the Net. Who knows? Maybe soon we'll actually be able to learn a musical instrument from a virtuoso over the Net. For now, we have large collections of lyrics, and irony of text-based material about non-text based subjects. But still, most schools don't have computer graphics capabilities yet. So perhaps what is now available on the Net *is* appropriate to our school's current capacities.

Lyrics & Discography—University of Wisconsin (Parkside)

Wondrous lyrics from the American patriot Frank Zappa are here, consorting with lyrics by the Andrews Sisters. Ancillary "discographic" information is abundant here, as well as graphics and sound files.

Where to find it

Anonymous FTP

Site	cs.uwp.edu or ftp.uwp.edu or 131.210.1.4
Directories	pub/music/folk
	pub/music/lyrics

HYDRA—The University of Western Ontario

Online newsletters and art exhibitions, and a wide variety of art-related materials reside at this Canadian FTP site.

Where to find it

Anonymous FTP

Site	`hydra.uwo.ca or 129.100.2.13`
Directory	`libsoft`
File	`ARTBASE.TXT`

ASTR-L

ASTR-L is the American Society for Theatre Research discussion list.

Where to find it

E-mail	`listserv@vmd.cso.uiuc.edu`
Body	`subscribe  ASTR-L Your Name`

CINEMA-L

This group discusses all forms of cinema, in all its aspects. Most people who watch and enjoy movies do so from a variety of personal points of view. This general, unlimited forum is desirable for both the integration and expansion of cinematic ideas, techniques, and understanding.

Where to find it

E-mail	`listserv@american.edu`
Body	`subscribe CINEMA-L Your Name`

This also is available as a Usenet newsgroup

```
bit.listserv.cinema-l
```

COMEDIA

COMEDIA is a discussion of Hispanic Classic Theater. The language used on this list usually is English, but some Spanish also is used.

Where to find it

E-mail   `listserv@arizvm1.ccit.arizona.edu`

Body   `subscribe COMEDIA` *Your Name*

For more information

E-mail   James T. Abraham

               `jabraham@ccit.arizona.edu`

PERFORM

PERFORM discusses Medieval Performing Arts.

Where to find it

E-mail   `listserv@iubvm.ucs.indiana.edu`

Body   `subscribe PERFORM` *Your Name*

Usenet Newsgroups on Theatre, Drama, Music, Dance, and Visual Arts

If you have access to Usenet newsgroups, the following are newsgroups to look for:

`alt.artcom`

`alt.binaries.pictures.fine-art.digitized`

`alt.binaries.pictures.fine-art.graphics`

`alt.binaries.pictures.fractals`

`alt.binaries.pictures.fine-art.d`

`alt.emusic`

`alt.exotic-music`

`alt.planning.urban`

`bit.listserv.allmusic`

`bit.listserv.cinema-l`

```
bit.listserv.emusic-l

bit.listserv.film-l

bit.listserv.geodesic

clari.news.arts

comp.music

k12.ed.music

rec.arts.cinema

rec.arts.comics

rec.arts.dance

rec.arts.fine

rec.folk-dancing

rec.arts.misc

rec.arts.movies

rec.arts.movies.reviews

rec.arts.theatre

rec.arts.tv

rec.audio

rec.audio.high-end

rec.music.classical

rec.video
```

REED-L

REED-L provides Records of Early English Drama Discussion. This is a private list, so your request must be approved by a moderator before you will begin to receive the discussion.

Where to find it

E-mail   listserv@vm.utcc.utoronto.ca

Body   subscribe REED-L *Your Name*

THEATRE

This group is for all those who are or want to be involved with theater as a hobby.

Where to find it

E-mail	`listserv@pucc.princeton.edu`
Body	`subscribe THEATRE` *`Your Name`*

TV-L

This group discusses all types of TV programs. Mail often is delayed going through this Listserv, so don't expect immediate replies.

Where to find it

E-mail	`listserv@vm3090.ege.edu.tr`
Body	`subscribe TV-L` *`Your Name`*

VIDPRO-L

This discussion involves various topics of professional video production. All levels of experience and expertise are welcome. This list also serves as a clearinghouse for video and/or media job openings.

Where to find it

E-mail	`listproc@bgu.edu`
Body	`subscribe VIDPRO-L Your Name`

Smithsonian Photographs

This a collection of the Smithsonian's photographs on a graphics Gopher! It also is available by FTP. You will need appropriate software and hardware to view these photo images. The `JPEG.faq` file tells you about the software and hardware needed, and the `Chapman.txt` file gives you a detailed description of each image, so that you will know which ones you want to see.

Where to find it

Gopher	`pipeline.com`
Choose	`Arts and Leisure`

Anonymous FTP

Site	`ftp.apple.com`
Directory	`alug/Smith`
Files	`JPEG.faq, Chapman.txt`
Directories	`alug/Smith/JPEG`
	`alug/Smith/JFIF`

DRAMA COLLECTION on the English Gopher Server

This extensive collection contains plays by many authors, including Aristophanes, Sophocles, Jonson, Goethe, Shakespeare (complete works), and Ibsen. There also are several links to other drama resources.

Where to find it

Gopher	`english-server.hss.cmu.edu`
Directory	`Drama`

Panda Lyric Server

Do you know the words to the song your youngster's been playing all day? Do you want to know? Here's how to find out.

Where to find it

Telnet

Site	`panda.uiowa.edu`
Choose	`4. Online Information Services`
	`11. Song Lyric Server`

BALLROOM

This group discusses ballroom and swing dancing. New subscriptions and unsubscriptions are processed on a two-week cycle, so you may not begin to receive messages for several days.

Where to find it

E-mail	ballroom-request@athena.mit.edu
Body	subscribe *Your Name*

DANCE-L

This list discusses folk dance and traditional dance. *DANCE-L* wants to motivate all the peoples of the world to get to know and to appreciate each other's dances, and to stimulate the use of computers in this field of human activities.

Where to find it

E-mail	listserv@hearn.nic.surfnet.nl
Body	subscribe *DANCE-L Your Name*

Health, Nutrition, Family Planning, and Sex Education

Parents and teachers will want to review these sites before they are made available to youngsters. Depending on the circumstances, each of these sites has very useful information, with proper supervision and preparation by adults. Some of the material is written for college freshmen, so, for example, it is likely to be valuable for some juniors and seniors in high school. Some of the anatomical files at the University of California at Irvine are very realistic and, therefore, not for the squeamish. This is an area for teacher and parental discretion.

HEALTHLINE

This excellent resource is the University of Montana Student Health Services Gopher. It covers physical and mental health (sexuality, drug and alcohol information, academic tips, and dietary facts), pointers to information for the disabled, information about the effect of computers on health, health-related USENET newsgroups, Electronic Books for the Blind and other similar projects, various "Extension Service" Gophers, environmental health and safety issues, and health-related information provided via U.S. Federal Agencies. Some of this Gopher's files were written by and for students, so they have a directness that is refreshing.

Where to find it

Gopher	`selway.umt.edu 700`

E-Text Archives—University of Michigan

The University of Michigan maintains a large archive of e-texts, where you will find both modern journals and items from the 15th century.

Where to find it

Anonymous FTP

Site	`etext.archive.umich.edu or 192.131.22.8`
Directory	`/pub/Politics/Feminism/Bibliographies`
File	`ethnicity+sexuality-bibliography`
Directory	`/pub/Politics/Feminism/Computing/ElectronicForums`
File	`family-violence-list`

GENDER

This is a moderated list devoted especially to scholarly discussion of issues pertaining to the study of communication and gender.

Where to find it

E-mail	`COMSERV@vm.its.rpi.edu`
Body	`subscribe Gender Your Name`

National Institutes of Health AIDS-Related Information

This site provides AIDS statistics, daily summaries of articles on AIDS in major newspapers, full text of AIDS Treatment News, reports from the National Commission on AIDS, pamphlets about AIDS, and more.

Where to find it

Gopher	odie.niaid.nih.gov
Choose	/AIDS related information

Library of Congress Marvel Gopher

This is a one-stop source for a multitude of government material, Congressional information, Census data, White House documents, crime statistics, State Department reports and more—taken from a variety of sources.

Where to find it

Gopher	marvel.loc.gov

National Referral Center Master File

This is a directory of more than 12,000 organizations qualified and willing to answer questions and provide information on many topics in science, technology, and the social sciences.

Where to find it

Telnet

Site	locis.loc.gov
Choose	organizations

World Health Organization

World Health Organization provides access to world health statistics, WHO press releases, full text of selected WHO publications, and more.

Where to find it

Gopher   gopher.who.ch

Gatekeeper

There are over 500 recipes in this FTP server, from soup to nuts, so to speak.

Where to find it

Anonymous FTP

Site   gatekeeper.dec.com
Directory   pub/recipes

Health Education and Promotion

This Gopher has reports on health promotion. You can use the keyword search function to find articles you might want, and then mail them to yourself.

Where to find it

Gopher   nightingale.con.utk.edu
Choose   /Research/Topical-index/Healtheducation andpromotion

Usenet Medical Newsgroups

If you have access to Usenet newsgroups, here are a few more to try out.

alt.image.medical

alt.support.arthritis

alt.support.attn-deficit

alt.support.big-folks

alt.support.cancer

alt.support.crohns-colitis

```
alt.support.depression

alt.support.diet

alt.support.eating-disord

alt.support.mult-sclerosis

alt.support.obesity

alt.support.spina-bifida

bit.listserv.autism

bit.listserv.deaf-l

bit.listserv.medforum

bit.listserv.medlib-l

bit.listserv.mednews

bit.listserv.transplant

clari.tw.health

clari.tw.health.aids

misc.health.diabetes

sci.med

sci.med.aids

sci.med.dentistry

sci.med.nursing

sci.med.nutrition

sci.med.occupational

sci.med.pharmacy

sci.med.physics

sci.med.psychobiology

sci.med.telemedicine

talk.politics.medicine
```

FTP Site at the University of California at Irvine

This archive contains years of software reviews from the *Journal of Family Practice* in text form, a state-by-state and country-by-country list of local telephone numbers for health-related BBSs, over a hundred issues of *Health InfoCom Network News*, a repository of medical education software and graphics, and is pretty easy to use, too. They seem to keep the README files (in this case some of the files are called 00index.txt) up-to-date, so you can find out the contents of a directory by getting the 00index.txt files.

> **Tip:** To save the steps of FTPing the README file, opening it with a text processor, and then re-FTPing to the site to get the rest of what you want, you can use an FTP trick. Rather than actually "getting" the file, you can print it to your screen, one page at a time, by using the following command:
>
> ```
> FTP> get readme ¦more
> ```
>
> This way, you can read the contents of the directory, note any files you want to get, and not clutter your hard drive with the README file.

Where to find it

Anonymous FTP

Site	ftp.uci.edu
Directory	med-ed/
File	README

Following is a sample of the material a K-12 teacher might adapt for classroom use:

```
00-index.txt
NOTE: This list was updated on 19 May 1994.
Some files may have been added or deleted since that date.
NOTE: Type B is Binary; Type A is ASCII; * = graphics required; + = text file
Directory MED-ED/MSDOS/EDUCATION
Filename    Type Length  Date    Description
============================================================================
AGETEST.ZIP   B   28296  921218  Determines your "medical" age.
ANATOMY.ZIP   B   14164  930423  Anatomy test. Requires BASCIA or GWBASIC.
BKACHE56.ZIP  B  190218  931201  Backache Relief Now!  Version 5.6
                                 Tutorial  discusses  back  pain  relief
                                 including spinal anatomy,  backaches and
                                 computer  operators,  arthritis,   the
                                 "slipped" disc, aging  and  back  pain,
                                 sports for back pain sufferers,  tumors,
                                 infectious   diseases,   posture,   new
```

medical technology, the orthopedic exam, chiropractic manipulation, pregnancy, little-known therapies, exercises, medications. By Jim Hood.

DIET.ZIP   B 112415 921223   Diet Disk weight control programs. For the serious dieter to get to and stay at Goal Weight. Written by a person who lost 100 pounds and has been a weight control counselor for 2 years.

ESTAT21.ZIP   B 396485 930825   *EASISTAT is a general-purpose statistics program which can perform a wide range of parametric and nonparametric statistics. Input can be interactive or from command files to carry out a number of analyses unattended. Complex logical and arithmetical expressions are available for data transformation and case selection. Also provided is EASIGRAF, a graph-drawing program which can display data from EASISTAT in a way which allows visualisation of a number of the statistical tests. Alternatively data from other sources may be displayed by specifying correctly formatted graph files. The EASISTAT package is shareware.

MATRIX.ZIP   B 272062 931201   HealthMATRIX is a Windows hypertext database of Internet health resources. The program allows subscription to medical newsletters, mailing lists and Usenet Newsgroups with point and click ease. HealthMATRIX offers point and click copying of email addresses to paste into your email editor. HealthMATRIX can be "dragged and dropped" into the same group as your favorite communications software. HEALTHTEL has sponsored the offering of this shareware as a public service. HealthMATRIX includes access to HEALTHTEL's medical librarian services by email. MSWindows required.

MENSTRUA.ZIP B 73751   940324   *MENSTRUA v.1.2, by Michael Schroda, Shannon Peak, and Louis Gross Institute for Environmental Modeling University of Tennessee Knoxville, TN. MENSTRU is a Charity-Ware MS-DOS program requiring a color monitor and an 8086 or higher machine. Purpose is to help women predict the probable day of ovulation, the probable beginning of the next menstrual cycle, the probable fertile days of the next cycle, and graph the past history of day types throughout the cycle. Ovulation prediction allows for

```
                              the   calendar   method   as   well   as   the
                              temperature  method  to  be  used,  if  the
                              user has temperature data available.
TEMPCONV.ZIP  B   1319  920922  Temperature conversion between several
                              systems.
```

and in another directory, you will find

```
Directory MED-ED/INFO
Filename        Type Length  Date    Description
===============================================================================
MED-INET.RES    A   154962  930618  +Internet/Bitnet Health Sciences Resource,
                                    (version 06-01-93). Extensive listing of
                                    various medically-related resources on the
                                    Internet. Includes Listservers, FTP sites,
                                    telnet addresses and more. Compiled by:
                                    Lee Hancock, Educational Technologist,
                                    Dykes Library, University of Kansas Medical
                                    Center. ASCII file.
HYTELN61.ZIP    B   384480  930127  HYTELNET version 6.1 gives  an  IBM-PC
                                    user instant-access to  information  and
                                    addresses of Internet-accessible library
                                    catalogs, Freenets, CWISs, Library BBSs,
                                    etc.  worldwide.  For   anyone
                                    interested  in  the   possibilities  of
                                    computer  networking  or  communications.
                                    V. 6.1 is a major upgrade. Note: the
                                    UNZIPPED  files  total  over  500,000
                                    bytes...but  remember,  you  can  always
                                    edit  out  any  information  you  do not
                                    need, in order to save space. Make sure
                                    you read the READNOW.!!! file for  info
                                    on   correct   installation!   The  file
                                    READNOW.!!!  gives full instructions for
                                    un-archiving HYTELNET.ZIP. Simply  put,
                                    you  **MUST** unZIP the file with the -d
                                    parameter  (PKUNZIP)  so  that  all  the
                                    subdirectories  will be recursed. MSDOS
                                    ONLY!
INFPOP21.ZIP    B   287744  920127  INFOPOP version 2.00, is memory-resident
                                    utility for MSDOS computers, designed to
                                    help you use Telnet and/or your modem to
                                    reach a variety of information  systems.
                                    Library  systems  in  the  US,  Canada,
                                    Australia and Europe accessible via  the
                                    Internet are covered,  as are commercial
                                    online systems like CompuServe, the Well
                                    and  a  couple  hundred  BBS   systems.
                                    Release  2.0  adds several new features:
                                    the ability to create your own databases
                                    for use with the  IP  (or  IPNR)  search
                                    engine;  completely reworked text search
                                    function.
SURFINET.TXT    A   62564  930127  +Surfing the INTERNET: an Introduction,
                                    version  2.0 December 3, 1992. by Jean
```

Armour Polly. This short, non-technical article is an introduction to Internet communications and how librarians and libraries can benefit from net connectivity. Following will be descriptions of electronic mail, discussion lists, electronic journals and texts, and resources available to those willing to explore. ASCII file.

RuralNet Gopher

The Marshall University Rural Health Gopher Server has resources for rural health concerns.

Where to find it

Gopher   ruralnet.mu.wvnet.edu

The Maternal and Child Health Network (MCH-Net)

Maternal and child health begins long before birth takes place. This Gopher has resources to improve the health of both mothers and their children.

Where to find it

Gopher   mchnet.ichp.ufl.edu

Department of Food Science and Nutrition—University of Minnesota

This group wants to provide consumer information on food safety, nutrition, food labeling, and food law with a new WWW server.

Where to find it

WWW

URL   http://fscn1.fsci.umn.edu

Internet/Bitnet Health Resources

This extensive compilation is maintained by Lee Hancock at the University of Kansas Medical Center. The final characters of the filename indicate the revision date for that version. (See Chapter 6 for more information about Lee's guides.)

Where to find it

Anonymous FTP

Site	`ftp.sura.net` or `128.167.254.179`
Directory	`/pub/nic`
File	`medical.resources.`*xxx* (where *xxx* is the latest release date)

Food and Nutrition Database

INFAN—International Food and Nutrition Database at the Agricultural College, Penn State University and Rutgers University. After choosing Penpages, you can do keyword searches of this site. A search of the word "nutrition" produced over 100 articles at this site.

Where to find it

Telnet

Site	`psupen.psu.edu`
Login	Your two-letter state abbreviation, or WORLD if you are not from the U.S.A.

Journalism

Four examples of the Net's usefulness to journalism are given in the following sections. These merely give teachers some ideas of how they can use the Net in their classrooms. Two student newspapers, a local newspaper indexing project, and an example of e-text distribution of otherwise printed material are given.

London Free Press Regional Index

This is an index of local and regional stories in the *London Free Press* (London, Canada). The index includes birth notices and obituaries. Editorials and letters to the editor on regional issues are indexed. Entries consist of the headlines of the stories, added keywords, date, and page number. Bylines are only included for opinion pieces.

Where to find it

Gopher	`gopher.lib.uwo.ca`
Choose	`Internet Resources/UWO Publications & Indexes/London-free-press-regional-index`

For more information

E-mail	Heather York-Marshall
	`york-marshall@uwo.ca`
Voice	519/661-3383, ext. 6661

GlasNews

This newsletter is published quarterly by the Communications Exchange Program, and is aimed at East-West communicators in fields such as journalism, advertising, public relations, and telecommunications.

Where to find it

Anonymous FTP

Site	`eskimo.com`
Directory	`GlasNews`

K-12 Online Student Newspaper

Vocal Point is a monthly newspaper created by the K-12 students of the Boulder Valley School District. The newspaper is designed to let the kids of Boulder express their ideas and the rest of us can listen in.

Each month, Vocal Point covers a local or national topic from the diverse perspectives of Boulder's youth. In the first edition, the topic was censorship. Vocal Point is created completely by the students in the school district. Noah Horton, a 13-year-old Centennial Middle School student, was the designer and creator of the HTML version of the online newspaper.

Where to find it

WWW

    URL   `http://bvsd.k12.co.us/cent/Newspaper/Newspaper.html`

For more information

    E-mail   Jill Tucker

                 `jtucker@knightridder.com`

    Voice   303/938-8427

Global Student Newswire

Student journalists, editors, and communicators around the world are invited to join the *Global Student Newswire,* an endeavor that attempts to develop a source of formal news stories written by students and uses the Internet as the distribution medium. The GSN attempts to connect students at the high school through graduate levels with the growing number of student publications on the Internet, and, in the process, provide a new learning tool for educators involved in teaching those subjects.

Where to find it

    URL   `http://www.jou.ufl.edu/features/gsn.htm`

Anonymous FTP

    Site   `cybernews.comm.cornell.edu` or `132.236.225.25`

    Directory   `pub/gsn`

    File   `gsnfaq.txt`

Mathematics, Algebra, Calculus, and Geometry

There are some useful projects and sites related to math of interest to teachers and students. These are a few, and some of the sites mentioned under science also have math-related information.

Solar Eclipse Project

A group of geometry teachers in Georgia and around the USA are working together to prepare lessons to take advantage of a Solar Eclipse within the next 5 to 10 years.

Kris Fitzgerald, Shiloh High School, Lithonia, GA

Trish Herndon, LaFayette High School, LaFayette, GA

Walter Brooks, Fitzgerald High School, Fitzgerald, GA

Martha Carter, Turner County High School, Ashville, GA

For more information

E-mail   Trish Herndon

`forum14@netcom.com`

OnLine Math Courses for K-8 Teachers

With support from the Annenberg/CPB Math and Science Project, Bank Street College of Education, in collaboration with the Education Development Center, will be offering 12 online mathematics forums beginning September 12, 1994. The Mathematics Learning Forums are to support classroom teachers in grades K-8 in learning new mathematics teaching practices in their classrooms, as recommended by current nationwide mathematics reform efforts.

Courses are offered for graduate credit, inservice credit, or personal enrichment through Bank Street's Graduate School of Education. Each course lasts for eight weeks and enrollment is limited to 10.

The forums can be accessed through a number of regional network services or directly through the Internet via telnet. Participants are expected to be online approximately three times a week.

For more information

E-mail   Nancy Ross

`nross@confer.edc.org`

Voice   212/807-4207

Following is a sample schedule of courses:

Mathematics Learning Forums Schedule

```
*September 12 - November 4*
Classroom Discourse: Talking and Writing Mathematics (K-4)
```

```
Teaching Probability (5-8)
Cooperative Learning: Working in Groups (K-4)
Investigating Patterns in Mathematics (K-4)
Fractions: Exploring Equivalent Forms (5-8)
Engaged Learning: When Does a Child Really Learn? (K-4)
*October 31 - December 23*
Teaching Probability (K-4)
Fractions: Parts of a Whole (K-4)
Cooperative Learning: Working in Groups (5-8)
Assessing Students Through Focused Observations (K-4)
Investigating Patterns in Mathematics (5-8)
Assessing Students Through Questioning Techniques (5-8)
*January 23 - March 17*
Classroom Discourse: Talking and Writing Mathematics (K-4)
Teaching Probability (5-8)
Cooperative Learning: Working in Groups (K-4)
Investigating Patterns in Mathematics (K-4)
Fractions: Exploring Equivalent Forms (5-8)
Engaged Learning: When Does a Child Really Learn? (K-4)
*March 20 - May 19*
Teaching Probability (K-4)
Fractions: Parts of a Whole (K-4)
Cooperative Learning: Working in Groups (5-8)
Assessing Students Through Focused Observations (K-4)
Investigating Patterns in Mathematics (5-8)
Assessing Students Through Questioning Techniques (5-8)
```

These courses are available for graduate and undergraduate credit, as well as for personal enrichment.

Explorer HomePage

This is a WWW source for Educational Curriculum, specifically Mathematics and Natural Sciences.

Where to find it

WWW

URL   http://unite.tisl.ukans.edu/xmintro.html

E-Math Gopher

Primarily for math educators and professionals, e-math provides online access to employment opportunities, software, and a variety of math publications. The American Mathematical Society (AMS) maintains and supports e-math. This contains sections on Mathematical Publications, Mathematical Preprints, Fermat's Last Theorem, Mathematical Discussion Lists and Bulletin Boards,

General Information of Interest to Mathematicians, Professional Information for Mathematicians, Mathematical Sciences Meetings and Conferences, Notes from MathSci, and Other Math-Related Gophers.

Where to find it

Gopher   e-math.ams.org or 130.44.1.100

Science—Biology, Chemistry, Physics, Astronomy, and Earth Science

The Internet is brimming over with science resources, with new sources coming online every day. Scientists have been using computers for a long time, so it's natural for them to use the Net, too. In fact, the history of the Net starts out with scientists and the military.

Project

High School Frog Dissection

High school students can develop very sophisticated abilities to use the Internet to search out useful information. Here is a biology assignment to locate Internet information on frogs prior to a unit on dissection.

Resources Hints

1. A Veronica search and a WebQuery should start the location of resources.
2. Check out Newton, the site sponsored by the Argonne National Laboratory Division of Educational Programs, using telnet to newton.dep.anl.gov and login as bbs.
3. Check out the following unusual WWW:

```
Virtual Frog dissection --frog dissection page
The Imaging and Distributed Computing Group of Lawrence Berkeley Laboratory
announces its interactive forms-based frog dissection kit.  Images of the
frog from various views, and in various stages of dissection, are generated
on-the-fly based on parameters set by the user.  The URL is http://
george.lbl.gov/ITG.hm.pg.docs/dissect/info.html
```

4. Locate lists and newsgroups related to biology and reptiles, and join the list. Locate an expert and directly e-mail them for information.

Biodiversity and Biological Collections Gopher

This Gopher, maintained at Harvard University, specializes in museum, herbarium and arboretum collection catalogs, and biodiversity information resources. It also has directories of biologists, biodiversity journals and newsletters, workshop information, standards organizations and reports software, and biological images.

Where to find it

Gopher   gopher huh.harvard.edu

ChemViz—Chemical Visualization project

ChemViz is an NSF funded grant to use High Powered Computing and Communications to help high school students better visualize abstract concepts of chemistry. Other supporters are the Benjamin Cummings Company, Apple Computer, and NCSA. It enables the student or teacher to make images and animations of calculated atomic and molecular orbitals. This project only supports Macintosh computers, and a color monitor is necessary to view these files.

Where to find it

Anonymous FTP

     Site   zaphod.ncsa.uiuc.edu

     Directory   Education/ChemViz

Computational Biology—Welchlab at Johns Hopkins University

This heavy-duty site has links to international sites for data and software in mathematics and biology, directories of biologists, and full text articles and newsletters.

Where to find it

Gopher   gopher.gdb.org

Earthquake Information

This site contains information for public use on recent events reported by the USGS National Earthquake Information Center. They use Universal Standard Time, which previously was referred to as Greenwich Mean time.

When it's noon in London, it's only 5 a.m. in Chicago!

Where to find it

Anonymous FTP

Site	`geophys.washington.edu`
Directory	`/pub/seis_net`

EarthNegotiations Bulletin

This is a daily, worldwide review of high level activities that may impact the planet and its ecosystems.

Where to find it

E-mail	`majordomo@.ciesin.org`
Body	`subscribe enb` *Your Name*

Energy and Climate Information Exchange (ECIX)

The *Energy and Climate Information Exchange* is a project of EcoNet aimed at educating environmental groups and the general public on the potential of energy efficiency and renewable energy to reduce the use of fossil fuels and their contribution to climate change. ECIX now offers free electronic information files on energy technologies and issues.

Subjects include biomass, electric vehicles, energy efficiency, fuel cells, geothermal energy, global warming, hydro power, solar energy, photovoltaics, social costs, sustainable development, transportation, wind energy, climate change, ozone, CO_2 Challenge Educators Kit, newsletters, and so on.

Where to find it

Anonymous FTP

Site	`igc.org or 192.82.108.1`
Directories	`ECIX`
	`ECIXfiles`
E-mail	`ecixfiles@igc.apc.org`

Environmental Protection Agency Gopher

This Gopher hole leads you to people at EPA who can give you more information about agriculture, air, water, land, energy graphics, industrial ecology, megatrends project, population, technology, tri-toxic release inventory, video examples, and other environmental Gophers.

Where to find it

Gopher   `futures.wic.epa.gov or info.umd.edu`

Geographic Name Server

The *Geographic Name Server* gives geographic information for U.S. cities, counties, and North American places by name, state/province, or ZIP code.

Where to find it

Telnet

Site   `martini.eecs.umich.edu 3000 or 141.212.99.9 3000`

IUBIO Archive for Biology—Indiana University

This archive specializes in molecular biology and fruit fly (drosophila) research. It includes software for Macintosh, DOS, and others.

Where to find it

Anonymous FTP

Site   ftp.bio.indiana.edu

IPAC Extragalactic Database

Infrared astronomy is the topic at the Infrared Processing and Analysis Center (*IPAC*). It is a project of the California Institute of Technology Jet Propulsion Laboratory, paid for by the National Aeronautics and Space Administration (NASA). It contains extensive cross-identifications for over 200,000 objects—galaxies, quasars, infrared and radio sources; positions, names, and basic data, such as magnitudes, redshifts; as well as bibliographic references, abstracts, and notes.

Where to find it

Anonymous FTP

Site   ned.ipac.caltech.edu or 134.4.10.119

Directory   pub/ned

Macintosh Science and Technology Archive

This is the Naval Research Lab's public archive. It specializes in Macintosh computing and programming. This site also contains materials on biology, geology, physics, and chemistry.

Where to find it

Anonymous FTP

Site   ra.nrl.navy.mil

Directory   /MacSciTech

File   _readme.txt, _all_files.txt

Material Safety Data Sheets

This is a database of over 20,000 chemical compounds (indexed by over 80,000 names). Search by name for prefix. It has trade names and synonyms, chemical family, molecular formula, molecular weight, ratings for health, fire, reactivity, and persistence hazards, components and contaminants, exposure limits, color, smell, taste, boiling point, melting point, specific gravity, vapor pressure, evaporation rate, solubility in water, vapor density, solvent solubility, flash point, fire-fighting information, transportation information, health effects and first aid, and protective equipment.

Nuclear Safety Gopher

The Nuclear Safety Gopher is operated by the Office of Environmental Safety and Health, Office of Nuclear Safety (EH-10), of the U.S. Department of Energy, and contains the Office of Nuclear Safety newsletter; *Department of Energy Information*.

Where to find it

Gopher   gopher.ns.doe.gov

Scientists on Disk

This is Johns Hopkins University's History of Science and Medicine Gopher. It includes material from the J. Robert Oppenheimer collection at the Library of Congress, transcripts of interviews with important figures from 20th Century Aerospace, *The Origin of Species* by Charles Darwin, lecture transcripts, an image-library of architectural photographs, American quilts, and so on.

Where to find it

Gopher   gopher.hs.jhu.edu

Smithsonian Photographs

To get these great graphics straight from the Institution, Office of Printing & Photographic Services, FTP to this site. A wide variety of subjects are covered with these digital images.

Where to find it

Anonymous FTP

Site   photo1.si.edu

Space Telescope Electronic Information System (STEIS)

STEIS contains information on the Hubble Space Telescope, links to astronomical Internet resources, access to Exploration In Education, including a series of Electronic PictureBooks that will run on any color Macintosh with HyperCard version 2.1.

Where to find it

Gopher   stsci.edu

SpaceLINK

This is a database of NASA aeronautics and space research. Also included are classroom activities that use NASA projects to teach scientific principles.

Where to find it

Telnet

Site   spacelink.msfc.nasa.gov or 192.149.89.61
Login   newuser

SpaceMet Internet

SpaceMet Internet is an online service for educators and students who are interested in space and space-related topics.

Where to find it

Telnet

Site   spacemet.phast.umass.edu or 128.119.50.48

Science and Technology Information System

STIS is an electronic dissemination system providing National Science Foundation (NSF) publications, including *The NSF Bulletin*, program announcements and *Dear Colleague* letters, general publications and reports, NSF Directions, press releases, NSF organization charts and phone books, NSF vacancy announcements, and Award abstracts (1989 to the present).

Where to find it

Telnet

Site	`stis.nsf.gov` or `128.150.195.40`
Login	`public`

The Scientist

This site provides text of each issue of *The Scientist*, a Philadelphia bi-weekly tabloid newspaper. Because the majority of the 30,000 subscribers are associated with the life sciences and biotechnology, life sciences are emphasized.

Where to find it

Gopher	`inforM.umd.edu`
Choose	`Educational_Resources/ReadingRoom/Miscellaneous/Science`

Anonymous FTP

Site	`ds.internic.net`
Directory	`/pub/the-scientist`

Kidlink Desertification Project

What is a desert? Why do we have them? This project will run for one year and involve classes from all over the world trying to answer these and similar questions.

The project "pre-announcement" is printed here for you to see the curriculum effort put into its design, and for you to get involved if you or your students are interested!

```
                THIS IS A PRE-ANNOUNCEMENT OF A KIDLINK PROJECT:
                "D E S E R T    A N D    D E S E R T I F I C A T I O N"
We invite Netters, teachers, students and researchers, to join us in
an adventure of learning about "Desert and Desertification".
This is a year long (September 1994 to May 1995) project, that has 4
Stages:
Stage I: (September 94 - October 94)
   * Main subjects: Introduction of students, Classes and area of living,
     collection of data, learning to use the INTERNET for sources and
     e-mail.
   * Suggested "Work Parcels": INTERNET Hunt, watching video movies,

Stage II: (November 94 - December 94)
   * Main subjects: The perception of the desert, The desert in
     literature, history and cultures, Names of the desert and of
     phenomena in the desert.
   * Suggested "Work Parcels": Study of Stereotypes and Prejudices,
     Understanding different cultures, Planning and a sociological
     study.

Stage III: (January 95 - February 95)
   * Main subjects: What is a desert? What is in a desert? The effect of
     man on the desert (development and/or desertification).
   * Suggested "Work Parcels": Presenting questions to experts, Use of
     Data bases, Study the Global Map of the deserts.

Stage IV: (March 95 - April 95)
   * Main subject: The Desert in the Future and the Future of the Desert.
   * Suggested "Work Parcels": Desert in Science Fiction literature (Dune
     by F. Herbert), Simulation of regional planning, A Case Study of
     planning or development, Becoming acquainted with the modern
     research of the desert.
A Final Happening (May 95)

Note that:
* According to KIDLINK policies, students participating in this project
  have to be at the age of 10-15, and should register to KIDLINK, and
  then also register to KIDPROJ.
  To get more information about KIDLINK, you can send a message to
  LISTSERV@VM1.NODAK.EDU
  (or for BITNET users - LISTSERV@NDSUVM1)
  and in the text of the message, write:
  GET KIDLINK MASTER
* We invite participants from all desert areas of the world, warm
    deserts as well as cold deserts, though you don't have to live in a
    desert in order to participate in this project.
* One does not have to participate at all stages of this project.
    Everyone is welcome to choose any part (or more than one part) of the
    project. The Israeli class will produce a summary and a report of each
    Stage, this report will be available from the KIDLINK Gopher.
   * The detailed program of the project will be sent to those who are
     interested. (Write to Email address: BOKER@ZEUS.DATASRV.CO.IL
     to request the full program).
     The program will include a Curriculum framework with suggestions for
```

```
        subjects and educational activities, as well as tips for the teachers.
        Teachers are invited to send us thoughts, suggestions and to be a part
        of designing this Curriculum.
    *   During Israeli spring (around April) there will be a desert experience
        in Midreshet Ben Gurion, the Negev, Israel. We invite representatives
        of classes that took part in this study to a week of real desert
        experience: visit to the desert research institute, field trips and
        workshops, a night in the desert and more.
    *   Students are invited to contribute pictures (as .gif files), desert
        sounds (as sound files) and suggest a logo (that can be used in
        electronic communication) for this project.
    *   We are planning to use various means of modern communication
        technology:
        E-mail, IRC (online conferencing), use of Gopher and Data bases,
        multi-media, video, picture and sound files, etc.
    *   This Project will be lead by Hannh Sivan, David Lloyd (teachers) and
        the 10th grade students of the High School for Environmental Studies
        in Midreshet Ben Gurion, The Negev, Israel. This group will send, at
        the beginning of each stage, instructions and tips to the teachers. At
        the end of each stage, this group will produce a final report of the
        input from the various groups.
        For further information contact Hannah Sivan or David Lloyd at:
        <boker@zeus.datasrv.co.il>
```

```
¦ David Lloyd, Hannah Sivan              ___                           ¦
¦ The High School for Environmental Studies  /    \ We teach IN the    ¦
¦ Sde-Boker, ISRAEL 84990                /         \   Environment, ON  ¦
¦ E-mail <boker@zeus.datasrv.co.il>   ___/          \   the Environment ¦
¦ Voice 972-7-565897                 /               \    and FOR the   ¦
¦ Fax 972-7-556286  -----------/                      \___ Environment ¦
```

Weather Underground

This is a very complete site for U.S. Weather Service information. Look up your local weather! This site is updated continuously, so that you can see three or more forecasts each day. This site also has long-range forecasts, ski conditions, earthquake reports, hurricane advisories, marine forecasts, a national weather summary, and severe weather advisories. It provides some information about Canadian weather and some other international data.

Where to find it

Telnet

Site   `madlab.sprl.umich.edu 3000` or `141.212.196.79 3000`

Project

Middle School Weather Project

This project is set up for working in teams of three and is separated into two weeks.

Week 1

Locate weather information on the Internet, including maps, .gif files, and text materials. Also, include materials from local newspaper weather reports.

Make a poster for each day (Monday through Friday) that indicates what the weather has been for each day.

Week 2

Each day, predict the local weather on the poster based on current information from the Internet. Have the groups of students write a paragraph describing how they arrived at their team forecast. See how accurate the forecast was for each day.

Resource Tips

1. Try a Veronica search for weather—this one located 10 screens of information. The following is just a sample:

```
              Internet Gopher Information Client v1.13
            Search GopherSpace by Title word(s) (via
NYSERNet): weather
  -->  1.  weather/
       2.  weather/
       3.  About News Events Weather.
       4.  About the Weather.
       5.  News, Events, Weather/
       6.  Weather/
       7.  Weather Maps and Satellite Images/
       8.  Weather Information /
       9.  News & weather . . . . . . News, weather &
sports/
      10.  News & weather . . . . . News, weather &
sports/
     • 11.  weather.gif <Picture>
      12. GC 1111    Science in Context: Weather and
Climate.
      13. GC 1111. SCIENCE IN CONTEXT: WEATHER AND
CLIMATE.
      14. Weather Information.../
      15.  Weather data.
      16.  weather data search.
      17. On the economic value of weather
forecasts in
wildfire suppressio.
      18. Effects of weather on capture of
stable flies
```

```
(Diptera: Muscidae).
        19. The influence of diurnal time and weather on sex
trap catches of.
This locates text files, gophers, and images.
```

2. Telnet to the Weather Underground—the complete U.S. Weather Service. This is an online weather service for regions, cities, long range forecasts, ski conditions, severe weather advisories, and more.

Where to find it

Telnet   madlab.sprl.umich.edu 3000 or 141.212.196.79 3000

Following is an example of a Weather Underground session:

```
telnet> open madlab.sprl.umich.edu 3000
Trying 141.212.196.79 ...
Connected to madlab.sprl.umich.edu.
Escape character is ^]
University of Michigan
University of Michigan
WEATHER UNDERGROUND
College of Engineering
Atmospheric, Oceanic, & Space Sciences
comments: sdm@madlab.sprl.umich.edu
Select an option:
-------------------------------------
1)      Forecast for a U.S. city
2)      National Weather Summary
3)      Current weather observations
4)      Ski conditions
5)      Long-range forecasts
6)      Latest earthquake report
7)      Special severe weather statement
X)      Exit program
C)      Change scrolling to screen
2

NWX1
NATIONAL WEATHER SUMMARY
NATIONAL WEATHER SERVICE KANSAS CITY MO
8 PM CDT FRI APR 26 1991

WEATHER RANGED FROM TORNADOES TO HEAVY SNOW.

A TORNADO WATCH HAS BEEN POSTED UNTIL 10 PM CDT OVER
PORTIONS OF EASTERN NEBRASKA...WESTERN IOWA AND
NORTHWEST MISSOURI.

A TORNADO WATCH WAS POSTED UNTIL 10 PM CDT ACROSS
PORTIONS OF CENTRAL AND EASTERN SOUTH DAKOTA.  A SEVERE
THUNDERSTORM WATCH HAS BEEN POSTED UNTIL MIDNIGHT CDT
```

```
OVER PORTIONS OF NORTHERN AND EASTERN ARKANSAS...AS WELL
AS WESTERN AND CENTRAL MISSISSIPPI.

A TORNADO WATCH WAS POSTED UNTIL MIDNIGHT CDT ACROSS
PORTIONS OF EASTERN SOUTH DAKOTA...NORTHWEST IOWA...AND
WESTERN THROUGH EXTREME SOUTHWEST MINNESOTA.

A TORNADO WATCH HAS BEEN POSTED UNTIL 1 AM CDT ACROSS
PORTIONS OF NORTHEAST TEXAS.
```

3. Try out the following Gophers:

Where to find it

Name	*U.S. Visible Satellite*
Type	`I`
Port	`70`
Path	`9/Images/North_America/cvis.gif`
Host	`groucho.unidata.ucar.edu`

Name	*Weather Maps and Satellite Images*
Type	`1`
Port	`70`
Path	`1/Online Books, Images, Journals, Preprints, Publishers, Tech Reports/Digital Images/Weather Maps and Satellite Images`
Host	`wave.scar.utoronto.ca`

4. Do a WebQuery about weather.

Where to find it

URL	`http://www.biotech.washington.edu/cgi-bin/WebQuery`

My search revealed three pages of links. Following is a sample:

```
WebCrawler Search Results (p1 of 3)
WebCrawler Search Results
   Search results for the query "weather":
   1000 National Weather Service (NOAA/NWS) Office Descriptions
   0861 Current weather - in Ft. Collins, and around the
nation
   0774 Weather.html
   0574 http://cscmosaic.albany.edu/news/sunya.html
```

```
0516 WEATHER
0505 WXP From Unidata
0484 Weather, weather, more weather
0484 LoanSTAR Database Statistics
0449 General Weather Forecasts
0442 Other Weather Gopher Servers
0430 Indiana University Weather Information
0415 The Agricultural Weather Information Service Home
Page
0387 SUNY Brockport WWW
0369 Weather World General Menu
0369 USL Welcome
0369 Weather Machine Server
```

Choosing North American Time Zones, you can find an explanation of Universal Coordinated time, and how those times are used in weatherh forecasting.
NORTH AMERICAN TIME ZONES AND GMT

Weather observations are always taken with respect to
time. Thus all observations have a corresponding time, and that time is
reported along with the measurement. By convention, weather scientists use
the twenty four hour clock, and use one time zone, Greenwich Mean Time (GMT).
This time also is known as Universal Time (UTC). To convert to local time, we
must know the time difference between GMT and local time for both standard
time and summertime (daylight savings time). Not all states use daylight
savings time in the summer.

The Time Zones across North America and Pacific from
East to West are:

	Standard Time	Daylight Savings Time
Atlantic		
Eastrn	EST	EDT
Central	CST	CDT
Mountain	MST	MDT
Pacific	PST	PDT
Alaska		
Hawaii		

Standard time:

GMT difference	ATL -4	EST -5	CST -6	MST -7	PST -8	ALA -9	HAW -10
00	8P*	7P*	6P*	5P*	4P*	3P*	2P*
01	9P*	8P*	7P*	6P*	5P*	4P*	3P*
02	10P*	9P*	8P*	7P*	6P*	5P*	4P*
03	11P*	10P*	9P*	8P*	7P*	6P*	5P*
04	12A	11P*	10P*	9P*	8P*	7P*	6P*
05	1A	12A	11P*	10P*	9P*	8P*	7P*
06	2A	1A	12A	11P*	10P*	9P*	8P*
07	3A	2A	1A	12A	11P*	10P*	9P*
08	4A	3A	2A	1A	12A	11P*	10P*
09	5A	4A	3A	2A	1A	12A	11P*
10	6A	5A	4A	3A	2A	1A	12A

5. FTP to igc.org, the Energy and Climate Information Exchange, and look at their materials on climate change, newsletters, and the educators kits.

WX-TALK

This Listserv is for discussion of all things weather-related.

Where to find it

E-mail	`listserv@vmd.cso.uiuc.edu.`
Body	`subscribe WX-TALK Your Name`

CHMINF-L

The *Chemical Information Sources List* is for chemistry and chemical compounds.

Where to find it

E-mail	`listserv@iubvm.ucs.indiana.edu`
Body	`subscribe CHMINF-L Your Name`

World Languages

The following sections discuss several sources to get you started in finding language information on the Internet. Several are specific to a single langauge, but the first two are more generic and cover several langauges.

The Online World Resources Handbook

Odd de Presno of Norway prepares and disseminates this handbook, which has a truly international flair. It contains information on learning foreign languages and finding foreign language books and assistance. This zipped file is over 300 Kb, so be sure you have room to receive it before you ask for it!

Where to find it

Anonymous FTP

Site	`oak.oakland.edu or 141.210.10.117`
Directory	`SimTel/msdos/info`
File	`online16.zip`

Word List Archive

This is a collection of dictionaries in eight languages. The dictionaries, which are actually word lists, are provided as a service for system administrators to use to check whether their users are using passwords that can be readily guessed.

Where to find it

Anonymous FTP

Site	`ftp.cs.vu.nl`
Directory	`dictionaries/words`

Two Chinese Web Sites

Here are two World Wide Web sites, the first in Taiwan and the second in Beijing.

Where to find it

Sites   `http://www.nthu.edu.tw/nthu.html`

`http://www.ihep.ac.cn:3000/ihep.html`

French Teachers Discussion List

This discussion list is for French language teachers, and covers all facets of teaching French.

Where to find it

Site	`listserv@vm.buffalo.edu`
Subscribe	`flteach Your Name`

From Here...

Chapters 7 through 9 on teaching and learning will give you more tips on using the Internet. Chapter 10 will give you information on learning on your own and provides information on ways to increase your own Internet skills.

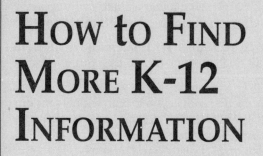

How to Find More K-12 Information

Something hidden. Go and find it. Go and look behind the Ranges.

Something lost behind the Ranges. Lost and waiting for you. Go!

Rudyard Kipling

Introduction to K-12 Information on the Internet

In Chapters 1 and 2, you looked at K-12 educational methods on the Internet and attained leads to resources for many specific curriculum areas. But what if *your* favorite area was omitted from Chapter 2? Or what if you want to make up a *new* educational method? How do you find more information specific to your needs?

Internet has many broad, generic resources. You can find material on curriculum areas not covered earlier, and you can *find your own way* to the cutting edge of educational methods!

Ideas in this chapter are less tightly focused to enable you to scan widely for your own interests. You'll see locations all over the realm. You also will need to be a little more self-sufficient, and a little more technically proficient.

One of the important ways to locate more information is to use the tools of the Internet—Gopher, Veronica, Archie, WebQuery, and the others. Appendix A outlines a few Internet tools, such as e-mail, Listservs, Gopher, WWW, FTP, and telnet, and *none* of them is too tough. In fact, they're getting easier and better all the time. You aren't the first to learn to use them, and you won't be the last!

Reach out and try some of these ideas—you will be rewarded. In this chapter, you will find information on

- Guides (and more!) for the Whole Net
- Gophers for You and Me
- WWW Home Pages
- E-mail Discussion Lists and Usenet Newsgroups
- Telnet Sites
- FTP Sites
- Software Archives
- Miscellaneous Resources

Tip: If you find yourself getting overwhelmed with the tech talk, don't forget that the quick guide in Appendix A can get your feet back on the ground.

Guides (and More!) for the Whole Net

First, let's look at some resources that cover the entire information spectrum, starting from K-12 education and spreading out from there. You'll glance at a couple guidebooks, check out a modern electronic library, and discover a group of educational library specialists just waiting at your beck and call!

Incomplete Guide to the Internet

The *Incomplete Guide* is aptly named. The Internet is in a constant state of flux, forever reinventing and reorganizing itself. How could a guide about an ever-changing thing be *complete*?

The *Incomplete Guide* is designed for beginner and intermediate Internet users. The full title tells its exact purpose: *The Incomplete Guide to the Internet and Other Telecommunications Opportunities Especially for Teachers and Students, K-12*. This guide is full of curriculum and project ideas for teachers and students. Here is just one example:

```
NEWSDAY Project

Project Name: NEWSDAY
Purpose:              To address and improve:
* Academic skills - reading, writing, editing, revising, interviewing, literature
appreciation and understanding
* Social Skills: cooperative learning, leadership, listening, discussing, encourag-
ing, sharing.
* Technical Skills: word processing, file management, keyboarding; telecommunica-
tions: terminal software commands, uploading and downloading.

Summary: NEWSDAY is a multi-curricular project in which students in each partici-
pating school produce a local newspaper based on the news dispatches submitted on
the NEWSDAY news wire by cooperating student correspondents. Students become news
gatherers and reporters, editors, layout and graphics artists, and publishers.
Participation on a national and international scale leads to understanding of broad
issues which transcend local concerns. This project can involve your students in
weeks of cross-curricular activity.

Schools may use a wide variety of methods to produce the papers, ranging from
simple word processor cut and paste to full DTP packages. Participants will receive
a newspaper produced by each of the other participants in the NEWSDAY project.

Grade Levels: Upper elementary, junior high, high school.
```

The National Center for Supercomputing Applications (NCSA) Education Group produced new editions of the Incomplete Guide dated July 1993, and another edition is expected in 1994. Needless to say, be sure you get the newest one available! The Incomplete Guide is available via anonymous FTP or in hard copy format.

Where to find it

Anonymous FTP

Site	`ftp.ncsa.uiuc.edu`
Directory	`/Education/Education_Resources/Incomplete_Guide/` `Dec_1993_Edition`
Subdirectory	`/MS_Word`
Subdirectory	`/postscript`

To decide which wordprocessor/text file format you want to receive, first get the README file and then, in your selected format, from the same directory, FTP the *Incomplete Guide* itself.

To order a paper copy, contact

NCSA Education Group

605 E. Springfield Ave.

Champaign, IL 61820

Internet Request for Comments (RFC) 1578, FYI #22

The real title on this easy-to-read document is *FYI on Questions and Answers— Answers to Commonly Asked "Primary and Secondary School Internet User" Questions.* Whew! You can expect to hear it called *RFC #1578*, or *FYI #22*, or simply "that neat Internet Q&A for K-12 schools."

Note: "FYI" means *For Your Information*. It also is the official designation for a series of informative reports. You also will see mention of *RFCs*. *RFC* means *Request For Comments*, which is another series of documents discussing issues in need of resolution.

Its author, Jennifer Sellers (`sellers@quest.arc.nasa.gov`), organized *FYI #22* as a set of commonly asked questions, each followed by their answers.

Because it was formally developed using the RFC process, this document is as definitive as they get. It also is recognized as a key Internet resource by being named an *FYI (For Your Information)*, which is a series of very informative papers about the Net.

This is one of the places to begin a search for answers to questions about how to

■ Use the Internet in K-12 educational settings

■ Find school support for an Internet connection

■ Solve start-up and technical problems

■ Deal with security, viruses, and ethics

■ Arrange educational collaboration and projects

■ Find the resources you need for a project

RFC 1578 also has a detailed, seven page glossary that you can use to broaden your understanding of the intricacies of the Net.

Where to find it

Anonymous FTP

North America

Site	`ds.internic.net or 198.49.45.10`
Directory	`/fyi`
Filename	`fyi22.txt`

Pacific Rim

Site	munnari.oz.au (128.250.1.21)
Directory	`/fyi`
Filename	`fyi22.Z`

These FTP sites are repositories of "official" Internet FYI documents. That means you can find any other FYI if you know its number. To get a copy of *FYI on "What is the Internet?"* (also known as *FYI #20* or *RFC #1462*), for example, change only the filename. Instead of getting `fyi22.txt`, you would get `fyi20.txt`.

> **Tip:** In Chapter 10, information is given on how to access the resource lists at the Clearinghouse of Content Oriented Guides at the University of Michigan via FTP, WWW, or Gopher. Have a look at the education lists.

A Guide to Internet Resources for K-12 School Librarians

Another really useful guide is *A Guide to Internet Resources for K-12 School Librarians*, prepared by Renee Troselius, of the Library/Media Education Department at Mankato State University in Minnesota, (`RTroselius@Vax1.mankato.msus.edu`). This guide is worth using, even if you aren't a librarian! Although it makes no claim to be comprehensive, this guide is organized in a way that is useful. The guide is organized into the following practical categories:

- Listservs
- Free-Nets
- Telnet Sites
- FTP Sites
- Gophers
- FAQs (Frequently Asked Question/Answer documents)
- Usenet Groups

Stumpers-List

The *stumpers-list* Listserv discussion group is primarily made up of reference librarians using the net. Although this Listserv is by and for reference librarians, others may subscribe.

When a library patron asks for something difficult to find, and one of these library reference experts is *stumped*, the others pitch in and help find the answer! Between them, these librarians have truly astounding abilities and access to information.

They request, but do not require, that you tell them in your question where you have already looked for the information you want. It sometimes helps motivate them if you've already tried the usual, expected places, but came up dry.

Where to find it

E-mail	`stumpers-list@crf.cuis.edu`
Subscribe address	`mailserv@crf.cuis.edu`
Moderator	`roslibrefrg@crf.cuis.edu`

Their work is intellectually demanding, and they use lots of humor to make it easier. Summer 1994 was rife with wombat jokes.

AskERIC and ERIC (Educational Resources Information Center)

AskERIC is an Internet-based question-answer service specifically for teachers, library media specialists, and administrators. Anyone involved with K-12 education can send an e-mail message to AskERIC. Drawing from the extensive resources of the ERIC system, AskERIC staff will respond with an answer within 48 working hours. If you have questions about K-12 education, learning, teaching, information technology, educational administration, these are the folks to contact.

The Gopher offers access to ERIC documents, education related documents, and AskERIC, the Internet-based K-12 question-and-answer service.

Where to find it

E-mail   askeric@ericir.syr.edu

Gopher

    Site   ericir.syr.edu 70

Surface mail

    AskERIC Network Information Specialists
    ERIC Clearinghouse on Information & Technology
    Syracuse University
    Syracuse, New York 13244-4100

    Voice   315/443-9114
    Fax   315/443-5448

The *Educational Resources Information Center* (ERIC) is a federally-funded national information system that provides access to an extensive body of education-related literature. ERIC provides a variety of services and products at all education levels, bibliographic information and abstracts for a variety of educational documents from the Educational Resources Information Center, and lesson plans by subject and grade level. ERIC documents include journal articles, conference papers, published research, and many other types of information. (For more information on ERIC, see Appendix B.)

You can access ERIC through many Gophers, including the previously mentioned address for AskERIC.

Colorado Alliance of Research Libraries (CARL)

CARL offers access to many databases: Academic and public library online catalogs; current article (and synopsis) indexes such as UnCover, ERIC and Magazine Index; databases such as the Academic American Encyclopedia and Internet Resource Guide; and a gateway to other library systems. Access to some items is limited.

CARL is a unique service. In some of the databases, after you search for references in which you are interested, and you find one that is especially valuable, they will photocopy it and surface mail it to you! Several restrictions apply, as you might imagine. The charge is calculated automatically when your search locates an item, and you are offered a chance to enter your credit card number to have it sent to you. If you don't want to buy it, you can copy down, or capture and print the bibliographic information, so that you can go to your local library and find it yourself.

To reach the company that provides CARL, you can use e-mail: help@carl.org.

Where to find it

    telnet csi.carl.org or telnet 192.54.81.18

When you telnet to CARL, you are prompted for a terminal type, so choose VT100, unless you have other instructions from your site.

Following is an example of the opening menu of a CARL telnet signon:

```
                 >>>  Systems That Inform  <<<

                 Welcome to the CARL System

                   (Release A.107.008)

         A Computerized Network of Systems and Services


       Developed by the Colorado Alliance of Research Libraries
           Marketed and supported by CARL Systems, Inc.
                 3801 East Florida St., Suite 300
                       Denver, Co. 80210
                   Voice:   303-758-3030
                   Fax:   303-758-0606
                   Internet:   help@carl.org

    PRESS <RETURN> TO START THE PROGRAM  (use //EXIT to return HOME)>>


           CARL Corporation offers access to the following
                     groups of databases:
```

```
      1. Library Catalogs
             (including Government Publications)

      2. Current Article Indexes and Access
             (including UnCover and ERIC)

      3. Information Databases
             (including Encyclopedia)

      4. Other Library Systems

      5. Library and System News

Enter the NUMBER of your choice, and press the <RETURN> key >>
```

Tip: You can break a telnet connection. As this little sample of CARL's interface shows, it is not quite as user friendly as it will someday need to be. For example, there is no visible option on the screen, but typing //**exit** works. Fortunately, because you accessed CARL by way of telnet, simply pressing Ctrl+] and pressing **q** or typing **close** breaks the connection!

I selected option 3, for Current Article Indexes because ERIC was mentioned.

```
Enter the NUMBER of your choice, and press the <RETURN> key >>3

WORKING...
  1. Libraries   2. Articles   3. Information  4. Other Systems  5. News

               INFORMATION DATABASES

               60. Choice Book Reviews (access restricted as of 9/1/93)
               61. Encyclopedia
               64. School Model Programs
               65. Internet Resource Guide
               66. Department of Energy
               67. Journal Graphics
                   (Television/Radio Transcripts)
               82. Company ProFile
               88. Federal Domestic Assistance Catalog
               89. Librarian's Yellow Pages
```

The Model School program listing #64 looked interesting, so I continued.

```
   Enter the NUMBER of your choice, and press the <RETURN> key >> 64

WORKING...

07/07/94
```

```
02:55 P.M.       SELECTED DATABASE:  School Model Programs

The School Model Programs database is a project of the Colorado
Department of Education, with federal funding provided through
Project LEAD (Leadership in Educational Administration Development).
The database provides access to information about educational programs
in Colorado that work in fostering school improvement.  Please contact
the schools listed for more information about their programs.


            Enter   N   for   NAME search
                    W   for   WORD search
                    B   to    BROWSE by program name
                    S   to    STOP or SWITCH to another database

            Type the letter for the kind of search you want,
            and end each line you type by pressing <RETURN>
                    SELECTED DATABASE:  School Model Programs
ENTER  COMMAND (?H FOR HELP) >>
```

CARL then offered me the opportunity to search the Model School Database by word, or browse the subheading program names.

Because it is so responsive, CARL is a good example of the service orientation many libraries will need to develop to remain state-of-the-art in the information age.

Internet Resource Directories (IRDs) for Educators

The *Internet Resource Directories* offers a set of documents, prepared and revised for and by educators. Three of the IRDs are about telnet sites, FTP sites, and e-mail Listserv discussion groups. The IRD on "infusion ideas" is a large collection of examples of how schools already have used the Internet in K-12 education.

Where to find it

Anonymous FTP

Site	tcet.unt.edu
Directory	/pub/telecomputing-info/IRD
Filenames	IRD-telnet-sites.txt
	IRD-ftp-archives.txt
	IRD-listservs.txt
	IRD-infusion-ideas.txt

The Internet Hunt

The *Internet Hunt* is a wonderful idea! Modeled on a scavenger hunt, it serves to interest students in the vastness and power of the Net, and gives them a way to demonstrate the skills they've learned. This example (June 1994) was limited to novices. September 1993 also was a novice hunt, and November 1993 was limited to K-12 students. All the Hunts are in the Hunt archives, so that you can have a look at past Hunts.

By reading the Hunt results and studying the Hunt archives, you can "stand on the shoulders of the giants." You can see where on the Net they look for items, and more importantly, how they structure their search strategies. Which tools do they use for different kinds of questions?

And, as mentioned in Chapter 1, having mini-hunts in your school is easy to do after reading the Hunt archives. There have been monthly Hunts since September 1992.

Just to show you the range and depth of the Hunts, following are extended excerpts of a Hunt in action.

Hunt results typically begin with a greeting, such as the following:

```
                        A Sample, Novice Hunt
*******************************************************************
                    THE INTERNET HUNT   *
*                       RESULTS         *
*                    FOR  JUNE, 1994    *
*******************************************************************

Greetings All!

The June novice-only Hunt is history, and our individual
winner is:
```

The winner is announced, the prizes (yes, prizes) are given, and scores accounted for. Information about the specific Hunt then is given, and in this example, it was a Hunt for novices.

```
The novices Hunt is always one of the most popular in terms
of number of participants. Most of these first-time
entrants performed quite well. As always, the best answers
are below.

Questions 4 & 7 turned out to be the most difficult.

If you need a beginner's Hunt to test out your skills, or to
use in a training exercise, this one, and the September,
1993 Hunt are the beginners Hunts to date. (In addition,
November, 93 was a K-12 only Hunt, and was a little easier
than most)
```

Next, the questions are given and the answers are outlined and explained, as in the following excerpts, which show just two questions and answers.

```
Question 7 (3 points)

(Question designed by Richard Lee Holbert, Billie Peterson,
Tony Safina & Dr Gerald R. Viers)

We are studying French history in my high school French IV
class.  Our instructor said there were two novels available
on the net that would help our understanding of two periods
in particular, the French Revolution of 1793 and the later
French Revolution of 1830.  I can't remember the names of
these novels for the life of me, but I believe he said
Charles Dickens wrote one of them and Victor Hugo wrote the
other one.  Can you tell me the names of these novels and
where on the Internet can I find them?

-------------------------------------
[We give here three answers to the question about the Dickens
and Hugo novels.  They used three different approaches to
arrive at the same correct answers: Dickens - A Tale of Two
Cities and Hugo - Les Miserables.  Many huntsters had
difficulty identifying the Hugo novel as it was not placed
in the Gutenberg files until May of this year, so, many
search engines had not yet picked up on it.]

-------------------------------------
[This answer utilized The World-Wide Web Virtual Library
which is a relatively new tool with which we should all
become familiar.]

   The World-Wide Web Virtual Library: Subject Catalogue
   http://info.cern.ch/hypertext/DataSources/bySubject/
   Overview.html

   Literature & Art
   http://info.cern.ch/hypertext/DataSources/bySubject/
   Literature/Overview.html

   Under English language Literature
   Gutenberg Master Index
   http://info.cern.ch/roeber/Misc/Gutenberg.html

   I paged down to "Literature, by Author":

   Charles Dickens

   A Tale of Two Cities
   ftp://mrcnext.cso.uiuc.edu/gutenberg/etext94/2city10.txt

   First page says:

     A Tale of Two Cities, by Charles Dickens
     [A story of the French Revolution]
      Victor Hugo

   Les Miserables
   ftp://mrcnext.cso.uiuc.edu/gutenberg/etext94/lesms10.txt
```

I'm assuming this is the correct book--I haven't read it.
Paging through the table of contents I see references to
France during the time periods mentioned. Also, the first
chapter mentions the French Revolution.

[From "Marge Gunter" <MGQ@tigger.ctd.ornl.gov>]

- -
[Steve utilized the Yanoff Guide - A MUST for any Internet
traveller. To find where to get your copy: Finger
Yanoff@csd4.csd.uwm.edu.]

I looked at Yanoffs internet resource list posted on
alt.internet.services
*LITERATURE/BOOKS- - - - - - - - - - - - - - -
Project Gutenberg
ftp mrcnext.cso.uiuc.edu or ftp 128.174.201.12
offers: Many books in print and almanac files.
cd pub/etext
ftp mrcnext.cso.uiuc.edu
login as anonymous
cd etext
searched indexes and found the following in INDEX200.GUT:

Jan 1994 A Tale of Two Cities, by Charles Dickens [CD#1]
[2city10x.xxx] 98

May 1994 Les Miserables, by Victor Hugo [in English]
[lesms10x.xxx] 135

cd to etext94
etext located in:
-rw-r--r-- 1 hart   787642 Dec 10 20:48 2city10.txt
-rw-r--r-- 1 hart   3334517 May 2 01:48 lesms10.txt

   To get to the answer

[From "Steve Sexton"<sexton@meaddata.com >]

- -
[This searcher utilized the Library of Congress resources
located at marvel.loc.gov to search for the texts.]

I hope it is alright to use what one knows and thus
tentatively identify the books in question as Dickens'
_Tale_of_Two_Cities dealing with the 1793 Revolution and
Hugo's_Les_Miserables_ dealing with the July Revolution of
1830. I proceeded on that assumption and confirmed it by
looking at the Table of Contents of the Hugo when when I
found it and in the head matter of the Dickens.

Now to find the text of these two novels on the Internet.

telnet marvel.loc.gov
 10. Global Electronic Library
   5. Language, Linguistics, Literature
    3. Literature
     7. Literature, Electronic Books
      85. A Tale of Two Cities

My memory did serve me correctly, the subtitle reads "A
story of the French Revolution."

```
Back up to the Literature menu
   4.  Electronic Text Archive, UMich
   10.  Gutenberg
      4.  Index200.GUT
```

The file list texts which have been added. The first item
on the list indicates that _Les_Miserables_ was added in
March 1994 and that the name of the file is lesms10x.xxx

Scanning through the very detailed table of contents
confirms that it definitely deals with France in the first
half of the 19th Century in general and near the end of the
book with the 1830 revolution in particular.

```
[From EANC-T-D-RLB@emh5.korea.army.mil]
```

```
***************************************************************************
```
Question 8 (3 points)
(question designed by Lu Wilson)

A teacher at my daughter's school developed this facinating
'Wolf Study' unit for her third grade pupils. She said that
she found much of the information at a gopher site on the
internet. She downloaded telemetry data, study guides,
behavioral data, photo-quality images, wolf howls and even the
utilities to convert the images and sounds - all in one place!
Where is this gopher and how can I find it?

```
- - - - - - - - - - - - - - - - - - - - - - - - - - - - - -
```

Used Veronica to search Gopherspace via U Texas, Dallas
search term - Wolf Study

Scanned the list of entries and selected Wolf Study Project/

Menu items included - Timber Wolf Unit Study Guide from the
Science Museum of Minnesota

Pressed the "=" key to see where this listing was coming
from. This revealed "host InforMNs.k12.MN.US"

Checked the list of gophers in Minnesota to verify the name
of the gopher:

telnet to   Info.umd.edu

select:

```
   10.  Search the internet
      11.Virtual Reference Desk
         2.Gophers - 22 different gopher groups
            1.United States gophers
            25.Minnesota
               11.K-12 Gophers - InforMNs (Minn. K-12 Project)
                  3.Minnesota K-12 Resources
                  18.Wolf Study Project
```

This verified that the gopher was located in Minnesota. Use
the path above to find it.

```
[From The Merry Married Librarians (Skip & Susan),
 Susan_KURZ@umail.umd.edu]

*************************************************************************
```

And every Hunt has a mystery question! The mystery question usually is one that the Huntmeisters do not know for sure if they can answer.

```
*************************************************************************
Mystery Question
(question asked by Rick Gates)

Has anybody found a picture of that galaxy-gobbling black hole that
the Hubble Space Telescope recently discovered?

-------------------------------------
[Rick: Jerry Eagle finds us what we need through Usenet.]

   Yes, indeed.  Using Usenet again, searching for "astro" I
   found the group "sci.astro" containing the following article
   titled "HST confirms black hole in M87 ...", and it lists
   the ftp reference:


   From: phfrom@nyx.uni-konstanz.de (Hartmut Frommert)
   Newsgroups: sci.physics,sci.astro,sci.chem,sci.bio Subject:
   Re: HST confirms black hole in M87 and the Loch Ness Monster
   Date: Mon, 30 May 1994 10:07:10 GMT Organization: University
   of Constance, Dept. of Physics Lines: 8 Message-ID:
   <phfrom.268.770292430@nyx.uni-konstanz.de> References:
   <2s379c$a1q@dartvax.dartmouth.edu>
   <2s42vf$2v5@netnews.ntu.edu.tw> NNTP-Posting-Host:
   maus.physik.uni-konstanz.de Xref: news.uoregon.edu
   sci.physics:82783 sci.astro:58958 sci.chem:23131
   sci.bio:19871

   b0202011@cc.ntu.edu.tw (ton) writes:

   >Is there any photo release of the "black hole"through ftp
   or www?

   ftp stsci.edu: /stsci/epa/gif/M87*.gif

   [From Jerry Eagle, jeagle@cie-2.uoregon.edu]
```

And the answer goes on for four more pages!

Many sites throughout the Internet have copies of the Internet Hunt. Several sites and lists also quickly make the questions available upon their release. Rick Gates, Internet maven, student, and lecturer at the University of Arizona in Tucson, and Internet Hunt Master, personally keeps the North American FTP locations up to date.

Where to find it

Anonymous FTP

North America

Site	`ftp.cni.org`
Directory	`/pub/net-guides/i-hunt/`
Filename	`00README`
Site	`ftp.cic.net`
Directory	`/pub/hunt/about`
Filename	`intro.txt`

Europe

Site	`ftp.nic.surfnet.nl`
Directory	`/mirror-archive/resources/internet-hunt/about`
Filename	`intro.txt`

Tip: Don't forget John December's Guides, *Nettools: The Guide to Network Resource Tools* and *Yanoff's Special Internet Connections*, mentioned in Chapter 10. They are great sources.

K-12 Gophers for You and Me

Gopherspace is one of the fastest expanding parts of the Net, and no wonder! *Gophers* are easy to use, can be run on inexpensive, less sophisticated equipment, and are very powerful! Check out Appendix A for more information on Gopher, and an even more powerful, related search tool called *Veronica* (Very Easy Rodent-Oriented Netwide Index to Computerized Archives).

United States Library of Congress

This is the greatest library in the modern world. And you can connect to it without even leaving your home town!

Where to find it

Gopher   marvel.loc.gov

The NYSERNet Newsletter and EMPIRE INTERNET SCHOOLHOUSE

The non-profit New York State Education and Research Network (NYSERNet) operates this excellent Gopher.

Where to find it

Gopher   nysernet.org 3000

E-mail   info@nysernet.org

Under the main menu, you will find an entry for the Empire Internet Schoolhouse that provides access to a broad range of K-12 information. It looks like this.

```
                    EMPIRE INTERNET SCHOOLHOUSE

—>  1. About the Empire Internet Schoolhouse.
    2. Assembly Hall for Projects and Discussions/
    3. Library & Internet Reference Tools/
    4. Academic Wings/
    5. School Reform and Technology Planning Center/
    6. Field trips to other school systems/
    7. ADAPT-IT ON-LINE WORKSHOP.
    8. Career and Guidance Office/
    9. Directory Services and Contacts Center/
   10. Electronic suggestion box (e-mail to Empire's staff)<TEL>
   11. The Grants Center/
```

CICNet K-12 on the Internet Gopher

Designed by a doctoral student of education at West Virginia University especially for K-12 teachers, the CICNet Gopher server includes summaries of several "Internet in the Classroom" projects.

Where to find it

Gopher   `gopher.cic.net`
Directory   `CICNet Projects and Gopher Servers`

OTPAD/ACT Gopher—New York Department of Education

One way to stay up with the flow of new things on the Net is to subscribe to *InterNIC Net-Happenings*, a Listserv list out of North Dakota run by Net luminary, Gleason Sackman. Among many other things, Net-Happenings frequently distributes a detailed update on the new diggings at the New York Department of Education Gopher built by George Casler. (You can subscribe to Net-Happenings via `net-happenings-request@is.internic.net`.)

To demonstrate how much upkeep a good Gopher requires, excerpts of three monthly updates are shown here. (The time period covered in these three examples is just 13 days, under 2 weeks.)

The OTPAD/ACT Gopher actually contains much more than is shown here. Only areas that have *new* material are listed in the updates. The + mark means that something new has been added to an existing "folder," or the folder itself is new.

> **Tip:** When George mentions a "folder" here, he means each of the options that will be listed for you to choose, when you use that level of the Gopher. "Folder" is the Macintosh term for what DOS calls a *directory* or *subdirectory*, and all contain files of information.

```
Date: Tue, 14 Jun 94 09:33:51 EDT
From: George Casler <act@unix5.nysed.gov>
Subject: NYSED's OTPAD/ACT Gopher

-----------------------------------------------------------
What's New on the OTPAD/ACT gopher - unix5.nysed.gov - 6/14/94
-----------------------------------------------------------
  To access, point your gopher client to unix5.nysed.gov
   HREF=gopher://unix5.nysed.gov

              —> NO public telnet access.  <—
-----------------------------------------------
In Conferences, Calls for Papers:
  - Founding meeting of Telecommunities Canada announced
  - Conference: Environments for Learning: Creating Interactive Learning
    Environments in Schools
```

```
   - First International Workshop of Community Networking: Integrated
     Multimedia Services to the Home
   - Panel Discussion by the Progressive Librarians Guild on The NII: Universal
     Access or Information Apartheid?
   - Fifth Solomons Interagency Conference on Public Access. Topic:
     Working with the Public to Ensure Public Access to Federal Information
     in an Electronic Age
   - U.S. Department of Ed satellite town meeting. Topic: Parental and Family
     Involvement in Education.

In the Education News folder:
   - California announces "Building the Future: K-12 Network Technology
     Planning Guide"
   - Global Classroom Youth Congress establishes website
   - Global Student Newswire announces temporary Webserver location
   - University of Southampton, U.K.,'s Interactive Learning Centre announces
     webserver
   - Summary of Nassau County (NY)-Hofstra University project offering
     10,000 free Internet passwords to students
   - MIT announces Weather Radar Laboratory website
```

Continuing on, it outlines new updates in the K-12 Resources folder.

```
In the K-12 Resources folder:
  + Arts & Humanities folder
  + Disability Resources & Information folder
  + English/Language Arts folder
  + General folder
  + Health, PhysEd & Home Ec folder
  + Languages Other than English folder
  + Math, Science & Technology folder
  + Occupation and Technical Folder
  + Other Educational Gophers folder
  + Social Studies folder
     - Link to the Historical Documents collection at Queens
         Public Library
```

It goes on to outline new holdings in the TelecommInfo folder, Higher Education and Education News Information now available on the Gopher; but then, only six days later, he has added more resources and reorganized the information for ease of use.

In the K-12 folder, the following have been added:

```
In the K-12 Resources folder:
  + Arts & Humanities folder
     - Link established to the John Hiatt Shot of Rhythm archive
     + Gallery - Works from the following artists have been added:
        - John Tenniell (Alice in Wonderland)
        - Thomas Cole
        - John Singleton Copley
        - Salvador Dali
        - Eugene Delacroix
        - Theodore Gericault
        - Francisco de Goya
```

```
+ Disability Resources & Information folder
+ English/Language Arts folder
+ General folder
   - Education Programs That Work 93
   - Education Programs That Work 94
```

A new folder has been created on Educational Technology.

```
A new folder -- Education Technology -- has been created under this
heading. The following items have been moved from the General folder
to the Education Technology folder:
- Answers to Commonly Asked "Primary & Secondary School Internet User"
   Questions
- California Technology Planning Guide
- COSN-FARNEt Final Report
- COSN-FARNet Issues Outline
- Distance learning Projects in the US K-12
- Grazint the net - Raising a Generation of Free Range Students
- The Interpedia Project
- Laserdisk Information
- Multimedia resources from Texas Tech
- Network Learning Success Stories
- "Networks: Where Have You Been All My Life" Essay Contest Winners
- "Prisoners of Time" - Report of Nat'l Comm on Time and Learning
- Things to do on the Internet
- Using the Internet in the Classroom
- Switched-on Classroom (Word 2.0- version) MASS report
- Switched-on Classroom (text version) MASS report
- The Public Domain & The WorldWide Web
Added to the Educational Technology folder are:
- Tools for Transforming Teaching and Learning, a report of the U.S.
   Department of Education
- Pointer to proceedings of the Secretary of Education's Educational
   Technology conference, held in May
```

... and just a week later:

```
In the K-12 Resources folder:
 + Arts & Humanities folder
    - A pointer to a small, informal collection of information on
      Jewelry making
    - Pointer to Fine Art Forum Online
```

Fortunately for us, there are many dedicated Internet experts who are willing to take on the challenge of trying to make sense of the hundreds of intricate Gopher holes now lacing through the Net. Arizona State University has the advantage of having such a person—Gene Glass. In this message, he promises to regularly review and repair or remove any broken connections. This type of dedication makes his Gopher one of the most valuable, so spend a moment reviewing the extensive holdings in this Arizona burrow.

Wouldn't the parents in your school district love to see your school listed here?!!

```
Date: Sun, 29 May 1994 22:28:50 MST
From: Gene Glass <ATGVG@asuacad.bitnet>
To: Multiple recipients of list AERA <AERA@asuacad.bitnet>
Subject: Education Gopher Servers
```

Dear Networkers:

Anyone who has spent any time navigating gopher space looking for
resources for professional educators knows how frustrating the search
can be. "Subject Trees" maintained at several sites can help, but
my recent experience with these collections of gopher "pointers" has
not been rewarding. The links that were once compiled to important
gopher sites are now often broken or dysfunctional. Duplications and
dead-end Telnet links add to the frustration.

I have compiled a collection of 16 electronic journals and about 75
education gophers (both listed below) and programmed links to them from
my local College of Education gopher. Furthermore, I am committed to
reviewing all these links periodically and removing broken ones. So by
accessing my College's gopher you can be assured of a fairly complete
and painless excursion into Gopherspace for the professional educator.
To get to these resources, gopher to info.asu.edu and enter the
ASU CAMPUS WIDE INFORMATION directory where you will find College of
Education. The pointers are in the Electronic Journals and Other
Education Related Gophers directories.

For Gopher administrators who wish to program a link, the specs are
Type=1; Host=info.asu.edu;Port=70; Path=1/asu-cwis/education/other and
1/asu-cwis/education/journals.

If you know of a gopher that is important for educators and that I
have missed, I would appreciate hearing about it. Thanks.
                                                   Gene Glass

LIST OF EDUCATION RESOURCES AT INFO.ASU.EDU:

                    Electronic Journals, Newsletters & More
     Daily Report Card News Service
     EDPOLYAN: A LISTSERV
     Education Policy Analysis Archives
     Education Policy Briefs from Arizona State University
     Education, Research and Perspectives (Journal from Australia)
     Electronic Journals at CICNet
     Interpersonal Computing & Technology
     Journal of Counseling and Development
     Journal of Distance Education & Communication
     Journal of Higher Education (from Ohio State)
     Journal of Statistics Education
     Journal of Technology Education
     New Horizons in Adult Education (from Ohio State)
     Psycoloquy
     Rasch Measurement Transactions
     The Chronicle of Higher Education

                    Other Education Related Gopher Servers
     ABCs of Teaching from Cal Berkeley
     AMI—A Friendly Public Interface
     Apple Computer Higher Education Gopher
     Arizona Board of Regents
     AskERIC at Syracuse University
     Australian Association for Research in Education
     BUBL Education Section - BH2B3
     Best of K-12 on the Internet (from TIES, Minn.)
```
```

Briarwood Educational Network K-12 Gopher
CAUSE--Information Technology in Higher Education
CICNet K-12 Gopher
CRESST/UCLA Research on Evaluation and Testing
California Department of Education
Center for Talented Youth (CTY)-Johns Hopkins University
Centre for Women's Studies in Education at OISE
Chicano/Latino Network
Confed. of Faculty Assoc. of Brit. Col.
Consortium for School Networking
Council for the Renewal of Undergraduate Education; Sweden
Curry School of Education at Univ of Virginia
EDUCOM
ERIC Clearinghouse on Assessment & Evaluation
East High School (Memphis, Tennessee)
Education Position Openings from Minnesota
Education Technology Centre of British Columbia
Electronic Government Information Service
Essays on Educational Topics
Grossmont Union High School District
Hacienda La Puente Unified School District
Hawaii Department of Education Gopher
IBM Kiosk for Education
Education Information by Subject at Rice University
K-12 Gopher at Univ. of Massachusetts
Lakeside School, Seattle, Washington
Learning Research and Development Center's Newsletters
Los Alamos Middle School
MDEnet - Michigan Department of Education Gopher
Maricopa County (AZ) Community College District Gopher Server
Minnesota Center for Arts Education
Missouri Department of Elementary and Secondary Education
Montgomery Blair High School
NASA K-12 Gopher
National Center for Adult Literacy
National Indian Policy Center
National School Network (Bolt, Beranek and Newman project)
National Science Foundation
New York State Dept of Education
New York State Educ & Res Network
Northwest Regional Educational Laboratories, Gopher
Ohio Education Computer Network
Ohio State Univ, ERIC Clearinghouse: Science, Math, Environ.
Ohio Department of Education
Ontario Institute for Studies in Education
Ontario, Ministry of Education and Training
Ralph Bunche Elementary School (NYC)
Research for Better Schools (RBS)
San Diego City Schools
Singapore Ministry Of Education
StarkNet (Stark County School District, Canton, Ohio, USA)
Subject Areas at University of Michigan
Teacher Education Internet Server in Virginia
Texas Higher Education Coordinating Board
The Evaluation Center at Western Michigan University
U.S. Government Gopher Servers
US Department of Education
Univ of California, Irvine, Education
Univ of California, Santa Barbara, Graduate School of Educ.
Univ of Hawaii, College of Education Server
Univ of Minnesota College of Education
Univ of South Florida, College of Education

```
Univ. of Mass. K-12 Education
Utah Education Network
Wisconsin Department of Public Instruction
k12net: Oak Ridge National Laboratories
```

Tip: Check out the Gopher Jewels entry in Chapter 10—it has even more pointers to Gophers for educators.

University of Michigan Library Gopher

This important Gopher includes news services, the original Clearinghouse for Subject Oriented Internet Resource Guides, access to the New York Public Library, and the capability to search for Internet resources by type, location, and subject.

Where to find it

Gopher   gopher.lib.umich.edu

Other Useful Gophers

Following are other gophers with very useful information for K-12 education.

Consortium for School Networking (CoSN) Gopher

CoSN's purpose is to promote development and use of computer network technology in K-12 education.

Where to find it

Gopher   digital.cosn.org

Wisconsin "Badger" Gopher

The Wisconsin Department of Public Instruction and Division for Libraries and Community Learning operates the Badger Gopher.

Where to find it

Gopher   `badger.state.wi.us`

North Carolina State University's "Library Without Walls"

This library contains dictionaries, directories, indices, and subject guides to literature and the Internet. It also has "Study Carrels" devoted to subject areas.

Where to find it

Gopher   `dewey.lib.ncsu.edu`

Directory   `/NCSU's "Library Without Walls"`

Services here include CNN Newsroom.

Internet for Minnesota Schools—Informnsnet

In addition to excellent links to many other K-12 educational resources, this Gopher has special areas for grant opportunities and for Spanish language Internet users.

Where to find it

Gopher   `Informns.k12.mn.us`

University of Massachusetts K12 Gopher

This Gopher includes EDNET, Kidsphere, and K12 Administration lists.

Where to find it

Gopher   `k12.ucs.umass.edu 70`

Ohio Education Computer Network

This Gopher is designed for use by K-12 students.

Where to find it

Gopher   `nwoca7.nwoca.ohio.gov`

MEMO Gopher

Where to find it

Gopher   `gopher.mankato.msus.edu`

CICNet

Where to find it

Gopher   `gopher.cic.net`

NASA's Network Applications and Information Center (NAIC)

Where to find it

Gopher   `//naic.nasa.gov/Guide to NASA Online Resources`

University of Manitoba

Where to find it

Gopher   `gopher.umanitoba.ca`

K-12 World Wide Web (WWW) Homepages

Because *World Wide Web* is a hypertext/hypermedia environment, WWW sites require a special access software, usually called a *browser*. Lynx and Mosaic are two popular browsers. Lynx operates in the hypertext environment as the lowest common denominator, but Lynx is *text only*. It can support the downloading of files and images, but you cannot view them online. Mosaic comes in a variety of versions for Macintosh, DOS/Windows, UNIX, and other platforms. Mosaic for Microsoft Windows requires a VGA monitor and a direct connection to the Internet—an element in short supply in most U.S. classrooms in 1994!

Mosaic has some flaws, and makes serious demands on the Net's precious bandwidth, but if you have the hardware, and can stand the Net-lags (waiting for a connection or a graphic file from a remote site), Mosaic has some nifty color graphics screens.

The `http://` (hypertext transfer protocol) addresses of each site conforms to the Uniform Resource Locator (URL) standard which makes the address part of the Web. All you need to access the site is the WWW browser software (such as Lynx, Mosaic, and so on) loaded and configured for your Internet-connected computer, and the URL you want to visit.

WWW has just begun to grow quite rapidly. The following sections discuss some sites you may want to visit.

> **Tip:** If you have no clue what WWW is, and want to try it out before you spend the effort to FTP (and install) the browser software, you can try it out over the Internet using telnet to `info.cern.ch`. This will bring you to the WWW Home Page at CERN, Switzerland. You now are using a simple line mode browser. To move around the Web, enter the number given with the item you want to see.

More Information on World Wide Web

Following are some primary resources for questions about World Wide Web and Hyper Text, and Hyper Text Markup Language (HTML):

Where to find it

Anonymous FTP

Site	`rtfm.mit.edu`
Directory	`pub/usenet/news.answers/www/faq`
File	`WWW-FAQ`
Site	`freehep.scri.fsu.edu`
Directory	`freehep/tutorials/`
Files	`how_to_write_HTML_*`

Choose the file format you want. The suffix .ps means *PostScript*, .txt means *ASCII*. Almost all word processors can read an ASCII file.

```
WWW
URL
http://www.vuw.ac.nz:80/who/Nathan.Torkington/ideas/www-faq.html
```

U.S. Department of Education (ED)/Office of Educational Research and Improvement (OERI)

Where to find it

URL   http://www.ed.gov/

Suggestions or questions?

E-mail   wwwadmin@inet.ed.gov

K12 Cyberspace Outpost

This site by Janice Abrahams has reliable examples of how the WWW medium can be used in K-12 education.

Where to find it

URL   http://k12.cnidr.org/janice_k12/k12menu.html

GNN Magazine (Global Network Navigator)

GNN Magazine published an "Education Issue" in January 1994. The Table of Contents is reproduced here, for you to sample. Several K-12 education uses of the Net are detailed.

Where to find it

Magazine URL   http://nearnet.gnn.com/mag/1_94/1_94.toc.html
Homepage URL   http://nearnet.gnn.com/GNN-ORA.html

Problems or questions?

E-mail   support@gnn.com

This is how the Table of Contents looks.

```
GNN Magazine January 1994

===================
TABLE OF CONTENTS
===================

The Internet -- An Education in Itself

- - - - - - - - - - - - - - - -
Feature Articles
- - - - - - - - - - - - - - - -

Remarks by Vice President Al Gore at National Press Club

    The Vice President sees a connection between the sinking
    of the Titanic, all roads leading to Rome, 24 hours of David
    Letterman, and yes, the information superhighway coming to you
    and me.  Stale jokes, clichés and classical allusions all included.
    What's important is the Administration's commitment to universal
    network access for schools.

Publishing for Professors
 by Dale Dougherty

    The _Chronicle of Higher Education_, the top publication for
    colleges and universities in America, is developing
    its own presence on the Internet, thanks to Judith Turner, the
    Director of Electronic Services.

Is the Surf Up?
 by Mitchell Sprague

    A teacher at a rural California high school writes about his
    discovery of the Internet and the direct effect it is having
    on his students.

Teaching and Learning in a Networked World
 by Donna Donovan

    Dr. Martin Huntley, scientist and educator with the Educational
    Technologies Department of Bolt, Beranek & Newman, Inc. (BBN) in
    Cambridge, Massachusetts, is a pioneer in the effort to bring
    technology to schools. Donna Donovan talked recently with Dr. Huntley
    about his ideas and concerns for networked classrooms.

Environmental Education on the Net
 by Laura Parker Roerden

    The Internet is making it helping students understand environmental issues.
    This article also catalogs many of the environmental education
    resources available on the Internet.

SchoolNet: Canada's Educational Networking Initiative
 by Tyler Burns
```

SchoolNet's goal is promote networking in Canadian elementary and secondary
schools and provide access to online national and international resources.

Academy One Introduces Classrooms to the Internet
 by Linda Delzeit

   Academy One is an online resource for educators, students, parents, and
   administrators of the kindergarten through high school age range. It
   is an international program of the National Public Telecomputing
   Network (NPTN).

KIDLINK - Global Networking for Youth 10 - 15
 by Odd de Presno

   KIDLINK is a grassroots movement established to get children between
   10 and 15 years of age involved in a global dialog. Since its launch
   in 1990, more than 10,000 children from 56 countries have participated
   in a project that has helped extend the limits of our global city.

Global Lab Project Cultivates Young Scientists
 by Boris Berenfeld

   The Global Lab Project integrates telecommunications,
   affordable scientific tools, and innovative
   curriculum to create a global community of student researchers.
   Students in the Global Lab project are engaged in real-world, hands-on
   investigations into local and global environments.

K-12 Schools on the Internet: One School's Experience
 by Mike Showalter

   Nearly two years after first gaining an Internet connection, faculty,
   administration, and students at the Bush School continue to be excited
   about the advantages of being online.

>From Littleton to Law on the Net
 by Peter Martin

   Martin, a law professor at Cornell, believes that the impact of
   information technology on legal research will change legal education
   as well as lay people's view of the legal system. Martin
   is also co-founder of the Legal Information Institute at Cornell Law
   School in 1992. One of the Institute's objectives is to provide legal
   information over the Internet.

Librarians and the Internet
 by Mary Ann Neary

   Librarians have embraced the Internet as a means of enhancing their
   information delivery capabilities. As a connector of people, files,
   and resources, the Internet is an ideal complement to the librarians'
   traditional role.

- - - - - - - - - -
GO FIND OUT
- - - - - - - - - -

Yanoff's Top Ten Education Resources
 by Scott Yanoff

```
Cruising the Web for College Information
 by Linda Mui

Environmental Education Resources
 by Laura Parker Roerden

Educator's Guide to e-mail Lists
 by Ellie Cutler

Knitting on the Net
 by Clairemarie Fisher O'Leary

Internet Kitchen
 by Miss Lorraine Quiche


--------
NET HEADS
--------

Learning from EXPO
 by Frans Von Hoesel

The Internet Service Station (#2)
 by Cricket Liu

Administrator's Handbook
 by Bryan Buus

The Wanderer
 by Matthew Gray


----
HOT AIR
----

Six Doonesbury strips on the Internet

Machinations by Odysseus
```

Global Network Academy (GNA) and Usenet University

GNA is an outgrowth of Usenet University and is developing into a credit and non-credit educational resource. (See Chapter 10 for more information.)

Where to find it

URL `http://uu-gna.mit.edu:8001/`

Questions or Suggestions?

E-mail `gna-webmaster@sun.dsy.de`

Clearinghouse for Subject-Oriented Internet Resource Guides at the University of Michigan

Mentioned previously, access to these useful guides can be made through a number of methods including FTP, Gopher, and WWW.

Where to find it

WWW

    URL   `http://http2.sils.umich.edu/~lou/chhome.html`

    or

               `http://www.lib.umich.edu/chhome.html`

The Department of Instructional Technologies at San Francisco State University WWW Server

This site has K-12 resources, and a great collection links to job listings.

Where to find it

    URL   `http://130.212.25.153/dit_home_page.html`

WisDPI Web Home Page—Wisconsin Department of Public Instruction

Special emphasis is placed on locating resources of interest to the K-12 and public library communities. In deference to these two groups who often have slower SLIP or PPP access (if they have any access at all!), all inline graphics in the WisDPI page total less than 5K! All clickable graphics include the file size in parentheses.

Where to find it

    URL   `http://badger.state.wi.us/0/agencies/dpi/www/`
               `dpi_home.html`

NASA's Network Applications and Information Center (NAIC)

This site compiles a guide that contains scientific, educational, and government resources of interest to both general Internet users and the NASA science community.

Where to find it

URL   `http://naic.nasa.gov/naic/guide/`

The Institute for the Learning Sciences

This site offers a hyperbook by Roger Schank and Chip Cleary, discusses what's wrong with the education system, how to reform it, and, especially, the role of educational technology in that reform.

Where to find it

URL   `http://www.ils.nwu.edu/~e_for_e/index.html`

K-12 Discussion Lists and Usenet Newsgroups

There are many interesting and useful discussion lists and newsgroups of interest to educators. Listservs and Usenet newsgroups operate a little differently, but accomplish the same purpose—to enable many people to discuss simultaneously interesting topics. For more information about these information tools, see Appendix A.

All Listservs have two or three addresses. One address is used to talk with *all* the other people on the list. There can be a few dozen or a few thousand people on a list, and each of your messages sent to this address goes to *everyone* on the list!

This e-mail address usually starts with the name of the list, as in the following:

```
Name-L@host.edu
```

A second e-mail address for every Listserv is for the software, or clerical robot program that takes care of subscribe, postpone, unsubscribe requests. This address commonly begins with:

```
listserv@    listproc@    majordomo@
```

Some especially good lists also have a third, prominent e-mail address. It's for the human being, usually the list owner or moderator, that you can write to if the list confuses or offends you, or if the Listserv software won't do what you want.

> **Tip:** Save all the information files sent back to you when you first subscribe. These files contain vital information about how to put a hold on your mail and to unsubscribe. Sometimes they even tell you the address of the list human who can help you when the robot won't.

Unfortunately, many less sophisticated Listservs have no filter to intercept messages sent to the wrong address. Even seasoned Listserv members sometimes lose control when a careless user sends clerical messages (unsubscribe, postpone) to the list *people* address rather than the list robot! To avoid getting flames, always check the address before you send a subscribe, unsubscribe, or postpone message, and always (always) use the Reply feature with caution. The software address should start with:

```
listserv@    listproc@    majordomo@
```

When you subscribe to a new Listserv, the clerical robot sends you back a message that has the other address in it—the address to use when you have something to say to the people on the list. Be sure not to mix up the addresses! List members don't appreciate getting mail that should be going to the robot.

Following are some useful lists, from among the thousands available.

KIDSPHERE Network

KIDSPHERE has been around for a long time by Net standards (since 1989) and serves to stimulate the development of an international computer network for the use of children and their teachers. KIDSPHERE includes issues surrounding handicapped access in K-12 education. A related list for kid-to-kid communication is called KIDS.

Where to find it

E-mail	kidsphere-request@vms.cis.pitt.edu
Body	subscribe kidsphere *Your Name*
E-mail	joinkids@vms.cis.pitt.edu
Body	subscribe kids *Your Name*

Postings to the people on the list (after you have joined using the subscribe procedure) are accomplished with mailings to the addresses.

```
kidsphere@vms.cis.pitt.edu

kids@vms.cis.pitt.edu
```

KidzMail List for Elementary Children

KidzMail's purpose is to promote "Kids Exploring Issues and Interests Electronically."

Subscription

E-mail	listserv@asuacad.bitnet
Body	subscribe kidzmail *Your Name*

KIDLIT-L (Children's Literature)

KIDLIT-L is a forum for faculty members, librarians, parents, researchers, teachers, and others interested in the study and teaching of literature for children and youth. This group discusses teaching strategies, innovative course ideas, and current research.

Where to find it

E-mail	listserv@bingvmb.bitnet
Body	subscribe KIDLIT-L *Your Name*

CoSNDISC (CoSN Discussion)

The *Consortium for School Networking* (CoSN) hosts a mailing list for discussion of the development of networking facilities for the K-12 community. The discussions are broad, and useful for anyone interested in school-based networking.

Where to find it

E-mail	listserv@bitnic.bitnet
Body	subscribe cosndisc *Your Name*

EdPOL-D (Education Policy Digest)

EdPOL-D (Education Policy Digest) is a moderated discussion list from Scholastic Incorporated without the techno-talk. EdPOL-Digest is for teachers, parents, administrators, researchers, policy-makers, and anyone else interested in the present and future of K-12 networking and technology.

Where to find it

E-mail   edpol-d-request@scholastic.com

Questions and Comments?

E-mail   SNEDITOR@aol.com

Following is a brief quote and table of contents from the premier issue of EdPOL-D:

```
WELCOME FROM THE EDITOR

Becoming an equal partner in the National Information Infrastructure is somewhat
problematic for K-12 educators. Although many educators have  access to electronic
communications technology, common access has not yet reached the majority of those
who work in K-12 public and private schools.

When educators are compelled to articulate the benefits telecommunications technol-
ogy can have in education, they are placed at a disadvantage. It is also difficult
for them to illustrate how technology will systematically impact teaching and
learning without having the resources and time to study the impact of  a technology
enriched environment on students.

For these reasons, it is important for a dialogue to open between all stakeholders
involved in building  telecommunications infrastructures. Educators, policy makers,
parents, commercial vendors and non-profit groups need to talk together to create
an understanding of the issues which need to be addressed. EdPOL-D has been
developed to help stimulate discussion and awareness of many of these issues.
Welcome to the start of our discussion group.


  ####################################################################
  @                                                                  @
  @   ########       ##  ######*      ######*    #*        #######    @
  @   #*            #*  #*    #*     #*     #*   #*        #*    #*    @
  @   ##            ##  ##    #*  ##         ##  ##        ##    ##    @
  @   #######*      #*  ######*   ##         ##  ##  xxx   #*     #    @
  @   ##        ##### ##  ##         ##         ##  ##        ##    ##    @
  @   #*       ## #*  #*        #*      #*   #####*   #*    #*    @
  @   ########  #####  ##         ######*    #####   ######*    @
  @                                                                  @
  @   >>>>>>>>>>>>>>>>>  Education Policy Digest  <<<<<<<<<<<<<<<<<<  @
  ####################################################################


  TABLE OF CONTENTS
  1. About EdPOL-D
```

```
  2. Publisher's Note
  3. Welcome from the Editor
  4. January Discussion:
     Building Consensus for Communications Infrastructures
  5. Upcoming in February:
        National Information Infrastructure (NII) - What is the role of
        the States?
  6. HOW TO SUBSCRIBE TO EdPOL-D
```

Additional Sample Of Listserv Lists

In addition to the previously mentioned lists, there are now thousands of Listserv lists. They cover every topic imaginable. You may want to listen in on some of these discussions to see if they meet your needs.

Subscriptions to these are accomplished using the standard Listserv procedures.

Tip: If you misspell or miscapitalize your own name when you subscribe to a Listserv, your mail will come that way. To change the way your name looks, unsubscribe, and then subscribe again.

Table 3.1 shows you some of the lists that might be of interest to K-12 educators, parents, and students.

Table 3.1 Lists for K-12 Interests

List Name	Subscription Address	Comment
BGEDU-L	listserv@ukcc.bitnet	Quality of education
Biopi-L	listserv@ksuvm.bitnet	Secondary Biology teachers
CSRNOT-L	listserv@uiucvmd.bitnet	Center for the Study of Reading
dts-L	listserv@iubvm.bitnet	Dead Teachers' Society
ECENet	listserv@uiucvmd.bitnet	Early childhood education (0-8 years)
ELED-L	listserv@ksuvm.bitnet	Elementary education
Gravity	listserv@uwf.bitnet	Gravity and space time
Kidcafe	listserv@ndsuvm1.bitnet	Youth dialog
Kidleadr	listserv@ndsuvm1.bitnet	Kidlink coordinator

List Name	Subscription Address	Comment
Kidlink	listserv@ndsuvm1.bitnet	Kidlink Project
Leadtchr	listserv@psuvm.bitnet	Networking lead teachers
LIBER	listserv@uvmvm.bitnet	Library/media services
LM_NET	listserv@suvm.bitnet	School library/media services
Multi-L	listserv@barilvm.bitnet	Language & multi-lingual education
NCPRSE-L	listserv@ecuvm1.bitnet	Science education reform
Penpal-L	listserv@unccvm.bitnet	Penpals
Physhare	listserv@psuvm.bitnet	High school physics
SUSIG	listserv@miamiu.bitnet	Teaching math
T321-L	listserv@mizzou1.bitnet	Teaching science in elementary schools
TALKBACK	listserv@sjuvm.bitnet	Kids forum, CHATBACK, disabled children
Tesl-L	listserv@cunyvm.bitnet	Teaching English as a second language
Teslec-L	listserv@cunyvm.bitnet	Electronic communication & pen pals
Teslff-L	listserv@cunyvm.bitnet	Fluency First and Whole Language list
UKERA-L	listserv@ukcc.bitnet	Educational reform
VT-HSNET	listserv@vtvm1.bitnet	VT K-12 School Network
Y-Rights	listserv@sjuvm.bitnet	Children's rights
Youthnet	listserv@indycms.bitnet	Youthnet

A Brief Sample Of Usenet Newsgroups

Usenet is a distributed messaging system that exchanges messages (sometimes called articles) among subscriber sites. The messages are accessed using software called *news readers* (such as *tin*, for example). See Appendix A for more information.

All newsgroups are not always available to all sites, even if you can access some Usenet groups, because local sites use discretion regarding the specific Usenet groups to carry. If they are available at a site to which you have access, try them out! If they are not, contact your local administrator to ask about the K-12 resources they do provide. Following are some newsgroups that may be of interest to educators:

```
alt.edu
alt.wais
alt.gopher
bit.listserv.edtech
k12.chat.elementary
k12.chat.junior
k12.chat.senior
k12.chat.teacher
k12.ed.art
k12.ed.business
k12.ed.comp.literacy
k12.ed.health-pe
k12.ed.life-skills
k12.ed.math
k12.ed.music
k12.ed.science
k12.ed.soc-studies
k12.ed.special
k12.ed.tag
k12.ed.tech
k12.lang.art
k12.lang.deutsch-eng
k12.lang.esp-eng
k12.lang.francais
k12.lang.russian
k12.library
k12.news
misc.education.multimedia
misc.kids
misc.kids.computer
rec.arts.books
```

Horizon (E-Mail) List and *On the Horizon* Newsletter

A publication called *On the Horizon* is a five-times a year newsletter that "keeps a weather eye" out for the trends and events that will affect the future of education. It costs $49.50 per year, or $124.50 for a site license. There is a related unmoderated e-mail list that discusses the newsletter and centers on the future of education.

Where to find it

E-mail	`listserv@gibbs.oit.unc.edu`
Body	`subscribe horizon` *Your Name*

Questions or Comments?

Telephone	919/962-2517

K-12 Telnet Sites

Telnet is one of the most under-used Internet tools, mostly because it is so simple—one computer connected to another computer. This method of Internet use sometimes is called *BBS*ing, and some Bulletin Board System (BBS) software actually is being used at telnet sites. This means that you can get color text at some sites, if your computer supports it.

The look and feel of telnet sites varies greatly. Sometimes it seems as if you're just logging on to your local mainframe (plain vanilla, "just the facts Ma'am"). But other times, multicolored menus appear and you sign on just like a local, telephone-based Bulletin Board System (BBS).

> **Tip:** Your first time on some BBS-type systems, you must give your name, address, phone number(s), sex, age, date of birth, and create a password. Subsequent visits usually will only require your name and password. Remember your password, or you need to fill in the newuser questionnaire again.

Federal Bulletin Board U.S. Government Printing Office (GPO)

This bulletin board service enables Federal agencies to provide, at reasonable rates, the public with immediate, self-service access to Government information in electronic form.

Where to find it

Telnet

Site   FEDERAL.BBS.GPO.GOV 3001 (162.140.64.8 3001)

Following is their opening menu:

```
H - What's New and HOT!              I - Information Center

              THE FEDERAL BULLETIN BOARD
                    MAIN MENU

    GENERAL SERVICES              FILES FOR DOWNLOADING

 1 - Order Products from GPO      A - Free Information
 2 - Electronic Mail             B - Congressional Information
 3 - Account/Registry Information C - Federal Register/CFR & Related
 4 - GO TO...                     D - Federal Agencies
 5 - Forums/SIG's                 E - Supreme Court & Federal Courts
 6 - File Library System          F - Subject Categories  ** NEW **
 7 - Administrative Maintenance   G - Federal Depository Library Files
                                  S - Search for Files
 X - EXIT (Logoff the Board)      T - Today's Files
```

Tip: The Library of Congress also is available using telnet to
marvel.loc.gov, and login as gopher.

WorldClassroom Network from Global Learning Corporation

Following is a sample of commercial educational services from Global Learning
Corporation, available over the Net.

Where to find it

Telnet

Site   GLOBAL1.GLC.DALLAS.TX.US (198.140.162.1)

Login   demo3 (lowercase)

Password WORLDCLASS (uppercase)

Once there, you will see

```
Welcome to the WorldClassroom Network from Global Learning Corporation!
Enjoy your visit! If you would like additional information about
WorldClassroom after your online tour, call 1-800-866-4452.

WorldClassroom Guest Menu
-----------------------
1  -  Introduction to WorldClassroom
2  -  Online Organization
3  -  Typical Session on WorldClassroom
4  -  Equipment Needed/Getting Started
5  -  Go to WorldClassroom Demonstration
0  -  Quit and Logoff

WorldClassroom is a global curriculum and information network for K-12
schools. By means of a microcomputer with a modem and a standard
telephone line, WorldClassroom links classes of students to work
together on structured curriculum activities in science, social studies,
language arts, foreign languages, and current events. WorldClassroom
also provides a series of Guest Speakers.
```

K-12 File Transfer Protocol (FTP) Sites

There are some interesting and useful FTP sites for K-12 educators. The following are just a few.

U.S. Department of Education (ED)/Office of Educational Research and Improvement (OERI)

Many full-text research reports are available here. The same site handles Gopher and WWW traffic, so several web and Gopher directories are full of incomprehensible or irretrievable stuff. You can see the directory, and sometimes some of the contents of the directory, but you can't get FTP to bring them home for you. The 00-INDEX file says the three directories mentioned below have material that is available for FTP.

Where to find it

Site	`ftp.ed.gov`
Directories	`/gopher/publications/full_text`
	`/ncesgopher/publications/youth_indic`
	`/pub`
File	`00-INDEX`

This is an example of what is available under recent publications:

```
ftp> cd recent_pub
250-
   Filename          Description
250--------          ----------
250-goals            National Education Goals
250-k-12             Elementary and Secondary Schooling and Reform
250-postsec          Postsecondary Education
250-pubintro.txt     About This Directory
250-special          Special Populations
```

KYBER-12 FTP Archive

The *KYBER-12* FTP archive is a repository for documents collected through Project KYBER-12, a worldwide study of K-12 telecommunications and information retrieval. This project will collect and archive information over a period of three years (from August 1992 through August 1995). The project will collect information on all facets of K-12 computer networking, including the following:

- Information on exemplary projects and programs
- The economics of these projects and programs
- Their planning and evaluation
- Information on inservice and teacher education for those involved in K-12 telecommunications, and biographies or profiles of leaders involved in K-12 telecommunications

Entries are in the form of articles, contacts, views, and opinions.

Where to find it

Anonymous FTP

Site	byrd.mu.wvnet.edu (129.71.32.152)
Directory	/pub/estepp/kyber-12
Files	KYBER-12.FTP.Index
	CHANDLER.research.report
	HAYES.weather.proposal
	Project.kyber-12

University of Maryland Information Database Archive

This FTP site contains state, local, national and international economic data; agricultural, chemical, statistical, women's studies, and many other resources.

Where to find it

Anonymous FTP

Site	`info.umd.edu or 198.213.2.6`
Directory	`/inforM/Educational_Resources/K-12/`
Subdirectories	`/CalDeptofEducation`
	`/K-12Networking`
	`/Kidlink`
	`/MDK12Stuff`
Directory	`/inform`
Directory	`/Data`

Tip: The files of the Library of Congress are accessible using anonymous FTP as well. FTP to `ftp.loc.gov`.

K-12 Software Archives

There are numerous sources of software useful in schools. Sometimes this software is shareware, so that it is free to try out. If you like it and use it, you then are obligated to pay a nominal fee ($5 to $30) to the programmer who created it. Software archives often contain reviews and evaluations of software, and sometimes contain software advertisements. The following sections outline samples of some useful sources and sites.

California Computer Software Clearinghouse

This warehouse of exemplary software is growing rapidly, and contains both shareware and reviews of commercially available software.

Where to find it

Gopher	198.49.171.206 70

Questions or Comments?

E-mail	jarenson@sierra.fwl.edu

University of Iowa Software Archive (UISA)

The University of Iowa Software Archive (UISA) contains software for several different computer systems, including Amiga, Apple II, Macintosh, MS-DOS, and UNIX. This well-developed site is heavy on the computing side of teaching, but also contains historical and scientific files. Because the urban legends and word etymology areas at UISA can be quite graphic, some teachers will want to avoid in-classroom use of this site.

Where to find it

Anonymous FTP

Site	grind.isca.uiowa.edu

Software Sources by Topic

These sites hold a large amount of software of various kinds, but they each have concentrations of software on the topic indicated.

> **Tip:** Remember to set your file type to binary when you are downloading executable or formatted files.

Where to find it

Anonymous FTP

Site	ftp.cica.indiana.edu
Directory	/pub/pc/win3
Topic	Windows software

Site	`ftp-os2.nmsu.edu`
Directory	`/pub/os2`
Topic	OS/2 software

Site	`sumex-aim.stanford.edu`
Directory	`/info/mac`
Topic	Macintosh software

Site	`mac.archive.umich.edu`
Directory	`/info-mac`
Topic	Macintosh software

Site	`prep.ai.mit.edu`
Directory	`/pub/gnu`
Topic	UNIX software

Site	`sunsite.unc.edu`
Directory	`/pub/micro/pc-stuff/ms-windows/`
Topics	Winsock, Windows applications

Site	`boombox.micro.umn.edu`
Directory	`/pub/gopher`
Topic	Gophers for PC, Mac, UNIX, NeXt, OS/2, VMS, X Window

Site	`info.cern.ch`
Directory	`/pub/www`
Topic	World Wide Web software

Site	`ftp.ncsa.uiuc.edu`
Directory	`/mosaic`
Topic	Mosaic software for several platforms

Site	`sumex-aim.stanford.edu`
Directory	`/pub/info-mac/comm`
Topic	Gopher client for the Mac—TurboGopher

Site	`lister.cc.ic.ac.uk`
Directory	`/pub/wingopher`
Topic	Hgopher for Windows

Site	`sumex-aim.stanford.edu`
Directory	`/info-mac/comm`
Topic	FTP—Fetch for the Mac and NCSA Telnet and FTP for Mac

Site	`biochemistry.bioc.cwru.edu`
Directory	`/pub/qvtnet`
Topic	WinQVT for Windows

Site	`ftp.ncsa.uiuc.edu`
Directory	`/mac/telnet`
Topic	NCSA Telnet and FTP for Mac

Site	`merit.edu`
Directory	`/pub/ppp/`
Topic	NCSA Telnet and FTP for DOS

Site	`ftp.ncsa.uiuc.edu`
Directory	`/pc/telnet`
Topic	NCSA Telnet and FTP for DOS

Site	`sumex-aim.stanford.edu`
Directory	`/info-mac/mac/comm`
Topic	Eudora for the Mac

Site	`ftp.qualcomm.com`
Directory	`/mac/eudora`
Topic	Eudora for the Mac

Site	`sunsite.unc.edu`
Directory	`/pub/micro/pc-stuff/ms-windows/winsock/apps`
Topic	Eudora for the PC

Site	`netcom1.netcom.com`
Directory	`/pub/mailcom/IBMTCP/ibmtcp.zip`
Topic	TCP/IP applications

The Garbo Software Collection

The Garbo collection from Finland is diverse, varied, and interesting.

Where to find it

Anonymous FTP

Site	`garbo.uwasa.fi`

Directory	/pub
Topic	A most ample variety of software

Following are Worldwide mirrors of the Garbo software site:

Site	wuarchive.wustl.edu
Directory	/mirrors/garbo.uwasa.fi
Site	Archie.au
Directory	/micros/pc/garbo
Site	nctuccca.edu.tw
Directory	/PC-MsDos/Garbo-pc

Other Software Repositories

There is a large collection of software on almost any subject maintained by SimTel. The collection is mirrored on several other sites—which means that the identical software is maintained at multiple sites.

Where to find it

Anonymous FTP

Site	oak.oakland.edu
Directory	/pub
Site	wuarchive.wustl.edu
Directory	/mirror
Site	archive.orst.edu
Directory	/pub/mirrors
Site	ftp.uu.net
Directory	/systems/simtel20
Site	nic.funet.fi
Directory	/pub
Site	src.doc.ic.ac.uk
Directory	/pub/computing/systems
Site	Archie/au
Directory	/micros

Site	nic.switch.ch
Directory	/mirror

Site	micros.hensa.ac.uk
Directory	/pub

Miscellaneous Resources

Here are several unusual resources that educators may find quite useful. They include a shareware book, information on Free-Nets, and some publications.

The Online World Resources Handbook v.1.6

This shareware e-book is an eclectic collection of resources that includes many unusual items. It is strong on foreign language learning/assistance and international affairs, including Asian and African matters. You'll find "cutting-edge" high-technology developments, too.

The handbook is large (312K) and compressed with PKZip, so you'll need to unzip it before you can load it into your word processor.

Where to find it

Anonymous FTP

Site	Oak.Oakland.Edu or 141.210.10.117
Directory	/SimTel/msdos/info
File	online16.zip

Free-Nets

There are a growing number of Free-Nets on the Internet, and many of them have an education section, often called the *School House*. Free-Nets are community-based BBS services, with a local flavor. In many cases, the Free-Nets provide Internet services to urban areas. For the most part, access is through dial-up or via terminals in public libraries. Many Free-Nets are open to guest logins, but sometimes they limit the services that guests are allowed to access. The menus usually are arranged with names for public services such as the library, the courthouse, and so on. Using telnet, check out the following Free-Nets.

Where to find it

Buffalo Free-Net (Buffalo, New York)

Address	`freenet.buffalo.edu`
Login	`freeport`

Cleveland Free-Net (Cleveland, Ohio)

Address	`freenet-in-a.cwru.edu`
	`freenet-in-b.cwru.edu`
	`freenet-in-c.cwru.edu`
Login	`2`
	`2`
	`2`

Columbia Online Inf. Net. (Columbia, Missouri)

Address	`bigcat.missouri.edu`
Login	`guest`

Denver Free-Net (Denver, Colorado)

Address	`freenet.hsc.colorado.edu`
Login	`visitor`

Heartland Free-Net (Peoria, Illinois)

Address	`heartland.bradley.edu`
Login	`bbguest`

National Capital Free-Net (Ottawa, Ontario)

Address	`freenet.carleton.ca`
Login	`visitor`

Tallahassee Free-Net (Tallahassee, Florida)

Address	`freenet.scri.fsu.edu`
Login	`visitor`

Vaasa FreePort BBS

Address	`garbo.uwasa.fi`
Login	`guest`

Victoria Free-Net (Victoria, BC, Canada)

Address	`freenet.victoria.bc.ca`
Login	`guest`

Youngstown Free-Net (Youngstown, Ohio)

Address	yfn.ysu.edu
Login	visitor

LEARNING—National Research Center on Student Learning

This newsletter is for anyone interested in education reform and research-based teaching methods. *LEARNING* focuses on the connection between research and practice in reading, math, science, geography, history, and other subject areas, highlighting applications designed to tap the full potential of teachers and students.

Where to find it

Gopher	`gopher.pitt.edu`
Telephone	412/624-4790

Scholastic Internet Services

Curriculum libraries and full-text articles are offered by *Scholastic Internet Services*. The Scholastic Internet Center will send access information upon request.

Where to find it

E-mail	`sninternet@aol.com`

The Consortium for School Networking (CoSN)

The *Consortium for School Networking* (CoSN) is a membership organization of institutions. Its purpose is to promote development and use of computer network technology in K-12 education.

The CoSN Curriculum Committee seeks to catalog current telecommunication projects and develop standards for excellence for future projects. For more information on the Curriculum Committee, send e-mail to gsolomon@nycenet.edu.

Where to find it

E-mail	cosn@bitnic.bitnet
Gopher	cosn.educom.edu
Surface Mail	P.O. Box 65193
	Washington DC 20035-5193
Telephone	202/466-6296
Fax	202/872-4318

Edutopia

Edutopia is a paper-based publication from the George Lucas Educational Foundation. It focuses on the use of multimedia and telecommunications in education. The latest issue, for example, featured articles on Community Involvement, Collaborative Power, Learning Alliances and Access to Information, and an interview about learning online.

For more information, contact them at

E-mail   edutopia@glef.org

The George Lucas Educational Foundation
P.O. Box 3494
San Rafael, CA 94912

The Internet Society (INET)

The *Internet Society* was created to promote the growth of the Internet, and to provide information about the Internet. This is a membership organization from individuals and organizations.

E-mail	isoc@isoc.org
Phone	703/648-9888
Fax	703/620-0913

INET—The Internet Society
1895 Preston White Drive #100
Reston, Virginia 22091
USA

They publish the *Internet Society News*, available by e-mail. Just write to the preceding e-mail address.

WIRED Magazine

The print magazine *WIRED* offers all of its articles, both features and departments, in ASCII text format, free for the asking. After the next issue of the printed-on-paper magazine appears on the newsstand, the files for the previous issue of *WIRED* appear on the `inforama@wired.com` server. So you can read the magazine *without* the advertisements, and only 30 days after the subscribers get it!

WIRED has printed several articles of interest to K-12 educators. To receive one about students mastering the Internet, *Kids Connecting* (by Jacques Leslie), send an e-mail message to `inforama@wired.com` with no subject and the following message:

```
get 1.5/features/kids.connecting
```

You will receive the text of the article by e-mail. For a brief help file to introduce you to the other services available from *WIRED*, send a blank to `info@wired.com`. Before you know it, you'll get back a lot of *WIRED* information.

From Here....

You may find a cruise of Chapter 10 especially useful at this point, as well as a look at Chapter 7 on teaching and learning issues.

PART

II

OFF TO COLLEGE AND GRADUATE SCHOOL

THE INTERNET AND HIGHER EDUCATION

Atque inter silvas Academi quaerere verum.

(And seek for truth in the groves of Academe.)

Horace

The Internet has, and is, changing higher education. It started quietly enough with the origins of the Internet in supporting research and defense, but now has become much more influential throughout academe. "Nightmare or Paradise?" asks Steven W. Gilbert in a May 23rd message to the AAHESGIT list—most likely, neither. Yes, the coming of the Internet has caused some problems such as security breaches, unsolicited e-mail, spamming, and so on, but it also has yet to fulfill its potential for research and academic support.

Academe very much has been the center of the development and support of the network, and yet its support of most areas of academe has just begun to be felt for the most part.

Background

Academe has a long history with the Internet. The Internet has its roots in the *ARPAnet*, established by the Advance Research Projects Agency, that connected various military and research sites in the early 1970s. One of its projects was to develop reliable networking capabilities. Some of the networking methods they developed include a protocol enabling dissimilar computer systems to communicate, and the development of methods for routing data through multiple communications paths using groups of data with their own destination addresses built in (packets). These methods were so successful that many other networks adopted these standards, known today as *TCP/IP*.

Beginning in the late 1980s, the *National Science Foundation* (NSF) started expanding incrementally its own NSFNET, using the technology developed by ARPAnet. This was done primarily to allow campuses and research centers to use NSF's supercomputers; but increasingly, the connections were used for e-mail and transferring data and information accurately and quickly between sites. Thus began the Internet.

The NSF backbone (the high capacity major communication links) connected major research centers, universities and defense-related companies. NSF developed a policy called *Acceptable Use* that outlines the appropriate and unacceptable uses for the NSF backbone. The following is an excerpt from the NSF Acceptable Use Policy:

```
THE NSFNET BACKBONE SERVICES ACCEPTABLE USE POLICY
                    1992
GENERAL PRINCIPLE:

(1) NSFNET Backbone services are provided to support open research and
education in and between US research and instructional institutions, plus
```

```
research arms of for-profit firms when engaged in open scholarly
communication and research. Use for other purposes is not acceptable.

SPECIFICALLY ACCEPTABLE USES:
(2) Communication with foreign researchers and educators in connection
with research or instruction, as long as any network that the foreign
user employs for such communication provides reciprocal access to US
researchers and educators.

(3) Communication and exchange for professional development, to maintain
currency, or to debate issues in a field or sub-field of knowledge.

(4) Use for disciplinary-society, university-association, government-
advisory, or standards activities related to the user's research and
instructional activities.

(5) Use in applying for or administering grants or contracts for research
or instruction, but not for other fund raising or public relations
activities.

(6) Any other administrative communications or activities in direct support
of research and instruction.

(7) Announcements of new products or services for use in research or
instruction, but not advertising of any kind.

(8) Any traffic originating from a network of another member agency of the

Federal Networking Council if the traffic meets the acceptable use policy
of that agency.
```

Many AUPs for regional, local, and national networks are under revision currently, and will reflect the growing commercialization of the Internet. Some commercial activity related to research and defense always has been allowed, and new interpretations of the commercial aspects of the Internet are forthcoming.

Early on in the development of the Internet, it was the domain of the hard sciences and computer sciences, and remained virtually unexplored by other disciplines. Even today, scholars and administrators on many campuses still have to "show cause" why they should be connected to the network.

Many colleges and universities are not yet connected to the Internet, and on many connected campuses, faculty, students, and administrators can gain only limited e-mail connections. In other cases, only those faculty in the hard sciences and computer science can gain access. System administrators have been, in some cases, of limited vision regarding the usefulness of Internet access to faculty and students; however, that appears to be changing. (I was informed fairly recently by a system administrator that our campus did not need Gopher, and he further suggested that faculty learn computer programming if they wanted to use the Internet. I'm still chuckling about that one.)

Currently, almost all major universities have some form of network access, but despite the current publicity about the network, many other campuses are not in any way connected to the network. Some campuses have hard-wired high-speed connections to all offices and dormitories, while some campuses offer nothing.

If your campus is still deciding whether to get rid of the horse troughs and whether the telephone is a fad, get a personal account through one of the commercial Internet access providers. It's inexpensive, and all the skills you learn and the resources you find can be carried over to a campus system when they finally do become connected.

Using the Internet in the Academy

Well then, is it Paradise? The Internet is exciting, stimulating, and offers untold opportunities for faculty administrators and students when they can gain access. Virtually all segments of the university community are using the Internet, including faculty, administrators, and students. It is being used in each of the traditional roles of academe, teaching/learning, research, and service.

Faculty

Faculty roles in higher education traditionally encompass teaching, research/ scholarship, and service. In all of these areas, the Internet has a presence. The following sections discuss how the Internet is affecting the work of faculty.

Teaching

Faculty members are using the Internet to support a variety of courses and teaching functions—they even are offering entire courses via the Internet. (For more information about how to teach and learn using the Internet, see Chapters 7 and 9).

In chemistry, for example, several professors are creating *QuickTime Movies* (electronically storable and transferable video files) for their intermediate and advanced undergraduates as demonstrations of particular lab techniques. Because these movies have been so successful, the faculty members are planning to offer them through an FTP site for access by Internauts everywhere.

Research/Scholarship

Professors and students are moving beyond data collection, analysis, and exchange into areas of preprints, online publications, and electronic scholarly journals. (You can find even more information on scholarly activities in Chapter 8.)

The Human Genome Project

In research, the *Human Genome Project* is one of the most well-known at this time. The NIH division of Research Grants Genome Study section is supporting The Human Genome Project—research in genetic map expansion, physical map development, DNA sequence determination, innovative development of technology, tools, and resources in genetics. This project is sharing data and analysis via the Internet on perhaps the largest scale of any single research project on the Internet. (There also are plant and animal genome projects communicating via the Internet, too.) The project maintains the GenBank database of all published sequences of nucleic acids. To find out what is being discussed, subscribe to the HUMAN-GENOME-PROGRAM Bulletin Board at biosci@genbank.bio.net. Two Usenet newsgroups discussing this research are bionet.molbio.genome-program, and bionet.molbio.genbank.

Another project that has wide participation via the Internet is *ProjectH*. ProjectH grew out of discussion on the Qualitative Research list. Using content analysis and quantitative methods, a very large group of researchers from around the world joined forces to research computer-mediated group discussion. Online together, they developed their hypotheses, design, methodology, analytic model, variables, and ethics and copyright guidelines. The pilot study as well was carried out online. The results have been analyzed and are being reported in several collaborative scholarly publications. The project is supported by a private discussion list sponsored by Comserve at RPI. More information is available at the FTP site archsci.arch.su.edu.au in the /pub/projectH/ subdirectory.

Grants

Obtaining grants to support research is an important faculty role, and the Internet is proving to be very useful in this activity.

Obtaining Grants

You can find announcements, such as the following, on several lists and newsgroups:

```
Return-path: <server@is.internic.net>
Date: Mon, 11 Apr 1994 21:20:20 -0700
From: Gleason Sackman <sackman@plains.nodak.edu>
Subject: Annenberg/CPB's new higher education guidelines are out (fwd)
Sender: net-happenings@is.internic.net
To: Multiple recipients of list <net-happenings@is.internic.net>

Forwarded by Gleason Sackman - InterNIC net-happenings moderator
*********************************************************************
```

The Annenberg/CPB Projects recently released the 1994 guidelines for its Higher Education Program. Proposals should address one of the following three Initiatives:

Initiative I is for the development of "coherent, course-sized bodies of rich instructional resources" whose content addresses one or more of the following priorities:

— completing the curriculum for a two-year degree

— developing materials in child care and parenting

— creating the means for learners and educators to understand and exploit emerging technology

— revising and augmenting materials currently in the Annenberg/CPB Collection.

Approximately $2.5 million is available for several projects. Typical projects should be completed in 1-2 years. Proposals are due July 1, 1994.

Initiative II is a call for preliminary proposals for an international co-production of introductory courses in Philosophy, Music, Religion, and Arts Appreciation. One to three preliminary proposals will be selected, taken to an international meeting of producers, and one selected to submit a final proposal. A one-page summary of your proposal is due May 2, 1994 and a ten-page preliminary proposal will be due June 10, 1994.

Initiative III relates to the development of "better means for faculty members to help one another rethink their courses in ways that take advantage of available technologies and teaching ideas."   Annenberg/CPB expects to fund five projects from a total pool of $600,000. Each project should involve a team of faculty from at least three institutions and should focus on one or more standard courses that some institutions have begun to

```
update and improve through uses of computers, video media,
and/or telecommunications.   Proposals submitted to Initiative
III are due by July 15, 1994.

To request a complete copy of the 1994 Higher Education
Guidelines, leave a message on the voice mail at 202-879-9644 or
send a fax to 202-783-1036.

Program guide avaialbe via E-Mail: annhe-guide-lines@chronicl.merit.edu
```

Grant information is available from a variety of sources—many Universities maintain grant information on their own Gophers. Historically, the first online grant information initiative is the NSF *STIS*—Science and Technology Information System. It is reachable using many of the Internet tools. The FTP site is `stis.nsf.gov`. Also, the `info.nsf.grants` and `info.nsfnet.status` newsgroups post information on NSF grant opportunities, guidelines, and updates.

Other examples of grant information sources are the following World Wide Web sites:

Where to find it

Linkname	NIH Grants and Contracts
Filename	http://www.nih.gov/grants
Linkname	Teacher's Guide to U.S. Dept of Ed: Table of Contents
Filename	http://www.ed.gov/pubs/tchr/index.html
Linkname	Funding Opportunities
Filename	http://medoc.gdb.org/best/fund.html

Chapters 5 and 8 have more information on research resources. The `sci.` and `bionet.` hierarchies have many newsgroups of interest to researchers, plus there are others, such as `alt.education.research`, that are focused on research.

Publication Opportunities

Electronic serials are growing in number and legitimacy. Some electronic journals mirror paper-based journals, and an increasing number exit only in electronic form. Additionally, both paper-based journals and e-journals often accept submissions and deal with editing via the Internet. The Library of Congress now will assign standard periodical numbers to e-journals and is working on methods to archive e-journals.

Journal Indexes

One of the vexing issues regarding scholarly journals is that credibility often resides with how and where the journal is indexed. Nowhere is that more true than in the health sciences. One electronic journal has made a breakthrough into a prestigious index—*Index Medicus*. The electronic journal, *The Online Journal of Current Clinical Trials*, now is indexed in the *Index Medicus*, which means that faculty and researchers can publish in the Journal, and know that its quality will not be questioned.

Interpersonal Computing and Technology: An Electronic Journal for the 21st Century, a refereed e-journal, is indexed in the Current Index to Journals in Education (CIJE), and also is selectively indexed in the Journal of Government Information.

There is an increasing number of electronic journals and pre-print opportunities. The *CICNet* (Committee on Institutional Cooperation) Gopher at gopher.cic.net houses a major collection of electronic journals in an archive.

Following are other useful links to electronic journals and preprints:

Where to find it

Linkname	Electronic Journals, Newsletters, and Texts
Filename	http://dewey.lib.ncsu.edu/stacks/index.html
Linkname	Preprints and Electronic Journals from around the World
Filename	http://www.geom.umn.edu/docs/worldpubs.html

Many scholarly journals have Tables of Contents, and excerpts available online as well, even if the full text is not available electronically. CARL and UnCover2 are notable suppliers of articles, mentioned in Chapter 8.

Tip: How do scholars cite electronic information gained on the Internet? This problem has been rumbling around for some time, and a sign of the times is that the new edition of the *APA Publication Manual* contains information on this, and a book called *Electronic Style: A Guide to Citing Electronic Information* by Crane and Li has been published.

Service

For faculty, service is a very broad role both within and outside of the university. It often includes committee work, activity in professional organizations, and non-scholarly publishing. Such service can be carried out via the Internet.

"What if you held a meeting and nobody came?" asks the *Chronicle of Higher Education* (July 15, p. A15). Well somebody did, and they didn't. The Association for Information Systems has used the Internet to debate and vote on a constitution and by-laws. Increasingly, access to the Internet and the creation of temporary lists and newsgroups are part of scholarly meetings. This type of Internet activity then can provide participation in professional organizations with the convenience of using the Internet. In times of limited funding, the Internet enables participation as well.

Many other professional organizations maintain an Internet presence.

Using E-Math

The *American Mathematical Society* (AMS) maintains the E-Math system available via Gopher at `e-math.ams.com`. E-Math contains all types of information for mathematicians, including calls for papers, information on conferences, and provides access to preprints and papers. A link to their "What's New" page is `http://e-math.ams.org/whatsnew.doc`.

An interesting WWW homepage at Stanford University titled "Organizations and Conferences" offers links to information on various types of scholarly organizations and groups, such as the American Philosophical Association, the American Psychological Association, and more.

Where to find it

Linkname	Cog & Psy Sci: Organizations & Conferences
Filename	`http://matia.stanford.edu/cogsci/org.html`

The page begins like this:

```
Cog &amp; Psy Sci: Organizations &amp; Conferences (p1 of 9)

                    ORGANIZATIONS & CONFERENCES

   Other sections: Academic Programs... Journals & Magazines... Usenet
   Newsgroups... Discussion Lists... Announcement/Distribution
```

```
Lists... Publishers... Miscellany... Acknowledgments... What's
New... Top Level


Contents: Am. Phil. Assn.... Am. Psych. Assn.... Am. Psych. Soc....
Am. Public Health Assn.... Assn. for Computational Ling.... Assn.
for Computing Machinery... Classification Soc. of N. Am.... Cog. Sci.
Soc.... Computers in Teaching Initiative... Euro. Networks of
Excellence... Euro. Assn. of Work & Org. Psych.... Foundazione Dalle
Molle... INRIA... Inst. for Computer-Based Learning... Intl. Media
Res. Found.... MacSciTech... Natl. Insts. of Health... Natl. Insts.
of Mental Health... Natl. Sci. Found.... Principia Cybernetica
Proj.... PsychNet (TM)... Psychonomic Soc.... PSYCGRAD Proj.... Soar
Proj.... Soc. for Computers in Psych.... Soc. for Math. Psych....
Swiss Informaticians Soc.... Other Conferences...
```

Following is the first page of information on APA:

```
American Psychological Association
    * Science Directorate: science@apa.org; +1 202 336-6000; 750 First
      Street NE, Washington DC 20002-4242.
    * Sponsors the electronic journal Psycoloquy (distribution list:
      PSYCOLOQUY; Usenet newsgroup: sci.psychology.digest).
    * Publishes the Psychology Research Funding Bulletin (distribution
      list: APASD-L).
    * Maintains the discussion list APAARIB (Animal Research Information
      Board).
    * Maintains the discussion list DIV28 (Psychopharmacology).
```

Locating Scholarly Locations

Jim Parrott, a librarian at the University of Waterloo, has located more than twenty scholarly associations around the world that offer information services via the Internet. Pointers to these are now located at the Gopher site uwinfo.uwaterloo.ca. In addition, you can reach the site at the same address using telnet, with a login as uwinfo.

Tip: The WebQuery function of WebCrawler is a useful WWW search tool, and is located at URL http://www.biotech.washington.edu/cgi-bin/WebQuery. Use it to look for your professional organization.

Conference announcements, calls for papers, and more, also are available online through discussion lists, WWW homepages, and Usenet newsgroups. These often provide scholars with an opportunity for electronic submissions.

Jobs in Academe

Faculty and other academic job openings increasingly are being listed at Internet sites. The best source of this information currently is the online *Chronicle of Higher Education*. The venerable *Chronicle* has a gopher with an opening menu that looks like the following:

```
             Internet Gopher Information Client v2.0.15

                  Home Gopher server: chronicle.merit.edu

   1.  NEW in "Academe This Week"
   2.  A GUIDE to The Chronicle of Higher Education, July 20, 1994/
   3.  EVENTS in Academe: July 19 to August 2/
   4.  BEST-SELLING BOOKS on campuses
   5.  ALMANAC: facts and figures on U.S. higher education
   6.  JOB OPENINGS in Academe from the July 20 Chronicle/
   7.  ABOUT The Chronicle of Higher Education
   8.  ABOUT "Academe This Week": search tips and more/
```

Choosing #6 takes you to the Job Openings menu, offering searchable entries by category:

```
SEARCH using The Chronicle's list of job titles

     1.  Faculty and research positions/
     2.  Administrative positions/
     3.  Executive positions/
     4.  Positions outside Academe/
```

Where to find it

The Chronicle site

URL	http://chronicle.merit.edu/
Linkname	top stories
Filename	http://chronicle.merit.edu:8082/.guide/.summary.html

The Online Career Center, maintained by MSEN, contains job openings in- and outside of academe. You can find it on the MSEN Gopher at `garnet.msen.com 70`. Following is their top menu:

```
            Internet Gopher Information Client v1.13

                    The Online Career Center

      1.  Questions and Comments to: occ@mail.msen.com.
      2.  About Online Career Center/
      3.  Company Sponsors and Profiles/
      4.  Employment Events/
      5.  Career Assistance/
      6.  FAQ - Frequently Asked Questions about OCC/
      7.  '94 College & University Resume Books/Diskettes/
      8.  * Search Jobs/
      9.  * Search Resumes/
      10. * Other Employment Databases//
      11. Recruitment Advertising Agencies/
      12. "Online Career Center" On Campus/
      13. Help Files: Keyword Search/Enter Resume/Print/
      14. How To Enter A Resume.
      15. Online Career Center Liability Policy.
```

The *Academic Position Network* (APN) puts job advertisements online for a fee to the employer. Job seekers can browse freely. Connect with the Gopher at `wcni.cis.umn.edu port 11111`.

There are many Usenet newsgroups that have information on jobs. You can find these under the `misc.` and `biz.` hierarchies, and under various country hierarchies, such as `uk.jobs` or `can.jobs`, regional hierarchies (`triangle.jobs`), states (`tx.jobd`), or cities (`milw.jobs`). Also, many universities maintain job information on their local Gophers.

Administration

Administrators also find that the Internet is creating an impact on their work. In addition to the increased availability of data and networking, many universities provide admissions information, public relations, sports, and other information on their Gopher in a *CWIS* (Campus Wide Information System). These sites often contain local information for local use by students, faculty, and administrators, and information meant to assist with recruitment, alumni relations, and other campus outreach. You often can find the following:

- Class schedules and syllabi
- Registration information

- Scholarship and Financial Aid information
- Alumni and development
- Public Relations
- Administrative and faculty phone numbers
- Announcements for faculty and students
- Events and academic deadlines and calendar information
- Student organizations
- Local restaurants, weather, and more

Locating School Information

Following is an example of a homepage that allows access to student, faculty, and alumni information (including a discussion list) at the School of Information and Library Science at the University of North Carolina at Chapel Hill:

```
         PEOPLE AT THE SCHOOL OF INFORMATION AND LIBRARY SCIENCE

    [IMAGE]

Students

    [IMAGE]
       * Student Organization and Participation

Administration and Staff

       * The University of North Carolina at Chapel Hill
       * School of Information and Library Science Administrative Board
       * School of Information and Library Science Administration and Staff

Faculty and Their Teaching and Research Interests

    [IMAGE]
       * Faculty
       * Adjunct Faculty
       * Emeritus Faculty
       * Visiting Faculty

Alumni

    The School's Alumni Association provides a network connecting current
    students with alumni. The Association assists the School in welcoming
    new students and in the provision of scholarship support, internship
    opportunities, career information, and job placement notices.

    Through its publication, News from Chapel Hill, and its sponsorship of
    reunions at major professional association meetings, the Association
    facilitates communication among the School's alumni.
```

```
The school also runs an electronic mail listserver for alumni. Alumni
can subscribe to the listserver by sending email to
listserv@ils.unc.edu with the words SUBSCRIBE ALUMNI-L Your Name in
the body of the message. For example: SUBSCRIBE ALUMNI-L John Smith.

[IMAGE]

[IMAGE] Return to Home Page
```

The University of Michigan, Dearborn, puts its Alumni Calendar of events at this WWW site:

Where to find it

Linkname   UM-Dearborn Alumni Society Calendar of Events

Filename   http://www.umd.umich.edu/events/alumcal5-9.html

Union College has a Web page of Welcome to Alumni, and even provides a page for alumni to put links to their personal homepages.

Linkname   Tardis Alumni Page

Filename   http://tardis.union.edu/alumni.html

In addition, many universities have begun to maintain links with vendors through the Internet, and are doing some purchasing online.

Using Electronic Services for Enrollment Info

There is an electronic service for campuses that want to share their data about enrollments and certain financial information. On the University of Virginia Gopher is the National Cooperative Data Share project. It provides access to current information on finances, salaries, and enrollments before those data are published by the U. S. Department of Education. The Gopher is gopher://gopher.uvirginia.edu:70/1. The information is found under the /Library Services/Social Science Data Center/National Cooperative Data Share menu path.

> ### E-mailing for Tickets
>
> The University of Denver is using e-mail to sell athletic event tickets. They have built in some incentives for e-mail ordering—you can purchase some tickets at half price, which has created a lot of interest among hockey fans. In addition, the athletic director has established a mailing list to distribute information to fans and supporters.

Students

Students are using the Internet to find data, complete assignments, network with other students, and for collaborative projects. (Chapter 7 discusses ways in which students use the Internet for learning.)

Student publications, sororities, and fraternities are going online. Many other student organizations have access to the Internet and are using Gophers and WWW documents to network and disseminate information. At the University of Minnesota, for example, the Association for Computing Machinery offers the following homepage:

```
University of Minnesota ACM Welcome Page (p1 of 2)

    [IMAGE]

    Welcome to the University of Minnesota, ACM! This is a very new but
    rapidly expanding web server. Information is being added almost daily
    so keep an eye out for new features.

ACM Information

        * Schedule of Events
        * ACM Introductory Guide to Unix
        * ACM Constitution
        * Info about Members

Miscellaneous

        * ACM Headquarters Home Page
        * Other ACM Chapter Home Pages
        * Internet Resources
        * Snow
```

Where to find it

Linkname	Association for Computing Machinery (ACM)
Filename	`http://leghorn.cs.umn.edu:80/acm/`

Alpha Phi Omega has a number of points of contact on the network, such as the following:

Linkname	Standard Chapter Articles of Association of Alpha Phi Omega
HTTP and Gopher	`/www.mit.edu:8001/hGET%20/people/jtkohl/aphio/std-arts.html`

E-mail Can Save Lives

A student at Mary Washington College used e-mail to talk to a person at the University of Denver who was threatening suicide, and probably saved her life. He talked to her until someone in Denver was able to make personal contact and offer assistance.

Useful Lists

There are two lists that discuss higher education and the Internet with a particularly high concentration of good information and high quality discussions: AAHESGIT and HEPROC-L.

AAHESGIT is the American Association for Higher Education's list for discussing the role of technology in higher education, among other things, as part of their commitment to building bridges between academic leaders, faculty, staff, and others.

The list addresses numerous subjects, including the role of technology in individual teaching and learning, the decline in student purchase of assigned textbooks, faculty uses of course packs in conjunction with textbooks, the application of information technology, and the role of academic departments in the changing curriculum and usage of technology. Members of the list include faculty, administrators, librarians, academic computing support staff, graduate students, publishers, and others. The Listserv address is aahesgit@gwuvm.gwu.edu or aahesgit@gwuvm.binet.

HEPROC-L (Higher Education Processes Discussion List) is a group that brings together diverse members of the higher education community in order to probe questions, problems, and solutions within higher education, and to distill, analyze, and electronically publish the results of that probing. This is a group of lists that is highly structured and moderated to ensure high quality discussion. Subscribe to HEPROC-L at `listserv@american.edu` or `listserv@auvm.bitnet`.

Challenges and Opportunities

Well then, is it a nightmare? The answer is the same as when asking if it was paradise: it might be. The Internet is causing academe to change, and that change can be difficult. The use of the Internet by faculty, administration, and students is starting some discussions on campus about many of the issues discussed in the following sections.

Promotion And Tenure (P&T)

Nothing is closer to the heart of academe than the process and rituals surrounding the promotion and tenuring of faculty. The Internet is inspiring a re-examination of all three of the traditional criteria: teaching, research/scholarship, and service.

Professors who spend time using the Internet for teaching and in support of teaching functions, such as advising, find that their colleagues may not appreciate or understand the new forms of teaching encouraged by the use of the Internet. As a consequence, they may find that they are not evaluated appropriately on this criteria for P&T.

While the use of the Internet for research is now old news, the use of the Internet for scholarship is creating some waves in higher education. Questions such as the following are beginning to be heard in promotion and tenure meetings:

- How does publication in an *electronic* journal compare to a paper-based journal?
- What does it mean to be an editor and referee for an electronic journal?
- Is a publication made available freely on the Internet a publication?

Service activities involving the Internet usually are not so problematic, because service often is more broadly defined, and in most circumstances, less important than scholarship and research.

The Haves and the Have Nots—Beyond Turf Issues

The divisions in higher education between the "haves" and the "have nots" extended deeply into the issues surrounding access to the Internet. Many colleges and universities do not feel that they can afford Internet access, or if they can afford some minimal access, faculty and student demand far exceeds their capability to provide services. Faculty from institutions that have rich resources are amazed that some other faculty have to fight to get any kind of access, even when they provide their own equipment.

Even at institutions that are well off financially, the faculty and students can be "have-nots" if the administration and computer systems administrators are unaware of what the Internet is, or feel that there is "no need for that Net stuff."

When universities make attempts to become more technologically up-to-date, new technology comes along to make it obsolete. In days of limited resources, some departments guard their computers and will not let other students or faculty use them. Turf issues abound in many institutions.

Students are required to pay stiff fees, and then feel that their access to the Internet is too limited. Often, students in Computer Science departments gain access for a single course, and then lose their account at the end of the semester. Other students may have no access at all.

Hacking and Censorship

Computer security issues are becoming more common on campus as students and others gain access to the Internet.

Some institutions provide Usenet newsgroups for campus use, but increasingly, issues of censorship are raised regarding the nature of some of these groups. When groups are removed, students, and to some degree faculty, feel that their access to information is being impaired. Freedom of speech and academic freedom discussions surrounding this issue are becoming common. At a major university recently, for example, a student distributed virulent anti-African-American messages to the community, and calls were made to silence the student through the revocation of his account. That case is still unresolved.

In some cases, students have sent e-mail falsely announcing the cancellation of classes and exams, and at another institution, a student was distributing pirated copyrighted software with his account.

Censorship in the Internet?

The electronic version of the 18th century novel *Fanny Hill* was removed from an Internet site at Indiana University. This action inspired considerable discussion on the newsgroup `alt.censorship`, and it remains unresolved.

These issues mirror the larger society—it is not just students at universities taking these types of actions. The Internet and campus communities have a long way to go before solving these problems, but overreacting to them and denying access to the Internet would be the educational equivalent of closing the campus library.

Libraries

Libraries are facing some of the most difficult adjustments to the ubiquitous Internet, ranging from copyright hassles to learning about and installing Internet tools and resources, working with CWIS, Gopher WWW, and developing new relationships with the computer center. The following are some areas where the Internet has had an impact on the campus.

- Two of the largest areas on campus most affected by the Internet is the Library and Computer Center. In the past, these were separate entities, but increasingly, they are tied together as libraries go online with the Internet. These somewhat uneasy alliances between library and computer services cause turf battles on some campuses, in which users are left wondering with whom to talk.

- Librarians and scholars are having to cope with increasing pressure on the copyright system, especially as it relates to materials available and placed on the Internet. This is causing considerable debate among librarians, and has caused some limitations on the access to the Internet that they are providing.

Faculty

In addition to the substantial issues raised in Promotion and Tenure assessments, there are many additional challenges to integrating the Internet into the work of faculty.

Faculty Development

On many campuses, there are no opportunities for faculty to learn about the Internet—no workshops, no training, no course development assistance, and no user services personnel. Techno-anxiety in many institutions is rampant, and faculty must learn on their own, which truly is a daunting experience.

Reward Structures

The reward structure for faculty regarding merit and pay often are based on very traditional criteria that do not recognize the use and adaptation of the Internet to teaching, research and service.

Teaching Assessment

Teaching evaluation schemes are not yet up to the task of evaluating the use of the Internet as a teaching vehicle or as a support system for the teaching function.

Teaching Loads

Where faculty are using the Internet to teach, little thought has been given to issues of faculty load. Is a class of 800 via the Internet equivalent to a face-to-face course of 20 students? How does preparation of an Internet course compare to preparation for a more traditional course? Where does advising by e-mail fit viz-a-viz office hours?

The Future of the Internet on Campus

The future of the Internet and higher education is a bright one: the challenges are numerous. Expect increasing use of the Internet for teaching and scholarship, both for faculty and students. Alliances of researchers will no doubt become even more common. Expect the unexpected, too.

Mosaic and Lynx are bringing the Internet to a more user-friendly level for all campus constituents, and the indications are that this will mean that HyperMedia and WWW will become a major component of campus administration, teaching, and research.

From Here...

Chapters 5 and 6 discuss the broad variety of undergraduate and graduate programs and related Internet resources and projects. Then, techniques for using the Internet in teaching and learning are discussed in Chapters 7, 9, and 10.

UNDERGRADUATE INTERNET RESOURCES BY SCHOOL

Knowledge is power.

Francis Bacon

There are Internet resources available for every school and department in the university—some departments have more than others, most notably the hard sciences, English, communications, and business. This chapter provides a large number of specific Internet resources for faculty and students in each school in the university. Assignment suggestions also are presented as starting points for learning more about what the Internet offers.

There are three resources organized by subject area of broad general interest—the World Wide Web Virtual Library, Riceinfo at Rice University, and the University of Michigan Clearinghouse for Subject-Oriented Internet Resources Guides. These can assist students and faculty in any school or department in locating information. Access to those resources is through the following:

Where to find it

The World-Wide Web Virtual Library: Subject Catalogue

Filename	`http://ai.iit.nrc.ca/shadow/Overview.html`
Name	`RiceInfo (Rice University CWIS)`
Host	`riceinfo.rice.edu`
Port	`70`
URL	`gopher://riceinfo.rice.edu:70/1`
Choose	Item #8 to get to `Information by Subject Area/`

The University of Michigan Clearinghouse for Subject-Oriented Internet Resources Guides

`http//:www.lib.umich.edu/chhome.html gopher//`
`:una.hh.lib.umich.edu/11/inetdirs`

`ftp//:una.hh.lib.umich.edu/inetdirsstacks`

School of Business and Computer Science

The following are some resources that should prove useful to faculty and students in computer science and business. The resources available within computer science are not as plentiful as those for business. Chapter 6 outlines additional significant resources for business.

The Homepage of the Department of Computer Science at the University of California, Davis has some useful files and links to other sites:

```
Computer Science Research Laboratories (p1 of 2)

                     DEPARTMENT RESEARCH LABORATORIES

Computer Science Department at UC Davis


   [IMAGE]

    * Artificial Intelligence Research Laboratory
    * Computer Architecture Research Laboratory
    * Computer Graphics Research Laboratory
    * Computer Security Research Laboratory
    * Multilingual Research Laboratory
    * Networks Research Laboratory
    *
    * Programming Languages & Verification Research Laboratory
    * Theory Laboratory
```

Where to find it

Linkname	Computer Science Research Laboratories
Filename	http://www.cs.ucdavis.edu/research_labs.html

A good example of how a Computer Science department could use WWW homepages is the system set up by Union College's Computer Science Department. They have faculty-oriented homepages and other departmental information, along with sound, image and movie files for use in program, and equipment testing.

Where to find it

URL	http://tardis.union.edu/cs_dept/cs_dept.html

```
THE UNION COMPUTER SCIENCE DEPARTMENT

    * Faculty interests of the Union Electrical Engineering and Computer
      Science department.
    * Course Descriptions of Union Computer Science classes, from the
      college catalog.
    * Schedule of classes offered through the Computer Science
      Department.
    * Faculty home pages of the Union Electrical Engineering and
      Computer Science department.
    _____

    * Sound testing
    * Movie test
    * MPEG Movie Archive
```

In business, one of the up-and-coming topics is business and the Internet. A good example of online business activity is the *Digital Equipment Company*, better known as DEC, which has created the Internet Electronic Connection. This is a free service that enables customers to get information about its products, prices, and orders.

Where to find it

URL	`http://www.dec.com/info.html`

Much of the Internet's computer science information is spread widely throughout many computer science department Gophers. There are fewer links between sites and fewer mega-sites in this field than in many others. Check these Computer Science department Gophers and homepages for general computer science information and to get an idea of the topics being studied at each school.

Where to find it

Linkname	`Harvard Computer Science Technical Reports`
Filename	`http://das-www.harvard.edu/techreports/tr.html`
Linkname	`U of MN Computer Science Department Home Page`
Filename	`http://www.cs.umn.edu/`
Linkname	`UT Austin Department of Computer Sciences`
Filename	`http://www.cs.utexas.edu/`

York University maintains a Gopher at `gopher.yorku.ca` that provides links through their menus to several universities:

Ohio State University, Department of Computer and Information

University of Kaiserlautern, Computer Science

University of Illinois at Urbana-Champagne, Department of Computer Science

University of Texas at El Paso, Computer Science Department

On the Gopher at `gopher.adfa.oz.au`, there are menu entries for linking to the following universities:

Columbia University, Computer Science

Portland State University, Computer Science

University of California at Berkeley, Computer Science, Tenet Group

University of Zurich, Computer Science Department

At the Gopher `gopher.gsfc.nasa.gov`, the following menus are available:

University of Bern, Switzerland, Department of Computer Science and Mathematics

University of Chicago, Computer Science Department

University of Lethbridge (Canada), Computer Science

University of Stuttgart, Computer Science

Purdue University maintains a Gopher at `arthur.cs.purdue.edu` with links to many other departments of Computer Science.

Australian National University, Computer Science Department

Boston University, Department of Computer Science

Carnegie-Mellon University, Computer Science Department

Michigan State University, Department of Computer Science

Rochester Institute of Technology, Department of Computer Science

University of Manchester, Department of Computer Science

University of Michigan, Electrical Engineering and Computer Science

University of Minnesota, Department of Computer Science

Washington University, Department of Computer Science

At the University of Utah `gopher.cc.utah.edu`, there are pointers to several Computer Science departments.

Brown University, Department of Computer Science

New York University, Computer Science

Princeton University, Department of Computer Science

University of Arizona, Computer Science Department

These are some useful Usenet newsgroups worth participating in for those in computer and information science:

Where to find it

American Society of Information Science

```
bit.listserv.asis-l
```

Campus-Wide Information Systems

```
bit.listserv.cwis-l
```

Information Graphics

```
bit.listserv.ingrafx
```

Information Technology and Africa

```
bit.tech.africana
```

Computer science education

```
comp.edu
```

Any discussion about information systems

```
comp.infosystems
```

Discussion of the Gopher information service

```
comp.infosystems.gopher
```

The Internet Encyclopedia

```
comp.infosystems.interpedia
```

The Z39.50-based WAIS full-text search system

```
comp.infosystems.wais
```

The World Wide Web information system

```
comp.infosystems.www
```

Announcements of Internet information services

```
comp.infosystems.announce
```

Theoretical Computer Science

```
comp.theory
```

Information Retrieval topics

```
comp.theory.info-retrieval
```

There are many newsgroups in the comp. hierarchy of interest to faculty and students in computing and information systems. The following are *hierarchies* that have sometimes as many as 10 to 15 groups organized under them:

```
comp.admin
comp.ai
comp.apps
comp.arch
comp.bugs
```

```
comp.cad

comp.compiler

comp.databases

comp.graphics

comp.infosystems

comp.lang

comp.mail

comp.networks

comp.org

comp.os

comp.protocols

comp.security

comp.soft-sys

comp.software

comp.sources

comp.specification

comp.std

comp.sys

comp.theory

comp.unix

comp.windows
```

School of Education

Educators have been developing a number of resources, especially in the K-12 sector. Part I of this book (Chapters 1 through 3) lists numerous resources and provides suggestions for their use. This section points to resources for pre-service teachers and for those in other specialized subject areas.

The Center for Teaching and Learning at Duke University has an interesting homepage located at URL http://www.ctl.duke.edu/#examples.

```
Center for Teaching and Learning at Duke:  Home Page (p1 of 15)

   [IMAGE]
                WELCOME TO THE CENTER FOR TEACHING AND LEARNING

   This is a new web server site for Duke's teaching and learning center.
```

```
The Center offers both resources and services to Duke's teaching
community. Part of our mission is to provide arenas for serious
discussion about issues regarding teaching. To facilitate this, we
make papers, articles, and letters with pedagogical themes available
electronically — through this web site as well as our gopher server.

You may find out more about the Center, if you like.

Many other brands and varieties of Information servers in and around
Duke are accessible through this site.
```

From their homepage, choose `Examples of Innovative Approaches to Technol-`
`ogy and Education` to reach a page of projects and links of considerable interest to
School of Education faculty and students:

```
Center for Teaching and Learning at Duke:  Home Page (p5 of 15)
Examples of Innovative Approaches to Technology and Education


    * NU Perseus Page
    * Globewide Network Academy
    * JASON Project
    * Trincoll multimedia journal
    * A Gallery of Interactive On-Line Geometry
    * Institute for Academic Technology
    * Diversity University MOO
    * Virtual Language Lab
    * UC ADFA Chemistry Department
    * Telemedia, Networks, and Systems Group
    * Art History at Australian National University
    * Exploration In Education - Electronic Picture Books
    * Virginia Tech Music Department Home Page
    * Visualization Lab at Virginia Tech providing assistance
      to the faculty, staff, and students in making data more
      understandable through use of visual methods.
    * Buckman School
```

One terrific homepage with K-12 information is `K12 Cyberspace Outpost` (by Janice
Abrahams) at URL `http://k12.cnidr.org/janice_k12/k12menu.html`.

The Homepage begins with the following:

```
K12 CYBERSPACE OUTPOST
   metapage at CNIDR...

   Raves and contributions welcome!!
    Email janice@k12.cnidr.org

   Welcome to the K12 OUTPOST. I have collected most of all that's N E W
   within k12 web-space.... and a lot of other things that relate to
   educational uses of the net.
```

```
        I am starting a new section janice's big RAVE this is a special
     section featuring the BEST and the newest use of web-space in education.

 * New and happening ART information page!!
       * other k12 metapages
       * K12 virtual libraries
       * Learn More!!
       * Cool stuff.
       * acceptable and unacceptable use of network resources: policies for
         K-12 schools (stored in the Armadillo gopher in Texas..)
       * NSF K-12 projects and experimental map
       * NSF project map
       * NSF Projects
       * Using technology to build a community of learners
```

The preceding homepage provides access to their Gopher as well, and lots of tutorial information and projects.

A useful homepage for exploring educational technology is located at The Department of Instructional Technologies at San Francisco State. Their World Wide Web server is found at http://130.212.25.153/dit_home_page.html. Not only does this site contain information and links to other IT resources, it also includes a collection of links to job listings.

For Vocational educators, VocServe is the National Center for Resources in Vocational Education's electronic Bulletin Board system, featuring online forums, publications for reading online or downloading, realtime conferencing, and private e-mail. You can reach VocServe using telnet at vocserve.berkeley.edu. VOCNET is NCRVE's Listserv discussion group. The VOCNET address is listserv@cmsa.berkeley.edu. A usenet newsgroup echoes VOCNET: bit.listserv.vocnet.

Project

Under the direction of professor Larry S. Anderson, students at Mississippi State University have developed a large database for the National Center for Technology Planning of information relating to technology planning aids. These include papers, reports from states all over the U.S., and provincial planning documents from Canada.

There are several points of access to the NCTP technology plans:

Where to find it

Anonymous FTP	ftp.msstate.edu
Subdirectory	/pub/archives/nctp

Gopher to	Gopher.MsState.Edu
Submenu	Resources Maintained at Mississippi State University/
Gopher to	digital.cosn.org
Submenu	Networking Information/
Mosaic (to MSU Homepage) using URL	http://www.msstate.edu

The U.S. Department of Education has established an archive of reports, information on legislation, and statistics, including the full text of *Goals 2000: Educate America Act*. You can reach this archive of information via Gopher, FTP, or WWW:

Where to find it

gopher://gopher.ed.gov

http://www.ed.gov

ftp://ftp.ed.gov

Tip: Don't forget; the resources of ERIC are huge and growing, including AskERIC. Appendix B lists all of the Clearinghouses.

NYSED Gopher is one of the very best education resources Gophers, offering folders for news, K-12 and Higher Education resources, and more. The URL is gopher://unix5.nysed.gov:70/1. New entries on this Gopher are reported regularly on the net-happenings list. Following is the current top menu:

```
Internet Gopher Information Client v2.0.15

                Home Gopher server: unix5.nysed.gov

     1.  About This Gopher
     2.  Conferences, Calls for Papers/
     3.  Education News/
     4.  GovernmentInfo/
     5.  Higher Education/
     6.  Internet Resources/
     7.  K-12 Resources/
     8.  Requests for Comment or Collaboration/
     9.  TelecommInfo/
    10.  TelecommNews/
    11.  NYSERNet's ftp site (test only)/
    12.  Search the Internet/
    13.  Search the New York State Library Catalog (OPAC) <TEL>
    14.  State Library's ftp site (test only)/
```

Choose #2, Conference, Calls for Papers, for the most recent entries:

```
                Internet Gopher Information Client v2.0.15

                     Conferences, Calls for Papers

 ->   1.   07-03-94 Habitat to benefit in database contest
      2.   07-03-94 Internet II - Implications for Librarians
      3.   07-03-94 Mosaic and the Web Conference
      4.   07-03-94 Plains Indians - Fact and Fiction
      5.   07-11-94 Leadership & Change
      6.   07-11-94 New Black eZine
      7.   07-12-94 Community Communications
      8.   07-12-94 Emotional Needs of Gifted
      9.   07-12-94 SOFSEM Seeking Papers
     10.   07-14-94 Higher Education Technology Conference
     11.   07-15-94 Canadian Community Network Conference
     12.   07-15-94 Computer Training and Support
     13.   07-15-94 Creating Communication Spaces
     14.   07-19-94 Safe Schools, Safe Students
     15.   07-25-94 What does it mean to be European? Conference
     16.   07-25-94 Wisdom Society seeks papers
```

Student/Parent Project

Pre-service teachers and professors in the Anglia Polytechnic University College of Education have put together an online reference for parents. The Parents Homepage is a reference for parents so that they can help their children with certain activities and assignments.

The Homepage begins this way:

```
Parents Home Page  (p1 of 2)

   [IMAGE] [IMAGE] [IMAGE]
   _____

                          PARENTS HOME PAGE

"Helping Your Child At Home With Computers".

   A useful booklet for parents everywhere.

Island sound radio interview

   A transcription of Phil Miles, "Island Sound" Radio, Malta talking to
   Professor Stephen Heppell, Anglia Polytechnic University about
   computers and education.
```

Where to find it

Parents Homepage

      Linkname   ULTRALAB Parents Home Page

      Filename   http://ultralab.anglia.ac.uk/Scripts/Homes/
                       parents.html

The Australian National University has a homepage of information about HyperMedia, and educational resources, that is of interest to faculty and students in the college of education. The URL is `http://life.anu.edu.au/education.html`.

Following is the first page of ANU's homepage:

```
ANU Educational resources (p1 of 4)

              [IMAGE] ANU HYPERMEDIA EDUCATIONAL RESOURCES

    As part of its service role for Australian universities, the
    Australian National University makes various resource material
    available via its hypermedia servers. The following educational
    resources are currently available:
    _____


    * Tutorials & lectures on-line
        + Art history works by Professor Mike Greenhalgh (ANU):
          ArtServe (ANU)
        + Complex systems: Cellular automata, L-systems, Fractals and
          scale, and Fuzzy logic
        + Landscape fires (Chris Trevitt)
        + Beginner's tutorial on GIS (USGS)
        + Esperanto HyperCourse
    * Software
```

This describes an example of a university laboratory school activity: University High School's Homepage. The laboratory high school of the University of Illinois has its own homepage, built and maintained by the students. Here is the first screen of the homepage:

```
                WELCOME TO UNIVERSITY HIGH SCHOOL


    Uni High is located in Champaign-Urbana, Illinois. It is a lab
    school of the University of Illinois.

    [IMAGE]
```

```
                        TOUR OF UNI

We are waiting for a really super-duper animation that some of the
students are doing, but we are having a little trouble. It should be
ready soon-ish. Meanwhile, look into the Art Department's art gallery,
Artspace, to view reproductions of works created by Uni art students.
Also, check out an article written for the Gargoyle (the school
newspaper) by a student in, and on, Mosaic.
```

Linkname	University High School's Homepage
Filename	http://superdec.uni.uiuc.edu/index.html

A useful Gopher for all educators, but of particular interest to special education is the Gopher at `services.dese.state.mo.us`. This Gopher is part of the Missouri Department of Elementary and Secondary Education (DESE) Technology Network Research Project. Their coverage includes K-12 and higher education, and has particular strength in curriculum.

Many universities maintain Campus Wide Information Servers (CWIS) as part of a local Gopher. To look at course materials and syllabi at one institution (Boston University, for example), point your Gopher to the following:

Where to find it

Host	gopher.bu.edu
Path	1/Resources At Your Fingertips/Undergraduate Course Catalog/School and College Catalog/School of Education/Course Descriptions/

In the same vein, the Gopher at Arizona State University (`info.asu.edu`) has an extensive collection of departmental information under their CWIS. Follow the menus to the School of Education.

The M-Link server at the University of Michigan contains links to information on a variety of subjects, but their collection under education is especially good. Point your Gopher to `vienna.hh.lib.umich.edu`.

The opening menu shows their subject menu tree:

```
   Internet Gopher Information Client v1.13
Root gopher server: vienna.hh.lib.umich.edu

 —>  1.  About Go M-Link/
```

```
 2.  Business and Economics/
 3.  Computers and Technology/
 4.  Education/
 5.  Entertainment and Recreation/
 6.  Environment/
 7.  Government and Politics/
 8.  Health and Nutrition/
 9.  Humanities/
10.  Libraries and Librarianship/
11.  Michigan/
12.  News Services, Newsletters and Journals/
13.  Reference Desk/
14.  Science/
15.  Social Issues & Social Services/
16.  The Internet & Its Other Resources/
```

Choose #4: Education, to access to the following:

```
 1.  Adult Education/
 2.  Briarwood Educational Network/
 3.  CAUSE gopher/
 4.  Distance Learning/
 5.  EDUPAGE Back Issues (EDUCOM)/
 6.  EDUPAGE Current Issue (EDUCOM).
 7.  ERIC Resources/
 8.  Education Resources on the Internet/
 9.  Education Statistics/
10.  FEDIX/
11.  Gifted/
12.  Higher Education/
13.  K-12 Education/
14.  Literacy/
15.  Michigan School Report/
16.  Research in Education/
17.  Resources for Educators/
18.  Scholastic Internet Center/
19.  Special Education/
20.  State Education Dept's/
21.  U.S. Department of Education Gopher/
```

Following are some additional interesting homepages:

Where to find it

Linkname   SCHOLASTIC RESOURCES

Filename   http://k12.colostate.edu/k12resources/scholastic/
scholastic.html

Linkname	The University of Washington Language Learning Center Home Page
Filename	http://d4.llc.washington.edu/

Virtual Reality for a Second Language

This example illustrates a virtual reality system for English as a second language. schMOOze University, a virtual reality designed for ESL/EFL students and teachers, is a system where students and teachers can meet, chat, and hold classes in a friendly, supportive environment. Using telnet, all communication takes place in realtime. Some of the activities that are available are language games, a grammar maze, "classroom" facilities, a Usenet feed, and Gopher access.

To connect to schMOOze U., telnet to morgan.dnsi.com 8888, and when connected, type **connect guest**.

Following are some Usenet groups of interest to those studying education, particularly special education.

Where to find it

Education for people with physical/mental disabilities

    alt.education.disabled

Autism and Developmental Disabilities List

    bit.listserv.autism

Library Access for People with Disabilities

    bit.listserv.axslib-l

Blindness Issues and Discussions

    bit.listserv.blindnws

Computer Access for People with Disabilities

    bit.listserv.easi

Handicap List (Moderated)

    bit.listserv.l-hcap

Educating students with handicaps and/or special needs

    k12.ed.special

Items of interest for/about the handicapped

    misc.handicap

Note: You will find many other newsgroups of broader interest to educators in Chapters 2 and 3, and in Chapter 6.

Lists Carry All Types of Information

Many lists carry announcements of products, software, and information. On the CoSN Discussion List (`cosndisc@yukon.cren.org`), recently, free software for School Bus Routing was offered to K-12 administrators or other interested individuals.

School of Fine and Performing Arts

Resources in the Fine and Performing Arts are being offered increasingly via WWW HyperMedia.

The Art History server at `http://137.141.153.38/art.html` offers links to a variety of topics and sites. Their homepage begins like the following:

```
Art and Music  (p1 of 4)

  [IMAGE]

Art and Music

  Art Serve
        This server offers a variety of image collections and small
        presentations, all of which deal in some way with Art History.
        The current setup is experimental, and will be improved from
        time to time.

  The Louvre
        The world-famous art museum is currently hosting three online
        exhibits: visit the French medieval art demonstration, a
        collection of well-known paintings from famous artists, or tour
        around Paris, the Eiffel Tower and the Champs-Elysees.
```

The 5th International Symposium on Electronic Art
        The 5th International Symposium on Electronic Art will take
        place in Helsinki, Finland in 1994, August 20 trough 25.
        ISEA'94 Helsinki will be a lively forum for scholars,
        artists,critics, scientists and educators - all those who
        share a professional interest in electronic art.

The International Conference on Color Education
        The aim of the Conference is to review the current state of
        colour teaching and its role in art and design education, to
        examine critically the position of established theories of
        colour in the visual arts and to provide an international forum
        for the exchange of ideas on teaching colour.

Ancestry, Religion, Death and Culture
        Appalachian artist Belinda Di Leo explores the interrelation
        ships between religion and the inevitability of death.

Michael's Interesting Music Network Locations
        Links to tons of other music info and lists of music lists;
        more every day!

Music Database
        A WWW Music Database.

Digital Photography '94
        This exhibit sought entrants nationwide from photographers
        whose work involved the techniques of "digital" (computer)
        photography.

Animation Index
        Currently 36 links to sites on the Web which serve Animations
        and Movies, and it is updated almost daily.

Music Pages
        A comprehensive list of music resources available on the Web.
        It currently has over 100 pointers, including over 40 different
        individual artists or bands.

ArtSource
        ArtSource is a gathering point for networked resources on Art
        and Architecture. The content is diverse and includes pointers
        to image collections, electronic exhibitions, art and
        architecture gopher sites, and electronic art journals, as well
        as original materials submitted by librarians, museums, art
        historians, etc.

 Syracuse University Computer Graphics for the Arts
        The hope is that this Web Server and other tools will
        facilitate the collaboration between artists here and others
        located across the Internet.

Cirque de la Mama
        Cirque was born to bring works of art to people and to bring
        people to works of art - to reach for people and to have people
        reach back.

ASCII art has grown rapidly on the Internet, and the ASCII Clip Art Collection contains more than 500 ASCII art images. ASCII is the text found on the Internet, so these images are not graphics, but are totally text-based. The Gopher at Texas Tech also contains a wealth of other graphical images as well. Point your Gopher to `cs4sun.cs.ttu.edu`. The ASCII images are located under the `Art and Images/ Clip Art` directory.

The ASCII Art Bazaar contains a collection of 24,000 art works in ASCII format. Point your Gopher to `twinbrook.cis.uab.edu` and look under the ASCII Art Bazaar.

The Indiana University Music Library has an extensive homepage (15 pages) of network resources related to Music.

Where to find it

Linkname   `Music Resources on the Internet`

Filename   `http://www.music.indiana.edu/misc/`
              `music_resources.html`

Their page begins like the following:

```
Music Resources on the Internet (p1 of 15)

                 MUSIC RESOURCES ON THE INTERNET

  This music resource list is offered as a service of the Indiana
  University Music Library.

  Standard Disclaimer: Due to the fact that these services are out of
  our control, The IU Music Library is not responsible for the
  availability or content of these links.

  To make a suggestion mail webmaster@www.music.indiana.edu or fill out
  this form.
  _____


  Index
     * Academic sites
     * User-maintained information
     * Non-academic sites
     * Geographically Local Sites
     * Artist-specific sites
     * Other lists and indices

Academic sites with music related information:

  World Wide Web
          + The Acoustic Music Server at the Advanced Computing Center
            for the Arts and Design at Ohio State.
```

+ Batish Institute of Indian Music and Fine Arts
+ The Bottom Line Archive, an electronic magazine for bassists
+ Bulgarian Folk Music
+ CAIRSS for Music database of music research literature
+ Ceolas Celtic Music Archive
+ CERL Sound Group
+ Chiba University's Server
+ Drum and Precussion Page
+ Electric Early Music
+ The English Server at Carnegie-Mellon University.
+ IRCAM: Institut de Recherche et Coordination
  Acoustique/Musique
+ Jazz WWW Server at Northwestern.
+ CHMA Mount Allison University's campus radio station 106.9 FM
+ Leeds University Department of Music
+ Music in Croatia
+ The Opera Schedule Server
+ Rare Groove: Tip Sheet at MIT
+ Song Lyrics, taken from the archive at cs.uwp.edu
+ The rec.music.bluenote Jazz Music Frequently Asked Questions
  list
+ Demonstrations of Renaissance Instruments
+ University of Notre Dame Marching Band
+ University of Oregon School of Music
+ Virginia Tech Music

Gopher

+ All-Music Guide music review databse
+ American Music Resource

MIT Press has a homepage entry that is useful to art, music, and theater majors and faculty. The URL is http://mitpress.mit.edu/jrnls-catalog/arts-toc.html. The homepage contains links to the Computer Music Journal, the Leonardo Electric Almanac, and TDR/The Drama Review.

Faculty Scholarship

Electronic communication facilitated the work of several tuba scholars, resulting in *The Tuba Source Book*. Eight editors of this book were able to work collaboratively, exchanging manuscripts across the Internet, using e-mail.

School of Health Sciences and Nursing

There are plentiful resources in the health sciences. Chapter 6 has additional resources on graduate schools related to medicine.

A good starting point is a list called hmatrix that deals with Internet resources broadly in the health sciences. The address is hmatrix-l@ukanaix.cc.ukans.edu.

At Warwick University in England, the School of Nursing is offering information through their NURSE Gopher.

Where to find it

Linkname	Nursing Information Systems
Filename	http://www.warwick.ac.uk:8000/nurse-info-systems.html
Filename	http://crocus.csv.warwick.ac.uk/nursing.html

```
NURSE (p1 of 8)

                              NURSE
           WARWICK UNIVERSITY NURSING (WWW) INFORMATION SERVICE
        ─────────────────────────────────────────────────────────

    For a brief description of NURSE click here.

    We are running a gopher nursing information service, which you can
    link straight to here [gopher] .

Contents

       * Introduction
       * Nursing Sites
       * Midwifery a new page for midwives.
       * Nursing Email Lists
       * USENET News, newsgroups for nurses.
       * Nursing Papers
       * Nursing Conferences
       * Nursing Jobs
       * Nursing Packages
       * Health Related Information Services
       * Other Information Services

Introduction

    Currently the WWW service is not indexed, but most of the NURSE
    information is on the gopher service, which is indexed, so if you want
    to search for an item click here.

    Tennesee also have a nursing gopher service NIGHTINGALE

    However many sites which run www are much better accessed via a proper
    www client, and we plan to have a www service to complement the gopher
    one. If you know of links to other sites which are useful, or if you
    wish to donate HTML documents (or ascii) for putting up on our new
    service please contact me :-
```

Warwick has a CWIS based on gopher called WINFO gopher WINFO and a WWW
server WWW WINFO

At Indiana University their motto is, "Medical and Bio Gophers of the World
Unite." The Medical/Bio page offers links to all manner of medical images. Their
address is `http://foyt.indyrad.iupui.edu/medres/fpage.html`. They cover almost
everything, including sites from Penn State to Switzerland, and NIH, the QUEST
Protein Database and the World Health Organization. This site specializes in
WWW sites.

Medicine Web links WWW medical and health information, and is a Web server
for information relevant to educational technology in the health professions. The
server is maintained by the Educational Technology Branch (ETB) at the National
Library of Medicine.

Where to find it

Linkname   `Medicine Web`

Filename   `http://www.medinfo.rochester.edu/pub/`
                 `MedicineWeb.html`

Scholarly Publishing

The publication of clinical and other material with significant numbers of pictures can prove prohibitively expensive; hence, many useful books are not
published. Edward Sylvester was told that his book *The Healing Blade: A Tale of
Neurosurgery*, had too many pictures of the surgeons and equipment, so they
were eliminating them due to cost considerations. In a creative solution, however, the images have been made available via FTP at `info.asu.edu` in the
subdirectory `/pub/cwis/journalism`.

Following are Usenet newsgroups that may prove useful to nursing faculty and
students:

Where to find it

Chronic Fatigue Syndrome Action Group

     `alt.health.cfids-action`

Computers and Health Discussion List

```
bit.listserv.c+health
c+health@Iubvm.cc.buffalo.edu (echo)
bit.listserv.c+health
```

Health Info-Com Network Newsletter

```
bit.listserv.mednews
```

International Nursing Student Group

```
bit.listserv.snurse-1
```

Disease, medicine, health care research

```
clari.tw.health
```

Health care business

```
clari.biz.industry.health
```

Nursing questions and discussion

```
sci.med.nursing
```

Physiological impacts of diet

```
sci.med.nutrition
```

Preventing, detecting, and treating occupational injuries

```
sci.med.occupational
```

Clinical consulting through computer networks

```
sci.med.telemedicine
```

The politics and ethics involved with health care

```
talk.politics.medicine
```

School of Liberal Arts

The School of Liberal Arts has a growing number of Internet resources. Some of these are discipline specific, while a great number are interdisciplinary in nature.

Located at the University of Kent in the U.K., the Anthropology Resources WWW page holds links to texts and images from around the world. Their URL is `http:/ /lucy.ukc.ac.uk`. Following is their homepage:

```
Anthropology Resources at the University of Kent (p1 of 3)

   [IMAGE]
   The CSAC Ethnographics Gallery is intended for the use of
   anthropologists and others to promote wider access to information. It
   is maintained by the

   Centre for Social Anthropology and Computing
       University of Kent at Canterbury.

   Please visit the CSAC Ethnographics Gallery Collection

   [IMAGE]

CSAC Projects

   CSAC Software Server [support for Applications in Computing for Social
Anthropologists updated 15-May-94
   Anthropology Intermedia Library updated 26-June-94
   Texts of Exploration updated 27-June-94
   45 Years in the Turkish Village updated 26-June-94
   Mauke Movie

Resources for Anthropologists

   UK University Seminar Schedules empty
   Internet resources of interest to anthropologists updated 9-May-94
       maintained by Allen Lutins (al2032@thor.albany.edu)
   Anthropology-related Gophers
   Anthropology Newsgroups
   WWW Virtual Library for Anthropology maintained by Michael Mascha of
       the Ethnographics Lab(USC)
   Theoretical Anthropology journal produced at the Institut fuer
       Voelkerkunde / University of Vienna - Austria
   Institute of Social and Cultural Anthropology (Oxford) publications,
       abstracts, references to other sites.
   QSR-NUDIST WWW server support for Qualitative Research and the Nudist
       Program (Australia)
```

The World Wide Web Virtual Library entry for Anthropology features information on anthropology; ethnography; paleontology; paleoclimatology; access to collections; institutions, such as the Ethnographic Lab, the Anthropology and Culture Archives at Rice University, the Bishop Museum, the Institute of Social and Cultural Anthropology at Oxford University, The Peabody Museum at Yale; and more. The World Wide Web Virtual Library: Anthropology can be found at http://Elab-server.usc.edu/ANTHROPOLOGY.HTML.

Another interesting resource for archaeology is ArchNet.

Where to find it

Linkname   ArchNet-University of Connecticut Anthropology
           Department

Filename   http://spirit.lib.uconn.edu/HTML/archnet.html

Of interest to a number of departments in the social sciences is the Demographic
and Population Resources page. This resource has great breadth and depth. The
homepage is located at http://www.pop.psu.edu/Demography/demography.html.

```
Demographic and Population Resources

   This page contains a listing of connections to
      * other demographic and population servers,
      * census and demographic data,
      * international information sources,
      * related fields such as statistical methods, economics, sociology,
        geography, anthropology, education, and health
      * demographic and other software.

   DEMOGRAPHIC AND POPULATION SERVERS
      * Australian National University Demography WWW server and gopher
        server
      * Florida State University Demography gopher
      * University of Pennsylvania Population Studies Center gopher
      * The Population Studies Center at the University of Michigan
      * United Nations Population Information Network [POPIN] gopher
      * A list of Demography Contacts courtesy of the Florida State
        University

   CENSUS AND DEMOGRAPHIC DATA
      * U.S. Census Bureau WWW server and gopher server
      * SIPP-on-Call (Survey of Income and Program Participation) data
        extraction from the Census Bureau
      * Listing of Census Data sources from the EINet Galaxy
      * Demographic data from Argentina, Canada, and the U.S. at Rice
        University and Texas A & M
      * Data from Africa, Latin America, the U.S. and Pennsylvania at the
      * State and U.S. census data from Missouri University and the
        University of Michigan
      * The Canadian Research Data Library at Simon Fraser University

   INTERNATIONAL INFORMATION SOURCES
      * The World Bank WWW server
      * The World Health Organization WWW server
      * The United Nations' World Demographic Trends
      * Information on the UN International Year of the Family
      * State Department Background Notes for countries around the world

   RELATED FIELDS
      * Statistical Methods
         + StatLib statistical resources and archives
```

```
        * Economics
            + The FINWeb Home Page, a listing of economic, business and
              financial data from the University of Texas
            + The University of Michigan Economics gopher server, and very
              complete listing of economic resources on the Internet
            + The Political Data Archive from Mississippi State University
            + A home page for the Center for Economic Studies at the Census
              Bureau, including discussion papers
            + EconDat at the University of Maryland
        * Sociology
            + The Social Sciences WWW Virtual Library from the Australian
              National University
        * Geography
            + The Project GeoSim server from Virginia Tech
            + A list of Internet Geography Resources
        * Anthropology
            + The Anthropology Server from the University of Southern
              California
        * Education
            + The AskERIC Virtual Library, at Syracus
        * Health
            + The Virtual Hospital from the University of Iowa
            + The Marshall University School of Medicine RuralNet, a rural
SOFTWARE
        * HumPop and IntlPop, tutorials for the IBM PC (with Mac and UNIX
          versions on the way)
        * EXTRACT: U.S. Bureau of Census software from the University of
          Nevada
        * FIVFIV Population Projection software
        * The POPULUS Population Modelling package from the University of
          Minnesota

    This listing is maintained by Michael Zimmerman. Please report any
    problems or suggestions to
      zimmer@pop.psu.edu
```

Another useful WWW repository for the Social Sciences is the WWW Social Science Information Gateway at http://sosig.esrc.bris.ac.uk/.

For linguists, and faculty and students in English, the Consortium for Lexical Research contains numerous links and items of interest:

Where to find it

Linkname	The Consortium for Lexical Research
Filename	http://crl.nmsu.edu/clr/CLR.html

A good site for academic resources for English is the English Server. It includes reference works, documents on language and linguistics, and dictionaries. The WWW access point is http://english-server.hss.cmu.edu.

The University of Montreal maintains one of the only Gophers focused on researching and teaching French Literature. The Gopheur Littertures specializes in Quebecois and francophone literatures. This Gopher is maintained in French and you can access it at gopher://gopher.litteratures.umontreal.ca:7070.

A very helpful Gopher for those in communications and journalism is the FCC Gopher:

Where to find it

Name	*Federal Communications Commission Gopher*
Type	1
Port	70
Host	fcc.gov

Following is their opening menu:

```
            Internet Gopher Information Client v1.13
            Federal Communications Commission gopher

  1.  IVDS_Auctions/
  2.  PCS_Auctions/
  3.  Cable/
  4.  Common_Carrier/
  5.  Daily_Business/
  6.  Daily_Digest/
  7.  Engineering_Technology/
  8.  Events/
  9.  Mass_Media/
 10.  Miscellaneous/
 11.  News_Releases/
 12.  Notices/
 13.  Orders/
 14.  Panel_Discussions/
 15.  Private_Radio/
 16.  Public_Notices/
 17.  Reports/
 18.  Speeches/
 19.  Wireless_PCS/
 20.  index.txt.
```

Following are some eclectic but useful Gophers for journalism:

Where to find it

Name	*Vanderbilt Television News Archive*
Type	1

Port	70
Host	tvnews.vanderbilt.edu
Name	*Netlink Journalism Resources*
Type	1
Port	1020
Path	#pnj/cl
Host	honor.uc.wlu.edu
Name	*Public Broadcasting System (PBS)*
Type	1
Port	70
Host	barkley.pbs.org
Name	*Univ. of Iowa, Communication and Mass Communication Resources [2270]*
Type	1
Port	2270
Host	iam41.arcade.uiowa.edu

An award winning service available through RPI called Comserve perhaps is the most complete service to communications scholars on the Internet. Comserve is a service of the Communication Institute for Online Scholarship. They provide a large number of lists covering human communication studies; news, jobs, new books, preview (which covers calls for papers, conferences, preprints, reviews, and more), Canadian communications, computer-mediated communications, communication in developing countries, students, history, speech disorders, education, practice, ethnomethodology, family, gender, health, mass communication, health, cross cultural, interpersonal, magazine, methods, organizational, political, and rhetoric. In addition, they support *EJCREC* (The Electronic Journal of Communication/La Revue Electronique), a refereed online scholarly journal. For information about CIOS and Comserve, send a message to support@rpitsvm.bitnet or support@vm.its.rpi.edu. Comserve provides services to the public, and to member organizations.

Following are some newsgroups that provide current information and collegial contacts for faculty and students in English and journalism. Some may contain divergent views, so exercise your judgment.

Where to find it

Shop talk by journalists and journalism students

> `alt.journalism`

I write, therefore I'm biased

> `alt.journalism.criticism`

Don't believe the hype

> `alt.news-media`

News & Talk about Digital Audio Broadcasting

> `alt.radio.digital`

U.S. National Public Radio: shows, stories, hosts, etc.

> `alt.radio.networks.npr`

PageMaker for Desktop Publishers

> `bit.listserv.pagemakr`

Electronic Publishing Discussion List

> `bit.listserv.vpiej-l`

Technical bookstore & publisher advertising & info

> `biz.books.technical`

Newspapers, publishers, magazines

> `clari.biz.industry.print_media`

Electronic prepress

> `comp.publish.prepress`

Technology & techniques of desktop publishing

> `comp.text.desktop`

Desktop publishing with FrameMaker

> `comp.text.frame`

WWW in Scholarly Publishing

Project MUSE is a scholarly publishing project at Johns Hopkins University aimed at making scholarly journals available on the Internet using the WWW protocol. The first journals put online were `Configurations` (a journal on technology and literature), `Modern Language Notes`, and `English Literary History`. In each case, the information is textual and visual and in several languages. The URL is `http://muse.mse.jhu.edu`.

Historians are making big moves on the Internet through several expanding sites.

The *H-Net* project at the University of Illinois at Chicago is an ambitious project which has set up 20 electronic mailing lists for historians on the Internet. There are more than 4500 subscribers from 50 countries. The H-Net lists are all located at `listserv@uicvm.uic.edu`.

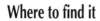

Where to find it

H-Net British and Irish History Discussion List

> `H-ALBION`

American Studies Discussion List

> `H-AMSTDY`

Civil War History Discussion List

> `H-CIVWAR`

H-DIPLO Diplomatic History Discussion List

> `H-DIPLO`

Ethnic History Discussion List

> `H-ETHNIC`

History of Film Discussion List

> `H-FILM`

H-Net History Graduate Students Discussion List

> `H-GRAD`

Jewish Studies Discussion List

> `H-JUDAIC`

H-Net Labor History Discussion List

> H-LABOR

Latin American History Discussion List

> H-LATAM

Legal History Discussion List

> H-LAW

H-Net Political History Discussion List

> H-POL

H-Net History Of Rhetoric Discussion List

> H-RHETOR

H-Rural & Agricultural History Discussion List

> H-RURAL

H-South U.S. Southern History Discussion List

> H-SOUTH

H-Net Teaching History Discussion List

> H-TEACH

H-URBAN Urban History Discussion List

> H-URBAN

H-WOMEN Women's History Discussion List

> H-WOMEN

Holocaust Studies, Anti-Semitism

> HOLOCAUS

Colonial America

> IEAHCnet

Yet another source of history information on the Internet is *HNSOURCE* at the University of Kansas. It is a repository of both information and a source of links to other sources. The URL is gopher://ukanaix.cc.ukans.edu:70/11/hnsource.

Following are some of the items to be found at *HNSOURCE*:

- ■ The Library of Congress' text and graphics files of their exhibit on Christopher Columbus

- Constitutional documents

- An extensive collection of material from the former Soviet Union

- The Electronic Newsletter of the American Academy of Research Historians of Medieval Spain

- An eclectic collection of classical documents including the Beinicke Papyrus Collection at Yale University

- Clinton White House materials

- Material from The Institute of Historical Research in London, which includes information organized by epoch and region

Electronic Sources For West European History And Culture, by Erwin K. Welsch, of the Memorial Library, University of Wisconsin-Madison is a thorough guide. It is available at the University of Michigan Subject-Oriented Clearinghouse mentioned in the beginning of this chapter.

The Welsch guide is quite comprehensive, covering text archives, lists, e-journals, and sources by epoch and sub-discipline. Following is an abbreviated listing of the contents:

```
      CONTENTS
I.    General History
      A. Listservers
      B. Electronic History Journals
      C. Other Resources
II.   Sources Arranged Chronologically By Approximate Period of
         Coverage:
III.  Sources arranged by country and chronologically within each:
IV.   History Sub-Disciplines
V.    Subjects Related to History (Alphabetically)
VI.   Text Archives
VII.  HISTORY NETWORKS
VIII. EUROPEAN CD-ROM SOURCES
IX.   RESOURCES IN EUROPE AVAILABLE THROUGH THE INTERNET
X.    ASSOCIATION FOR HISTORY AND COMPUTING
XI.   EUROPEAN EXHIBITS IN THE LIBRARY OF CONGRESS
XII.  GENERAL ONLINE BIBLIOGRAPHIC DATABASES
      A. Library of Congress
GLOSSARY
BIBLIOGRAPHY
```

Medieval Studies resources of interest include *The Labyrinth*. The Labyrinth provides everything from information on research in Italy and religious studies, to job listings. It also offers material that professors have produced for teaching medieval studies. The collection of material and links is quite impressive, and can be found via `http://www.georgetown.edu/labyrinth/labyrinth-home.html`.

Mdvlphil (`mdvlphil@lsuvm.sncc.lsu.edu`) is a list devoted to the discussion of the philosophy and socio-political thought of the Middle Ages. Subscribe using standard Listserv protocol.

Using the Internet in Teaching

A seminar on the fourth-century philosopher Augustine taught by James O'Donnell was "advertised" on several lists on the Internet. This resulted in the 10 University of Pennsylvania graduate students being joined for the course by upwards of 350 Internauts. All students received the same syllabus, notes were posted after each class meeting, and class discussions moved online. Participant locations ranged from Turkey to Wales.

The International Philosophical Preprint Exchange provides prepublication works in philosophy for critique and commentary by interested readers. This Gopher also maintains listings of calls for papers, philosophical conferences, and points to other information. The address is `gopher://apa.oxy.edu`.

Tip: For Mosaic users, the creators of Mosaic—the folks at the National Center for Supercomputing Applications—have asked that you change your homepage from theirs to any other. They are overloaded with traffic.

The Yale Peabody Museum Gopher is online with access to its collections of data at `gopher.peabody.yale.edu`, port `70`. The initial Gopher collection is 255,268 specimens/lots, which translates to a little under a million individual specimens—the + means under construction:

Curatorial Division	Cataloguing Methodology	Number of Items	Items On Gopher
Anthropology	Lot	267,000	+
Botany/ Paleobotany	Individual	360,000	16,809
Entomology	Indiv./Lot	900,000	5,705
Invertebrate Paleontology	Lot	300,000	24,189
Invertebrate Zoology	Lot	300,000	8,584

Curatorial Division	Cataloguing Methodology	Number of Items	Items On Gopher
Meteorites	Indiv./Lot	500	+
Mineralogy	Individual	40,000	29,115
Scientific Instruments	Individual	2,000	573
Vertebrate Paleontology	Individual	120,000	28,132
Vertebrate Zoology			
VZ-Herpetology	Individual	14,400	+
VZ-Ichthyology	Lot	9,908	9,908
VZ-Mammalogy	Individual	4,806	4,806
VZ-Ornithology	Individual	113,648	113,648
VZ-Osteology	Individual	13,799	13,799

Syracuse University has a project to disseminate government information over the Internet. The Electronic Government Information Services are Gopher-based resources that provide copies of government reports. This would provide data to faculty and students in sociology, political science, and government. The address is eryx.syr.edu, in the subdirectory called Other Gopher and Information Services/North America/USA/General/EGIS.

Faculty Using the Internet in Teaching

Two Virginia professors at the University of Virginia and Virginia Commonwealth University professors are running an electronic political market similar to a futures/commodity market. Participants have the opportunity to buy stock in political candidates in the U. S. Senate race from Virginia. Participants invest $5 to $500. If you just want to see what is going on, telnet to iem.biz.uiowa.edu and then choose 26. This server at the University of Iowa hosts other simulations of this kind as well.

The Russian and East European Studies Homepages at the University of Pittsburgh cover language, literature, music, art, culture, government, science and technology, engineering, communication, business, finance, economics, history, geography, sociology, and others. Links are maintained to text sources, databases, directories, software and multimedia. The address is http://www.pitt.edu/~cjp.

Internet used to Augment Courses

Gary M. Klass at Illinois State University at Normal teaches his course "Race, Ethnicity, and Social Inequality" to students on campus, and draws in additional participation from all over the world via a discussion list on Internet. As a part of the course, students must review five books, and post their reviews to the discussion list `pos302-l@ilstu.edu`.

An interesting resource for many of the Liberal Arts is the EXPO collection of electronic materials, including material from the Library of Congress' recent exhibit—Rome Reborn: The Vatican Library and Renaissance Culture. This particular exhibit contained in excess of 200 images of selected manuscripts. The full-color images are particularly stunning, and are available for downloading. The EXPO address is `http://sunsite.unc.edu/expo/ticket_office.html`.

Using Lists for Scholarship

Jeffery Walker, a professor from the University of Arkansas at Little Rock, has created a list for scholars in criminal justice to release copies of papers on a variety of topics, and then discuss the papers through a group of interlocking lists. To participate, sign up for the CRIMECON list at `mailserv@ualr.edu`.

Internet resources in psychology are plentiful. Among them are the following:

Validata (`validata@ua1vm.us.edu`) focuses on the development, testing a validation of psychological measures.

There are two new lists dealing with schizophrenia. *Schizoph* (`schizoph@vm.utcc.utoronto.ca`) is a list for exchanging information about schizophrenia, and `schiz-l@umab.umd.edu` has a similar charter.

The Coombspapers—Social Sciences Research Data Bank at Australia National University is a very large project focusing on social science and humanities resources.

Where to find it

Name	*COOMBSQUEST Soc.Sci & Humanities Inf.Facility at ANU*
Type	1
Port	70
Host	coombs.anu.edu.au

or

FTP	coombs.anu.edu.au
Path	/coombspapers

Following is the opening message on Coomsquest:

```
ABOUT THE COOOMBSQUEST GOPHER

Gopher Name:
============
COOMBSQUEST Social Sci.& Humanities Inf.Facility (ANU)

Gopher Description:
============
This is the world-wide Social Sciences and Humanities Information
Service of the Coombs Computing Unit, Research Schools of Social
Sciences & Pacific and Asian Studies, Australian National University,
Canberra, Australia.

Services:
=========
- Direct access to the COOMBSPAPERS SOCIAL SCIENCES RESEARCH DATA BANK
anon. FTP Archive on coombs.anu.edu.au machine and to its major mirrors
in USA and other countries.
        [The COOMBSPAPERS were established in Dec.1991 to act as the
world's major electronic repository of the social science & humanities
papers, documents, bibliographies, directories, theses abstracts and
other high-grade research material dealing with Australia, Pacific
Region, SouthEast and NorthEast Asia, as well as Buddhism, Taoism,
Shamanism and other oriental religions].

- On-line searching of the ANU-xxx-xxx series of WAIS format databases:

- Unique directory of pointers to the world's leading soc.sci. and
        humanities gophers
- Unique directory of pointers to the world's leading electronic
- On-line searching of the ANU-xxx-xxx series of WAIS format databases:

- Unique directory of pointers to the world's leading soc.sci. and
        humanities gophers
- Unique directory of pointers to the world's leading electronic
        archives,dbases and inf. facilities dealing with:
        (a) Aboriginal Studies;
        (b) Asian Studies (esp. China,Indonesia, Philippines, Thailand,
            Tibet);
        Buddhist Studies (esp. Zen and Tibetan Buddhism);
        Linguistics (esp. Australia and Pacific region);
        Prehistory & Archaeology (esp. Australia and Pacific region);

- Pointer to the East Asia/Pacific Wireless Files (US Information
        Service/ANU)
- Pointer to the ELISA - Electronic Library Information System (ANU)
        gopher

Contact person: Dr T.Matthew Ciolek <tmciolek@coombs.anu.edu.au>.
```

School of Science, Technology, and Engineering

Departments in the School of Science, Technology, and Engineering will find a wealth of Internet resources that are useful in teaching and research.

Indiana University maintains *IUBio*, which contains a large collection of materials related to biological research, including gene sequence data from Genbank, tables of contents for molecular biology journals, and software for biologists. The Gopher address is `gopher://ftp.bio.indiana.edu`.

In Geneva, Switzerland, the Geneva University Hospital maintains a database of protein sequences, and other biological data at `http:/expasy.hcuge.ch`.

Those interested in fish ecology can sign up for `fish-ecology@searn.sunet.se`. This European list discusses empirical and theoretical issues related to fish and fisheries, and ecology.

The American Chemical Society maintains a Gopher that contains the tables of contents to it publications, and some full text articles. These journals include the *Journal of Chemical Education* and the *Journal of Chemical Education: Software*. Point your Gopher to `jchemed.chem.wisc.edu`.

In the United Kingdom is an interesting resource called *Chemical On-line Presentations and Talks*. This resource uses World Wide Web: `http://www.ch.ic.ac.uk/talks/`. These presentations use the WWW online.

The following are some active newsgroups for chemists.

Where to find it

Chemical production

    relcom.commerce.chemical

Chemistry and related sciences

    sci.chem

The field of electrochemistry

    sci.chem.electrochem

Organometallic chemistry

    sci.chem.organomet

All aspects of chemical engineering

    sci.engr.chem

There are two entries in the WWW Virtual Library that are useful to faculty and students in engineering: the Civil Engineering page and the Materials Engineering page:

Where to find it

Linkname	The World-Wide Web Virtual Library: Civil Engineering
Filename	http://howe.ce.gatech.edu/WWW-CE/home.html
Linkname	The World-Wide Web Virtual Library: Materials Engineering
Filename	http://m_struct.mie.clarkson.edu/VLmae.html

The Civil Engineering page contains links to the following:

```
Web Server:Carleton University
            This server offers information concerning the Civil
            Engineering Department at Carleton University. It also
            contains the catalog for The Engineering Case Library —
            a set of case studies useful for education. The catalog
            may be searched for all cases relevant to Civil
            Engineering.

Web Server:Georgia Institute of Technology

            This server offers information concerning the School of
            Civil Engineering at the Georgia Institute of Technology,
            Atlanta, Georgia USA. The information includes the
            faculty, staff, students, research centers, projects,
            courses, and admission information.

Web Server:University of Ljubljana, Slovenia, Department of Civil
            Engineering.

            The server contains information about their university
            and a related project ICARIS which has many good links to
            other sources.
```

The Materials Engineering page contains links to the following:

```
Web server: Clarkson University Center for Advanced Materials
        Processing.

Web server: Los Alamos National Lab Materials Science & Technology
        Group.
```

Following are a large number of diverse Usenet newsgroups used by engineers:

Where to find it

Parametric Technology's Pro/Engineer design package

```
comp.cad.pro-engineer
```

Discussions of the Ethernet/IEEE 802.3 protocols

```
comp.dcom.lans.ethernet
```

VHSIC Hardware Description Language, IEEE 1076/87

```
comp.lang.vhdl
```

Issues and announcements about the IEEE & its members

```
comp.org.ieee
```

Software Engineering and related topics

```
comp.software-eng
```

Women In Science and Engineering NET

```
info.wisenet
```

Technical discussions about engineering tasks

```
sci.engr
```

Discussing the field of biomedical engineering

```
sci.engr.biomed
```

All aspects of chemical engineering

```
sci.engr.chem
```

Topics related to civil engineering

```
sci.engr.civil
```

The engineering of control systems

```
sci.engr.control
```

The field of mechanical engineering

```
sci.engr.mech
```

All aspects of materials engineering

```
sci.materials
```

General Announcements for IEEE community

```
ieee.announce
```

Postings about managing the ieee.* groups

```
ieee.config
```

IEEE—General discussion

```
ieee.general
```

Discussion & tips on PC-NFS

```
ieee.pcnfs
```

Regional Activities Board—Announcements

```
ieee.rab.announce
```

Technical Activities Board—Announcements

```
ieee.tab.announce
```

Technical Activities Board—General Discussion

```
ieee.tab.general
```

The Technical Committee on Operating Systems

```
ieee.tcos
```

USAB—Announcements

```
ieee.usab.announce
```

USAB—General Discussion

```
ieee.usab.general
```

Note: The IEEE is willing to distribute these newsgroups via NNTP to any site that desires to carry them. If you would like a feed of these newsgroups, have the news administrator for your site contact usenet@ieee.org for a feed.

Useful Software for Teaching

Information on the McDonnell Douglas Human Modeling System (DHMS) is available at `http://pat.mdc.com/LB/LB.html`. The McDonnell Douglas Human Modeling System (MDHMS) is an interactive 3-D modeling system offering the capability to analyze human body fit and function within a geometric structure. This resource is used extensively in mechanical engineering courses.

There are many actively updated resources in climatology; among them is the UIUC Weather Machine maintained by the Atmospheric Sciences Department at the University of Illinois. The data are updated every hour and include color images of the U.S. The images also include current and projection maps showing precipitation, isobars, and fronts. The images are located at `gopher://wx.atmos.uiuc.edu/11/Images`.

Using the Internet for Professional Advancement

Two young physicists believe that the Internet helped them to get elected to the board of the American Physical Society. The two put out a petition on the Young Scientists Network mailing list to solicit signatures—and they got them. Usually, these petitions and signatures are sought via snail mail and the telephone.

There are newsgroups covering most aspects of modern physics, including the now infamous one dealing with cold-fusion:

Where to find it

The Science of Sounds

    alt.sci.physics.acoustics

Scientific theories you won't find in journals

    alt.sci.physics.new-theories

The Science and Profession of Biophysics

    bionet.biophysics

Biophysical Society Official Announcements

    bionet.prof-society.biophysics

K-12 Physics List

`bit.listserv.physhare`

Forum in Astronomy/Astrophysics Research

`sci.astro.research`

Semiconductor devices, processes, materials, physics

`sci.engr.semiconductors`

Issues of physics in medical testing/care

`sci.med.physics`

Physical laws, properties, and so on

`sci.physics`

Particle accelerators and the physics of beams

`sci.physics.accelerators`

Computational Fluid Dynamics

`sci.physics.computational.fluid-dynamics`

Electromagnetic Theory and Applications

`sci.physics.electromag`

Information on fusion, especially "cold" fusion

`sci.physics.fusion`

Particle Physics Discussions

`sci.physics.particle`

Plasma Science and Technology

`sci.physics.plasma`

Current Physics Research

`sci.physics.research`

Now for something a little off-beat. The Mini-Annals of Improbability Research is available over the Net. This humorous approach to scientific practices can be enjoyed by faculty and students in almost any discipline. Following is their announcement:

The mini-journal of inflated research and personalities.
Published by The Annals of Improbable Research (AIR)
at The MIT Museum

```
************************************************************************
1994-03-9        Purpose of mini-AIR (*)
```

The mini-Annals of Improbable Research (mini-AIR) publishes news
about improbable research and ideas. Specifically:

A) Haphazardly selected superficial (but advanced!) extracts of
research news and satire from The Annals of Improbable Research.

B) News about the annual Ig Nobel Prize ceremony.

C) News about other science humor activities intentional and
otherwise.

WHAT IS AIR? (An introduction, of sorts)
AIR is a new magazine produced by the entire former editorial
staff (1955-1994) of "The Journal of Irreproducible Results
(JIR)," the world's oldest satirical science journal. The new
magazine's co-founders are Marc Abrahams, who edited JIR from
1990-1994, and Alexander Kohn, who founded JIR in 1955 and was its
editor until 1989. AIR is published at the MIT Museum in
Cambridge, MA. AIR's editorial board consists of more than 40
distinguished scientists from around the world including seven
Nobel Laureates. Every October, AIR and the MIT Museum produce the
Ig Nobel Prize Ceremony, honoring people whose achievements cannot
or should not be reproduced.

```
— — — — — — — — — — — — — — —
1994-03-12       How to Receive to mini-AIR, etc.(*)
```

mini-AIR is an electronic publication, available over the
Internet, free of charge. It is distributed as a LISTSERV
application. We publish approximately 12 issues per year.
To subscribe, send a brief E-mail message to either of these
addresses:
        LISTSERV@MITVMA.MIT.EDU   or   LISTSERV@MITVMA
The body of your message should contain ONLY the words "SUBSCRIBE
MINI-AIR" followed by your name.
Here are two examples:
        SUBSCRIBE MINI-AIR Irene Curie Joliot
        SUBSCRIBE MINI-AIR Nicholai Lobachevsky
To stop subscribing,
send the following message to the same address:
        SIGNOFF MINI-AIR
To obtain a list of back issues,
send this message:
        INDEX MINI-AIR
To retrieve a particular back issue,
send a message specifying which issue you want.
For example, to retrieve issue 94-00001,send this message:
        GET MINI-AIR 94-00001

To obtain a somewhat complete list of gopher sites that maintain
mini-AIR, email us a request.

And for something not very scientific, a Gopher at UCLA maintains a collection of wisdom and lore, including I Ching, biorhythms, and Tarot cards at `http://cad.ucla.edu/repository/useful/useful.html`.

From Here...

Just as this chapter offered specific Internet resources and examples for undergraduate education, Chapter 6 provides resources for graduate faculty and students.

ON TO GRADUATE SCHOOL

*A university should be a place of light,
of liberty and of learning.*

Benjamin Disraeli

Graduate education is increasingly involved in using the Internet for teaching and research. The following are the most popular university graduate schools:

- The "B" school (School of Business)
- The School of Library Science and Information Studies
- The Law School
- The Medical School

This chapter provides a large number of specific Internet resources for faculty and students in each of these areas. In addition, suggested assignments are presented as a starting point for learning more about what the Internet offers each discipline.

The "B" School

Business oriented resources are appearing on the Internet at a rate that may exceed all other categories. The subjects and data available cover the full range of business activities and are available abundantly through many Internet tools and resources, including the following:

- Unique Sites
- Gophers and WWW Sites
- FTP Sites
- Guides
- Discussion lists
- Usenet newsgroups

Unique sites

The next sections discuss several unique sites that make excellent starting points for business information searches.

Washington and Lee

One of the largest collections of business related information can be accessed using the WWW site at Washington and Lee Law Library. The URL is `http://honor.uc.wlu.edu:1020`.

Washington and Lee has menus, arranged by subject, that show the breadth of their links:

```
by SUBJECT   (p1 of 3)

       * Non-classified
       * General Reference
       * Philosophy
       * Psychology, Mental Health
       * Religion
       * History
       * Directories of People/Institutions
       * Geography
       * Oceanography
       * Anthropology, Archeology
       * Games, Sports, Recreation
       * Social Science
       * Social Science Statistics, Census
       * Economics
       * Film, Television, Radio
       * Commerce, Business, Accounting
       * Careers, Jobs, Employment
       * Retail Trade
       * Grants, Funding
       * Politics
 -- press space for next page --
  Arrow keys: Up and Down to move. Right to follow a link; Left to go back.
 H)elp O)ptions P)rint G)o M)ain screen Q)uit /=search [delete]=history list
                            #hf/cl (p1 of 3)
```

Choosing the Commerce, Business, Accounting link locates 321 links for those subjects. Here are just a few from the beginning of the listing:

```
       * ..Restrict by Subject
       * ..Restrict by Type (Telnet, Gopher, WWW)
       * ..Sort: Date (for date coded entries) [321 items]
       * ..Sort: Geographic [321 items]
       * Agricultural Commodity Market Reports, USGS (WAIS db)
       * Agricultural Market News (search)
       * Andrews University, School of Business
       * ANet, The International Accounting Network
       * Arizona State Economic Development Database (ASEDD)
         (Login: => at userid;enter HELLOASU;)
       * Arizona State Economic Development Database at ASU
         (Login: helloasu)
       * Asia and Pacific Rim Agriculture and Trade Notes
       * Asia Pacific Business & Marketing Resources
       * Automated Trade Library Service: ATI-Net
         (Login: => at login;enter super;)
       * Bank of England: Quarterly Bulletin Time Series Data
         (Login: => at login;enter janet;at pass;enter ;at hostname;enter
         uk.ac.swurcc;at username;pause 1;enter ;pause 5;enter ;at
         service;enter PMAC;)
       * Banking
       * Best Market Reports
```

```
* BI / Norwegian School of Management
* Bibliographic Information Retrieval ONline (BIRON)
  (Login: biron(passwd=norib))
* Bibliographies in Economics (University of Michigan)
* Branch Information Services Gopher
* British Columbia. Ministry of Small Business, Tourism and Culture
  (Victoria)
* British Telecom's "Electronic Yellow Pages" Service (Imperial
  College)
  (Login: => at login;enter eyp;pause 4;enter \r;)
* British Telecom's "Electronic Yellow Pages" Service
  (Login: => at login;enter janet;at pass;enter ;at hostname;enter
  uk.ac.niss;at call;at niss;pause 2;enter U;at information;pause
  2;enter E;at password;pause 2;enter \r\r;pause 1;enter ;pause
  2;enter \r;at vt100;pause 1;enter 1;)
* Building and Real Estate (Hong Kong)
* Bureau of Labor Statistics (BLS), FTP Site
* Bureau of Labor Statistics (BLS) Databases
* ..Show Remaining 299 Items
```

In addition, business related information can be located under `Careers`, `Jobs and Employment`, `Retail Trade`, and others.

Project

Goal: To increase awareness of the unique advantages and restrictions of Internet aided business activities.

Write a marketing plan for a business wanting to do business on the Internet. Explore the issues surrounding Acceptable Use and commercial activity on the network and incorporate them in the plan. Working in teams of four research, write, and present the plan.

Following are some hints for locating resources:

1. Check out CommerceNet. It is oriented specifically to the commercial user. The URL is `http://www.commerce.net/`.

2. Look at InterBEX (Business Exchange), a commercial information service. For a current index of advertisements, send an e-mail message to `InterBEX-index@intnet.bc.ca`.

3. Go to the `Commercial Use of the Net` Page at URL `http://pass.wayne.edu/business.html`. and the Commercial Sites on the Web at URL `http://tns-www.lcs.mit.edu/commerce.html`.

Tip: To request Web pages via e-mail. send an e-mail message to `test-list@info.cern.ch`, with a message containing the URL in which you are interested, preceded by the command send:

```
send http://www.service.digital.com/html/emall.html
```

4. The Gopher at Kent State University has an excellent set of business-related information that could be useful in this assignment:

```
        Kent State University.
        --> 1.  An Introduction to BSN.
    2.  BSN.ACCOUNTING.
    3.  BSN.COMPUTER.
    4.  BSN.ECONOMICS.
    5.  BSN.FINANCE.
    6.  BSN.GENERAL.
    7.  BSN.INVESTMENTS.
    8.  BSN.LOCATION.
    9.  BSN.MANAGEMENT.
   10.  BSN.OPERATIONS.
   11.  BSN.PERSONNEL.
   12.  BSN.STATISTICS.
```

This site is available via WWW or directly by pointing a Gopher to

Name	*Business Sources on the Net (Special Project)*
Path	`D-1:2577:Business`
Host	`refmac.kent.edu`
Port	`70`
Type	`1+`
URL	`gopher://refmac.kent.edu:70/1D-1:%3a2577%3aBusiness`

5. Join the `inet-marketing` list (Internet Marketing) on `listproc@einet.net`. The list discusses marketing, demographics and advertising via the Internet."

6. Look into a couple of online bookstores, such as `wordsworth.com`, or online libraries to see what books and journal articles exist concerning this topic.

CareerMosaic

CareerMosaic is the first World Wide Web guide to in-depth information regarding employers. It profiles employers, such as National Semiconductor, Read-Rite, Symantec, Tandem Computers, and US WEST. CareerMosaic has been developed and presented by Bernard Hodes Advertising. You can access it via any World Wide Web browser at `http://www.careermosaic.com/cm/`.

ANet Accounting Gopher

ANet is an international accounting network run from Southern Cross University in New South Wales, Australia. The ANet Accounting Gopher is a useful site for accounting and related information. The URL & link info is

Where to find it

Type   1+

Path   1/anet

Host   anet.scu.edu.au

Port   70

URL   gopher://anet.scu.edu.au:70/11/anet

You can obtain more information on ANet by sending an e-mail with the message left blank to anet@scu.edu.au. A help file will be returned automatically. The top level menu for this Gopher is as follows:

```
                ANet- The Accounting Network

    1.  Details on A-Net/
    2.  Calendar of Coming Events in Accounting/
    3.  Upcoming conferences - Details/
    4.  Accounting Departments-Details/
    5.  Accounting and Auditing Journals-Details/
    6.  Accounting Organisations/
    7.  Archives of A-Net Mailing Lists/
    8.  Accounting Gophers & Other Services/
    9.  Other Resources/
    10. Key Search All ANet Items <?>
```

IAWWW—Internal Auditing World Wide Web

The purpose of the *IAWWW* is to provide online information on auditing broadly, including the profession, help and access, audit information, and industry specific information. The following is their introductory material:

```
What can be done with IAWWW?

The IAWWW will be able to provide an auditor with:

*       Internet resources of general interest
```

```
*        Physical conferences and seminar listings
*        Vendor, product, and service information
*        News:
         *        IAWWW
         *        Internal auditing
         *        General and public
*        Electronic professional participation forms
*        Profession-specific and Internet resources for:
         *        Managerial auditing
         *        Operational auditing
         *        Fiscal and financial auditing
         *        Information and knowledge auditing
         *        Audit management
         *        Audit committees
*        Viewing industry-specific topics
*        Geographic-specific domains:
         *        Country
         *        USA/State
         *        Country/Provinces
*        Electronic discussion groups ordered by subject matter
*        White papers
*        Multimedia audit-specific documents, movies, pictures, etc.
```

Where to find it

URL   http://mmm.dartmouth.edu/pages/dhmc/IAWWW-FOLDER-V1.0/
       DARTHOME-IAWWW-EXEC.HTML

The National Institute for Management Technology

A new WWW server has been added for the *National Institute for Management Technology* (NIMT) in Cork, Ireland. This server provides information in executive support systems, groupware, strategic/management use of IT, multimedia, and trends.

Where to find it

URL   http://www.nimt.rtc-cork.ie/nimt.htm

GNN Personal Finance Center

The *GNN Personal Finance Center* (PFC) features numerous links to the vast personal finance and investment resources of the Internet. In addition, it contains original articles and columns.

Where to find it

URL   `http://nearnet.gnn.com/gnn/meta/finance/index.html`

Brookfield Business Answer(TM)

The Brookfield Business Answer (TM) is a free service for small business owners. You can ask any business-related question, and they will put it into their free newsletter, stripped of identification. Questions and answers are compiled and made available on a mailing list. To subscribe, send e-mail to `brookfld@netcom.com`, with the subject SUBSCRIBE BBA *your_real_first_name your_real_last_name*. The message itself should be left blank. Monitoring this newsletter can help to keep Business School members up-to-date on concerns of small businesses. The following is an excerpt from their informational message:

```
TYPICAL QUESTIONS FOR BROOKFIELD BUSINESS ANSWER

How to hire (or fire) without risk of litigation

Asset protection strategies

Landlord tenant questions and problems

Debt collection (if you owe or someone owes you)

Employee ownership and profit sharing plans

Compensation strategies

Independent contractors versus employees

Incorporating -- when, why and how

Negotiating a lease -- how to do it

Test marketing strategies

Estate Planning for the small business owner
```

ARIAWeb

ARIAWeb is the homepage of an academic association called the *American Risk and Insurance Association*. It includes pointers to all sorts of information on risk and insurance, including working papers, and conference information.

Where to find it

URL   `http://riskweb.bus.utexas.edu/whataria.html`

QuoteCom

QuoteCom provides a variety of free and subscription services, such as providing 15-minute delayed stock quotes.

Where to find it

URL   `http://www.quote.com/`

You can obtain stock quotes from `http://www.quote.com/demo-chrt.html`.

The following is from QuoteCom's information screen:

```
                Stock Quotes on the Internet!

QuoteCom is a new service, dedicated to bringing quality financial
market data to the Internet community.  This includes:

o  Up to 5 quotes per day FREE to registered users
o  Delayed (15 minutes typical) quotes available on all domestic
   stock and commodity exchanges, mutual and money market funds
o  Access via WWW, telnet, email, and ftp


Besides these free services, we provide much more quality
information for investors at very low prices ($10-25 per month)

o  Up to 100 (15-minute delayed) quotes per day
o  End-of-day portfolio updates sent automatically via email
o  Real-time alarm monitoring of items in your portfolio
o  Automatic tagging of news items to stocks in your portfolio
o  End-of-day updates downloaded for 45,000+ symbols
o  Historical data
o  Business news, market analysis, and commentary supplied by
   Standard & Poor's MarketScope
o  Fundamental (balance sheet) data supplied by Standard &
   Poor's Stock Guide
o  In-depth company and industry profiles supplied by Reference
   Press, Inc.
o  Coverage of international exchanges, including Canadian stock
   exchanges and many European exchanges
o  On-line charts with user-specifiable parameters for WWW users
o  BusinessWire earnings reports and press releases (coming soon)
```

For more information, send a blank e-mail message to info@quote.com, or access information via FTP at ftp://ftp.quote.com/pub/info.

InterNet Info: Venture Capital Firms on the Net

InterNet Info has researched venture capital firms on the Internet, and provides an update to the Internet community monthly, as in the following example:

```
                    Venture Capital Firms on the Net
                           June 15, 1994


Venture Firm                      Domain Name        Office Location

Accel Partners                    ACCEL.COM          Princeton
Atlas Venture                     AVENTURE.COM       Boston
Bessemer Venture Partners         BESSEMER.COM       Wellesly
Canaan Partners                   CANAAN.COM         Menlo Park
Colorado Bio/Medical Venture Ctr  CBVC.COM           Lakewood
Enterprise Partners               ENT.COM            Los Angeles
General Atlantic Partners         GAPARTNERS.COM     New York
GeoPartners Research Inc.         GEOPARTNERS.COM    Cambridge
Greylock Mangement Corp.          GREYLOCK.COM       Boston
Highland Capital Partners         HCP.COM            Boston
Hummer Winblad Venture Partners   HUMWIN.COM         Emeryville
Kleiner, Perkins, Caufield et al  KPCB.COM           Palo Alto
Menlo Ventures                    MENLOVEN.COM       Menlo Park
Merrill, Pickard, Anderson et al  MPAE.COM           San Francisco
Mohr, Davidow Ventures            MDV.COM            Menlo Park
New Enterprise Associates         NEA.COM            Menlo Park
Oak Investment Partners           OAKWEST.COM        Menlo Park
Onset Ventures                    ONSET.COM          Palo Alto
Sequoia Capital                   SEQUOIACAP.COM     Menlo Park
Sierra Ventures                   SIERRAVEN.COM      Menlo Park
Sigma Partners                    SIGMPTRS.COM       Menlo Park
Sutter Hill Ventures              SHV.COM            Palo Alto
TA Associates                     TA.COM             Palo Alto
```

Contact Internet Info for more information by sending a blank e-mail message to info@internetinfo.com.

Patent Titles via E-mail

Gregory Aharonian offers a free patent information service via an e-mail Listserver. It is a weekly mailing of all patents issued by the Patent Office during the previous week. For each patent, the patent title and number is listed. Each mailing contains three files—one each with mechanical patents, chemical patents, and electronic patents.

Where to find it

patents-request@world.std.com

Gophers and WWW

As with other subject areas, Gophers provide a rich and reasonably user-friendly access to Internet information. The following sections discuss some sites that are particularly useful in the study of business.

Economic Bulletin Board

The *Economic Bulletin Board* is a huge repository of information which is available using either Gopher (login as gopher), telnet, or FTP.

The ebb FTP subdirectory or Gopher menu item provides access to many other resources. This site provides data from the Department of State's Economic Bulletin Board. The range of data available is truly amazing.

Where to find it

FTP   una.hh.lib.umich.edu
Subdirectory   /ebb

Point your Gopher to the same site.

RiceInfo

The Gopher at Rice University (*RiceInfo*) has a substantial amount of useful business related information. Point a Gopher at riceinfo.rice.edu. This Gopher, called *RiceInfo*, has information arranged by subject such as Government, Business, Political Science, and Law, in which there are more than 200 entries, including items such as About the Iowa Political Stock Market, How to Use the Government Documents Database, Other U.S. Government Gophers to Search, United States Government Programs, and Various U.S. State Laws.

J. L. Kellogg Graduate School of Management

The Gopher of the J. L. Kellogg Graduate School of Management at Northwestern University has an excellent collection of business information.

Where to find it

skew.kellogg.nwu.edu

The following screen appears:

```
    Internet Gopher Information Client v1.13

1.  Business Data Processing (Jacobs)/
2.  Minority Business Development Agency/
3.  Business Administration Building/
4.  Volume 5. Business Affairs/
5.  HF   Commerce/
6.  Intl. Chamber of Commerce Arbitration, 2-e (Craig et al)/
7.  Oregon Business/
8.  Business/
9.  Economic Bulletin Board of the U.S. Department of Commerce/
10. Business/
11. International Business Management/
12. Business and Accountancy/
13. Business/
14. alt.business.multi-level/
15. Unused - Economics and Business/
16. Aarhus School of Business/
17. relcom.fido.spb.business/
18. Commerce Business Daily/
19. Master of International Business/
20. Business & Management/
21. Business, Economics, Publishing and News/
22. Other Business School Gophers/
23. Missouri Small Business Development Centers/
24. Economics and Business/
25. Business Administration/
26. City of Tucson's Small Business Financial Info Guide/
27. About Business & Industry/
28. MBA ISM Concentration/
29. New Jersey Business Corporations (Law and Practice) (John R. MacK/
30. International Business (under development)/
31. Asia Pacific Business & Marketing Resources/
32. * Business, Economics, Marketing/
33. Business Writing & Editing/
34. Business/
35. Federal Register and Commerce Business Daily /
36. Business Services (organizationalUnit)/
37. market/
38. Faculty of Business Administration/
39. Market News Reports - Monday/
40. Business/
41. business/
42. Business/
43. Students For Responsible Business Mailing List/
```

Choosing #22 can take you to other Business School Gophers.

```
Internet Gopher Information Client v1.13
Other Business School Gophers

1.   Other Business School Gophers.
2.   Carlson School of Management, University of Minnesota Gopher/
3.   Graduate School of Business, Stanford University/
4.   Harvard Business School (Courses)(BUS) 93-94/
5.   Macquarie Graduate School of Management (Australia)/
6.   Stern School of Business, New York University/
7.   University of Texas at Austin Gopher/
8.   Wharton School, University of Pennsylvania Gopher/
```

The University of Missouri, St. Louis

The University of Missouri, St. Louis has an extensive collection of business related information available through their Thomas Jefferson Library Gopher, under the menu for Business, Economics, Marketing.

```
Internet Gopher Information Client v1.13

          * Business, Economics, Marketing

1.   Economics & Business Information via NCSU Library Without Walls/
2.   Economics & Business Information via Library of Congress MARVEL/
3.   -----------------------------------------.
4.   International Economic Information Resources/
5.   United States Economic Information Resources/
6.   --------- Other Resources -----------.
7.   AARNET Guide to Internet Business Resources.
8.   Kovacs Guide to Internet Business Resources.
9.   EDGAR project - Electronic SEC files original announcement.
10.  EDGAR gopher  - Electronic SEC files, 1/1/1994 - Present/
11.  National Trade Data Bank (NTDB) gopher/
```

Where to find it

Name	*University of Missouri—St. Louis*
Path	11/academic/busdiv
Type	1
Port	70
Host	umslvma.umsl.edu

Other Gopher Sites

This list of Gopher sites includes not only sites similar to those mentioned previously, but also examples of both business and Business School's use of Gopher.

Where to find it

Name	*All Bills about Competitive Business Practices; Restraint of Trade*
Type	`1`
Port	`7000`
Path	`1/Legislation/103/alpha/C/Competitive business practices; restraint of trade/all`
Host	`mudhoney.micro.umn.edu`

Name	*Minority Business Development Agency*
Type	`1`
Port	`7000`
Path	`1/Legislation/103/alpha/D/Department of Commerce/Minority Business Development Agency`
Host	`mudhoney.micro.umn.edu`

Name	*Oregon Business*
Type	`1`
Port	`70`
Path	`1/portland/pubs/ob`
Host	`gopher.teleport.com`

Name	*Economic Bulletin Board of the U.S. Department of Commerce*
Type	`1`
Port	`70`
Path	`1/h_huni/info_forras/hytelnet/sites2/fee000/fee056`
Host	`miat0.vein.hu`

Name	*International Business Management*
Type	`1`
Port	`70`
Path	`1/.aom/.app/.im`
Host	`mccool.cbi.msstate.edu`

Name   *Business and Accountancy*
Type   1
Port   70
Path   1/Academic departments/Business and Accountancy
Host   gopher.wfu.edu

Name   *Commerce Business Daily*
Type   1
Port   70
Path   1/Commercial Services/Commerce Business Daily
Host   teal.csn.org

Name   *Business Administration*
Type   1
Port   70
Path   1c:\nic\09crs\bus
Host   matthew.nic.bc.ca

Name   *City of Tucson's Small Business Financial Info Guide*
Type   1
Port   70
Path   1/biz/.finance
Host   econ.tucson.az.us

Name   *About Business & Industry*
Type   1
Port   70
Path   1/vv/business/about
Host   slonet.org

Name   *MBA ISM Concentration*
Type   1
Port   3004
Path   11/MBAProgram/Concentrations/MSIS
Host   gopher.cc.utexas.edu

Name   *Asia Pacific Business & Marketing Resources*
Type   1
Port   70

Path   `1/dlam/business`

Host   `hoshi.cic.sfu.ca`

Name   ** Business, Economics, Marketing*

Type   `1`

Port   `70`

Path   `1/library/refdesk/subjects/business`

host   `umslvma.umsl.edu`

Name   *Business Writing & Editing*

Type   `1`

Port   `70`

Path   `1/.browse/.METAOUTSU/.OUTSU37/.OUTSU3701/`

Host   `gopher.adp.wisc.edu`

Name   *Federal Register and Commerce Business Daily*

Type   `1`

Port   `70`

Path   `1/Federal/FedRegister`

Host   `solar.rtd.utk.edu`

Name   *Faculty of Business Administration*

Type   `1`

Port   `70`

Path   `1/cinfo/admin/inf/td/FTD/BAF`

Host   `gopher.cuhk.hk`

Name   *Students For Responsible Business Mailing List*

Type   `1`

Port   `70`

Path   `1/library/greengopher/res/econ/srb`

Host   `ecosys.drdr.Virginia.edu`

Name   *The Business And Professional Listing In The White Pages*

Type   `1`

Port   `8010`

Path   `1/govt/blue_pages/mpls`

Host   `neural.med.umn.edu`

Name   *MBA (Distance Learning Programme)*
Type   `1`
Port   `70`
Path   `1/Academic/A-E/DUBS/mbadlp`
Host   `delphi.dur.ac.uk`

Name   *Business Sources on the Net*
Type   `1`
Port   `70`
Path   `1gopher_root:[bus.bsn]`
Host   `vaxvmsx.babson.edu`

Name   *School of Business Administration*
Type   `1`
Port   `70`
Path   `1/ACADEMIC/BUSDIV`
Host   `UMSLVMA.UMSL.EDU`

Name   *Doing Business with NEARNET Members*
Type   `1`
Port   `70`
Path   `1/doing-business-with-nearnet-members`
Host   `gopher.near.net`

Name   *Business and Financial Pages*
Type   `1`
Port   `9001`
Path   `1/news/Clarinet/biz`
Host   `gopher.cc.umanitoba.ca`

Name   *market*
Type   `1`
Port   `70`
Path   `1/Network information/UCSC public ftp service/news/archive/`
        `ba/market`
Host   `darkstar.ucsc.edu`

Name   *School of Business*
Type   `1`

Port	70
Path	1/.students/.open-section/.METAREGSU/.REGSUBROWSE/.REGSU07/
Host	burrow.adp.wisc.edu

Name	*Executive MBA Students*
Type	1
Port	70
Path	1/StudentInfo/ExecMBA
Host	mercury.stern.nyu.edu

Name	*School of Business and Management*
Type	1
Port	70
Path	1/School of Business and Management
Host	astro.ocis.temple.edu

Name	*Swedish Business University*
Type	1
Port	70
Path	1/internet/hytelnet/sites1/sites1b/fi000/fi007
Host	gopher.cc.umanitoba.ca

Name	*Business, Consumers, Labor, and Trade*
Type	1
Port	70
Path	1/.dir/clinton.business.dir
Host	gopher.tamu.edu

Name	*Business Administration*
Type	1
Port	2760
Path	1VV21
Host	cwis.c-fiber.siu.edu

Name	*Texas Department of Commerce*
Type	1
Port	70
Path	1/subject/gov/state/agencies/agency/TDOC
Host	info.texas.gov

Name *Swedish Business University*

Type 1

Port 70

Path 1/hytelnet/sites1/sites1b/fi000/fi007

Host gopher.isnet.is

Name *Business and Economics*

Type 1

Port 70

Path 1/Business and Economics

Host newshost.sju.edu

Name *Business & Economics*

Type 1

Port 7000

Path 1/Research/Resources by Discipline/Business & Economics

Host picasso.cc.rochester.edu

Name *Sasin Graduate Institute of Business Administration*

Type 1

Port 70

Path 1/Specific Information/Graduate Institutes/Sasin Graduate
Institute of Business Administration

Host chulkn.chula.ac.th

Name *Minority Business Enterprise Program*

Type 1

Port 70

Path 1/MDInfo/Agencies/General Services, Department Of (DGS)/
Minority Business Enterprise Program

Host seymour.md.gov

Name *Maryland Wholesale Seafood Market*

Type 1

Port 70

Path 1/MDInfo/Agencies/Food Center Authority, Maryland (MFCA)/
Maryland Wholesale Seafood Market

Host seymour.md.gov

Name	*Business Administration*
Type	1
Port	70
Path	1/AISESnet Gopher/AISESnet Resumes/Business Administration
Host	bioc02.uthscsa.edu
Name	*FISCAL_BUSINESS*
Type	1
Port	70
Path	1/MGG/A&P_Positions/FISCAL_BUSINESS
Host	elm.circa.ufl.edu
Name	*Business Development Group*
Type	1
Port	70
Path	1/MDInfo/Agencies/General Services, Department Of (DGS)/ Minority Business Enterprise Program
Host	seymour.md.gov
Name	*Internet Business Journal*
Type	1
Port	70
Path	1/e-serials/general/business/internet-business-journal
Host	gopher.cic.net
Name	*Subject Area Resources (e.g., Biology, Education, Business)*
Type	1
Port	70
Path	1//LIBRARY/SUBJECTS
Host	UMSLVMA.UMSL.EDU
Name	*Business & Industry*
Type	1
Port	70
Path	1/other_servers/business_industry
Host	slonet.org
Name	*Students for Responsible Business*
Type	1

Port   70
Path   1/StudentInfo/MBA/StudentClubs/SRB
Host   mercury.stern.nyu.edu

Name   *Business News (Southeast Asia)*
Type   1
Port   70
Path   1/e-serials/general/business/business-news
Host   gopher.cic.net

Name   *Business Process Re-engineering—Selection*
Type   1
Port   1075
Path   1/vc/stream/section2
Host   apollo.adcom.uci.edu

Name   *relcom.commerce.transport*
Type   1
Port   74
Path   1/russian/relcom/news/relcom.commerce.transport
Host   infomeister.osc.edu

Name   *Doing Business with NREL*
Type   1
Port   70
Path   1/business
Host   nrelinfo.nrel.gov

Name   *Economics and Business*
Type   1
Port   70
Path   1/Tietopalvelut/tieteen/Gopher-Jewels/Economics_and_Business
Host   messi.uku.fi

Name   *School of Business Administration*
Type   1
Port   70
Path   1//ACADEMIC/BUSDIV
Host   UMSLVMA.UMSL.EDU

Name *Programs to Improve Manufacturing with Consultation for Small Business*

Type   `1`

Port   `70`

Path   `1/CPR-Cooperative Programs for Reinvestment/Programs Orga-nized by Goals/Programs to Improve Manufacturing/Programs to Improve Manufacturing with Consultation/Programs to Improve Manufacturing with Consultation for Small Business`

Host   `asc.dtic.dla.mil`

Name *SMALL BUSINESS ADMINISTRATION*

Type   `1`

Port   `70`

Path   `1/CPR-Cooperative Programs for Reinvestment/Programs Orga-nized by Agency/SMALL BUSINESS ADMIN`

Host   `asc.dtic.dla.mil`

Name *Economics and Business*

Type   `1`

Port   `70`

Path   `1/library/disciplines/economics`

Host   `dewey.lib.ncsu.edu`

Name *Center for Study of Japanese Business*

Type   `1`

Port   `70`

Path   `1/AcademicProgs/ResearchCenters/JapanCenter`

Host   `is-2.stern.nyu.edu`

Name *Swedish Business University*

Type   `1`

Port   `70`

Path   `1/h_huni/info_forras/hytelnet/sys000/sys014/fi007`

Host   `miat0.vein.hu`

Name *Business, Economics, Publishing and News*

Type   `1`

Port   `3050`

Path   `1m/kovac-list-ti/acadlist.7.ti`

Host   `lib-gopher.lib.indiana.edu`

Name *Business Affairs, Miscellaneous*

Type 1

Port 70

Path `1/igp/bu/busaf`

Host `ux1.cts.eiu.edu`

Name *Berkeley Business Guides*

Type 1

Port 70

Path `1/resdbs/econ/busiguides`

Host `infolib.lib.berkeley.edu`

Name *Graduate School of Business Administration*

Type 1

Port 70

Path `1/University_Information/Catalogue/`
`School_of_Business_Administration/`
`Graduate_School_of_Business_Administration`

Host `cwis.usc.edu`

Name *Missouri School/Business/Community Partnerships*

Type 1

Port 70

Path `1/el.sec.school.info/ed.progs/PARTNERS.TXT`

Host `services.dese.state.mo.us`

Name *Office of Business Analysis*

Type 1

Port 7000

Path `1/Regulations/agency/doc/100569/oba`

Host `mudhoney.micro.umn.edu`

Name *Business, Labor, and Trade*

Type 1

Port 70

Path `1/.dir/bush.business.dir`

Host `gopher.tamu.edu`

Name *Business and Innovation Centre*

Type 1

Port 70

Path 1/.gopherdir/ctu/Business-Innovation

Host isdec.vc.cvut.cz

Name *Business Information*

Type 1

Port 7001

Path 1/Refspecific/Business

Host gopher-server.cwis.uci.edu

Name *Economics and Business*

Type 1

Port 72

Path 1gopher_root1:[_jewels.12]

Host nwoca7.nwoca.ohio.gov

Name *Simon Graduate School Of Business Administration (Winter)*

Type 1

Port 7000

Path 1/Course Descriptions & Class Schedules/Course Schedules by
      College II/SIMON GRADUATE SCHOOL OF BUSINESS
      ADMINISTRATION(WINTER)

Host picasso.cc.rochester.edu

Name *Business and Economics Resources*

Type 1

Port 70

Path 1/busecon.resources

Host uncgopher.univnorthco.edu

Name *Business, Economics, Marketing*

Type 1

Port 70

Path 1/LIBRARY/REFDESK/SUBJECTS/BUSINESS

Host UMSLVMA.UMSL.EDU

Name *Institute of Business Management*

Type 1

Port 70

Path 1/General Information/College Information and Services/
Marriott School of Management/Institute of Business Management

Host ucs2.byu.edu

Name *Business and the Arts*

Type 1

Port 70

Path 1/govt/columbia/reports/CreativeColumbia/03-
BusinessAndTheArts

Host bigcat.missouri.edu

Name *Insurance, Real Estate & Business Law*

Type 1

Port 70

Path 1ftp:SHARED:CSUEB:Faculty Positions by Discipline:Business &
Management:Insur, Real Estate, Bus Law

Host edu-53.sfsu.edu

Name *Small Business Administration State Profiles*

Type 1

Port 70

Path 1//LIBRARY/GOVDOCS/STATES

Host UMSLVMA.UMSL.EDU

Name *Business and Engineering Extension*

Type 1

Port 70

Path ~db.CYNET FRAMES/fd.BEE

Host isumvs.iastate.edu

Name *0313 Business Gold: National Technology Transfer Center*

Type 1

Port 70

Path 1/h_huni/info_forras/hytelnet/new_hytelnet/oth128

Host miat0.vein.hu

Name *Department of Commerce*

Type 1

Port 7000

Path   1/Legislation/103/sort/Federal Agencies/Department of
        Commerce

Host   mudhoney.micro.umn.edu

Name   *Business Journal*

Type   1

Port   70

Path   1/portland/pubs/bj

Host   gopher.teleport.com

Name   *Centers for teaching and research in the School of Economics and
        Commerce*

Type   1

Port   70

Path   1/monash/Academic/business/clayton/centres

Host   info.monash.edu.au

Name   *Business Administration, Management Sci Group*

Type   1

Port   70

Path   1/phones/browse-by-dept/busi-admi-mana-sci-grou

Host   chaos.dac.neu.edu

Name   *Business News (Southeast Asia)*

Type   1

Port   70

Path   1/ser/alphabetic/b/business-news

Host   info.anu.edu.au

Name   *School of Business Administration*

Type   1

Port   71

Path   1/ACADEMIC/BUSDIV

Host   UMSLVMA.UMSL.EDU

Name   *College of Business*

Type   1

Port   70

Path   1/On_Campus/RegnRec/summer94/cb

Host   rodeo.uwyo.edu

Name	*Office of Inspector General—Commerce*
Type	1
Port	`7000`
Path	`1/Legislation/103/alpha/D/Department of Commerce/Office of Inspector General-Commerce`
Host	`mudhoney.micro.umn.edu`
Name	*(400) Agricultural Business Management*
Type	1
Port	`70`
Path	`1/atinet/agteach/core/core400`
Host	`caticsuf.csufresno.edu`
Name	*Business Videos*
Type	1
Port	`70`
Path	`1/lssinf/mediacat/vid/nonlang/ag/bn`
Host	`polyglot.lss.wisc.edu`
Name	*Governmental Bodies Affecting Business*
Type	1
Port	`4070`
Path	`1/other/gov`
Host	`postoffice.cob.fsu.edu`

Discussion Lists

There are hundreds of discussion lists that can provide information and opportunities for personal networking for faculty and students in the School of Business. Following are a few of the more popular ones:

Where to find it

AIS Task Force Technology Business Management

    aistftbm@cuvmc.bitnet

Commerce Business Daily-Awards

    awards-b@osuvm1.bitnet

Commercial Real Estate

```
commercial-realestate@syncomm.com
```

Society of Computational Economics

```
csemlist csemlist@hasara11.bitnet
```

Eastern Europe Business Network

```
e-europe@pucc.bitnet
e-europe@pucc.princeton.edu
```

The Electronic Journal of Finance

```
finance@templevm.bitnet
finance@vm.temple.edu
```

Great Lakes Econ Dev Research Group

```
gled@uicvm.bitnet
gled@uicvm.uic.edu uicvm.cc.uic.edu
```

Global Marketing Consortium Discussion List

```
globalmc@tamvm1.bitnet
globalmc @tamvm1.tamu.edu
```

Human Resource Development Group List

```
hrd-l@mizzou1.bitnet
hrd-l@mizzou1.missouri.edu
```

Industrial Psychology Forum

```
ioobf-l@uga.bitnet
ioobf-l@uga.cc.uga.edu
```

Industrial Design Forum

```
idforum@yorkvm1.bitnet
idforum@vm1.yorku.ca
```

Manufacturing Strategy (subscribe using the mailbase protocol)

```
mfn-strategy@mailbase.ac.uk
```

Mineral Economics and Management Society

```
memsnet@uabdpo.bitnet
memsnet@uabdpo.dpo.uab.edu
```

North American Service Industries Research

```
nasirn-l@ubvm.bitnet
nasirn-l@ubvm.cc.buffalo.edu
```

Pacific Business Researchers Forum

```
pcbr-l@uhccvm.bitnet
pcbr-l@uhccvm.uhcc.hawaii.edu
```

Progressive Economists Network

```
pen-l@uscvm.bitnet
pen-l@vm.usc.edu
```

The Financial Economics Network is a large group of related lists, with more than 5,000 subscribers. The Network consists of a master subscription, called AFA-FIN, with 40 channels or sublists:

AFA-ACCT	(Accounting and Finance)
AFA-ACTU	(Actuarial Finance)
AFA-AGE	(Gerontology Finance)
AFA-AGRI	(Agricultural Finance)
AFA-AUDT	(Auditing)
AFA-BANK	(Banking)
AFA-CORP	(Corporate Finance)
AFA-CFA	(Financial Analysts)
AFA-DER	(Derivative Securities)
AFA-DEF	(Defense/Military Reconfiguration)
AFA-ECOM	(Electronic Commerce)
AFA-ECMT	(Econometrics and Finance)
AFA-EDU	(Education Finance)
AFA-EMKT	(Emerging Markets)
AFA-ENGR	(Financial Engineering)
AFA-ENVI	(Environmental Finance)
AFA-GORE	(FinanceNet)
AFA-HEAL	(Health Finance)
AFA-INST	(Teaching/Instruction)
AFA-INT	(International Finance)
AFA-INV	(Investments)

AFA-JOB	(Job Postings)
AFA-LDC	(Bank/Finance in Less Developed Countries)
AFA-LE	(Law & Economics)
AFA-MATH	(Mathematical Finance)
AFA-MKTM	(Market Microstructure)
AFA-PERS	(Personal Finance)
AFA-PUB	(Public Finance)
AFA-REAL	(Real Estate)
AFA-REG	(Regulation)
AFA-RES	(Resumes)
AFA-RMI	(Risk Management & Insurance
AFA-S-IV	(Small Investor)
AFA-SBUS	(Small Business Finance)
AFA-SINV	(Social Investing)
AFA-SOFT	(Financial Software)
AFA-TECH	(Technological Investment Analysis)
AFA-THRY	(Financial Theory)
AFA-VCAP	(Venture Capital)
AFA-WA-R	(Real Estate in WA State)

For subscription information, contact Wayne Marr at `marrm@clemson.clemson.edu`.

Usenet Newsgroups

There are many Usenet Newsgroups of interest to faculty and students in the "B" School. Following is a sample:

Where to find it

All aspects of commerce

`alt.business.misc`

Multilevel (network) marketing businesses

`alt.business.multi-level`

Business Libraries List

`bit.listserv.buslib-l`

Eastern Europe Business Network (Moderated)

```
bit.listserv.e-europe
```

Japanese Business and Economics Network (Moderated)

```
bit.listserv.japan
```

MBA Student curriculum Discussion

```
bit.listserv.mba-l
```

AmeriCast Announcements

```
biz.americast
```

Samples of AmeriCast

```
biz.americast.samples
```

Technical bookstore & publisher advertising & information

```
biz.books.technical
```

Announcements about ClariNet

```
biz.clarinet
```

MCSNet

```
biz.comp.mcs
```

Generic commercial service postings

```
biz.comp.services
```

Generic commercial software postings

```
biz.comp.software
```

Biz Usenet configuration and administration

```
biz.config
```

Announcements from Digex

```
biz.digex.announce
```

Digital Equipment Corp. news & announcements

```
biz.digital.announce
```

Digital Equipment Corp. newsletter, catalog, and journal

```
biz.digital.articles
```

Position announcements

```
biz.jobs.offered
```

Miscellaneous postings of a commercial nature

```
biz.misc
```

New product announcements for the NeXT

```
biz.next.newprod
```

New product announcements from O'Reilly and Associates

```
biz.oreilly.announce
```

Postings about stolen merchandise

```
biz.stolen
```

Biz newsgroup test messages

```
biz.test
```

Zeos Product Announcements

```
biz.zeos.announce
```

Zeos technical support and general information

```
biz.zeos.general
```

Discussion on operating a business

```
misc.entrepreneurs
```

The International Association of Business and Commerce Students

```
soc.college.org.aiesec
```

The ClariNet Usenet newsgroup hierarchy consists of groups provided by commercial news services and other sources. A feed of the ClariNet groups requires payment of a fee and execution of a license by your Internet access provider. Many commercial and academic Internet access providers carry these ClariNet hierarchies. For more information, send e-mail to info@clarinet.com. Following are some of these ClariNet hierarchies:

Where to find it

Hourly business newsbrief from the AP

```
clari.apbl.biz.briefs
```

Headlines of top business stories

```
clari.apbl.biz.headlines
```

Hourly newsbrief from the Associated Press

```
clari.apbl.briefs
```

Chicago Board of Trade report

```
clari.apbl.reports.commodity
```

Daily gold and dollar prices

```
clari.apbl.reports.dollar_gold
```

General economic reports

```
aclari.apbl.reports.economy
```

Reports on the money supply

```
clari.apbl.reports.finance
```

Daily review of the news

```
clari.apbl.review
```

General stock market reports

```
clari.apbl.stocks
```

Market analysis from the insiders

```
clari.apbl.stocks.analysis
```

Dow Jones averages

```
clari.apbl.stocks.dow
```

ClariNews TechWire stock reports

```
clari.apbl.stocks.tech
```

World weather reports

```
clari.apbl.weather
```

Miscellaneous weather-related articles

```
clari.apbl.weather.misc
```

Major storms

```
clari.apbl.weather.storms
```

U.S. weather reports

```
clari.apbl.weather.usa
```

Business newsbriefs

```
clari.biz.briefs
```

Businesses' earnings, profits, losses

```
clari.biz.earnings
```

U.S. Economic News

```
clari.biz.economy
```

News of the world's economies

```
clari.biz.economy.world
```

Business feature stories

```
clari.biz.features
```

Interest rates, currencies, government debt

```
clari.biz.finance
```

Agriculture, fishing, forestry

```
clari.biz.industry.agriculture
```

The car and truck industry

```
clari.biz.industry.automotive
```

Airlines and airports

```
clari.biz.industry.aviation
```

Banks and S&Ls

```
clari.biz.industry.banking
```

The television and radio industry

```
clari.biz.industry.broadcasting
```

The construction industry

```
clari.biz.industry.construction
```

Consumer goods, clothing, furniture

```
clari.biz.industry.dry_goods
```

Oil, gas, coal, alternatives

```
clari.biz.industry.energy
```

Food processing, markets, restaurants

```
clari.biz.industry.food
```

The health care business

```
clari.biz.industry.health
```

The insurance industry

```
clari.biz.industry.insurance
```

Heavy industry

```
clari.biz.industry.manufacturing
```

Mining for metals, minerals

```
clari.biz.industry.mining
```

Newspapers, publishers, magazines

```
clari.biz.industry.print_media
```

Housing and real estate

```
clari.biz.industry.real_estate
```

Retail stores and shops

```
clari.biz.industry.retail
```

Consulting, brokerages, services

```
clari.biz.industry.services
```

The tourism and hotel industry

```
clari.biz.industry.tourism
```

Trains, buses, transit, shipping

```
clari.biz.industry.transportation
```

Commodity reports

```
clari.biz.market.commodities
```

Bonds, money market funds, and other instruments

```
clari.biz.market.misc
```

News affecting the financial markets

```
clari.biz.market.news
```

International Market Reports

    `clari.biz.market.report`

Asian Market Reports

    `clari.biz.market.report.asia`

European Market Reports

    `clari.biz.market.report.europe`

Overview of the markets

    `clari.biz.market.report.top`

U.S. Market Reports

    `clari.biz.market.report.usa`

New York Stock Exchange Reports

    `clari.biz.market.report.usa.nyse`

Mergers, acquisitions, and spinoffs

    `clari.biz.mergers`

Other business news

    `clari.biz.misc`

Daily review of business news

    `clari.biz.review`

High-priority business news

    `clari.biz.top`

Breaking business news

    `clari.biz.urgent`

GATT, free trade, and trade disputes

    `clari.biz.world_trade`

Commodity news and price reports

    `clari.biz.commodity`

Lawsuits and business related legal matters

    `clari.biz.courts`

Earnings and dividend reports

```
clari.biz.finance.earnings
```

Personal investing & finance

```
clari.biz.finance.personal
```

Banks and financial industries

```
clari.biz.finance.services
```

News for investors

```
clari.biz.invest
```

Strikes, unions, and labor relations

```
clari.biz.labor
```

American Stock Exchange Reports and News

```
clari.biz.market.amex
```

Dow Jones NYSE Reports

```
clari.biz.market.dow
```

NYSE Reports

```
clari.biz.market.ny
```

NASDAQ Reports

```
clari.biz.market.otc
```

Important new products and services

```
clari.biz.products
```

Newsbytes business and industry news

```
clari.nb.business
```

Canadian Business News

```
clari.world.americas.canada.business
```

Canadian Business Summaries

```
clari.canada.biz
```

Computer and technology stock prices

```
clari.tw.stocks
```

Relcom is the hierarchy of Russian-language newsgroups distributed, for the most part, in the former Soviet Union. Many of these groups also are available in Europe and Northern America.

Newsgroups under the hierarchy `relcom.commerce` contain classified advertisements, and can be valuable for researchers and students interested in the first-hand information on the economics of former Soviet Union countries. They are, however, in the Russian language and will require software that can handle Cyrillic letters. Contact Eugene Peskin at `eugene@rd.relcom.msk.su` for more information. The following is a sample of the relcom hierarchy:

Where to find it

Discussions on banking technologies

    relcom.banktech

Computer hardware

    relcom.commerce.computers

Gas, coal, oil, fuel, generators, etc.

    relcom.commerce.energy

Information services

    relcom.commerce.infoserv

Jobs offered/wanted

    relcom.commerce.jobs

Machinery, plant equipment

    relcom.commerce.machinery

Medical services, equipment, and drugs

    relcom.commerce.medicine

Metals and metal products

    relcom.commerce.metals

Credits, deposits, and currency

    relcom.commerce.money

Books and publishing services

    relcom.commerce.publishing

Stocks and bonds

    relcom.commerce.stocks

Money matters in the former Soviet Union

    relcom.currency

Discussion on market development /ASMP/

    relcom.infomarket.talk

Political & economic news digest

    relcom.spbnews

Investments and the handling of money

    misc.invest

Forum for sharing info about stocks and options

    misc.invest.stocks

Guides

There are a number of useful guides to business information available online via the Internet. These guides list, often with annotations, online resources within a certain topic or area of interest.

A good general guide, *Government Sources of Business and Economic Information on the Internet*, by Terese Austin and Kim Tsang is available via anonymous FTP at una.hh.lib.umich.edu in the subdirectory /inetdirsstacks as file govdocs:tsangaustin. You also can find this guide on many Gophers. The URL for the guides on the University of Michigan Gopher is gopher://una.hh.lib.umich.edu/00/inetdirsstacks.

Another business-oriented guide which is organized by subject is the Business Sources On The Net. This guide is available via anonymous ftp to ksuvxa.kent.edu in the /library sub-directory. BSN also is available at the Kent State University Gopher refmac.kent.edu 70 under business sources on the net. The following subjects are currently covered:

- Accounting and Taxation
- Computer Science (as it relates to business)
- Corporate Finance and Banking
- Economics
- Foreign Statistics, Economic Trends and International Management

- General Business Internet Sources
- Human Resources and Personnel Management
- Management Science, Statistical Methods and Productions/Operations
- Management
- Management and the Management of Public and Nonprofit Organizations

Resources for Economists on the Internet, by Bill Goffe, is a helpful guide available through the Usenet archives at `rtfm.mit.edu` as `econ-resources-faq` in the `/pub/usenet-by-groups/sci.econ.research` subdirectory, and through the University of Michigan as mentioned elsewhere.

The Law School—L1 And After

The quantity and breadth of the material available on the Internet to law students and professors on the Internet is amazing. There are current citations and rulings, electronic journals, Supreme Court rulings and history, state and local legal information, and information on legal matters ranging from rental contracts to maritime and space law. These resources include the following:

- Gophers and WWW sites
- FTP sites
- Guides
- Discussion lists
- Usenet newsgroups
- telnet sites

Telnet Sites

While many law-oriented sites now offer services directly through Gopher or WWW, there are some sites best accessed through telnet. Here are two examples:

Where to find it

Washburn University Law Library LAWNET

Telnet	`acc.wuacc.edu`
Login	`lawnet`

This is a World Wide Web server containing several resources of interest to law-yers and law librarians, such as bibliographies and pathfinders on various topics created by advanced legal research students at Washburn University Law School.

Where to find it

Cleveland Free-Net

Telnet	freenet-in-a.cwru.edu
	freenet-in-b.cwru.edu
	freenet-in-c.cwru.edu
Login	guest

The Cleveland Free-Net is the largest and most famous site of the *National Public Telecomputing Network* (NPTN). NPTN promotes the creation of community computer systems throughout the United States and Canada.

Sponsored by Case Western Reserve University, the Cleveland Free-Net is organized on the model of a city, so it includes a Medical Arts Building, a Courthouse and Government Center, a Post Office, and so on. There is a collection of Supreme Court materials at this site provided through Project HERMES.

Project

Goal: To increase awareness of the depth and breadth of legal information available on the Internet.

An assignment for Constitutional Law might include a debate regarding upcoming Supreme Court decisions, to be researched solely using the Internet.

You are to prepare yourself to debate the key elements and precedence for the assigned case.

1. Locate Gopher, WWW, telnet, and FTP sites containing information on Supreme Court decisions.
2. Retrieve related information and documents.
3. Analyze the materials, and prepare the case.
4. Prepare a 15 page case brief.
5. Post a two page version of the brief to the class conference.
6. Prepare your oral arguments for class.

Following are some hints for resources for this assignment:

1. Try the Gophers at the University of Massachusetts, and Pennsylvania State University.

Name	*UNITED STATES SUPREME COURT JUDICIAL DATABASE, 1953-1989 TERMS*
Type	0
Port	4999
Path	0/data_files/all_else/ICP_9422
Host	titan.ucs.umass.edu

Name	*Index to Supreme Court Decisions*
Type	0
Port	70
Path	1gopher_root:[_shelves._govandlaw._legalinfo]
Host	psulias.psu.edu

2. Look at the following two FTP sites:

FTP	ftp.cwru.edu
Login	anonymous
Password	*your_e-mail_address*
Subdirectory	/hermes

FTP	ftp.uu.net
Login	anonymous
Password	*your_e-mail_address*
Subdirectory	/government/usa/supreme-court

3. Do a Veronica search for supreme court. Following is a small percent of the documents and directories found by Veronica in a recent search:

```
Internet Gopher Information Client v1.13
Search GopherSpace by Title word(s) (via NYSERNet): supreme court
      1.   nc-supreme-court.src.gz.
      2.   supreme-court.src.gz.
      3.   U.S. Supreme Court Decisions/
      4.   U.S. Supreme Court Decisions/
      5.   United States Supreme Court/
      6.   The Supreme Court/
      7.   Project Hermes:  U.S. Supreme Court Opinions.
      8.   The Poor in Court: The Legal Services Program
and Supreme Court Decisions
      9.   About Project Hermes: U.S. Supreme Court
Opinions.
```

```
    10. Project Hermes: U.S. Supreme Court Opinions/
    11. Supreme Court Cases/
    12. Index to Supreme Court Decisions.
    13. Index to Supreme Court Decisions.
    14. Supreme Court /
    15. Supreme Court /
    16. UNITED STATES SUPREME COURT JUSTICES
BIOGRAPHICAL DATA, 1789-1958
    17. SUPREME COURT CERTIORARI STUDY, 1947-1956
    18. UNITED STATES SUPREME COURT JUDICIAL DATABASE,
1953-1989 TERMS
    19. ABC NEWS SUPREME COURT NOMINATION POLL, JULY
1991
    20. 94-0077 Supreme Court decisions.
    21. 94-0089 Finding Supreme Court Opinions.
    22. 94-0090 More on Supreme court Opinions.
    23. 94-0103 Supreme Court footnotes.
    24. Supreme Court Opinions and Decisions/
    25. 94.03.22.MEDIA ADVISORY - California Supreme
Court Justice Malcolm
    26. Supreme_Court-Judicial_Politics/
    27. Supreme Court Decisions/
    28. Supreme Court Cases, Briefs, and Records.
    29. Supreme Court Rulings (CWRU)/
    30. Government, 17 Supreme Court Decision on 1st
Amendment Right (11).
    31. Government; Researching State and Supreme Court
decisions (11-12).
    32. U.S. History; How the Supreme Court affects our
freedoms (9).
    33. Cass Gilbert, Supreme Court, Washington, D.C.;
1935;  <Picture>
    34. 93-09-28 New Biography of Oliver Wendell Holmes
Jr.
    35. 94-05-18 Biography of Justice Lewis Powell Draws
on Personal Files...
    36. 93-10-13-11: Supreme Court, Civil Rights,.
    37. 94-02-06-03: ~ Supreme Court Death Penalty Demo.
    38. 94-01-31-11: Supreme Court Death Penalty Demo.
Wow, now that is handy, a picture of Cass Gilbert from 1935.
```

4. Try the WWW site at Cornell Law School (fatty.law.cornell.edu)—it is quite extensive. Following is their homepage as seen in Lynx. Notice that items appear in brackets, such as [Image], and in Mosaic, these items would appear in a graphical way instead:

```
Legal Information Institute (p1 of 4)
  WWW-SITE MAINTAINED BY
The Legal Information Institute
Cornell Law School [IMAGE]

   This WWW-server integrates both the Gopher-based and the WWW-based
offerings of the Legal Information Institute (LII), Cornell Law School.
```

```
All Internet hypertext (HTML) publications of the LII are mounted here,
with links to other relevant legal materials on the LII's Gopher server
and elsewhere on the Internet.
    This server offers the LII's hypertext front-end to recent Supreme Court
decisions (which are distributed on the day of decision under project Hermes)
and the LII's e-mail address directory of faculty and staff at U.S. law
schools. It also is host to the Nasdaq Financial Executive Journal. It
provides full information about Cello, the LII's Internet browser, and
about LII published hypertext law materials on disk.

    New Items Main Menus About WWW and LII Other WWW Sources
SUPREME COURT DECISIONS (p1 of 2)

[Credits and Conditions] [Context] [Structure] [Your Comments]
_____

    ____
    A Hypertext Publication
    of LII - Legal Information Institute - Cornell Law School
_____
DECISIONS OF THE U.S. SUPREME COURT
    Recent Decisions
 1990-1994
        Indexed by Topic
        Key Word Search
 Most Recent Term (Oct. 1993 - June 1994)
        Arrayed by Date of Decision
      SUPREME COURT DECISIONS
  1994   Indexed by Party Name: First Party, Second Party
  1993   Indexed by Party Name: First Party, Second Party
  1992   Indexed by Party Name: First Party, Second Party
  1991   Indexed by Party Name: First Party, Second Party
  1990   Indexed by Party Name: First Party, Second Party
    Historic Decisions
  * Roe v. Wade
```

5. Explore Washington and Lee using Gopher or WWW

6. Do a WebCrawler WebQuery.

Gopher and Web Resources

There are a number of particularly good Gopher and WWW sites of interest to those in the Law School. These are discussed in the following sections.

Washington and Lee Law Library Netserver

One of the most complete and useful sites for legal information and linkages is the Washington and Lee Law Library. You can reach it through a variety of means including, Gopher and WWW (http://honor.uc.wlu.edu:1020), or telnet (`liberty.uc.wlu.edu`, login as `lawlib`). Following is the WWW presentation of the beginning of the menu:

```
Washington and Lee Law Library

http://honor.uc.wlu.edu/

Law resources


    * ..Restrict by Subject
    * ..Restrict by Type (Telnet, Gopher, WWW)
    * ..Sort: Date (for date coded entries) [435 items]
    * ..Sort: Geographic [435 items]
    * AALS Section on Law & Computers, Uses of the Internet (Jan 1993
      Meeting)
    * About Villanova Tax Law Compendium
    * ACCESS: Legislative Information Service, Hawaii State Legislature
      (Login: => note: no login script needed;)
    * ACCORD (Advisory Committee on Copyright Registration and Deposit)
    * ACLU (American Civil Liberties Union) [6601]
    * Admissibility in Federal Courts of Hypnotically Assisted
      Testimony...
    * Agreement Relating to the International Telecommunications
      Satellite Organization "INTELSAT" (with annexes and Operating
      Agreement)(1971)
    * Alaska's Statewide Library Electronic Doorway
      (Login: => note: no login script needed;)
    * American University, Washington College of Law, Library (LEAGLE)
      (Login: => at login;enter library;)
* American University, Washington College of Law
    * Americans With Disabilities Act
    * Ananse International Trade Law
    * Atmosphere and Space
    * Available Information from UNCJIN
    * Aviation
    * Bamako Convention on the Ban of the Import into Africa and the
      Control of Transboundary Movement and Management of Hazardous
      Wastes Within Africa (1991)
    * Basic Law of Hong Kong (FTP)
    * Bell Atlantic Gopher
    * Berkeley Software Design, Inc. [Berkeley Unix] (BSDI)
    * BH2B8C - Copyright FAQ in 6 parts
    * Bodleian Law Library, Oxford University (OLIS)
      (Login: => at terminal;enter VT100;)
    * Boston University, Library
      (Login: => at login;enter library;)
    * ..Show Remaining 413 Items
    * ..Show All 435 Items
    * ..Text copy of links

This is a searchable index.  Use 's' to search
  Arrow keys: Up and Down to move. Right to follow a link; Left to go back.
  H)elp O)ptions P)rint G)o M)ain screen Q)uit /=search [delete]=history list
```

Cornell University School of Law

The Cornell University School of Law has an extensive collection of useful and interesting information. The WWW/Mosaic server is particularly easy to use.

Where to find it

Cornell University School of Law

```
http://fatty.law.cornell.edu
```

A major law school publishing project using WWW is under development by the Legal Information Institute at Cornell University School of Law. This site includes hypertext versions of the U.C.C., Federal Intellectual Property statutes, U.S. Supreme Court opinions, and other items. The site also is accessible by way of Gopher.

```
Internet Gopher Information Client v1.13

                  Cornell Law School (experimental)

     1.  Cornell Law School Information/
     2.  Directory of Legal Academia/
     3.  Discussions and Listserv Archives/
     4.  U.S. Law: Primary Documents and Commentary/
     5.  Foreign and International Law: Primary Documents and Commentary/
     6.  Other References Useful in Legal Education and Research/
     7.  Government (US) and Agency Information/
     8.  Information Services: Academic Institutions/
     9.  Library Resources (online catalogs)/
     10. Periodicals, News, and Journals/
     11. Other Gophers and Information Services/
     12. WAIS-based information/
     13. Internet (FTP sources, Archie, listserv directory)/
     14. Locators (where to find people and things)/
     15. Miscellaneous/
     16. Other Internet Law Sites/
     17. +--+ Please give us feedback! +--+.
```

Item #4 offers a menu for primary documents and commentary on U.S. Law:

```
Internet Gopher Information Client v1.13

              U.S. Law: Primary Documents and Commentary

     1.  Copyright Law/
     2.  Patent Law/
     3.  Trademark Law/
```

```
    4.  Commercial Law/
    5.  Americans With Disabilities Act (and related material)/
    6.  Laws relating to the Net and Computer Use (EFF)/
    7.  State and Local Government Information (U.S.)/
    8.  Supreme Court Decisions (WWW) <TEL>
    9.  WorldWideWeb material (LII) <TEL>
```

From the main menu again, choose #6, Other Useful References In Legal Educa-tion And Research to display this menu:

```
Internet Gopher Information Client v1.13

         Other References Useful in Legal Education and Research

  --> 1.  Basic Legal Citation/
      2.  Citation Standards by Jurisdiction/
      3.  ABA Draft Accreditation Standards for Law Libraries/
      4.  American Philosophical Association BBS <TEL>
      5.  Columbia Law School Directory of Legal Employers (text search) <?>
      6.  Commerce Business Daily/
      7.  Directory of Legal Academia/
      8.  Economics resources/
      9.  Historical documents/
     10.  Law and Politics Book Review/
     11.  Tables of Contents of International Legal Journals/
```

Other WWW and Gopher Sites of Interest

The Indiana University School of Law provides access to an electronic version of the Federal Communications Law Journal, and other legal sources.

Where to find it

Indiana University School of Law

    http://www.law.indiana.edu

This Saint Louis University Law Library site provides an extensive number of Gopher pointers to legal information (numbering in excess of 1,100). Following is a sample of Gopher sites of interest:

Where to find it

The Saint Louis University Law Library

    http://lawlib.slu.edu/home.html

All of these are located at mudhoney.micro.umn.edu 7000.

Where to find it

Name *Legal Services Corporation*
Path `1/Legislation/103/alpha/D/Department of Veterans Affairs/ Legal Services Corporation`

Name *Administrative law, rules and procedure*
Path `1/Legislation/103/alpha/A/Administrative law, rules and procedure`

Name *Federal Law Enforcement Training Center*
Path `1/Legislation/103/alpha/F/Federal Law Enforcement Training Center`

Name *Federal law enforcement officers*
Path `1/Legislation/103/alpha/F/Federal law enforcement officers`

Name *International Law*
Path `1/Legislation/103/sort/Foreign relations/International law`

Name *Legal Division*
Path `1/Regulations/agency/iegc/fdic/ld`

Name *Law enforcement policy and management*
Path `1/Legislation/103/alpha/L/Law enforcement policy and manage-ment`

Name *Administrative law, rules and procedure*
Path `1/Legislation/103/sort/Governmental affairs/Administrative law, rules and procedure`

Name *University of Pennsylvania Law School Library*
Path `1/h_huni/info_forras/hytelnet/sys000/sys007/us180`

Name *0327 Washington College of Law*
Path `1/h_huni/info_forras/hytelnet/new_hytelnet/us524`

Name *George Washington University Law Center*
Path `1/h_ekez/info_forras/hytelnet/sys000/sys007/us463`

Name *Catholic University of America Law Library*
Path `1/h_noekez/info_forras/hytelnet/sys000/sys007/us350`

Name *John Marshall Law School*
Path `1/h_huni/info_forras/hytelnet/sys000/sys007/us351`

Name   *Legal Information Institute Directory Server*

Path   `1/h_ekez/info_forras/hytelnet/sites2/dir000/dir017`

Name   *Georgetown University Law Library*

Path   `1/h_huni/info_forras/hytelnet/sys000/sys007/us462`

Name   *New York University Law Library (JULIUS)*

Path   `1/h_ekez/info_forras/hytelnet/sys000/sys007/us166`

The following Gophers are located at various sites throughout the world:

Where to find it

Name   *Faculty of Law*

Type   `1`

Port   `70`

Path   `1gopher_root:[QUT.LAW.LAWI]`

Host   `GOPHER.QUT.EDU.AU`

Name   *Government and Law*

Type   `1`

Port   `70`

Path   `1/Schoolhouse/carrels/Law`

Host   `crusher.bev.net`

Name   *Law Library Bulletin*

Type   `1`

Port   `70`

Path   `1/Library Services/pub/Law Library Bulletin`

Host   `info.utas.edu.au`

Name   *Law and Legislation*

Type   `1`

Port   `70`

Path   `11/starters/library/social/law`

Host   `cln.etc.bc.ca`

Name   *West's Legal Directory via WAIS*

Type   `1`

Port   `70`

```
Path    .dir/wld
Host    wld.westlaw.com

Name    Legal-Law Information
Type    1
Port    70
Path    1/dirofdirs/legal
Host    ds2.internic.net

Name    Law Related Information
Type    1
Port    70
Path    1e:/usm/law/lri
Host    gopher.usmacs.maine.edu

Name    American Association of Law Libraries—Legal Info Service
Type    1
Port    70
Path    1/e-serials/alphabetic/a/aall-lisp
Host    gopher.cic.net

Name    Law and Legal
Type    1
Port    99
Path    1/directory_780/directory_781
Host    hnt.com

Name    0214 Yale University Law Library
Type    1
Port    9001
Path    1/internet/hytelnet/new_hytelnet/us433
Host    gopher.cc.umanitoba.ca

Name    United States Legal Materials
Type    1
Port    70
Path    1/library/reference/guides/subguides/uslegal
Host    dewey.lib.ncsu.edu
```

Name   *George Washington University Law Center*

Type   1

Port   70

Path   1/hytelnet/sites1/sites1a/us000/us000law/us463

Host   gopher.isnet.is

Name   *Villanova Tax Law Compendium*

Type   1

Port   70

Path   1/.taxlaw/

Host   ming.law.vill.edu

Name   *VII_-_International_Law*

Type   1

Port   70

Path   1/.united.nations/UN_Background_Info/Basic_Facts_about_UN/
       VII_-_International_Law

Host   mirna.together.uvm.edu

Name   *Legal Studies*

Type   1

Port   70

Path   1/gophers/umass/law

Host   gopher.ucs.umass.edu

Name   *Fletcher School of Law & Diplomacy (Multilateral Conventions)*

Type   1

Port   70

Path   ftp:jade.tufts.edu@pub/diplomacy/

Host   infoserver.ciesin.org

Name   *Law_of_the_Sea*

Type   1

Port   70

Path   1/University_Information/News_Service/Experts_Directory/
       Experts_Directory/Law/Law_of_the_Sea

Host   cwis.usc.edu

Name   *0214 University of Southern California Law Library*

Type   1

Port   70

Path   1/internet/hytelnet/new_hytelnet/us504

Host   gopher.cc.umanitoba.ca

Name   *Legal Foundations*

Type   1

Port   1901

Path   1/other/national-orgs/ngltf/ftr/ngltf-ftr/legal

Host   uclink.berkeley.edu

Name   *Constitutional_Law*

Type   1

Port   70

Path   1/University_Information/News_Service/Experts_Directory/
       Experts_Directory/Law/Constitutional_Law

Host   cwis.usc.edu

Name   *Religion_&_the_Law*

Type   1

Port   70

Path   1/University_Information/News_Service/Experts_Directory/
       Experts_Directory/Law/Religion_&_the_Law

Host   cwis.usc.edu

Name   *The Villanova Information Law Chronicle*

Type   1

Port   70

Path   1/.chron/

Host   ming.law.vill.edu

Name   *Political Science, Law, Government*

Type   1

Port   70

Path   1gopher_root:[polisci]

Host   gopher.gvltec.edu

Name   *Hamline University Law Library*

Type   1

Port   70

Path   1/internet/hytelnet/sites1/sites1a/us000/us000law/us324

Host   gopher.cc.umanitoba.ca

Name   *Internet Law Related Libraries*

Type   1

Port   70

Path   pub/internetlibraries

Host   holmes.law.cwru.edu

Name   *Foreign Law Programs*

Type   1

Port   70

Path   1/Legal Information Resources/Legal Education Resources/
       Foreign Law Programs

Host   trout.ab.umd.edu

Name   *Case Law (Court Reports)*

Type   1

Port   70

Path   1/departments/Library/finding/general/Government informa-
       tion/canada/Law/Case Law (Court Reports)

Host   watserv2.uwaterloo.ca

Name   *Current Index to Legal Periodicals*

Type   1

Port   70

Path   1/.library/.periodicals/.cilp

Host   lawnext.uchicago.edu

Name   *Human Rights and International Law Resources*

Type   1

Port   70

Path   1gopher$root:[data21._library_services._lawlib._intlaw]

Host   sluava.slu.edu

Name   *Antitrust_Law*

Type   1

Port   70

Path   1/University_Information/News_Service/Experts_Directory/
       Experts_Directory/Law/Antitrust_Law

Host   cwis.usc.edu

Name	*0214 Temple University School of Law Library*
Type	1
Port	9001
Path	1/internet/hytelnet/new_hytelnet/us405
Host	gopher.cc.umanitoba.ca

Name	*Legal Sources*
Type	1
Port	70
Path	1s/SCOUG/legal
Host	bairn.gslis.ucla.edu

Name	*Widener University School of Law*
Type	1
Port	70
Path	1/hytelnet/sys000/sys007/us349
Host	gopher.isnet.is

Name	*Law and Politics Book Review*
Type	1
Port	70
Path	1/Northwestern/journal
Host	casbah.acns.nwu.edu

Name	*Law and Related Guides*
Type	1
Port	70
Path	1/infoguide/resources/law
Host	ds.internic.net

Name	*Law & Legal Issues*
Type	1
Port	70
Path	1/Resources by Discipline/Law & Legal Issues
Host	seagull.rtd.com

Name	*Legal or Law related*
Type	1

Port 70

Path 1/Gopher_Jewels/Gopher_Jewels/Legal_or_Law_related

Host cwis.usc.edu

Name *New York University Law Library (JULIUS)*

Type 1

Port 70

Path 1/hytelnet/sites1/sites1a/us000/us000law/us166

Host gopher.isnet.is

Name *Temple University School of Law Library*

Type 1

Port 70

Path 1/internet/hytelnet/sys000/sys007/us405

Host gopher.cc.umanitoba.ca

Name *Law Topics*

Type 1

Port 70

Path 1/gov/law/progressive

Host gopher.igc.apc.org

Name *Law Students' Society (LSS)*

Type 1

Port 70

Path 1/Faculty Information/Faculty of Law/Law Students' Society
(LSS)

Host gopher.queensu.ca

Name *Legal Studies Archives*

Type 1

Port 70

Path 1/academic/law/archives

Host gopher.ucs.umass.edu

Name *Other Law Sources and Services*

Type 1

Port 70

Path 1/English/lawsites

Host gopher.droit.UMontreal.CA

Name   *American Journal of International Law*
Type   1
Port   2100
Path   1/category/international/ajil
Host   gopher.internet.com

Name   *California Law and Regulations*
Type   1
Port   70
Path   1/policy/ca
Host   netinfo.berkeley.edu

Name   *Copyright Law*
Type   1
Port   70
Path   1/uslaw/copyright
Host   gopher.law.cornell.edu

Name   *Legal Bytes*
Type   1
Port   70
Path   1/e-serials/alphabetic/l/legal-bytes
Host   gopher.cic.net

Name   *0214 University of Pennsylvania Law School Library*
Type   1
Port   70
Path   1/internet/hytelnet/new_hytelnet/us180
Host   gopher.cc.umanitoba.ca

Name   *0214 WASHLAW: A Law related "Gopher" System*
Type   1
Port   9001
Path   1/internet/hytelnet/new_hytelnet/oth073
Host   gopher.cc.umanitoba.ca

Name   *Courses on Women and the law*
Type   1
Port   70
Path   pub/women+law/courses
Host   holmes.law.cwru.edu

Name   *Law Enforcement*

Type   1

Port   70

Path   1/vv/public_safety/law

Host   slonet.org

Name   *University of Southern California Law Library*

Type   1

Port   70

Path   1/hytelnet/sys000/sys007/us504

Host   gopher.isnet.is

Name   *College of Law*

Type   1

Port   70

Path   1/depart/College of Law

Host   jupiter.willamette.edu

Name   *0214 Indiana University School of Law WWW Server (WWW)*

Type   1

Port   70

Path   1/internet/hytelnet/new_hytelnet/www010

Host   gopher.cc.umanitoba.ca

Name   *Pre-Law, Legislation, Court Decisions*

Type   1

Port   70

Path   1/readings/social-sciences/law

Host   grace.skidmore.edu

Name   *University of Texas at Austin Tarlton Law Library (TALLONS)*

Type   1

Port   70

Path   1/hytelnet/sys000/sys007/us227

Host   gopher.isnet.is

Name   *Media_Law*

Type   1

Port   70

Path   1/University_Information/News_Service/Experts_Directory/
        Experts_Directory/Law/Media_Law

Host	cwis.usc.edu
Name	*united_kingdom.law*
Type	1
Port	70
Path	m/Law Documents/Collection of various Laws (mainly from U.S.)/united_kingdom.law
Host	sulaw.law.su.oz.au
Name	*Foreign and International Law Librarians Archive*
Type	1
Port	70
Path	1/listservs/intlaw
Host	gopher.law.cornell.edu
Name	*Law related items*
Type	1
Port	70
Path	GOPHER:SUBJ_TREE:LAW:
Host	gopher.ufsia.ac.be
Name	*University of New Mexico Law School*
Type	1
Port	70
Path	1/hytelnet/sys000/sys007/us228
Host	gopher.isnet.is
Name	*0214 Catholic University of America Law Library*
Type	1
Port	9001
Path	1/internet/hytelnet/new_hytelnet/us350
Host	gopher.cc.umanitoba.ca
Name	*Judiciary & Law Enforcement*
Type	1
Port	1250
Path	1/.gov/.nat/.judge
Host	garnet.berkeley.edu

Name *John Marshall Law School*

Type 1

Port 70

Path `1/hytelnet/sys000/sys007/us351`

Host `gopher.isnet.is`

Name *Department of Mental Health Law and Policy*

Type 1

Port 70

Path `1/mhlp`

Host `hal.fmhi.usf.edu`

Name *Law Library Information*

Type 1

Port 70

Path `1e:/usm/law/lib`

Host `gopher.usmacs.maine.edu`

Name *Administrative Law*

Type 1

Port 70

Path `1/Legal Information Resources/Research Resources/Resources by Subject/Administrative Law`

Host `trout.ab.umd.edu`

Name *Browse Courses in BUSINESS LAW*

Type 0+

Port 70

Path `0/student/COURSES/B-C/BLAW`

Host `gopher.Hawaii.Edu`

Name *Legal and Economic Information on the Internet*

Type 1

Port 70

Path `1/.internet`

Host `lawnext.uchicago.edu`

Name *prison-legal-news*

Type 1

Port 70

Path	1/ser/alphabetic/p/prison-legal-news
Host	info.anu.edu.au

Name	*Law Library*
Type	1
Port	70
Path	1/monash/Library/newbooks/law
Host	info.monash.edu.au

Name	*The CWRU Law School Gopher*
Type	0
Port	70
Path	0h/about
Host	holmes.law.cwru.edu

Name	*New York State Department of Law*
Type	1
Port	70
Path	1/New York State Government Information Locator/New York State Executive Branch/New York State Department of Law
Host	unix2.nysed.gov

Name	*Law Library Newsletter*
Type	1
Port	70
Path	1e:/usm/law/lib/cn
Host	gopher.usmacs.maine.edu

Name	*Legal Studies Course Syllabi*
Type	1
Port	70
Path	1/academic/law/archives/syllabi
Host	gopher.ucs.umass.edu

Name	*Political Science and Law*
Type	1
Port	9999
Path	1gopher_root:[academic.poly]
Host	merlin.hood.edu

Name   *World Law Index*
Type   1
Port   70
Path   0/Library_Resources/experimental/.forms/Stanford23
Host   jupiter.cc.gettysburg.edu

Name   *Canadian Academic Law Libraries Resource Sharing*
Type   1
Port   70
Path   1/Faculty Information/Faculty of Law/Canadian Academic Law
        Libraries Resource Sharing
Host   gopher.queensu.ca

Name   *Butterworth Legal Publishers*
Type   1
Port   4323
Path   g2go4 gopher.infor.COM 4800 1
Host   thor.ece.uc.edu

Name   *Law Library Resources (On Line Catalogues)*
Type   1
Port   70
Path   1/Law Library Resources (On Line Catalogues)
Host   sulaw.law.su.oz.au

Discussion Lists

There are hundreds of discussion groups which specifically relate to the concerns of law and the legal profession. Each has its own personality and quality level. There is no substitute for signing up temporarily to each to evaluate it's value to you. Following are some of the top contenders:

Where to find it

Lists with Listserv subscription protocols

Administrative Law teaching (law professors)

    adminlaw@chicagokent.kentlaw.edu

Agricultural Law

    aglaw-l@acc.wuacc.edu

Artificial Intelligence & Law

    ail-l@austin.onu.edu

Bioethics Law

    bioethicslaw-l@acc.wuacc.edu

AALS Section on Business Associations

    bizlaw-l@umab.bitnet

Computer-Assisted Legal Instruction List

    cali-l@chicagokent.kentlaw.edu

Journal of Criminal Justice and Popular Culture

    cjmovies@albany.bitnet

Criminal Justice Discussion

    cjust-l@iubvm.bitnet

Civil Rights Discussion Group (law professors)

    civilrts@chicagokent.kentlaw.edu

Copyright Discussion List

    cni-copyright@cni.org

Computers and Legal Education

    comlaw-l@ualtavm.bitnet

Communications Law

    comlaw-l@acc.wuacc.edu

Teaching and Applications of Contracts Law

    contracts@austin.onu.edu

Computer Professionals for Social Responsibility

    cpsr@gwuvm.bitnet

Law and Policy of Computer Networks

    cyberia-l@listserv.cc.wm.edu

Dispute Resolution

    `dispute-res@fatty.law.cornell.edu`

Law and Economics

    `econlaw@gmu.edu`

Education law

    `edlaw@ukcc.uky.edu`

Family Law

    `familylaw-l@acc.wuacc.edu`

Forensic Economics list

    `forensiceconomics-l@acc.wuacc.edu`

Federal Taxation/Accounting

    `fedtax-l@shsu.bitnet`

Discussions about Feminist Legal Issues

    `femjur@suvm.bitnet`

Health Law

    `healthlaw-l@acc.wuacc.edu`

History of Law (Feudal, Common, Canon)

    `hislaw-l@ulkyvm.bitnet`

History of Law (general)

    `h-law@uicvm.bitnet`

Human Rights Law

    `humanrights-l@acc.wuacc.edu`

International Law Students Association list

    `ilsa-l@chicagokent.kentlaw.edu`

Jewish Law Professors' List

    `jewishlawprof-l@acc.wuacc.edu`

Jewish Law Students List

    `jls@austin.onu.edu`

Law and Society

    `lawand@polecat.law.indiana.edu`

Clinical law teaching and clinical legal education

    `lawclinic@acc.wuacc.edu`

Law School Deans and Associate Deans

    `lawdeans-l@acc.wuacc.edu`

Law job postings

    `lawjobs-l@acc.wuacc.edu`

Law Journal and Law Review Discussion List

    `lawjournal-l@acc.wuacc.edu`

Law school professors only

    `lawprof@chicagokent.kentlaw.edu`

Internet Resources on Law

    `lawsrc-l@fatty.law.cornell.edu`

Law School Financial Aid

    `lawaid@rutvm1.bitnet`

Law School Discussion List

    `lawsch-l@auvm.bitnet`

Legal writing instructors

    `legwri-l@chicagokent.kentlaw.edu`

Oil and Gas Law List

    `oilgaslaw-l@acc.wuacc.edu`

Psychology and Law

    `psylaw-l@utepa.bitnet`

Law School Computer Service Providers

    `teknoids@fatty.law.cornell.edu`

Telecommunications Regulation

    `telecomreg@relay.adp.wisc.edu`

Law of Torts

```
tortslaw@ulkyvm.bitnet
```

Following is a list with Majordomo subscription protocols:

Where to find it

Issues for Non-Profit Organizations

```
usnonprofit-l@rain.org
```

Following is a list using mailserv subscription protocols:

Where to find it

Environmental law students

```
envirolaw@oregon.uoregon.edu
```

Environmental law professors

```
envlawprofs@oregon.uoregon.edu
```

SouthWest Association of Law Libraries

```
swall-l@post-office.uh.edu
```

Following are lists using the mailbase (join vs subscribe) protocol in the UK:

Where to find it

Law and Economics Law

```
economics@mailbase.ac.uk
```

European Law

```
europe@mailbase.ac.uk
```

Family Law, especially U.K. and Europe Law

```
family@mailbase.ac.uk
```

UK Public/Constitutional Law

```
public@mailbase.ac.uk
```

Following are lists using the listname-request format (`forens-l-request@`):

Where to find it

Forensic Medicine and Science

> `forens-l@acc.fau.edu`

Canadian Law and Society

> `lawsoc-l@cc.umanitoba.ca`

Usenet Newsgroups

There are quite a few Usenet newsgroups that are of interest to law students and lawyers. Quality varies from group to group and from time to time. Here are some interesting lists for those in the Law School:

> alt.child-support
> alt.dads-rights
> alt.discrimination
> alt.politics.usa.constitution (constitutional law)
> alt.society.civil-liberty
> alt.tv.la-law
> clari.news.issues.civil_rights
> clari.news.law
> clari.news.law.civil
> clari.news.law.crime
> clari.news.law.crime.sex
> clari.news.law.crime.trial
> clari.news.law.crime.violent
> clari.news.law.drugs
> clari.news.law.investigation
> clari.news.law.police
> clari.news.law.prison
> clari.news.law.profession
> clari.news.law.supreme
> comp.patents (computers and patents, also software patents)
> comp.software.licensing

gnu.misc.discuss (some patent and copyright discussions)

misc.consumers (legal issues of consumer recourse arise)

misc.int-property (intellectual property rights)

misc.legal (miscellaneous legal issues)

misc.legal.moderated ("The Legal List" is posted here)

misc.legal.computing (legal issues related to computers)

misc.taxes (Tax laws and advice)

usa-today.law (the legal portion of a paid information feed)

FTP Sites

While most of the archives at FTP sites are accessible more conveniently via Gopher, there are two sites that are worth browsing if you are researching the Supreme Court:

Where to find it

FTP	`ftp.cwru.edu`
Login	`anonymous`
Password	*your e-mail address*
Subdirectory	`/hermes`
FTP	`ftp.uu.net`
Login	`anonymous`
Password	*your e-mail address*
Subdirectory	`/government/usa/supreme-court`

Guides of Interest to Legal Scholars

The Clearinghouse of Subject Oriented Guides maintains several guides of law and legal information, either by way of Gopher at `una.hh.lib.umich.edu`, or FTP to the same address and look in the `/inetdirsstacks` subdirectory. In addition, here are some guides and sites that may prove useful:

■ "Where to Start" for New Internet Users, is available by anonymous FTP from `sluaxa.slu.edu`, directory `/pub/millesjg`, filename `newusers.faq`. You also can obtain it e-mail by sending a message to `listserv@ubvm.cc.buffalo.edu` containing only the line GET NEWUSERS FAQ NETTRAIN F=MAIL. It also may be obtained by e-mail by sending a message to `listserv@ubvm.cc.buffalo.edu` containing only the line GET NEWUSERS FAQ NETTRAIN F=MAIL.

- A list of law related Internet resources by Mary Jensen contains sections on electronic conferences and lists related to law, politics, government, and librarianship; law library catalogs on the Internet; interesting FTP sites related to law, politics and government; a selection of usenet newsgroups related to law, politics, government, and librarianship, and more.

- "The Legal List, Law-Related Resources on the Internet and Elsewhere" by Erik J. Heels, (legal-list@justice.eliot.me.us) Legal Resources; E. Heels is designed to provide a consolidated listing of all of the law-related resources on the Internet. It is available via anonymous FTP from ftp.midnight.com in the pub/LegalList/ subdirectory as the file legallist.txt. By Gopher, it is available from gopher.usmacs.maine.edu in the submenus /Campus Information by Department/LS Law School/ Related Information/Legal List Version 3.1.

LEXIS/NEXIS

The *LEXIS/NEXIS* system is a fee-based system that is important for legal scholars. Access usually is available to professors and students through their own law library.

For information on LEXIS/NEXIS, contact

Mead Data Central
P.O. Box 933
Dayton, OH 45401
Phone: 1-800-543-6862 or (513) 859-1608

Where to find it

LEXIS/NEXIS is accessible via the following:

Telnet lex.meaddata.com
Telnet hermes.merit.edu

The School of Library Science

Libraries developed some of the first independent networks and developed in-depth bibliographic databases. Currently, library science information is available abundantly through the following Internet services:

- Gophers
- Guides

■ Software information

■ Discussion lists

■ Usenet newsgroups

Project

Goal: Increase awareness and knowledge of the unsolved legal issues pertaining to the increased availability of materials on the Internet, electronic archiving, and data exchange relating to library operations.

A useful investigation for graduate students in Library Science is to examine current copyright law as it pertains to electronic publication, including proposed changes in those laws.

You could include the following elements in the assignment:

1. Use Veronica and WebCrawler to search for Gopher and WWW sites particularly helpful for investigating copyright law.
2. Use Archie Search for FTP sites particularly helpful for investigating copyright law.
3. Join several library and copyright related lists and observe the topics being discussed.
4. Retrieve supporting information and documents from the Gopher, WWW, and FTP sites, and list archives.
5. Analyze the materials.
6. Prepare a 15 page position paper regarding current law and practices relative to electronic publishing; identify possible and proposed changes.
7. Post an abstract of the paper to an online class conference.
8. Present findings orally in class.

Following are hints for resources for this project:

1. Check out the Library of Congress Gopher, which is LC MARVEL (marvel.loc.gov).

```
              Internet Gopher Information Client v1.13
                    Library of Congress (LC MARVEL)
      1.   About LC MARVEL/
      2.   Events, Facilities, Programs, and Services/
      3.   Research and Reference (Public Services)/
      4.   Libraries and Publishers (Technical Services)/
```

```
-->  5.  Copyright/
     6.  Library of Congress Online Systems/
     7.  Employee Information/
     8.  U.S. Congress/
     9.  Government Information/
    10.  Global Electronic Library (by Subject)/
    11.  Internet Resources/
    12.  What's New on LC MARVEL/
    13.  Search LC MARVEL Menus/
```

Look under `Copyright`, #6.

```
Copyright
     1.  Introduction to the Copyright Office.
     2.  Copyright Basics (Circular 1).
     3.  Copyright Information Circulars (under
construction)/
     4.  Copyright Registration/
     5.  Research in Copyright Office Files/
     6.  Copyright Office Announcements (notice of
actions: regulations, et../
     7.  Other Copyright Topics/
     8.  ACCORD (Advisory Committee on Copyright
Registration and Deposit)/
     9.  CARP & Licensing Information/
    10.  What's New in the Copyright Office/
    11.  Other Internet Copyright Resources/
```

In the menus that follow, you will find numerous entries dealing with copyrights, regulations, various official circulars, and more.

2. Look in Gopher Jewels, under Library Science.

3. Do a Veronica search of `gopherspace`.

4. Obtain the Copyright FAQ. This FAQ is available via anonymous FTP from `rtfm.mit.edu`, in directory `pub/usenet/news.answers/law/Copyright-FAQ`, files `part1` - `part6`. If you do not have access to FTP, you can obtain the FAQ using e-mail. Send a message to `mail-server@rtfm.mit.edu` with the following message in the body:

```
send usenet/news.answers/law/Copyright-FAQ/part1
send usenet/news.answers/law/Copyright-FAQ/part2
send usenet/news.answers/law/Copyright-FAQ/part3
send usenet/news.answers/law/Copyright-FAQ/part4
send usenet/news.answers/law/Copyright-FAQ/part5
send usenet/news.answers/law/Copyright-FAQ/part6
quit
```

Following is the Gopher reference for this FAQ:

Name   *copyright.faq*

Type	0
Port	70
Path	`0/PCERT/docs/copyright.faq`
Host	`arthur.cs.purdue.edu`

5. Obtain from the following Gopher a copy of *Copyright and the Electronic Library* by Scott Seaman:

Name	*Copyright and the Electronic Library*
Type	0
Port	70
Path	`0/University of Colorado, Boulder Information/CUline`
Gopher	`(experimental)/CAMPUS SERVICES/Computing on Campus/The DIGIT/May-June 1994/Copyright and the Electronic Library`
Host	`gopher.Colorado.edu`

6. Using WebQuery, investigate copyright issues.

7. Try out the "Study Carrels" at North Carolina State University, where they offer a discipline-specific Internet resources link to Library and Information Science resources:

Linkname	`Discipline-specific Internet resources ("Study Carrels")`
URL	`http://dewey.lib.ncsu.edu/disciplines/index.html`

and

Linkname	`Library and Information Science`
Filename	`http://dewey.lib.ncsu.edu/disciplines/library.html`

9. Join CNI's Copyright and Intellectual Property discussion list—`cni-copyright`—using the standard listproc protocol, `listproc@cni.org`, with a message of **subscribe cni-copyright *yourfirstname yourlastname***.

10. Check out the Copyright Gopher in the next section on "Gophers Containing Information for Library Science."

Gophers Containing Information for Library Science

Gopher sites with substantial quantities of Library Science information are plentiful. The following sections discuss some sites that are particularly rich in resources, and an excellent place to start a search for information.

Library of Congress

The Library of Congress contains a wealth of information for those teaching and studying Library Science.

Where to find it

Name   *Library of Congress (LC MARVEL, LOCIS)*

Type   1

Path

Port   70

Host   marvel.loc.gov

The following is the opening menu for the LC Gopher:

```
      Internet Gopher Information Client v1.13
Library of Congress (LC MARVEL, LOCIS)

1.  About LC MARVEL/
2.  Events, Facilities, Programs, and Services/
3.  Research and Reference (Public Services)/
4.  Libraries and Publishers (Technical Services)/
5.  Copyright/
6.  Library of Congress Online Systems/
7.  Employee Information/
8.  U.S. Congress/
9.  Government Information/
10. Global Electronic Library (by Subject)/
11. Internet Resources/
12. What's New on LC MARVEL/
13. Search LC MARVEL Menus/
Press ? for Help, q to Quit, u to go up a menu
Page: 1/1


Choosing 1 will give us a look at the Welcome screen:



    ************************************************************
    *                                                        *
    *                WELCOME TO LC MARVEL                     *
    *                                                        *
    *             MACHINE-ASSISTED REALIZATION               *
    *           OF THE VIRTUAL ELECTRONIC LIBRARY            *
    *                                                        *
    ************************************************************

The Library of Congress (LC) Machine-Assisted Realization of the Virtual Electronic
Library (MARVEL) is a Campus-Wide Information System that combines the vast
collection of information available about the Library with easy access to diverse
electronic resources over the Internet.  Its goal is to serve the staff of LC, as
well as the U.S. Congress and constituents throughout the world.  It is available
on the Internet and uses the Gopher software from the University of Minnesota.
During the preliminary stages of development, the posting of information on LC
```

MARVEL will be coordinated by the "LC MARVEL Design Team" in cooperation with
service units and divisions throughout the Library. The Information Technology
Services (ITS) service unit has sponsored this effort in conjunction with recommendations coming from the staff organization -- The Internet Users Group (IUG).

Since the information offered by the system will be viewed by both staff members
and users outside of the Library from workstations with varying ranges of characteristics and capabilities, the format of documents on LC MARVEL will, for the
most part, adhere to the "lowest common denominator" -- plain ASCII text. In some
cases files will be listed that are not in ASCII format (i.e., graphic images from
the Library's exhibits) which can be saved, but not viewed through LC MARVEL. It
may be possible in the near future to view images and more richly formatted textual
works.

The American Library Association

The *American Library Association* maintains a Gopher with the following welcome
as a way of noting that certain features are under construction:

Welcome to the ALA Gopher. Our Gopher is a young critter, recently born, and not
yet fully developed.

Staff in ALA's divisions and offices are currently formatting documents and posting them on the Gopher.

Where to find it

Name *American Library Association (ALA) (Under Construction)*

Type 1

Port 70

Path 1/library/ala

Host gopher.uic.edu

Following is ALA's top Gopher menu:

```
    Internet Gopher Information Client v1.13
American Library Association (ALA) (Under Construction)

1.   I.About this gopher.
2.   II.About ALA (news, directories, etc.)/
3.   III.ALA and Division Conferences/
4.   IV.Publications (Electronic and other)/
5.   V.ALA's Council and Executive Board/
6.   VI.ALA, Division, and Round Table Elections/
7.   VII.ALA, Division, and Round Table Committee Charges and Rosters/
8.   VIII. ALA Policy Manual and Constitution & Bylaws/
9.   IX.ALA and Division Standards & Guidelines/
10.  X.ALA Intellectual Freedom Statements/
```

```
11. XI.Legislation Affecting Libraries/
12. XII.Awards and Scholarships/
13. XIII. ALA's Divisions/
14. XIV.ALA's Round Tables/
15. XV.ALA's Offices and Other Units/
16. XVI.ALA Chapters and Affiliates/
Press ? for Help, q to Quit, u to go up a mePage: 1/1
```

ALA also posts ALANEWS:

Where to find it

Name	*ALANEWS*
Type	1
Port	70
Path	1/library/stacks/alanews
Host	dewey.lib.ncsu.edu
URL	ftp://dewey.lib.ncsu.edu/pub/stacks/alanews/alanews-940411

A typical news article selection menu looks like this:

```
NEWS RELEASES

April 11, 1994

This batch contains:

1.   ABC public service campaign directs public to libraries
2.   BRASS Disclosure Student Travel Award recipient named
3.   Collection development policies for electronic formats RASD program topic
4.   LAMA preconference to focus on preventing violence in libraries
5.   LAMA to offer telecommunications wiring for libraries preconference
6.   Legislative Advocacy Workshop planned for ALA Annual Conference
7.   May 1 EBSCO ALA Conference Sponsorship Award deadline
8.   "Miami Hot Stuff" Swap and Shop theme
9.   Multitype library networks and the Internet ASCLA program topic
10.  1994 National Library Week Power Programs planning Grants awarded
11.  National School Library Media Program of the Year finalists announced
12.  National Library Week highlights
13.  YALSA preconference celebrates 25 years of Best Books
```

In addition, ALA offers the ALCTS (Association for Library Collections & Technical Services) Network News via:

Where to find it

Name   *ALCTS Network News*

Type   1

Port   70

Path   1/library/stacks/ann

Host   dewey.lib.ncsu.edu

URL   ftp://dewey.lib.ncsu.edu/pub/stacks/ann/ann-v7n06

Coalition for Networked Information (CNI)

The *Coalition for Networked Information* is a joint project of EDUCOM, the Association of Research Libraries, and CAUSE. Its purpose is to promote the creation of and access to information resources in networked environments in order to support scholarship and to enhance intellectual productivity. CNI supports many activities including mailing lists, and the following Gopher:

Where to find it

Name   *Coalition for Networked Information (CNI)*

Type   1

Port   70

Host   gopher.cni.org

```
Internet Gopher Information Client v1.13
Coalition for Networked Information (CNI)

1.  About the Coalition for Networked Information.
2.  Coalition BRS-SEARCH Services/
3.  Coalition FTP Archives (ftp.cni.org)/
4.  Coalition Working Groups/
5.  Association of Research Libraries Services/
6.  CAUSE Gopher Services/
7.  Educom Gopher Services/
8.  Other Gopher Services/
Press ? for Help, q to Quit, u to go up a meu
Page: 1/1
```

CNI also sponsors a number of interesting discussion lists:

Where to find it

CNI's News Announcement Network

    cni-announce@cni.org

CNI's Copyright and Intellectual Property Forum

> `cni-copyright@cni.org`

CNI's Directories and Resource Information Services Working Group

> `cni-directories@cni.org`

CNI's Legislation, Codes, Policies, and Practices Working Group

> `cni-legislation@cni.org`

CNI's Management and Professional and User Education Working Group

> `cni-management@cni.org`

CNI's Modernization of Scholarly Publication Working Group

> `cni-modernization@cni.org`

CNI's Access to Public Information Working Group

> `cni-pubinfo@cni.org`

CNI's Teaching and Learning Working Group

> `cni-teaching@cni.org`

CNI's Transformation of Scholarly Communication Working Group

> `cni-transformation@cni.org`

Note: All CNI lists use the `listproc@site` subscription addressing conventions.

Acquisitions Librarians Electronic Network

The *Acquisitions Librarians Electronic Network* (ACQNET) provides a way for acquisitions librarians and others to exchange ideas, information, and to participate in problem-solving. It is not a Listserv; rather it is more like a BBS and newsletter rolled into one. The editor receives all potential postings, organizes them, edits them, summarizes them, and distributes them to the membership.

Where to find it

Name   *ACQNET*
Type   1
Port   70

Path   `1/library/stacks/acq`

Host   `dewey.lib.ncsu.edu`

```
          Internet Gopher Information Client v1.13
                        ACQNET

   1.   About ACQNET.
   2.   Retrieving ACQNET back files and back issues via anonymous FTP
   3.   FTP to the ACQNET archives/
   4.   Search ACQNET (freeWAIS) <?>
   5.   Volume 1 (1991)/
   6.   Volume 2 (1992)/
   7.   Volume 3 (1993)/
   8.   Volume 4 (1994)/
```

The Bulletin Board for Libraries (BUBL)

BUBL is a large scale service for librarians in the UK, that also provides information of interest to library science professionals in other countries.

Where to find it

Name   *BUBL, Bulletin Board for Libraries*

Type   `1`

Port   `7070`

Host   `bubl.bath.ac.uk`

Located on their Gopher is the BUBL Leaflet that describes their pupose.

```
The BUBL Leaflet
                          ================
                              April 1994
                          ........................
                          B U B L  Leaflet Side A
                          ........................


The BUBL Information Service serves UK Library and Information Science
Professionals and the wider academic and research community they support. The MAIN
MENU gives a broad idea of coverage:

- BUBL Beginners, Updates, Contacts, News, Sponsors..
- Library & Information Science on and via BUBL
- Internet Resources by Subject; Reference Tools, Electronic Texts & Journals
- BUBL's Latest Additions and Amendments (files only)
- The BUBL Subject Tree Project
- Keyword Searching: BUBL Files, Internet: Archie, Veronica, WAIS
- NISS, Mailbase, SALSER, HENSA, CONCISE, etc
```

```
- Services by Type: OPACs, Gopher Jewels, Gophers, WWW, WAIS
- Networks and Networking: Tools, User guides  Training...


LIBRARY & INFORMATION SCIENCE ON BUBL:
---------------------------------------
BUBL began life as the Bulletin Board for Libraries and its major aim is
still to inform, support, educate, and represent the interests of, the UK LIS
community. Choose option 2 on the BUBL top level menu to get the Library &
Information Science sub-menu, which includes the following:

- Information Networking
- New Publications in Library & Information Science
- Directories of Internet and  LIS oriented resources
- Current Contents of Computing and LIS Journals
- Electronic Mail Discussion Lists
- LIS: Services, Education, Surveys, News, Organisations
- LIS Glossaries, Acronyms and Definitions
- LIS Education, Including Network Use Exercises
- Electronic Journals and Texts
- Traditional Divisions of Librarianship
- Library Systems & Software Resources
- CTILIS: Computers in Teaching Initiative
```

Citations for Serial Literature

This Gopher, called Citations for Serial Literature, provides access to a collection of information about Serial Literature of all kinds, for example, *The Journal of the United Kingdom Serials Group, Newsletter on Serials Pricing Issues,* and *Issues in Science and Technology Librarianship.*

Where to find it

Name *Citations for Serial Literature*

Type 1

Port 70

Path 1/library/stacks/csl

Host dewey.lib.ncsu.edu

```
Internet Gopher Information Client v1.13
Citations for Serial Literature

1.   Search Citations for Serial Literature (freeWAIS) <?>
2.   Volume 1 (1992)/
3.   Volume 2 (1993)/
4.   v3/
Press ? for Help, q to Quit, u to go up a menu    Page: 1/1
```

Selecting #4 takes you to the following:

```
Citations for Serial Literature v3n04 (April 3, 1994)
URL = ftp://dewey.lib.ncsu.edu/pub/stacks/csl/csl-v3n04

CITATIONS FOR SERIAL LITERATURE          ISSN 1061-7434
Volume 3, number  04 April 3, 1994
-----------------------------------------------------------------

In this issue:

Serials: The Journal of the United Kingdom Serials Group, vol. 7, no. 1,
    Mar. 1994
Newsletter on Serials Pricing Issues, NS 110, March 17, 1994
Newsletter on Serials Pricing Issues, NS 111, April 2, 1994
Issues in Science and Technology Librarianship, No. 9, March 1994 (selective)
Serendipitous Citings
```

An excerpt from Volume 7, Number 1 reads

```
-----------------------------------------------------------------

    SERIALS: THE JOURNAL OF THE UNITED KINGDOM SERIALS GROUP
          Volume 7 Number 1 (March 1994)

      Pg    CONTENTS

      3     Editorial
      3     UKSG News
      4     UK Serials Group Roadshow       Margaret Graham
      8     News
     11     News from North America
     16     Letters
     17     Electronic serial publishing and its effect on the
            traditional information chain Gerard A J S van
            Marle
     29     The impact of electronic information on serials
            collection management Hazel Woodward
     37     Will you survive the electonic library? Janet
            Tomlinson
     43     Plugging into the network       Will Wakeling
     46     The Tironet shared library resources project
            Nigel Butterwick
     50     The Logos experience       Gordon Graham
     53     The story of STM       Lex Lefebvre
     57     The Directory Publishers Association       Rosemary
            Pettit
     60     Three hundred years of women's magazines, 1693-
            1993       Jill Allbrooke
     65     1993 CAPP book and journal spending report
            Claire Waddell
     69     The importance of Follett       Maurice B Line
     73     The Scientific, Technical and Medical Information
            System in the UK: a report published by the Royal
            Society, 1993       Dennis Pilling
     77     ICEDIS, the international committee on electronic
            data interchange for serials       Brian Cox
     79     Subscription agencies: fewer, tougher, more agile
            - and beleaguered       Wim Luijendijk
```

Copyright Law, Fair Use & Libraries

This Gopher pointer, called Copyright Law, Fair Use & Libraries, is to a collection of information and legal cases about copyright law, recent developments in copyright law and procedures, and related information.

Where to find it

Name   *Copyright Law, Fair Use & Libraries*

Type   1

Port   70

Path   1/alpha/copyright

Host   gopher.lib.virginia.edu

```
Internet Gopher Information Client v1.13
Copyright Law, Fair Use & Libraries

1.  About these resources.
2.  U.S. 1976 Copyright Act, Section 107 (Fair Use).
3.  U.S. 1976 Copyright Act, Section 108 (Libraries).
4.  Copyright Law, Libraries & Universities, by Kenneth D. Crews (ASCI...
5.  Copyright Law, Libraries & Universities, by Kenneth D. Crews (PS).
6.  Copyright Law, Libraries & Universities, by Kenneth D. Crews .. <HQX>
7.  Copyright Law, Libraries & Universities, by Kenneth D. Crews .. <Bin>
8.  TEXACO - Summary of Leval, by Ritchie Thomas.
9.  TEXACO brief, March 1993 (ASCII).
10. TEXACO brief, March 1993 (PS) <Bin>
11. TEXACO reply brief, May 1993 (ASCII).
12. TEXACO reply brief, May 1993 (PS) <Bin>
13. TEXACO - ARL etc. Joint AMICUS (ASCII).
14. TEXACO - ARL etc. Joint AMICUS (WP5.1) <Bin>
15. TEXACO - ALA AMICUS 3/93 (ASCII).
16. TEXACO - ALA AMICUS 3/93 (PS) <Bin>
17. TEXACO - Association of American Publishers Brief 4/93 (ASCII).
18. TEXACO - Association of American Publishers Brief 4/93 (PS) <Bin>
19. Copyright FAQ, part 1.
20. Copyright FAQ, part 2.
21. Copyright FAQ, part 3.
22. Copyright FAQ, part 4.
```

```
23. Copyright FAQ, part 5.
24. Copyright FAQ, part 6.
Press ? for Help, q to Quit, u to go up a menu  Page: 1/1

Receiving Information../
```

Software Archive

This is an archive of library related software, available via both Gopher and FTP, called *LIBSOFT*. This archive contains programs of general interest to librarians. You can locate the file and program descriptions in the file INDEX.TXT. Before transferring files, read this file because it will give you an idea of the content and size of files. In addition, LIBSOFT contains files that can help librarians make use of the Internet.

Where to find it

Name *LIBSOFT, an archive of library related software*

Type 1

Port 70

Path ftp:sunsite.unc.edu@/pub/docs/about-the-net/libsoft/

Host dewey.lib.ncsu.edu

```
     Internet Gopher Information Client v1.13


LIBSOFT, an archive of library related software

1.   .cache.
2.   aaa_readme.1st.
3.   agguide.dos.
4.   agguide.wp.
5.   archie.com.
6.   archie_guide.txt.
7.   artbase.txt.
8.   aut103-4.txt.
9.   aut1101.txt.
10.  binaries.txt.
11.  binaries_ftp.txt.
12.  bitnet_ftp.txt.
13.  boombox.lst.
14.  bsd.zip.
15.  carl.txt.
16.  cassy.exe.
```

```
17. cassy.txt.
18. catalist.txt.
19. cdlock.com.
20. cdn_internet_libs.txt.
21. cdnap.com.
22. cdplay.exe.
23. college_email.txt.
24. cwis.txt.
25. dialog.exe.
26. download.txt.
27. dtsearch.txt.
28. dtsearch.zip.
29. ejournals.txt.
30. email_address.txt.
31. email_guide.txt.
32. email_services.txt.
33. explorer.doc.
34. explorer.zip.
35. file_transfers.txt.
36. freebies.txt.
37. ftp_guide.txt.
38. ftp_help.txt.
39. ftp_how_to.txt.
40. ftp_list.txt.
41. ftp_sites.txt.
42. fullcat.exe.
43. geac_docs.exe.
44. goftp.com.
45. govdox.exe.
46. govmain.prg.
47. guide1.txt.
48. guide2.txt.
49. hwguide.txt.
50. hwguide.zip.
51. hyclass.com.
52. hyglos.doc.
53. hyglos.zip.
54. hyperdiss.doc.
55. hyperdiss.exe.
56. hyperdiss.txt.
57. hyperrez.exe.
58. hytelnet.dir.
59. index.txt.
60. infnetnews1.txt.
```

... and on for a total of 150 plus items.

Useful Guides

There are many useful guides to library resources available on the Internet. You can retrieve Internet Accessible Library Catalogs and Databases compiled by Art St. George and Ron Larsen via FTP at `ariel.unm.edu`, in the directory `/library`, as the file `internet.library`. Library-Oriented Lists and Electronic Serials by Charles W. Bailey, Jr. is available at `dewey.lib.ncsu.edu` via gopher under the menus

NCSU's `"Library Without Walls"/Study Carrels/Library & Information Science/Library-oriented Lists`, and at the University of Michigan Library Gopher site mentioned earlier.

Discussion Lists

The following discussion lists cover a broad range of Library Science issues. As with all discussion lists, expect the postings to range from inspired to inane. These lists are excellent places to network with colleagues. The following table shows a variety of discussion lists that may be of interest to those in Library science. Where the address looks like this—`ACRL@UICVM`—it is a BITNET address; otherwise, they are Internet addresses:

Where to find it

Association of College and Research Libraries

    `acrl@uicvm`

African American Studies and Librarianship

    `afas-l@kentvm`

Academic Librarian's Forum

    `alf-l@yorkvm1`

Archives and Archivists List

    `archives@miamiu`

Art Libraries Association of North America

    `arlis-l@ukcc`

American Society for Information Science

    `asis-l@uvmvm`

Library Cataloging and Authorities Discussion Group

    `autocat@ubvm`

Discussion of Software for Citations and Bibliographies

    `bibsoft@indycms`

Bibliographic Instruction

    `bi-l@bingvmb`

Business Librarians

    `buslib-l@idbsu`

CARL Users

    `carl-l@uhccvm`

CD-ROMs

    `cdrom-l@uccvma`

Circulation and Access Services

    `circplus@idbsu`

Library Collection Development List

    `colldv-l@uscvm`

ACRL College Libraries Section

    `collib-l@willamette.edu`

Committee on South Asian Libraries and Documentation

    `consald@utxvm`

Cooperative Cataloging Discussion Group

    `coopcat@nervm`

Campus-Wide Information Systems

    `cwis-l@wuvmd`

Doctoral Students in Library and Information Studies Programs

    `docdis@ua1vm`

OCLC Documentation

    `doc-l@oclc.org`

ASEE Engineering Libraries Division

    `eldnet-l@uiucvmd`

Open Library/Information Science Research

    `eleasai@arizvm1`

Library Automation in Greece

```
ellasbib@grearn
```

Management and Preservation of Electronic Records

```
erecs-l@albnyvm1
```

Electronic Text Centers

```
etextctr@rutvm1
```

Rare Books and Special Collections

```
exlibris@rutvm1
```

Fee-Based Information Service Centers in Academic Libraries

```
fisc-l@ndsuvm1
```

Transborder Libraries Forum

```
foro-l@arizvm1
```

Geoscience Librarians and Information Specialists

```
geonet-l@iubvm
```

Library Gopher Developers

```
go4lib-l@ucsbvm
```

Government Documents

```
govdoc-l@psuvm
```

Interlibrary Loan

```
ill-l@uvmvm
```

Indexer's Discussion Group

```
index-l@bingvmb
```

Innovative Interfaces Users

```
innopac@maine
```

Foreign and International Law Librarians

```
int-law@uminn1
```

Open Library/Information Science Education Forum

```
jesse@arizvm1
```

Library Administration and Management

> `libadmin@umab`

Exhibits and Academic Libraries Discussion List

> `libex-l@maine`

Library Master Bibliographic Database

> `libmastr@uottawa`

Library Personnel Issues

> `libper-l@ksuvm`

University Library Planning

> `libpln-l@ukanvm`

Libraries and Librarians

> `library@miamiu`

Discussion of Library Reference Issues

> `libref-l@kentvm`

Library Support Staff

> `libsup-l@uwavm`

Library and Information Science Students

> `lis-l@uiucvmd`

School Library Media & Network Communications

> `lm_net@suvm`

Maps and Air Photo Forum

> `maps-l@uga`

Internet/BITNET Network Trainers

> `nettrain@ubvm`

Announcements of New Electronic Journals

> `newjour-l@e-math.ams.org`

National Information Standards Organization

> `niso-l@nervm`

OCLC Electronic Journal Publishing

    `oclc-journals@oclc.org`

OCLC Press Releases

    `oclc-news@oclc.org`

Off-Campus Library Services List

    `offcamp@waynest1`

Public-Access Computer Systems Forum

    `pacs-l@uhupvm1`

PACS-L Publications Only

    `pacs-p@uhupvm1`

Public Libraries

    `publib@nysernet.org`

Internet Use in Public Libraries

    `publib-net@nysernet.org`

Library Services to Children and Young Adults in Public Libraries

    `pubyac@nysernet.org`

Serials Users Discussion Group

    `serialst@uvmvm`

Special Libraries Association Employment Opportunities

    `slajob@iubvm`

Special Libraries Association—Physics, Astronomy, and Mathematics

    `sla-pam@ukcc`

Discussion Group for Technical Services in Special Libraries

    `sla-tech@ukcc`

OCLC Technical Bulletins

    `techbul-l@oclc.org`

Texas Documents Information Network

    `txdxn-l@uhupvm1`

Veterinary Medicine Library Issues and Information

```
vetlib-l@vtvm1
```

Strategic Visions Steering Committee Electronic Discussion Forum on the Future of Librarianship

```
visions@library.sdsu.edu
```

Publishing E-Journals: Publishing, Archiving, and Access

```
vpiej-l@vtvm1
```

Don't forget `stumpers-l`, a list for difficult reference questions. Subscribe using `mailserv@crf.cuis.edu`. This is a moderated list.

There are other lists of interest in Library Science, and you can obtain more information on those from the University of Michigan's Subject Oriented Guides. Look for the 8th Revision Directory of Scholarly Electronic Conferences, by Diane Kovacs, and Library-Oriented Lists and Electronic Serials by Charles W. Bailey, Jr.

Electronic Journals

There are a growing number of electronic journals available that may be of interest to librarians. Subscriptions to the following are through listserv@site in BITNET format (unless noted).

Where to find it

The Acquisitions Librarian's Electronic Network

```
acqnet@cornell.edu
```

ALA Washington Office Newsline (ALAWON)

```
alawon@uicvm
```

NETWORK NEWS

```
alcts@uicvm
```

Citations for Serial Literature

```
sercites@mitvma
```

An Electronic Newsletter (subscription requests go to `edupage@educom.edu`)

```
edupage@eucom.edu
```

Electronic Journal on Virtual Culture

```
ejvc-l@kentvm
```

Information Bits

```
infobits@gibbs.oit.unc.edu
```

Information Retrieval List Digest

```
ir-l@uccvma
```

Journal of Academic Media Librarianship

```
mcjrnl@ubvm
```

LC Cataloging Newsline

```
lcnn@ sun7.loc.gov
```

Library and Information Science Research Electronic Journal

```
libres@kentvm
```

Network News

```
nnews@ndsuvm1
```

Many of these electronic journals also can be found on Gophers, and WWW. The following, for example, is the pointer for Network News:

Where to find it

Name	*Network News*
Type	1
Port	70
Path	1/library/stacks/nnews
Host	dewey.lib.ncsu.edu

When you use this Gopher, you will find menu items for current and back issues and a change to a keyword search of Network News. Here are some excerpts from Network News.

```
Internet Gopher Information Client v1.13
Network News

1.   Search Network News (freeWAIS) <?>
2.   1991/
3.   1992/
4.   1993/
5.   1994/
```

```
Press ? for Help, q to Quit, u to go up a menu    Page: 1/1


     Internet Gopher Information Client v1.13
1994


 -->  1.  Network News 13 (March 28, 1994).

Network News 13 (March 28, 1994)
URL = ftp://dewey.lib.ncsu.edu/pub/stack/nnews/nnews-13




========================================================================
              N   N   N   N   EEEEE   W   W   SSSSS
              NN  N   NN  N   E       W   W   S
              N N N   N N N   EEE     W W W   SSSSS
              N  NN   N  NN   E       WW WW       S
              N   N   N   N   EEEEE   W   W   SSSSS
========================================================================
    an update to libraries and information resources on the Internet
                       sponsored by Metronet
========================================================================
Number 13                     NETWORK-NEWS                    March 1994


TABLE OF CONTENTS:

      New Guides
      WWW - World Wide Web
      Keeping up with the Usenet Newsgroups
      The Top Ten List for Internet Novices
      Software Toolbox


==========
NEW GUIDES
==========


At long last the revision of A Guide to Internet/Bitnet is complete. It's a
bit shorter (50 pages), has a few new sections, and a longer bibliography. The
guide is available as GUIDEV2 NNEWS on the listserv@ndsuvm1.bitnet or via FTP
from vm1.nodak.edu in the NNEWS directory.

Most of the library specific material from the original guide has
been moved to LIBCAT: A Guide to Library Resources on the Internet.This guide
(110+ pages) includes 750+ library catalog listings, an extensive list of
special collections and databases, selected lists for librarians, and a
smattering of Gopher and World Wide Web listings. The LIBCAT files also are
available via FTP from the site listed above.
```

Following is a Gopher pointer to a collection of electronic journals in Library Science:

Where to find it

Name   *Library Journals Online*

```
Type   1
Port   70
Path   1/librariess/journals
Host   vienna.hh.lib.umich.edu
```

Usenet Newsgroups

Usenet newsgroups of interest to those teaching and studying Library Science are as yet fairly limited. A few of the more useful ones include the following:

Where to find it

Discussing electronic libraries (Moderated)

```
comp.internet.library
```

Library Cataloging and Authorities List

```
bit.listserv.autocat
```

Library Access for People with Disabilities

```
bit.listserv.axslib-l
```

Circulation Reserve and Related Library Issues

```
bit.listserv.circplus
```

Library Reference Issues (Moderated)

```
bit.listserv.libref-l
```

Library and Information Science Research (Moderated)

```
bit.listserv.libres
```

Library and Information Science Students

```
bit.listserv.lis-l
```

Music Library Association

```
bit.listserv.mla-l
```

Implementing info technologies in school libraries

```
k12.library
```

In the preceding listing, *Moderated* indicates that the list is moderated, as opposed to simply accepting all postings as they come in.

The Medical School

The Internet is bristling with resources for medical school faculty and students. The array is daunting. There are guides, Gophers, WWW sites, lists, and groups that can be useful in sorting through the information.

Guides

There are several guides to resources that are especially useful. You can retrieve all of them from the University of Michigan's Subject Oriented Clearinghouse at the Gopher una.hh.lib.umich.edu 70.

The Medical List and Health Matrix

The most complete and accessible guide to medical information is called the *Medical List* by Dr. Gary Malet, a family physician (gmalet@surfer.win.net) and Lee Hancock, an educational technologist (le07144@ukanvm.cc.ukans.edu).

Gopher access to this guide is available via the Clearinghouse of Subject-Oriented Internet Resource Guides mentioned previously at URL gopher://una.hh.lib.umich.edu/11/inetdirsstacks. The most recent version of this document also can be retrieved via anonymous FTP from ftp2.cc.ukans.edu pub/hmatrix in the file /medlst*.

Following is what the contents of the Medical List look like:

```
- TABLE OF CONTENTS -

1   INTRODUCTION TO "THE MEDICAL LIST"
    1.1   PURPOSE AND HISTORY
    1.2   AN INTRODUCTION TO INTERNET HEALTH AND MEDICAL RESOURCES
    1.3   "BEST" OF INTERNET MEDICAL RESOURCES
        1.3.1   MOSAIC AND IMAGE RETRIEVAL
        1.3.2   DISEASE CATEGORIZED INFORMATION
        1.3.3   SPECIALTY CATEGORIZED INFORMATION
        1.3.4   FEATURED DOCUMENTS AND PROGRAMS
        1.3.5   EMPLOYMENT/CLASSIFIEDS
        1.3.6   INTERNET USERS' RECOMMENDATIONS
        1.3.7   CANCERNET-GUIDE TO CANCER TREATMENT
        1.3.8   NLM's PRACTICE GUIDELINES-HSTAT
        1.3.9   NIH'S CLINICAL ALERTS
        1.3.10  WWW ACCESS TO THE HEALTH SECURITY ACT
    1.4   NEWS AND NEW RESOURCES
    1.5   E-MAIL-ACCESSIBLE RESOURCES
    1.6   THE HMATRIX MAILING LIST-ONLINE HEALTH RESOURCES
    1.7   DESCRIPTION OF "MEDICAL LIST" ENTRIES
    1.8   DISCLAIMER
```

```
2  GETTING AND REDISTRIBUTING "THE MEDICAL LIST"
      2.1  WHERE TO GET THE LATEST VERSION
      2.2  HEALTH MATRIX- HOW TO ACQUIRE THE WINDOWS
                VERSION OF  THIS DATABASE


3  MEDICAL MAILING LISTS AND LISTSERVS
      3.1   MAILING LISTS OVERVIEW
      3.2   HOW TO ADDRESS MAILING LISTS
      3.3   ETIQUETTE
      3.4   COMMMANDS
      3.5   MEDICAL MAILING LISTS
               [listnames omitted]
4  FTP RESOURCES
      4.1.  FTP OVERVIEW
      4.2   COMMANDS
      4.3   FTP VIA E-MAIL
      4.4   ARCHIE
      4.5   MEDICAL FTP RESOURCES
      4.5.1       ANESTHESIOLOGY ARCHIVES  files/ programs
      4.5.2       BIOMEDICAL INFORMATICS, CAMPINAS, BRAZIL
      4.5.3       M-MEDIA medical applications
      4.5.4       MAC ARCHIVES SECTION AT  U. OF MICHIGAN software
      4.5.5       MEDTBOOK  contributions/textbook
      4.5.6       MIRROR FTP SITE-PUB. DOMAIN MEDICAL SOFTWARE
      4.5.7       NIH SERVER articles
      4.5.8       THE UCI MED. EDUCATION SOFTWARE REPOSITORY
      4.5.9       VOXEL-MAN 3D Interactive atlas


5   DATA ARCHIVES
      5.1   MEDICAL DATA ARCHIVES
      5.1.1       ANESTHESIOLOGY ARCHIVES
      5.1.2       CANCERNET- NATIONAL CANCER INSTITUTE, NIH
      5.1.3       CDC WONDER- Centers for Disease Control
      5.1.4       CHAT-Conversational Hypertext Access Technology
      5.1.5       FEDERAL FOOD AND DRUG ADMINISTRATION
      5.1.6       MEDLINE
      5.1.7       SOUTH EAST FLORDIA AIDS INFORMATION NETWORK


6   GOPHER RESOURCES
      6.1   GOPHER OVERVIEW
      6.2   GOPHER MEDICAL RESOURCES
      6.2.1       AIDS RELATED INFORMATION
      6.2.2       ANESTHESIOLOGY INTERNET GOPHER
      6.2.3       CAMIS- Center for Advanced Med. Informatics at Stanford
      6.2.4       CANCERNET INFORMATION
      6.2.5       FAM-MED MEDICAL REFERENCES- Comp. in family med.
      6.2.6       HEALTHLINE GOPHER SERVER- Patient health info.
      6.2.7       NIAID- National Institute  allergy and infectious disease
      6.2.8       NIGHTINGALE-Nursing community communication
      6.2.9       RURALNET GOPHER-Rural health programs and research
      6.2.10   SCI.MED.TELEMEDICINE
      6.2.11   TJGOPHER -- Thomas Jefferson University's gopher
      6.2.12   WHITE HOUSE HEALTH GOPHER
      6.2.13   YALE BIOMEDICAL GOPHER


7  WWW-ACCESSIBLE AND MOSAIC RESOURCES
      7.1   WWW AND MOSAIC OVERVIEW
      7.2   WWW MEDICAL RESOURCES
      7.2.1       AIDS INFORMATION
      7.2.2       BREAST CANCER INFORAMTION CLEARINGHOUSE
      7.2.3       GEMA GLOBAL EMERGENCY MEDICINE ARCHIVES
```

```
15  COMPUTER RESEARCH
    15.1        MEDLINE
    15.2        PHYSICIANS ON LINE
```

In addition, the Medical List is a part of a database called Healthmatrix—Guide to Online Health Resources. Healthmatrix is a Windows Help, icon driven, hypertext, online presentation of this text of the Medical List in Mosaic homepage format. For information or to send requests for the Healthmatrix program (approximately a quarter of a megabyte) contact `gmalet@surfer.win.net`.

Other Guides

Lee Hancock's other guide, Internet/Bitnet Health Sciences Resources, is exhaustive, and covers resources reachable via telnet, Gopher, FTP, and an extensive listing of Internet/BITNET discussion lists. For the most recent files, telnet (login as `kufacts`) or Gopher to `ukanaix.cc.ukans.edu`. Look under Departmental Information, Medical Center Resources, or the University of Michigan listed previously.

Health Sciences Resources On The Internet by Nadia J. Martin (`nadia.martin@um.cc.umich.edu`), Pat Redman (`patricia.redman@um.cc.umich.edu`), and Gale Oren (`gale.oren@um.cc.umich.edu`) contains a good listing of discussion groups and pointers to Gopher and FTP resources.

Medical Practice/Medical Personnel/Patients, compiled by Jeanne M. Langendorfer (`JLANGEND@kentvm.kent.edu`) is part of the Directory of Scholarly Electronic Conferences. It covers the scholarly discussion lists related to medical practice, personnel, and patient, and can be obtained from the University of Michigan site mentioned previously.

Medical Imaging and The Virtual Hospital and Library

In terms of medical information, Mosaic (and WWW) is becoming an important part of the use of the Internet by physicians, students and other medical personnel. Mosaic displays high resolution graphical images from distant sites, providing one of the greatest potential medical applications of Internet. Medical institutions are providing numerous images, including pathologic slides, X rays, and photographs. An excellent example of this application is The Virtual Hospital (VH) from the University of Iowa.

The *Medical Imaging Networked Consortium* (MINC) is currently being used by clinicians and researchers to beta-test several digital consultation software packages that have been developed at the Department of Pathology at the University of

Medicine and Dentistry of New Jersey. It has a growing library of public medical images. In the near future, MINC will grant public access to relational databases of pictorial data related to molecular biology, cytology, and clinical pathology.

Where to find it

Name	Medical Imaging Networked Consortium (MINC)
Host	`mirage.umdnj.edu`
Path	
Port	`70`
Type	`1`

The Virtual Hospital(VH)

The *Virtual Hospital* (VH) is a medical multimedia database. The VH provides patient care support and distance learning to practicing physicians. The VH makes the latest medical information available to physicians, students and individuals. The information may be used for Continuing Medical Education(CME). The VH uses the World Wide Web (WWW) software technology to store, organize, and distribute multimedia textbooks (MMTBs) contained within it. You can access the VH using any WWW browser, at the URL `http://indy.radiology.uiowa.edu/VirtualHospital.html`.

For more information, send e-mail to: `librarian@indy.radiology.uiowa.edu`.

The WWW Virtual Library—Medicine (Biosciences)

This is a comprehensive listing of WWW resources for medicine and the biosciences. The URL is `http://golgi.harvard.edu/biopages/medicine.html`.

Massachusetts General Hospital Webserver—Department of Neurology

This Web site contains information, research, and clinical areas. The Webserver has PI research interests, unit descriptions, and staff. It even includes "mini-CVs" with photographs. The entry on current events in Neurology is useful, and it contains pointers to other pertinent medical/neurological webservers, as well as general information about the Internet. The URL is `http://132.183.145.103`.

Discussion Lists and Electronic Journals

There are a number of very interesting and useful electronic journals and discussion lists for faculty and students in the medical school. The following list is just a sample. Unless otherwise noted, the addresses are all BITNET addresses (`listname@node.bitnet`).

Where to find it

Mature discussion of various addictions

> `addict-l@kentvm`

AIDS/HIV News (refereed)

> `aidsnews@rutvm1`

Anesthesiology

> `anest-l@ubvm`

Research in auditory perception

> `auditory@mcgill1`

Research on low back pain and disability

> `backs-l@uvmvm`

Association of Biomedical Communication

> `biomed-l@mcgill1`

Biomedical Ethics

> `biomed-l@ndsuvm1`

Mind-brain discussion

> `brain-l@mcgill1`

Computers and health

> `c+health@iubvm`

History of Medicine

> `caduceus@utmbeach`

Cancer discussion

> `cancer-l@wvnvm`

Clinical Alerts from NIH

    `clinalrt@umab`

Communication in health care

    `comserv@rpiecs`

International Research Project on Diabetes

    `diabetes@irlearn`

Support and discussion of weight loss

    `diet@indycms`

Drug abuse education information and research

    `drugabus@umab`

Academic Family Medicine

    `family-l@mizzou1`

Fetal and Perinatal Care

    `fet-net@hearn`

Healthcare Financial Matters

    `finan-hc@wuvmd`

Wellness, Exercise, and Diet

    `fit-l@etsuadmn`

Molecular Biology

    `forumbio@bnandp11`

Clinical Human Genetics

    `genetics@indycms`

Geriatric Healthcare

    `gerinet@ubvm`

Management of Health Care Organizations

    `healthmgmt@chimera.sph.umn.edu`

Health Care Reform

    `healthre@ukcc`

Laser Medicine

```
lasmed-l@taunivm
```

Lyme Disease

```
lymenet-l@lehigh.edu
```

Medical Consulting and Case Description

```
medcons@finhutc
```

Menopause

```
menopaus@psuhmc
```

Minority Health Issues in the U.S.

```
minhlth@dawn.hampshire.edu
```

Network of Centers of Excellence in Respiratory Health

```
nce-resp@mcgill1
```

NIH Grants and Contracts Distribution List

```
nihguide@ubvm
```

Nursing Informatics

```
nrsing-l@nic.umass.edu
```

Perinatal Outcomes

```
prenat-l@albnydh2
```

Radiology Special Interest Group

```
radsig@uwavm
```

Medical decision making

```
smdm-l@dartcms1
```

Carpal Tunnel Syndrome and Tendonitis

```
sorehand@ucsfvm
```

Cerebrovascular accidents

```
stroke-l@ukcc
```

Coping with endometriosis

```
witsendo@dartcms1
```

Women's Health

```
wmn-health@uwavm
```

Electronic Journals and Newsletters

Amyotrophic Lateral Sclerosis

```
bro@huey.met.fsu.edu.
```

```
als digest
```

Chronic Fatigue Syndrome Newsletter

```
cfs-news@nihlist
```

Handicap Digest

```
l-hcap@ndsuvm1
```

MEDNEWS@asuacad (weekly)

```
heath infocom newsletter
```

History and Analysis of Disabilities Newsletter

```
fcty7310@ryerson
```

Consciousness and its relation to the brain (refereed)

```
psyche-l@nki
```

Psychology, Neuroscience, Behavioral Biology

```
psycoloquy@pucc
```

The Directory of Electronic Journals and Newsletters includes some 100 scholarly journals and newsletters. It is available in plain text by sending the following e-mail message to `listserv@acadvm1.uottawa.ca`.

```
get ejournl1 directry f=mail
    get ejournl2 directry f=mail
```

Note the unusual spelling of `directory`—many people spell it wrong when they get these files.

Usenet Newsgroups

There are a number of lists that are of interest to those in the Medical School, ranging from image exchanges to biomedical research. Here are some particularly good ones:

Where to find it

Minority scientists and students in biomedical research

```
alt.bio.minority
```

Medical image exchange discussions

```
alt.image.medical
```

Chronic Fatigue Syndrome Action Group

```
alt.health.cfids-action
cfids-l@american.edu
alt.health.cfids-action
```

Computers and Health Discussion List

```
bit.listserv.c+health
c+health@Iubvm.cc.buffalo.edu
bit.listserv.c+health
```

Deaf Issues

```
bit.listserv.deaf-l
```

Medical Students Discussions

```
bit.listserv.medforum
```

Medical Libraries Discussion List

```
bit.listserv.medlib-l
```

Health Info-Com Network Newsletter

```
bit.listserv.mednews
```

Disease, medicine, health care research

```
clari.tw.health
```

HIV and AIDS research, politics

```
clari.tw.health.aids
```

The health care business (Moderated)

```
clari.biz.industry.health
```

Digital Imaging and Communications in Medicine

```
comp.protocols.dicom
```

Health and Physical Education curricula in grades K-12

    k12.ed.health-pe

Forum for paramedics & other first responders

    misc.emerg-services

Alternative, complementary, and holistic health care

    misc.health.alternative

Discussion of diabetes management in day to day life

    misc.health.diabetes

Discussing the field of biomedical engineering

    sci.engr.biomed

Medicine and its related products and regulations

    sci.med

Medicine

    sci.med

Dental related topics; all about teeth

    sci.med.dentistry

AIDS discussion

    sci.med.aids

Nursing questions and discussion

    dsci.med.nursing

Physiological impacts of diet

    sci.med.nutrition

Preventing, detecting and treating occupational injuries

    sci.med.occupational

The teaching and practice of pharmacy

    sci.med.pharmacy

Issues of physics in medical testing/care

    sci.med.physics

Dialog and news in psychiatry and psychobiology

```
sci.med.psychobiology
```

All aspects of radiology

```
sci.med.radiology
```

Clinical consulting through computer networks

```
sci.med.telemedicine
```

The politics and ethics involved with health care

```
talk.politics.medicine
```

Medical services, equipment, drugs (Russian)

```
relcom.commerce.medicine
```

Gophers

There are a large number of Gophers with information useful to medical school faculty, students, and others.

A Veronica search for medically related gopher information nets 192 entries. Following is a sample of those entries:

```
     Internet Gopher Information Client v1.13
 1.  Health Resources & Services Administration/
 2.   Title VIII : Health & Health Related Programs of the Federa/
 3.  0214 Texas Health Science Libraries Consortium/
 4.  Health Professions/
 5.  Doctor of Philosophy/
 6.  9211017_The Quenched Approximation in Health and in Sickness, Clau../
 7.  Health Policy and Admin/
 8.  Health Sciences Library (organizationalUnit)/
 9.  Agency for Health Care Policy and Research/
10.  health-pe/
11.  Health and social services/
12.  Creighton University Health Sciences Library/
13.  Doctor.Fun/
14.  AMER HEALTH ASSISTANCE FDN  (1 entries)/
15.  Animal Health and Biomedical Sciences/
16.  Cabin Creek Health Center, Cabin Creek, WV/
17.  Comp-Health-94/
18.  Public Health Library Selected New Acquisitions Lists/
19.  Health Security Act - Legislation/
20.  Ch 4: The Economics of Health Care/
21.  Health and Health Care/
22.  Health Services/
23.  To Your Health (Information for a healthier you)/
24.  Texas Health Science Libraries Consortium/
```

```
25. Safety & Health Office/
26. Health Plan/
27. Health and Welfare Benefit Plans (A Legal Guide to Planning and M/
28. OTHER NAT INSTITUTE OF HEALTH (6 entries)/
29. 315 SUNY Health Sci Ctr Brooklyn/
30. PHYSICAL ACTIVITY HEALTH (1 entries)/
31. Toxicology/Occupational Health Resources/
32. Uniformed Services University of the Health Sciences/
33. Occupational_Safety_&_Health/
34. Health Sciences Institutions/
35. National Institutes of Health/
36. 0214 University of Virginia Health Sciences Library/
37. National Institutes of Health (NIH) Clinical Alerts/
38. Environmental Health & Safety/
39. NATL INST CHILD HEALTH HUM DEV  (3 entries)/
40. health/
41. Computers and Health/
42. Uniformed Services University of the Health Sciences/
43. Health Care Reform Info/
44. Emotional Health/
45. Health Benefits/
46. Agency for Health Care Policy & Research/
```

Here are some additional Gophers of possible interest:

Where to find it

Name   *Health Resources*

Type   1+

Port   70

Path   /Research/Life Sciences/Health

Host   galileo.cc.rochester.edu

Name   *Creighton University Health Sciences Library*

Type   1

Port   70

Path   1/hytelnet/sites1/sites1a/us000/us000med/us293

Host   gopher.isnet.is

Name   *Public Health Library Selected New Acquisitions Lists*

Type   1

Port   70

Path   1/resdbs/publ/phlinfo/acqlist

Host   infolib.lib.berkeley.edu

Name   *Health and Health Care*

Type   1

Port 70

Path 1s/Bureau/Pr/Subject/Health

Host gopher.census.gov

Name *Health and Welfare Benefit Plans (A Legal Guide to Planning and Medicine)*

Type 1

Port 4800

Path exec:R614992-616593-/.text/main:/.bin/views

Host infx.infor.com

Name *Toxicology/Occupational Health Resources*

Type 1

Port 70

Path 1/resdbs/publ/tox

Host infolib.lib.berkeley.edu

Name *Occupational_Safety_&_Health*

Type 1

Port 70

Path 1/University_Information/News_Service/Experts_Directory/
Experts_Directory/Safety/Occupational_Safety_&_Health

Host cwis.usc.edu

Name *Health Sciences Institutions*

Type 1

Port 70

Path 1/ogophers/hs-insts

Host medstat.med.utah.edu

Name *National Institutes of Health (NIH) Clinical Alerts*

Type 1

Port 70

Path 1/alerts

Host gopher.nlm.nih.gov

Name *Environmental Health & Safety*

Type 1

Port 70

Path 1/./SBNEWS/admserv/ehs

Host adam.cc.sunysb.edu

Name   *Computers and Health*
Type   1
Port   4001
Path   1/.p/ist/Oct92/GD/.s1
Host   istpub.berkeley.edu

Name   *Health Care Reform Info*
Type   1
Port   70
Path   FuturesMonster:Gopher Server:zzzlink:zzGov:Health Care
        Reform Info:
Host   futures.wic.epa.gov

Name   *Emotional Health*
Type   1
Port   70
Path   1/.browse/.METACACDI/.CACDI05/.CACDI0506/
Host   gopher.adp.wisc.edu

Name   *World Health Organization (WHO)*
Type   1
Port   170
Path   1gopher_root:[_shelves._govandlaw._intinfo._who]
Host   psulias.psu.edu

Name   *HEALTHNEWS Health Center*
Type   1
Port   70
Path   HEALTHNEWS
Host   ns3.CC.Lehigh.EDU

Name   *Health Security Act*
Type   1
Port   70
Path   ICHP I:ICHP Gopher Server:Health Security Act:
Host   QM-Server.ichp.ufl.edu

Name   *Health Resources*
Type   1

Port 70

Path 1/CSU Hayward Services and Information/ALSS -- School of Arts, Letters and Social Sciences/Human Development Department/Health Resources

Host s1.csuhayward.edu

Name *Title III : Public Health Initiatives*

Type 1

Port 70

Path 1/LIBRARY/HSLIB/HPLEGIS/HPLEG03

Host UMSLVMA.UMSL.EDU

Name *U.S. Policy Documents (Budget, Health, NAFTA, NII, NPR)*

Type 1

Port 70

Path 1/reference/docs/policy

Host infopath.ucsd.edu

Name *Mayo Clinic Family Health Book, Interactive Edition*

Type 1

Port 2100

Path 1/bookstore/ww/software.1

Host gopher.internet.com

Name *Bouve College Pharmacy & Health Science*

Type 1

Port 70

Path 1/phones/browse-by-dept/bouv-coll-phar-heal-sci

Host chaos.dac.neu.edu

Name *Title I: Health Care Security*

Type 1

Port 70

Path 1/LIBRARY/GOVDOCS/HPLEGIS/HPLEG01

Host UMSLVMA.UMSL.EDU

Name *Affil Health Care & Rsrch Facil*

Type 1

Port 70

Path 1/Resources At Your Fingertips/Undergraduate Course Catalog/
School and College Catalog/Sargent College/Affil Health Care
& Rsrch Facil

Host software.bu.edu

Name *The Health Sciences Campus*

Type 1

Port 70

Path 1/The_Health_Sciences_Campus

Host cwis.usc.edu

Name *Browse through abstracts about SYSTEMS, HEALTH*

Type 1

Port 70

Path 1/exchange-library/browse-subject/systems-health

Host cause-gopher.Colorado.EDU

Name *Federal Programs/Health-Related*

Type 1

Port 70

Path 1/.vine/links/FED/FEDHEAL

Host gopher.harvard.edu

Name *Domestic Affairs (Health Care)*

Type 1

Port 70

Path 1/.dir/pres.1992/pres.gen.dir

Host gopher.tamu.edu

Name *Public Health Resources*

Type 1

Port 70

Path 1/.public

Host count51.med.harvard.edu

Name *University of Utah, Eccles Health Sciences Library*

Type 1

Port 70

Path 1/internet/hytelnet/sys000/sys018/us189

Host gopher.cc.umanitoba.ca

Name *Stress and Mental Health*
Type 1
Port 4600
Path exec:R4984674-4986053-/.text/Main:/.bin/views
Host infx.infor.com

Name *Oregon Health Sciences University*
Type 1
Port 70
Path 1/internet/hytelnet/sys000/sys014/us302
Host gopher.cc.umanitoba.ca

Name *Physician Assistant Program*
Type 1
Port 70
Path 1/.students/.open-section/.METAREGFA/.REGFABROWSE/.REGFA06/
.REGFA0621/
Host burrow.adp.wisc.edu

Name *Work, Occupational Safety & Health*
Type 1
Port 70
Path 1/Biomed/Work
Host linux2.mic.ki.se

Name *Health Science Libraries*
Type 1
Port 70
Path 1/databases/health
Host salix.lib.washington.edu

Name *Health Policy Information*
Type 1
Port 70
Path 1/Academic Department Information/Policy Science (POSI)/
Health Policy Information
Host umbc4.umbc.edu

Name   *MEDCAT*
Type   1
Port   70
Path   1/library/medcat
Host   mchip00.med.nyu.edu

Name   *Department of Mental Health Law and Policy*
Type   1
Port   70
Path   1/mhlp
Host   hal.fmhi.usf.edu

Name   *Sexual Health & Education*
Type   1
Port   70
Path   1/SERVICE/general/health/sexuality
Host   nuinfo.nwu.edu

Name   *Medicine and Health*
Type   1
Port   4600
Path   1.browse/YOUNG ADULT/Medicine and Health
Host   infx.infor.com

Name   *HEALTH information and services (SW Med. Library)*
Type   1
Port   70
Path   1/healthinfo
Host   gopher.metronet.com

Name   *Health Sciences Libraries Consortium CBL Software Database*
Type   1
Port   70
Path   1/h_ekez/info_forras/hytelnet/sites2/ful000/ful050
Host   miat0.vein.hu

Name   *Medical and Health Science Libraries*
Type   1
Port   70

Path   1/Libraries and Reference Works/Medical and Health Science
        Libraries

Host   itsa.ucsf.edu

Name   *Physical Sciences, Health, and Medicine*

Type   1

Port   70

Path   1gopher_root:[physci]

Host   Gopher.gvltec.edu

Name   *Health Sciences*

Type   1

Port   70

Path   1/referencenew/healthsciences

Host   bigcat.missouri.edu

Name   *General Health Care Information*

Type   1

Port   70

Path   1/health/General

Host   Gopher.IC.Mankato.MN.US

Name   *Community Health Education Opportunities*

Type   1

Port   70

Path   1/hospital/comhealth

Host   yfn.ysu.edu

Name   *Women's Health*

Type   1

Port   70

Path   Moore Media:gopher server:UHS: General: Women's Health:

Host   bio-13.bsd.uchicago.edu

Name   *HPCC and Health Care Visualization*

Type   1

Port   70

Path   1/News Releases/HPCC and Health Care Visualization

Host   gopher.osc.edu

Name	*Environmental Health Newsletter...*
Type	1
Port	70
Path	1/.ehe/.news
Host	gopher.who.ch
Name	*Health Related Services*
Type	1
Port	2101
Path	1/Commercial/Services
Host	gopher.internet.com
Name	*School of Hygiene and Public Health Computing Center*
Type	1
Port	70
Path	1/.infotech/.shph
Host	jhuniverse.hcf.jhu.edu
Name	*Medicine & Health Sciences*
Type	1
Port	70
Path	1/gopherspace/Science/Medicine
Host	ocf.berkeley.edu
Name	*Health Sciences Resources on the Internet*
Type	1
Port	70
Path	1c:/resource
Host	el-gopher.med.utah.edu
Name	*Community Health Programs*
Type	1
Port	70
Path	1gopher_root:[depts.health.community]
Host	gopher.mala.bc.ca
Name	*HEALTH Studies & Issues in the Great Lakes*
Type	1

Port   2200

Path   1/health

Host   gopher.great-lakes.net

Name   *WHO (World Health Organization), Geneva*

Type   1

Port   8000

Path   1/info_coop/partners/region/europe/Switzerland/WHO

Host   infoserver.ciesin.org

Name   *National Institute of Health Catalog*

Type   1

Port   70

Path   1/Biomedical.../catalogn.../National Institute of Health Catalog

Host   gopher.library.upenn.edu

Name   *Health Care Briefings, Remarks, & Town Halls*

Type   1

Port   70

Path   1/.dir/pres.health.stuff

Host   gopher.tamu.edu

Name   *Health information*

Type   1

Port   70

Path   1/HEALTH

Host   gan.ncc.go.jp

Name   *Health Science Libraries*

Type   1+

Port   70

Path   1/databases/health

Host   salix.lib.washington.edu

Admin   Thomas Dowling, U of Washington Libraries, 206-685-8372
        <tdowling@u.washington.edu>

ModDate Thu Apr 7 14:38:10 1994 <19940407143810>

URL   gopher://salix.lib.washington.edu:70/11/databases/health

Other Resources of Interest to All Graduate Faculty and Students

All graduate faculty and students are engaged in research, and there are some resources of interest relating to methodology, statistics, and grants.

Lists and Newsgroups

Because the Internet began as a network for educational and governmental researchers, there are literally thousands of lists on topics useful to faculty and students. These are just a few of the research-related lists.

Where to find it

Methods

Material Culture Study and Methods

    `artifact@umdd.umd.edu`

Preprint Server for Computational Methods

    `comp-gas@jpnyitp.bitnet`

Electronic Research Methods

    `erm-l@emuvm1.cc.emory.edu`

Ethnomethodology/Conversation Analysis

    `ethno@vm.its.rpi.edu`

Social Science Research Methods Instructors

    `methods@unmvma.unm.edu`

Research Methodology

    `methods@vm.its.rpi.edu`

Q Methodology Network

    `q-method@kentvm.kent.edu`

Forum of Quantitative Methods in Geoscience

    `stat-geo@ufrj.bitnet`

Virtual Storage Access Method

`vsam-l@vm3090.ege.edu.tr`

Qualitative

Irish and British Ethnographic Research List

`ethnet-l@ysub.ysu.edu`

Quantitative Methods: Theory and Design

`qnteva-l@psuvm.psu.edu`

Qualitative Research List

`qual-l@psuvm.psu.edu`

Qualitative Research for the Human Sciences

`qualrs-l@uga.cc.uga.edu`

Qualitative Research in Education

`qualrsed@unmvma.unm.edu`

Quantitative and Statistical

Forum da Associacao Brasileira de Estatisti

`abe-l@brlncc.bitnet`

Quantitative Methods of Research on Agriculture

`camase-l@nic.surfnet.nl`

Teachers Int. Study Program in Statistics

`isps@cc1.kuleuven.ac.be`

EARN Statistics Group

`earnstat@vm.gmd.de`

EARN Statistics Group

`earnstat@earncc.bitnet`

Open discussion list for the Statistical Sciences

`genstat@ib.rl.ac.uk`

Psychology Statistics Discussion

`psysts-l@mizzou1.missouri.edu`

Quantitative Methods: Theory and Design

    qnteva-l@psuvm.psu.edu

Forum of Quantitative Methods in Geoscience

    stat-geo@ufrj.bitnet

General and Miscellaneous Research

Open Lib/Info Sci Research Forum

    xeleasai@arizvm1.ccit.arizona.edu

AERA-D Division D: Measurement and Research

    aera-d@asuvm.inre.asu.edu

Educational Research List

    erl-l@asuvm.inre.asu.edu

Researchers In Population Aging

    aging-l@brownvm.brown.edu

Research on Higher Education in Latin America

    hilat-l@bruspvm.bitnet

Electronic Research Methods

    erm-l@emuvm1.cc.emory.edu

Research & Teaching in Global Info Tech

    gtrti-l@gsuvm1.gsu.edu

Collaborative Research in the Health Science

    healr-l@gsuvm1.gsu.edu

AJCU Conference on Research

    ajcures@guvm.ccf.georgetown.edu

Human Evolutionary Research Discussion List

    humevo@gwuvm.gwu.edu

The National Indian Policy Research Institute

    niri@gwuvm.gwu.edu

Research Animals Topics Discussion Forum

    rat-talk@nic.surfnet.nl

European Association for Research on Learning

    `earli-ae@nic.surfnet.nl`

Discussion on Hungarian Academic & Research

    `h-net@huearn.sztaki.hu`

Discussion Research in Education and Didactic Systems

    `red-net@icineca.cineca.it`

Research Network

    `irl-net@irlearn.ucd.ie`

Cosine Project—Dental Research

    `dental-l@irlearn.ucd.ie`

International Research Project on Diabetes

    `diabetes@irlearn.ucd.ie`

International Discussion on Health Research

    `health-l@irlearn.ucd.ie`

Research on the Diatom Algae

    `diatom-l@iubvm.ucs.indiana.edu`

Consultation and Discussion of Research

    `conslt-l@iubvm.ucs.indiana.edu`

Library and Information Science Research

    `libres@kentvm.kent.edu`

Behavioral Research In Transplantation

    `brit-l@ksuvm.ksu.edu`

Research in Auditory Perception

    `auditory@vm1.mcgill.ca`

Teaching and Research in Economic History

    `econhist@miamiu.acs.muohio.edu`

Brain Tumor Research/Support

    `braintmr@mitvma.mit.edu`

Political Science Research and Teaching List

    `psrt-l@mizzou1.missouri.edu`

African-American Research

    `afam-l@mizzou1.missouri.edu`

Applied Expert Systems Research Group List

    `aesrg-l@mizzou1.missouri.edu`

Sociocultural Research Group

    `scrg@msu.edu`

Social Network Researchers

    `socnet@nervm.nerdc.ufl.edu`

Researchers in Population Aging

    `niatrn-l@list.nih.gov`

Research on Disability and Long-Term Care

    `ltcare-l@list.nih.gov`

Research Computing Forum

    `res-comp@nki.bitnet`

Classroom assessment and classroom research

    `ca-cr-l@nmsu.edu`

Operations Research/Computer Science

    `orcs-l@vm1.ucc.okstate.edu`

Communication Research and Theory Network

    `crtnet@psuvm.psu.edu`

Language Testing Research and Practice

    `ltest-l@psuvm.psu.edu`

Vision Research Group

    `vision-l@psuvm.psu.edu`

Public Management Research Exchange

    `pubmax-l@qucdn.queensu.ca`

Current Research in Human Communication

 `preview@vm.its.rpi.edu`

Discussion Forum on Camels Research

 `camel-l@sakfu00.bitnet`

Research Libraries' Network Administrators' List

 `bibtech@searn.sunet.se`

Swedish Initiative for Research and Education

 `siren@searn.sunet.se`

Nordic Initiative for Research and Education

 `nordren@searn.sunet.se`

Great Lakes Research Consortium Information

 `glrc@suvm.syr.edu`

Photosynthesis Researchers' List

 `photosyn@vm.tau.ac.il`

Stuttering: Research and Clinical Practice

 `stutt-l@vm.temple.edu`

Western Canadian Dairy Research and Technology

 `wcdrt-l@vm.ucs.ualberta.ca`

Research and Advanced Study: Canada and Italy

 `caci-l@vm.ucs.ualberta.ca`

North American Service Industries Research

 `nasirn-l@ubvm.cc.buffalo.edu`

Florida Artificial Intelligence Research

 `flairs@ucf1vm.cc.ucf.edu`

Association for Chinese Music Research Network

 `acmr-l@uhccvm.uhcc.hawaii.edu`

Pacific Business Researchers Forum (PCBR-L)

 `pcbr-l@uhccvm.uhcc.hawaii.edu`

Association of College and Research Libraries

> acrl@uicvm.uic.edu

Great Lakes Economic Development Research Group

> gled@uicvm.uic.edu

Computer-assisted Reporting & Research

> carr-l@ulkyvm.louisville.edu

Braille Research Center forum

> brctr@ulkyvm.louisville.edu

Clinical and Basic Science Research of Schizophrenia

> schiz-l@umab.umd.edu

Conferences on Chemistry Research and Education

> chemconf@umdd.umd.edu

CROSS-L Cross Cultural Research

> cross-l@vm1.spcs.umn.edu

Operations Research

> orms-l@umslvma.umsl.edu

Canadian Theatre Research

> candrama@unbvm1.csd.unb.ca

Social Science Research Methods Instructors

> methods@unmvma.unm.edu

BATLINE: Bat Research Information Exchange

> batline@unmvma.unm.edu

Marine Mammals Research and Conservation

> marmam@uvvm.uvic.ca

Institutional Researchers/University Planner

> air-l@vtvm1.cc.vt.edu

APA Research Psychology Network

> apasd-l@vtvm1.cc.vt.edu

Small Sociometric Research Project

```
clastalk@wcupa.edu
```

Spirochete Research Discussion Group

```
spiroc-l@wvnvm.wvnet.edu
```

Nonlinear Dynamics Research Group

```
ndrg-l@wvnvm.wvnet.edu
```

American Schools of Oriental Research in Canada

```
castor@vm1.yorku.ca
```

Usenet Newsgroups

There are many Usenet newsgroups with a Research focus. The range is broad from the sciences, social sciences, and the humanities, to research methods.

Where to find it

Information about Funding Agencies

```
bionet.sci-resources
```

Psychology Grad Student Discussions

```
bit.listserv.psycgrad
psycgrad@acadvm1.uottawa.ca
bit.listserv.psycgrad
```

Qualitative Research of the Human Sciences

```
bit.listserv.qualrs-l
```

The Nature of Research in Japan

```
comp.research.japan
res-japan-group@cs.arizona.edu
comp.research.japan
```

The SAS Statistics Package

```
comp.soft-sys.sas
```

The SPSS Statistics Package

    comp.soft-sys.spss

NSF Grant Notes (grants@note.nsf.gov)

    info.nsf.grants

General issues related to graduate schools

    soc.college.grad

Information about graduate schools

    soc.college.gradinfo

The use of computers as tools in scientific research

    sci.comp-aided

Research, teaching, and application of operations research

    sci.op-research

Research methods, funding, ethics, and so on

    sci.research

Issues relevant to careers in scientific research

    sci.research.careers

Anything about postdoctoral studies, including offers

    sci.research.postdoc

Statistical Consulting

    sci.stat.consult

Statistics Education

    sci.stat.edu

From Here...

To learn more about teaching and learning with the Internet, including Computer-Mediated Communication, continue on to Chapter 7. For more information on scholarship, research, and libraries, see Chapter 8.

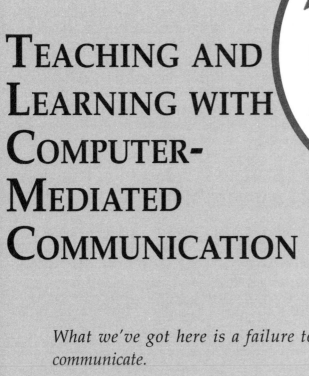

Teaching and Learning with Computer-Mediated Communication

What we've got here is a failure to communicate.

from *Cool Hand Luke* (Donn Pearce)

Teaching and learning using the Internet are multifaceted processes that can include using the Internet to access and investigate information, interactive collaborative learning groups, e-mail advising, and even the presentation of whole courses online.

Using the Internet presents some unique opportunities and challenges, because communication and teaching/learning via the Internet is different from communication in a traditional classroom. In some cases, the activities are so different that it presents some situations that require new communication techniques and new understandings of how people learn. Underlying all of the activity in education on the Internet is *Computer-Mediated Communication*. This means that all our communication—oral and visual—is conducted using computers in some way. All that we do involves computers in the interaction.

Computer-Mediated Communication

When using the Internet, we are using Computer-Mediated Communication (CMC). CMC is the name given to all types of functions where computers are used to facilitate and support human communication activity. This can be person-to-person, human-to-computer, and human-assisted by the computer. It touches on all uses of the computer in the educational enterprise. Grasping the concept of these computer-assisted interactions will give you a better understanding of how the process can work well, and how the process sometimes gets off-track.

CMC Via the Internet

CMC can offer new and enhanced avenues for teaching and learning: it can help break down time and location barriers, it can allow for interpersonal distance, enable students to access information in a self-paced exploratory fashion, reinforce learning, and allow for and encourage self-directed learning. CMC can involve a large range of activities—e-mail, use of Listservers, computer conferencing, the use of databases, collaborative projects, real-time chat, and more. CMC can include all the permutations of teacher-student, teacher-teacher, and student-student interactions as well.

The communication involved can be private, for example, between student and teacher via e-mail, or it can involve broad participation with public postings on a list, in an open conference or class conference. The interactions can be didactic—from one-to-many, without feedback similar to lectures, or it can be interactive (many-to-many), among collaborative groups or classes.

CMC is used at home, at work, at school, or anywhere people are using computers for their work, entertainment, or learning. This type of activity has grown exponentially in the last decade.

There are three main modes of computer-mediated communication:

■ *Human-to-Human Using a Computer*

In person-to-person communication using the computer, the computer is the vehicle for interaction and information exchange. The computer routes the exchanges, and this is typified on the Internet by e-mail, computer conferencing, and so on.

■ *Human-to-Computer for Information Maintenance and Retrieval*

Computers are capable of the storage of vast quantities of information in text, databases, images, and so on. In these cases, the computer is a resource for information storage and retrieval. These are very common activities on the Internet, involving FTP and CWIS, particularly in the case of accessing libraries and archives.

■ *Human-to-Computer for Process Assistance*

The computer also can be used to facilitate learning through *Computer Assisted Instruction* (CAI) and similar systems. The computer presents choices and threads to follow in the accomplishment of tasks. The computer is doing more than just following instructions; it is in a basic form, interacting with the user.

Resource

To show you how you can use the Internet to find information about a subject, here is an example of a first pass at learning about computer-mediated communications using computer-mediated communications. The idea is not to attempt a full thorough study of CMC, but rather to get the big picture of what information is available, and to get enough information to more carefully focus subsequent online sessions.

Note: See Appendix A for specific instructions on how to use the following Internet tools.

I started with a Veronica search for `computer-mediated communication`, and netted 200 files and Gopher menus. The first screen of matches looked like the following:

```
Internet Gopher Information Client v2.0.15

Search GopherSpace by Title word(s) (via SCS Nevada ): computer mediated comm...

 --> 1.  Computer Mediated Communication (CMC) Sources on the Internet (1 of..
      2.  Computer Mediated Communication (CMC) Sources on the Internet (2 of..
      3.  The Internet and computer-mediated communication
      4.  Computer_Mediated_Communication_(CMC)_Sources_on_the_Internet_(1_of..
      5.  Computer_Mediated_Communication_(CMC)_Sources_on_the_Internet_(1_of..
      6.  Computer_Mediated_Communication_(CMC)_Sources_on_the_Internet_(2_of..
      7.  Computer_Mediated_Communication_(CMC)_Sources_on_the_Internet_(2_of..
      8.  Computer_Mediated_Communication_(CMC)_Sources_on_the_Internet_(3_of..
      9.  Internet-and-Computer-Mediated-Communication  [17Sep93, 46kb]
     10.  Internet-and-Computer-Mediated-Communication
     11.  ...Internet & Computer-Mediated Communication
     12.  Information Sources: the Internet and Computer-Mediated Communicati..
     13.  "Information Sources: the Internet and Computer-Mediated Communicat..
     14.  Educational Computer-Mediated Communication: Recent Research
     15.  Instructional Design For Computer-Mediated Communication
     16.  _Inst. Science_: Computer-Mediated Communication.
     17.  _Inst. Science_: Computer-Mediated Communication.
     18.  Computer-Mediated Communication Part 1
     19.  Computer-Mediated Communication Part 2
     20.  Information Sources: Internet and Computer-Mediated Communication /
     21.  Computer Mediated Communication Resources
     22.  The Internet and Computer-Mediated Communication
     23.  Computer-Mediated Communication Forums/
     24.  Computer-mediated communication (the December list)
     25.  Infosources (Internet & Computer Mediated Communication) (04.04.93)
     26.  Info Sources: Internet & Computer-Mediated Communication (04_04_93)
     27.  Re: Computer Mediated Communication
     28.  Re: Computer Mediated Communication
     29.  computer-mediated.communication
     30.  4.25 Computer mediated communication -- research project
     31.  COMPUTER-MEDIATED COMMUNICATION--------------------+-----------
     32.  Information Sources: Internet & Computer-Mediated Communication
     33.  Information Sources: Internet & Computer-Mediated Communication
     34.  Computer_Mediated_Communication_(CMC)_Sources_on_the_Internet_(1_of..
     35.  Computer_Mediated_Communication_(CMC)_Sources_on_the_Internet_(2_of..
     36.  Computer_Mediated_Communication_(CMC)_Sources_on_the_Internet_(3_of..
     37.  Computer_Mediated_Communication_(CMC)_Sources_on_the_Internet_(1_of..
     38.  Computer_Mediated_Communication_(CMC)_Sources_on_the_Internet_(2_of..
     39.  Computer_Mediated_Communication_(CMC)_Sources_on_the_Internet_(3_of..
     40.  Computer_Mediated_Communication_(CMC)_Sources_on_the_Internet_(1_of..
     41.  Computer_Mediated_Communication_(CMC)_Sources_on_the_Internet_(2_of..
     42.  Computer_Mediated_Communication_(CMC)_Sources_on_the_Internet_(3_of..

Press ? for Help, q to Quit, u to go up a menu          Page: 1/5
```

I chose number 15, Instructional Design for Computer-Mediated Communication, and received a paper by Maurice Mitchell that begins:

```
Instructional Design For Computer-Mediated Communication
                        Maurice Mitchell
           University of Nevada System Computing  Services
    Association for the Development of Computer Based Instructional Systems
                         San Diego, CA
                        October 30, 1990
                 Copyright, 1990, Maurice Mitchell
                 ************************
```

Abstract

Computer-mediated communication (CMC) seems to be the latest fad in the
use of computers in instruction. Much of the early use of CMC was ad hoc
and haphazard in design. However, as CMC has grown in popularity,
faculty who embrace it are beginning to ask questions about how to improve
the instructional experience. This session will review a simple
instructional design guide for using CMC in instructional systems.

Objectives

Upon completion of the presentation the participants should be able to:

A   describe computer-mediated communication (CMC) and discuss the
     implications this technology has for instructional systems
     development;

B.   employ the distributed design guide in applying CMC in their courses.

Because this looked useful, I then e-mailed the document to myself to read later,
offline. Next, I explored an announcement of the opening of the Computer-Mediated Communication Studies Center and the first issue of an online CMC
related magazine.

From daemon Sun Jun 08 01:50:01 1994
From: <decemj@rpi.edu>
Newsgroups: comp.infosystems.announce
Subject: the Opening of the Computer-Mediated Communication Studies Center /
Organization: Michigan State University
Date: Sat, 7 May 94 12:50:37 EDT

Announcing: the Opening of the Computer-Mediated Communication Studies
Center and first issue of _Computer-Mediated Communication Magazine_

The Computer-Mediated Communication Studies Center, a set of web
pages dedicated to serving the needs of researchers, students, teachers,
and practitioners interested in computer-mediated communication
(CMC), is now open. This Center helps people share information, make
contacts, collaborate, and learn about developments and events related
to CMC. This center includes the first issue of _Computer-Mediated
Communication Magazine_, links to people who are interested in CMC, a
resources collection, and pointers to activities. If you are interested in
CMC studies, you are invited to participate.

About the CMC Studies Center

MISSION

   * To provide a forum for the exchange of information about CMC
   * To foster community-building among CMC scholars students,
     developers, and users through collaboration and information exchange.
   * To articulate and define CMC studies
   * To inform and educate interested persons about CMC issues and
     scholarship

I also e-mailed this one to my account as well, and subscribed to the magazine.

My next step in looking for information on CMC was to do a *WebQuery* using a WWW site called *WebCrawler*. Following is the URL:

```
http://www.biotech.washington.edu/WebCrawler/WebQuery.html
```

WebQuery is a nifty search tool for WWW that is similar to Veronica for Gopherspace. It is very powerful and can be used to search the WebCrawler database for any kind of WWW information. Using any WWW browser (such as WWW, Lynx, and Mosaic) you can go to the following homepage (I used Lynx):

```
WebCrawler Searching

                 [IMAGE] SEARCH THE WEB

   To search the WebCrawler database, type in your search keywords here.
   This database is a indexed by content. That means that the contents of
   documents are indexed, not just their titles and URLs. It will help to
   include both general and specific queries about your search.
   _____
      (*)AND words together        Search


   If you're having trouble using the WebCrawler, here are some helpful
   hints for searching. The WebCrawler also can answer questions about
   the graph structure of the Web; that capability is used to build the
   WebCrawler Top 25 List. For more information on the WebCrawler, and
   how the index is created, see this description. To compare the
   WebCrawler with other indexes of the Web, check out this list of Web
   indexes.

   _____


bp@cs.washington.edu
```

I entered `computer AND mediated` in the search, and discovered

```
      WebCrawler Search Results (p1 of 2)

WebCrawler Search Results

   Search results for the query "computer AND mediated":

   1000 Guides and Tutorials
   0818 CMC Magazine Masthead
   0777 John December Index Page
   0674 ProjectH Information
   0666 CMC Study Center Resources
   0567 JASON Project
   0548 ExCITE Background Info
   0491 Documents intéressants
   0482 Computer-Mediated Communication Studies Center
   0478 http://lib-gopher.lib.indiana.edu/other-service.html
   0455 Access to Network Software
```

```
0444 Zines
0444 Papers by ProjectH'ers
0437 Other Lists of Bibliographies
0429 WWW Servers Outside of Chalmers
0424 http://cpsr.org/cpsr/gender/ejvc_special_issue_cfp
0423 Internet Catalogues
0414 CityScape Internet Services
0392 CMC Study Center Resources
0388 http://eies.njit.edu:5230/pub/cccc.html
0388 Selected Web server sites
0388 Index of Services at Virginia Tech CS Dept.
0378 APANA Sydney infomation
0373 Scott's Home Page
0373 Glen (Gub) Daniels' Home Page
0373 Scott's Home Page
0372 Naval Postgraduate School (NPS) World-Wide-Web Home Page
0357 http://it.njit.edu/njIT/Department/CCCC/eies.html
0355 Cog & Psy Sci: Miscellany
0355 Other Internet Information Sources
0345 Vanessa Wilburn's home page
0345 Arachnophilia's Pointers to Publications on the Web
0333 Computer Mediated Communication Survey
0326 Internet Tools Summary
0321 Selections from franklin@uci.edu hotlist
0314 NCSU Computing Information and Resources
0311 CCCC @ NJIT Information Selection
0307 CCCC @ NJIT Information Selection
0305 Other World Wide Web Servers
0294 Non-LeRC resources
0286 Internet Tools Summary
0282 A Bison's Library of Dreams
0271 Internet Services, etc...
0270 The Australian Defence Force Academy
0268 Internet Tools Summary
0266 Brian Wilson's Home Page
0262 The Netizen's Cyberstop
0253 Internet Tools Summary
0251 Index of Services at Virginia Tech CS Dept.
0239 Florida Institute of Technology "What's New on the Web" Page
```

Whew! There is a lot here to look at and most of these were not identified in the Veronica search. My curiosity got the better of me so I took a look at 0282 A Bison's Library of Dreams, where I discovered a link to a WWW Human Computer Interaction and CMC Index:

```
A Bison's Library of Dreams (p1 of 3)

                      A BISON'S LIBRARY OF DREAMS

    [IMAGE]

    The Management is Not Responsible for Anything Lost or Found Herein.

The Catalogues

    The following list provides pointers to general subject indexes and
    keyword search programs covering the World Wide Web.
```

```
     * The WWW Virtual Library Subject Catalogue
     * The Clearinghouse for Subject-Oriented Internet Resource Guides
     * Joel's Hierarchical Subject Index
     * Libby Black's List of Subject Servers
     * Distributedly Administered Categorical List of Documents
     * EINet Galaxy
     * Index to Multimedia Information Sources
     * Internet Resources Metamap
     * The Mother-of-all BBS
     * World Wide Web Wanderers, Spiders & Robots (keyword search
       catalogues)
     * Search ALIWEB
     * Search the WebCrawler Index
     * U.C. Berkeley Library Gopher
     * HCI & CMC Materials
```

The HCI & CMC Materials item lead to this

```
                    INDEX OF HCI-RELATED MATERIAL

     [ HCI picture ]

     This index-page points to Human-Computer Interaction (HCI) related
     material in the World Wide Web. If you know of material that should be
     included in this list, but isn't, let me know by sending e-mail to:
     J.J.deGraaff@TWI.TUDelft.NL.

     I hope you find this page useful.
      Hans de Graaff
```

In just a few minutes I was able to get an overview of the depth and breadth of Internet CMC resources and several hundred leads for further research.

Communicons: Emoticons, Smiley Faces, Emphasis, and Stage Directions

On the Internet, it often is difficult to express emotions, context, moods, and emphasis in the text-based messages of private e-mail and public postings to discussion lists and Usenet newsgroups. After all, how do you express irony without being able to make your voice rise and fall and a shrug of your shoulders?

When you try to express humor, surprise, anger, sarcasm, and so on, the text-based nature of Internet messages makes that difficult because the non-verbal components of human communication are missing; however, there are a variety of communicons (communication + icon) that can be used to make up for this loss of the non-verbal expressions.

The most popular of these communicons are called *smileys* or *smiley faces*. The simplest of these is a colon combined with a right parenthesis (tilt your head to the left to see it).

:)

If you include a joke or humorous comment in a message or posting, put a smiley after it so that no one interprets your joke as being your genuine opinion or understanding of the situation. Other communicons have been created and used to help the message reader understand the "inflection" intended by the writer to indicate the context of the message. There are hundreds of these. Following are some of the most common with the usual interpretation of some of the symbols you might see:

```
:)    your basic smiley

:-)   another simple smiley with a nose added

;)    a wink

:->   another simple smiley

;>    a winking mischievous smile

:]    a goofy grin

:-o   surprise

:-O   shock

8-)   a smiley wearing glasses

:-¦   a blank look

:(    a frown

:-<   a sad face
```

You can create your own. =8-0, for example, might be a frightened or alarmed communicon with the hair standing up, and the eyes and mouth wide open. Have fun!

Project

A good project for K-6 is to have each child invent his or her own communicon to try out in an e-mail message with a pen pal. Older youths might want to try to create a personal icon, and discuss the emotion or mood they are trying to convey. At the collegiate level, students could study how the use of various symbols causes variations in the interpretation of messages and in their impressions of the sender.

Another set of communicons encompass a form of shorthand for common phrases. Following are some of the most common abbreviations:

<g>	Grin
AKA	Also Known As
BTW	By The Way
IMHO	In My Humble Opinion
IMO	In My Opinion
GD&R	Grinning, Ducking, and Running
LD&R	Laughing, Ducking, and Running
L8R	Later
LOL	Laughing Out Loud
OTOH	On The Other Hand
SYSOP	SYStem OPerator
TIC	Tongue In Cheek
TTFN	Ta Ta For Now

The standard ASCII characters in use on the Internet provide no direct way to underline, use fonts, italics, or other ways of highlighting a word or phrase. Internauts have created several ways of working around this to show emphasis for text:

■ _psuedo-underlining_

Putting an underline before and after the word or phrase indicates that it would be underlined in normal text.

■ *using asterisks*

Putting asterisks—stars in Internet lingo—around a word or phrase emphasizes what might have been bolded in other circumstances.

■ USING ALL CAPITAL LETTERS

Another way to show emphasis is to capitalize a word or phrase.

Tip: Using ALL CAPS ALL THE TIME is considered "shouting" and annoys some people—they will ask you to quit!

Another way to help the reader understand your meaning is to include stage directions and/or written gestures in your message. For example I might say

```
[as I get up on my soapbox]

    and then enter my message, and then put

[stepping down off of my soapbox]
```

This lets the reader know that I am aware of the controversial nature of my statement and that I want to isolate this portion of my message from the other portions.

Following is another popular stage direction:

```
[set flame on]

    message text

[set flame off]
```

In this type of message, everyone knows that the text in the middle is critical or somewhat negative, but that the writer is trying to soften the criticism.

Another approach to these stage directions or asides is to use the following method:

```
I don't know <shrug> what do you think?
```

There are only a few specific asides and stage directions that are commonly used—they are usually made up fresh on the spot to more accurately communicate the *whole* message.

Communicons help convey a message in a more complex and expressive way. Often it is _how_ we say something that makes a substantial difference—try using a few of these methods for enhancing text-based messages.

Example

Consider the difference in the following messages:

```
Bob,
How could you ever say that?
------------------------------
Bob,
How could you ever say that?  GD&R  ;>
------------------------------
Bob,
How could you ever say that?  :(
------------------------------
Bob,
How could *you* ever say that? <shaking his head in disbelief>
```

Learning Implications of CMC and Learning Styles

There are many things that influence us when we use the Internet for CMC in teaching and learning. One of the most important is the learning styles of those being taught.

Learning Styles, CMC, and the Internet

Understanding *learning styles* is complex because it involves an understanding of the interaction of personality, cognition, conceptualization, information processing, effect, and behavior, among others. These involve the basic patterns of personal style including personality and preferences. When they affect learning, we refer to these patterns as learning styles.

There are many existing learning style inventories or assessments for children, youths, and adults, as well as many approaches to the notion of individual differences. Several different assessment instruments have been developed, including *Kolb's Learning Styles Inventory*, *The Gregorc Style Delineator*, *The Furman Jacobs Learning Interaction Inventory*, and others.

To illustrate one learning style categorization and its influence on teaching and learning using the Internet, I will use Kolb's Learning Styles Inventory (LSI).

David Kolb developed his LSI to measure relative differences in the way people approach learning: how they perceive or understand experience and information (concrete versus abstract; sensing/feeling versus thinking), and how they process or convert experience and information (active versus reflective and doing versus observing). The LSI was designed to describe learning styles as an indicator of behaviors consistent with experiential learning theory. The LSI presents items for learners to rank using a scale with numbers from 1 to 4, corresponding to their perception/interpretations in relation to their learning preferences. Individuals score the LSI themselves. It then offers comparisons between individuals and a norm, measuring the strength of each learning style category.

The learning is categorized by Kolb into four styles.

Concrete Experience (CE)	Experience based
	Peer oriented
	Emphasizing feedback and discussion
Abstract Conceptualization (AC)	Analytical
	Oriented toward things and symbols

	Authority directed impersonal learning situations
Active Experimentation (AE)	Active orientation Focused on "doing" Project oriented
Reflective Observation (RO)	Reflective Observational approach Prefer lecture situations

There are many of these learning style classification schemes. Using Kolb as an example, look at what each style might mean to a learning situation involving the Internet.

Concrete Experience	A person with a learning preference in this area would want to actively experience the Internet with others—to get on the Internet and take part in an activity working on a team, followed by discussions.
Abstract Conceptualization	This individual would want to begin by planning and analyzing the activity, and carry out alone a leader/teacher structured activity on the Internet, followed by formal feedback of information.
Active Experimentation	A person with these learning preferences would want to jump right in and complete on the Internet with less preparation and little follow-up a project.
Reflective Observation	This individual would want a lecture before beginning an activity on the Internet, followed by a demonstration. He or she also would like to work in a pair in order to observe online a partner's activities.

Structuring the learning activities to meet learning styles especially is important when using the Internet. Because of the relatively "cool" nature of the medium, planning for a variety of activities can prove useful. Plan some with teams, some alone, some with hands-on experiences, and some with didactic elements.

Levels of Learning

The successful use of CMC with the Internet in teaching or learning depends upon the application of four levels of developmental teaching and learning. Each level of the learning requires mastery of the previous level.

Level 1: Why Are We Doing This?

Level 1 teaching and learning involves the mastery of the general context for the other learning tasks, answering questions such as "What are we trying to accomplish? What is expected? How can the Internet be useful?" Essentially, this tier lays the groundwork for the entire activity; the student must have a context for the more specific learning, and must understand the role and value of CMC in that learning. In effect, they must see the connection between what is being taught (the content) and the vehicles (methods and media) for that teaching.

Level 2: Learning the Technology

This builds on Level 1, and involves introductory hands-on learning of the technical aspects of access and process that students must acquire in order to start using the various technologies and tools. These are the skills, or the "how to" operational level tasks: the rules of interaction. Typically, this means learning how to use a terminal and/or PC (if they do not already know how) in order to access the Internet. Typical questions include "How do I sign on? How do I use this communication program?" This involves using the hardware, and learning the various software and protocols involved in connecting, access, e-mail, up- and downloading, and using a computer conferencing system, such as VAXnotes.

Level 3: Mastering the Tools

This involves learning the search tools of the Internet, such as Gopher, WWW, and so on, and gaining real confidence in the basic skills. In this level, students need to gain proficiency and mastery of the tools so that those tools become second nature and don't form a barrier to carrying out the assignment or activity. Both teacher and learner must have sufficient expertise and familiarity with the tools so that the tools themselves are not a communication barrier.

Level 4: Applying What Has Been Learned For Problem Solving

This is the level at which the student should start to see, through personal experience, the value of the Internet in gathering information and solving problems. These problems and challenges first can come as assigned tasks that use the Internet as a tool and then as student-defined problems and needs. This level results in the actual utilization of the Internet in problem solving, information gathering, negotiating, and turning in assignments.

The Internet is reputed to have a very steep learning curve and a user-unfriendly (often called *savage* on the Internet itself) interface. The steepness of the learning curve has been exaggerated. When time is spent moving through the levels of learning (outlined previously), and the learning tasks have been broken down into coherent units, the up-front learning is much easier, quicker, and smoother.

The issues surrounding the savage interface too are somewhat exaggerated. Many systems can make use of Lynx, and some can use Mosaic, which can help with this problem. In addition, new Internet tools and user interfaces are continuing to make Internet access easier and more intuitive. And again, where the levels of learning are moved through carefully, even the dreaded % or $ prompt can be much less intimidating.

All too often, faculty and teachers want to use the Internet as an enhancement or as a major delivery system, but they overlook the need to provide Level 2 technical "how to" information. They will, for example, ask students to sign on to the system and use Gopher to find something. The students have no clue how to do this and do not dare to reveal that they don't know how. They also do not know who else to get the answer from—and, frustrated, they do not complete the assignment.

Resource

There are many online resources for finding training materials related to helping others gain facility with the Internet and the Internet tools. For example, there are two ERIC clearinghouses that maintain useful materials, and they have e-mail addresses to request more information—the *ERIC Clearinghouse on Adult, Career, and Vocational Education* at `ericacve@magnus.acs.ohio-state.edu`. You can reach the ERIC Clearinghouse on Assessment and Evaluation using e-mail to `eric_ae@cua.edu`. ERIC materials are available online through a variety of sources.

Another service from ERIC, called AskERIC, can be reached by pointing your Gopher at `ericir.syr.edu`. The Gopher at Arizona State University especially is fertile for the educator. Point your Gopher to `info.asu.edu port 70/asu-cwis/ education`.

John Makulowich has created a WWW resource called the *Awesome List* to offer links to training materials and items for demonstrating the Internet. Reach this resource at `http://www.clark.net/pub/journalism/awesome.html`.

The *Internet Resource Directory for Educators* (IRD) is available for anonymous FTP from `tcet.unt.edu` in the `/pub/telecomputing-info/IRD` subdirectory. The IRD has four sections, each contained in ASCII text files, including `IRD-telnet-sites.txt`, `IRD-ftp-archives.txt`, `IRD-listservs.txt`, and `IRD-infusion-ideas.txt`.

St. John's University has both learning styles and useful educational information that can be accessed by pointing your Gopher to `sjuvm.stjohns.edu` (`149.681.1.10`). To obtain learning styles information, choose the menu item `education & teaching resources`, and then from the next menu, choose `learning styles`.

You can find an outline of an introductory session on WWW and Mosaic at `http://www.cs.princeton.edu/grad/Dan_Wallach/www-talk/talk0.html`.

Here is a very abbreviated Archie search hunting for `training`.

```
world% Archie -s training

Host life.anu.edu.au


Host ccadfa.cc.adfa.oz.au

    Location: /pub/tex/ctan2/fonts/postscript/adobe/Documents
        FILE -r--r--r--       4698  Jul  9 1992  training.info

Host ic16.ee.umanitoba.ca

    Location: /pub/Database/Images/Grey/People/512x512
        FILE -rw-r--r--        375  Dec  8 1992  Training_sequence

Host nic.switch.ch

    Location: /docs/GAO-Reports
        FILE -rw-rw-r--     184883  May  1 1990  GAO-Training-Strategies
    Location: /mirror/ucsd/races
        FILE -rw-rw-r--       2063  Sep 14 1992  training.asc
Host world.std.com

    Location: /src/wuarchive/packages/TeX/fonts/postscript/adobe/Documents
        FILE -r--r--r--       4698  Jul  9 1992  training.info

Host think.com

    Location: /cm
      DIRECTORY drwxrwxr-x        512  May  6 02:23  training

Host athene.uni-paderborn.de

Location: /doc/FAQ/news.answers/dogs-faq
        FILE -rw-r--r--      39615  May 23 22:41  training
    Location: /doc/FAQ/rec.answers/dogs-faq
        FILE -rw-r--r--      39615  May 23 22:41  training
    Location: /doc/FAQ/rec.pets.dogs
        FILE -rw-r--r--      39615  May 23 22:41  Dog_FAQ
```

```
Host ftp.denet.dk

    Location: /pub/security/NIST
       DIRECTORY drwxr-xr-x        1024  Apr  5 09:29  training

Host archive.cis.ohio-state.edu

    Location: /pub/internic/resources/.cap
          FILE -r--r--r--          18  Aug 10 1993  training.Z
    Location: /pub/internic/resources
       DIRECTORY drwxr-xr-x         512  Jun 18 08:12  training

Host gogol.cenatls.cena.dgac.fr

    Location: /pub/docs/ada/tools
          FILE -rw-r--r--         5467  Apr 24 1992  Training_Education.txt.Z

Host ghost.dsi.unimi.it

    Location: /pub/net-bib
          FILE -rw-r--r--        12120  Feb 16 1993
a_list_of_training_materials.network-training-materials-project.newcastle-
university.nov-1992.Z

Host nctuccca.edu.tw

DIRECTORY drwxr-xr-x        2048  Dec 30 00:00  training
    Location: /documents/networking/Internet/InterNIC-InfoGuide/resources
       DIRECTORY drwxr-xr-x       2048  May  8 00:00  training
    Location: /documents/networking/guides/InterNIC.Directory.of.Directories
       DIRECTORY drwxr-xr-x       2048  Jun  9 00:00  training
    Location: /documents/security/NIST
       DIRECTORY drwxr-xr-x       2048  Jun  8 00:00  training
```

This is just a sampling of the files and directories Archie found in this search. And, as with any search (whether Veronica, WebCrawler, Archie, or others), you can always expect to find both gems and those way off the track (such as the "dogs-faq" and the dog training files). To get a more refined list you can repeat the search to filter out unwanted matches, for example, by searching for training AND internet NOT dog. (See Appendix A for more details.)

Collaborative Learning

In the traditional classroom, collaborative learning is an instructional method that requires students to work together on academic tasks. It is especially well-suited to Internet tasks. This can involve a wide range of cooperative activities requiring active peer involvement and participation using shared resources, and results in a common experience of shared success or failure. Collaborative learning in Computer-Mediated Learning involves small groups of students, generally four to six, who investigate, research, discuss, present facts and opinions, and arrive at consensus regarding a topic assigned by the instructor or agreed on by the group and the teacher.

A major goal of collaborative learning is the involvement of students in *active* learning activities. By using massive, open-ended data from the Internet rather than just selecting facts memorized from the traditional lecture, students must find and process information as they will have to when they are not in the controlled environment of school. Students who become responsible for their own learning and collaboration are more likely to acquire lifelong learning skills. Even very young students can learn to think for themselves more and to respect the opinions and judgments of others.

The development of consensus is important to collaborative learning. Without inhibiting individuality, members of a group gain a stake in collective projects when given the goal of finding consensus. This is consensus as a practical matter; it is not just reconciling differences through role playing or "ideal" conversation.

The term "collaborative learning" can be applied to peer tutoring, group projects, shared writing, co-authoring, and so on. It involves the achievment of individual goals and the completion of projects along with a group of learners within the context-bound classroom. By using the Internet, this group can extend across continents.

The role of the teacher in the collaborative learning process is to facilitate the learners' expanding knowledge base, assist them in asking the right questions, and provide guidance toward appropriate answers. Instructors have the opportunity through groups to challenge students' intellects and prepare them for "real world" fields, which depend on effective interdependence and consultation to achieve excellence. This can be achieved with a sliding scale of independence ranging from a considerable amount of guidance with modest goals for K-6 students, through increasing independence for 7-12 students, and greater independence at the collegiate level.

The creation of a positive climate for collaboration depends on the instructor's attention to the learning environment, willingness to "let them stew" a little, a willingness on the part of the teacher to operate in the role as facilitator, and for the students to take some responsibility for their own learning.

The purpose, process, and goals of collaborative groups should be well understood before students embark on working together. After an introduction to the group process, the instructor must step back and allow the groups to function. With college-age students, if the instructor intervenes more than to answer a question of format or operation, students revert to the "teacher as authority model" that they learned through most of their schooling and the collaborative cord is broken. Even younger students to a degree need help in finding their own way.

The role of the student shifts from the relatively passive "listener, observer, note-taker" to "problem-solver, contributor, and discussant" in the small group, from "competitor" to "collaborator," and from learning independently to learning interdependently.

The processes of creating, analyzing, and evaluating (higher level thinking skills in *Bloom's Taxonomy*) in collaboration with others strengthen socialization skills, increase cross-cultural awareness and appreciation, and increase general interest, focus, and synthesis efforts. (Thanks to Barbara Tew for discussions that helped clarify collaborative learning concepts.)

Okay, Now What?: Useful Vehicles for Teaching and Learning with the Internet

All this information about computer-mediated communication, learning styles, and collaborative learning can be applied directly to using the Internet for education. The Internet can be useful both in gaining content (alpha learning) and in reinforcement such as asking questions (beta learning).

The four typical Internet vehicles for interacting with, and among, students and others on the Internet are e-mail, conferencing, MOOs and MUDs, and interactive messaging, such as Internet Relay Chat (IRC) and Talk. The other major activity is the acquisition of information.

You can use *e-mail* to provide a variety of types of interactions, such as student-to-student interaction, where students can communicate and complete assignments, discuss class-work (both processes and content), and so on. Student-to-faculty and faculty-to-student interaction, encompassing a full range of communication such as advising, explanations, course content, evaluation, and the turning in of written assignments, also can be accomplished using e-mail. The best way to learn more about your mail program is to talk with your SYSOP.

Assessment and evaluation activities also can be carried out online at a variety of levels, and usually are accomplished using e-mail. Specific assignments can be critiqued and evaluated, as well as provide a forum for less formal assessment activities. The Internet provides "on-the-fly" opportunities for networking and mentoring, as well.

Conferencing usually involves a private computer conference (exclusive to class members) using VAXNotes, for example, set aside to provide shared, posted views, ideas, and collaborative writing activities, including peer-to-peer interactions. You also can use didactic postings, involving one way communication for the purpose of making assignments. Postings in the computer conferences can be quite broad, ranging in their purpose, level of formality, and intent. There are numerous packages of conferencing software, depending upon your computing resources.

Internet Relay Chat (IRC) can provide interactive messaging across huge distances where a student in California, for example, can talk directly with those in Russia, or a class can directly discuss an author's book with him or her. IRC requires that all parties be online simultaneously. You can obtain more information on IRC on the newsgroup `alt.irc`, which covers Internet Relay Chat material, and via FTP to `cs.bu.edu` as `/irc/support/tutorials`.

MUDs and *MOOs* are increasingly popular as educational Internet tools that enable learners and others to interact in a virtual environment. Multi-User Dialog/Dimension/Dungeons (MUD) are text-based virtual environments that enable groups and individuals to interact in real-time. MUD Object Oriented (MOO) is a MUD, based on an object-oriented language, which offers a more complex experience than MUD. Multi-User Simulation Environment (MUSE) is a facility that combines elements of Internet Relay Chat and role-playing games. Each person creates his or her own virtual reality, or can participate in existing scenarios. MIT maintains a virtual reality called *MicroMuse* designed to enable students to explore a twenty-fourth century science fiction environment and design their own world. Telnet to `michael.ai.mit.edu` (`18.43.0.177`), and then at login, type **guest**. If you see a `TERM+(vt100)` prompt, press Enter. At the `MicroMuse` prompt, type **connect guest**. For more information, FTP to `chezmoto.ai.mit.edu` and look in the `/muse` subdirectory.

CU-SeeMe is a video conferencing facility using the Internet. While not accessible yet for most educational institutions, Cornell University software is being use to conduct video conference over the Internet. It would allow video to accompany interactive messaging technology. For information on CU-SeeMe, contact Richard Cogger at `R.Cogger@cornell.edu`.

A very useful FAQ on the Internet is called *Internet Services Frequently Asked Questions and Answers*. It covers a very broad range of topics, including what is telnet, FTP, Usenet, finger, IRC, Veronica, MUDs, and discusses how to send e-mail on the Internet, getting more information, and more. Maintained by Kevin Savetz, you can obtain it via FTP from `rtfm.mit.edu` in the `/pub/usenet/news.answers/internet-services` subdirectory as file `faq`.

In addition to the more serious teaching and learning activities, you can use the Internet as relief from stress. There are lots of humorous, lighthearted lists and newsgroups that can provide entertainment.

From Here...

To learn more about the Internet and distance learning, continue on to Chapter 8. For tips about learning on your own, see Chapter 10.

SCHOLARSHIP, RESEARCH, LIBRARIES, AND RESOURCES

I always imagined that Paradise would be a kind of Library.

Jorge Luis Borges

Research and scholarships in higher education have been changed by the Internet. Traditional research methods involve on-site examination, extensive note taking, and photocopying of paper-based journals and books. It also involves using indices and abstracts, such as ERIC and Psychological Abstracts. For an increasing number of faculty, however, the Internet has been improving dramatically the speed and quality of their work.

Now, it is increasingly common for a faculty member to use remote databases, exchange mail with far-flung colleagues, collaborate on research, and get copies of the latest journals, all online, and without even going into the office.

Many teachers and faculty members strive to be on the cutting edge—and increasingly this means going far beyond traditional hard-copy journals and books. Opportunities abound for the scholar on the Internet. Where else can you meet new colleagues in Ulan Bator, locate a vast storehouse of resources, and use distant libraries easily. You can even talk in real-time with others halfway around the world. The resources available to faculty and teachers include library catalogs, databases, indices, electronic journals, electronic texts, papers, images, sound and music files, discussion groups, Usenet newsgroups, and more. Each of these offer tools to the educator.

Books, chapters and articles are written, presentations are planned, and research in carried out on the Internet. I have frequently collaborated on research and writing with colleagues I have never met face to face.

Research and scholarship on the Internet includes access to vast store houses of information and raw data, access to analytic tools, and access to people and ideas. So how does research and scholarship work now, as opposed to the "olden" days? Take a look at some of the ways in which the Internet has become integral to scholarship and research.

- Discussion Lists
- Usenet Newsgroups
- Libraries
- Electronic Journals
- Electronic Texts
- Discipline Specific Information
- Conferences and Calls for Papers
- Syllabi
- Globalization

Discussion Lists and Scholarship

The Internet discussion lists are excellent sources of up-to-date information and resources for world-wide collegial networking. You can send trial balloons of your ideas, ask for help in locating information and experts, send out a draft of a paper for informal reactions, and receive thoughtful, insightful assistance from across the world (and the campus) often in minutes. Through these activities, it is easy to locate colleagues who are interested in the same issues and ideas. All these activities and more happen on the discussion lists and newsgroups.

These lists and groups provide opportunities for writing articles and carrying out research collaboratively, for professional networking, and the posting of calls for papers and grant opportunities. For example, I have written books, chapters, and articles, and worked through the refereeing and editing processes entirely online with colleagues I have met on the lists. In addition, these lists are one of the best ways to keep your finger on the pulse of a discipline and/or organization.

 Note: For the standard procedures involved in subscribing to discussion lists, see Appendix A.

Diane Kovacs from Kent State University, along with several colleagues, maintains extensive listings of scholarly discussion lists categorized by discipline. You can find these listings on many Gophers, including the University of Michigan Clearinghouse (`una.hh.lib.umich.edu port 70`).

Following are the relevant files regarding the scholarly discussion lists:

`acadlist.readme`	Explanatory notes
`acadstac.hqx`	Binhexed, self-decompressing, HyperCard stack, keyword searchable
`acadlist.file1`	Education, library, and information science
`acadlist.file2`	Humanities, Part one
`acadlist.file3`	Humanities, Part two
`acadlist.file4`	Social Sciences
`acadlist.file5`	Biological Sciences
`acadlist.file6`	Physical Sciences
`acadlist.file7`	Business, economics, publishing, and news
`acadlist.file8`	Computer science, social, cultural, and political aspects of computing and academic computing support, research related

acadlist.file9	Computer science, social, cultural, and political aspects of computing and academic computing support, non-specific including public domain software
acadwhol.hqx	Binhexed self-decompressing Macintosh document of all files

You can retrieve these files from `listserv@kentvm.kent.edu` or `listserv@kentvm.bitnet` by sending the e-mail message **get Filename Filetype** to the Listserv (leave the subject line blank). To retrieve the file containing lists on the physical sciences, for example, send the message **get acadlist file4**. The files also are available via FTP from `ksuvxa.kent.edu` in the `/library` subdirectory.

Kovacs uses this format to present information about each discussion list:

```
LN: List Name
TI: Topic
SU: Subscription
ED: Edited - yes or no
AR: Archived? if Yes, frequency
MO: Name of moderator or listowner
SA: Institutional affiliation
KE: Key subject words
```

Following is a sample of the 24 of listings in Business, Economics, Publishings and News:

```
File Seven; (Business, Economics, Publishings and News) (p2 of 24)
─────────────
LN: BUSFAC-L
TI: The purpose of this list is to provide business faculty an arena
to share ideas for research, curriculum and discuss solutions to
problems.
SU: (B) LISTSERV@CMUVM (I) LISTSERV@CMUVM.CSV.CMICH.EDU
ED: Yes
AR: Yes, Monthly, Private
MO: Syed Shah (B) 3M3EPLG@CMUVM (I) 3M3EPLG.CMUVM.CSV.CMICH.EDU
SA: (I) BUSFAC-L@CMUVM.CSV.CMICH.EDU
KE: Faculty  - Business
─────────────
LN: CTI-ACC-AUDIT
TI: Open to anyone interested in Auditing and wanting to be in
contact with others with similar interests. Sponsored by the CTI
Centre for Accounting Finance and Management at the School of
Information Systems, University of East Anglia.
SU: (I) MAILBASE@MAILBASE.AC.UK
ED: No
AR: Yes, Monthly
MO: (I) cti-acc-audit-request@mailbase.ac.uk
SA: (I) CTI-ACC-AUDIT@MAILBASE.AC.UK
KE: Accounting - Auditing - International
─────────────
LN: CTI-ACC-BUSINESS
```

```
TI: For the use of those interested in the use of computers in the
teaching of Accounting Finance and Management. Sponsored by the CTI
Centre for Accounting Finance and Management at the School of
Information Systems, University of East Anglia.
SU: (I) MAILBASE@MAILBASE.AC.UK
ED: No
AR: Yes, Monthly
MO: (I) chem-mod-request@mailbase.ac.uk
SA: (I) CTI-ACC-BUSINESS@MAILBASE.AC.UK
KE: Finance Accounting Management - International
```

Following are some useful lists I have discovered that pertain to higher education, faculty activities, and the academic community:

```
AACIS-L       American Association for Collegiate Independent Study
              listserv@ecnuxa.bitnet
              listserv@bgu.edu
```

AACIS-L is sponsored by The American Association for Collegiate Independent Study. It focuses on correspondence, independent study, and distance learning.

```
AEDNET        Adult Education Network
              listserv@alpha.acast.nova.edu
```

AEDNET is an international electronic network that includes approximately 750 individuals from 12 countries who are broadly interested in adult education issues.

```
ALTLEARN      Alternative Approaches to Learning Discussion
              listserv@sjuvm.bitnet
              listserv@sjuvm.stjohns.edu
```

The *Alternative Approaches to Learning* discussion list is broadly concerned with learning strategies at all levels of education.

```
DTS-L         Dead Teachers Society Discussion List
              listserv@iubvm.bitnet
              listserv@iubvm.ucs.indiana.edu
```

The *Dead Teachers' Society Discussion List* is for discussions of all kinds related to teaching and learning.

```
EDNET         Education Net
              listproc@nic.umass.edu
```

EDNET is for those interested in exploring the educational potential of the Internet. Discussions range from K-12 through postsecondary education.

```
EDPOLYAN       Educational Policy Analysis
               listserv@asuacad.bitnet
               listserv@asuvm.inre.asu.edu
```

The *EDSTYLE* list focuses on educational policy analysis. This is an active, lively list, where issues surrounding all levels of education are discussed, often from a philosophical perspective.

```
EDSTYLE        The Learning Styles Theory and Research List
               listserv@sjuvm.bitnet
               listserv@sjuvm.stjohns.edu
```

The *Learning Styles Theory and Research* list discusses all aspects of learning styles.

```
HILAT-L        Higher Education in Latin America
               listserv@bruspvm.bitnet
```

HILAT-L provides a means of interchange about research on Higher Education in Latin America. Postings are mostly in English, but are also welcome in Spanish and Portuguese.

```
IPCT-L         Interpersonal Computing and Technology
               listserv@guvm.bitnet
               listserv@guvm.ccf.georgetown.edu
```

IPCT-L is focused on Computer-Mediated Communication, and teaching and learning broadly, and usually is an animated and thought-provoking list.

```
NEWEDU-L       New Patterns in Education List
               listserv@uhccvm.uhcc.hawaii.edu
```

New Patterns discusses education very broadly, including delivery systems, media, collaborative learning, learning styles, and more.

```
POD            Professional Organizational Development
               listserv@lists.acs.ohio-state.edu
```

The *POD* network is aimed at faculty development, instructional, and organizational development in higher education.

```
STLHE-L        Forum for Teaching & Learning in Higher Education
                    listserv@unbvm1.bitnet
                    listserv@unbvm1.csd.unb.ca
```

STLHE-L focuses on all facets of post-secondary education, and many conference announcements and calls for papers appear on the list.

```
TEACHEFT       Teaching Effectiveness
                    listserv@wcu.bitnet
                    listserv@wcupa.edu
```

TEACHEFT treats teaching effectiveness and a broad range of teaching/learning interests.

Tip: Do not send subscription requests to the list itself. Send them through the list processor, Listserver, or majordomo. See Appendix A for more information on how to do this.

Other lists of possible interest include those found in table 8.1.

Table 8.1. Lists Broadly Related to Teaching and Learning

List Addresses	List Name
AERA-C@asuvm.inre.asu.edu	AERA-C Division C: Learning and Instruction
AERA-D@asuvm.inre.asu	AERA-D Division D: Measurement and Research
AERA-J@asuvm.inre.asu.edu	AERA-J Division J: Postsecondary Education
AERA-VC@unbvm1.csd.unb.ca	VirtCon: AERA's Virtual Conference
AJCURES@guvm.ccf.georgetown.edu	AJCU Conference on Research
AAHESGIT@gwuvm.gwu.edu	AAHE Info. Tech. Activities & Projects
CL_NEWS@iubvm.ucs.indiana.edu	News on Teaching With Collaborative Learning
CMC@vm.its.rpi.edu	Computer-Mediated Communication

continues

Table 8.1. continued

List Addresses	List Name
DGTLCLAS@vm1.McGill.CA	Discussion on Digital Media and MultiMedia
EARLI-AE@nic.surfnet.nl	European Association for Research on Learning
EDTECH@msu.edu	EDTECH - Educational Technology
EDUTEL@vm.its.rpi.edu	Education and Information Technologies
EUITLIST@bitnic.educom.edu	Educational Uses of Information Technology
EMAILMAN@vtvm1.cc.vt.edu	Learning about Accessing Electronic Information
ENET-L@uhccvm.uhcc.hawaii.edu	AERA Electronic Networking SIG Discussion List
ERL-L@asuvm.inre.asu.edu	Educational Research List
ERM-L@emuvm1.cc.emory.edu	Electronic Research Methods
GRANT@gwuvm.gwu.edu	Fulbright Awards and Grants for Faculty
GRANT-L@ua1vm.ua.edu	OSP Funding Alert List
GTRTI-L@gsuvm1.gsu.edu	Research & Teaching in Global Information Technology
IRL-NET@irlearn.ucd.ie	Research Network
LISRSC-L@nmsu.edu	ACRL Research - Scholarly Communication
LRNASST@arizvm1.ccit.arizona.edu	Open Forum for Learning Assistance
MEDIA-L@bingvmb.cc.binghamton.edu	Media in Education
METHODS@vm.its.rpi.edu	Research Methodology
PLA-L@ADMIN.HumberC.ON.CA	Prior Learning Assesment
PRISON-L@dartcms1.dartmouth.edu	Prison Teacher's Discussion List
QUAL-L@psuvm.psu.edu	Qualitative Research List
QUALRS-L@uga.cc.uga.edu	Qualitative Research for the Human Sciences
QUALRSED@unmvma.unm.edu	Qualitative Research in Education
SATEDU-L@wcupa.edu	Satellite Education List

List Addresses	List Name
SOCNET@nervm.nerdc.ufl.edu	Social Network Researchers
T-ASSIST@unmvma.unm.edu	University Teaching Assistant Discussion List
T_LEVAL@arizvm1.ccit.arizona.edu	CNI Teaching & Learning Working Group
TEACH-L@uicvm.uic.edu	Classroom Dynamics
TEACHER@vm.utcc.utoronto.ca	Seminar for Teachers of Computing in the Humanities
WIOLE-L@mizzou1.missouri.edu	Writing Intensive Online Learning Environment
WISP-L@iubvm.ucs.indiana.edu	Women in Scholarly Publishing Discussion

Tip: Remember not to send personal messages to the whole list—use the reply feature carefully. If you need help, consult the list's guidelines or refer to Appendix A.

The following announcement is quite typical on the discussion lists—this is from the Adult Education Network (AEDNET):

```
Date: Sun, 26 Jun 94 12:56:20 -0400
From: Jim Harrison<jharris@opus.mse.edu>
Reply to: aednet@alpha.acast.nova.edu
To: je@world.std.com
Subject: New mailing list

A new electronic mailing list is available for people who are interested
in Jungian analytical psychology. Subscription to the list is free for
anyone with Internet access.

To sign up for this list, send a subscription message to:

     majordomo@creighton.edu

The text of the message should read:

     subscribe jung-psyc <your email address here>


Please note that MAJORDOMO (the list manager program) requires your email
address, and not (as in LISTSERV managers) your name.
```

There are many other sources of information about lists. See Chapter 10 for more information.

Useful Usenet Newsgroups

There are many hundreds of Usenet newsgroups that focus on information useful to faculty and students in many disciplines. The comp. groups, for example, have information for computer science study, and anyone using DOS, OS/2, Microsoft Windows, Amigas, IBM, Macintosh, UNIX, and VAX machines have separate groups dealing with that platform, software or interest. The following is just a sample of the newsgroups available of academic interest. To give you an idea of the number of messages that each group might contain, the following list shows the currently active messages at one site when this listing was made. See Appendix A for information on accessing and using Usenet newsgroups.

```
alt.agriculture.misc: 836
alt.architecture: 2544
alt.education.disabled: 1029
alt.education.distance: 1591
alt.education.research: 457
bionet.agroforestry: 624
bionet.announce: 1073
bionet.biology.computational: 537
bionet.biology.grasses:
bionet.biology.n2-fixation: 160
bionet.biology.tropical: 385
bionet.biophysics: 228
bionet.cellbiol: 452
bionet.cellbiol.cytonet: 52
bionet.chlamydomonas: 175
bionet.drosophila: 327
bionet.general: 8446
bionet.genome.arabidopsis: 1995
bionet.genome.chrom22: 123
bionet.genome.chromosomes: 202
bionet.immunology: 1224
bionet.info-theory: 1836
bionet.journals.contents: 1184
bionet.journals.note: 269
bionet.metabolic-reg: 210
bionet.microbiology: 62
bionet.molbio.ageing: 663
bionet.molbio.bio-matrix: 480
bionet.molbio.embldatabank: 297
bionet.molbio.evolution: 1387
bionet.molbio.gdb: 196
bionet.molbio.genbank: 1580
bionet.molbio.genbank.updates: 120590
bionet.molbio.gene-linkage: 325
bionet.molbio.genome-program: 715
bionet.molbio.hiv: 342
bionet.molbio.methds-reagnts: 13348
bionet.molbio.proteins: 1763
```

```
bionet.molec-model: 71
bionet.mycology: 478
bionet.neuroscience: 3066
bionet.parasitology: 130
bionet.photosynthesis: 311
bionet.plants: 2374
bionet.population-bio: 622
bionet.prof-society.biophysics: 3
bionet.protista: 71
bionet.sci-resources: 979
bionet.software: 7052
bionet.software.acedb: 210
bionet.software.gcg: 525
bionet.software.sources: 42
bionet.structural-nmr: 45
bionet.users.addresses: 1653
bionet.virology: 494
bionet.women-in-bio: 907
bionet.xtallography: 815
misc.creativity: 609
misc.education: 18632
misc.education.adult: 109
misc.education.language.english: 996
misc.education.multimedia: 111
soc.college: 21788
soc.college.grad: 6344
soc.college.gradinfo: 5698
soc.college.org.aiesec: 489
soc.college.teaching-asst: 1297
sci.aeronautics: 6862
sci.aeronautics.airliners: 1394
sci.agriculture: 787
sci.answers: 1078
sci.anthropology: 3276
sci.anthropology.paleo: 621
sci.aquaria: 6127
sci.archaeology: 5561
sci.archaeology.mesoamerican: 1
sci.astro: 42932
sci.astro.hubble: 1134
sci.astro.planetarium:606
sci.astro.research: 1
sci.bio: 14102
sci.bio.ecology: 4393
sci.bio.ethology: 707
sci.bio.evolution: 1249
sci.bio.herp: 522
sci.bio.technology: 1646
sci.chaos: 282
sci.chem: 13641
sci.chem.electrochem: 71
sci.chem.organomet: 283
sci.classics: 3612
sci.cognitive: 2614
sci.comp-aided: 543
sci.cryonics: 1380
sci.crypt: 19950
sci.data.formats: 454
sci.econ: 21027
sci.econ.research: 1004
sci.edu: 4015
sci.electronics: 64758
```

```
sci.energy: 20360
sci.energy.hydrogen: 881
sci.engr: 8928
sci.engr.advanced-tv: 1085
sci.engr.biomed: 2104
sci.engr.chem: 2826
sci.engr.civil: 1839
sci.engr.control: 2063
sci.engr.lighting: 668
sci.engr.manufacturing: 1151
sci.engr.mech: 3549
sci.engr.semiconductors: 352
sci.environment: 36195
sci.fractals: 2685
sci.geo.eos: 79
sci.geo.fluids: 1918
sci.geo.geology: 10455
sci.geo.hydrology: 119
sci.geo.meteorology: 7692
sci.geo.satellite-nav: 681
sci.image.processing: 7577
sci.lang: 18365
sci.lang.japan: 11473
sci.logic: 5960
sci.materials: 4118
sci.math: 41663
sci.math.num-analysis: 11349
sci.math.research: 2339
sci.math.symbolic: 10815
sci.mech.fluids:
sci.med: 52871
sci.med.aids: 8043
sci.med.dentistry: 1741
sci.med.nursing: 271
sci.med.nutrition: 10233
sci.med.occupational: 1441
sci.med.pharmacy: 1160
sci.med.physics: 2099
sci.med.psychobiology: 1004
sci.med.radiology: 142
sci.med.telemedicine: 1409
sci.military: 33635
sci.misc: 4578
sci.nanotech: 2414
sci.nonlinear: 1029
sci.op-research: 1088
sci.optics: 4718
sci.philosophy.meta: 9373
sci.philosophy.tech: 11671
sci.physics: 48187
sci.physics.accelerators: 741
sci.physics.computational.fluid-dynamics: 163
sci.physics.electromag: 802
sci.physics.fusion: 12344
sci.physics.particle: 704
sci.physics.plasma: 0
sci.physics.research: 1240
sci.polymers: 654
sci.psychology: 11101
sci.psychology.digest: 381
sci.psychology.research: 83
sci.research: 3958
sci.research.careers: 3070
```

```
sci.research.postdoc: 774
sci.skeptic: 48681
sci.space.news: 5164
sci.space.policy: 309
sci.space.science: 44
sci.space.shuttle: 14184
sci.space.tech: 171
sci.stat.consult: 4555
sci.stat.edu: 1036
sci.stat.math: 920
sci.systems: 407
sci.techniques.mag-resonance: 1
sci.techniques.microscopy: 413
sci.techniques.spectroscopy: 270
sci.techniques.xtallography: 534
sci.virtual-worlds: 11258
sci.virtual-worlds.apps: 291
soc.answers: 941
soc.college: 21788
soc.college.grad: 6344
soc.college.gradinfo: 5698
soc.college.org.aiesec: 489
soc.college.teaching-asst: 1297
soc.culture.afghanistan: 5090
soc.culture.african: 23522
soc.culture.african.american: 44657
soc.culture.arabic: 21595
soc.culture.argentina: 3916
soc.culture.asean: 18332
soc.culture.asian.american: 50876
soc.culture.australian: 18605
soc.culture.austria: 3230
soc.culture.baltics: 6277
soc.culture.bangladesh: 19953
soc.culture.bosna-herzgvna: 14204
soc.culture.brazil: 13189
soc.culture.british: 68871
soc.culture.belgium:
soc.culture.bulgaria: 7065
soc.culture.burma: 576
soc.culture.canada: 36599
soc.culture.caribbean: 5367
soc.culture.celtic: 28539
soc.culture.chile: 4563
soc.culture.china: 116432
soc.culture.colombia: 1
soc.culture.croatia: 11393
soc.culture.czecho-slovak: 3978
soc.culture.esperanto: 9745
soc.culture.europe: 33161
soc.culture.filipino: 15707
soc.culture.french: 36140
soc.culture.german: 38775
soc.culture.greek: 34431
soc.culture.hongkong: 69811
soc.culture.indian: 149376
soc.culture.indian.info: 225
soc.culture.indian.telugu: 11030
soc.culture.indonesia: 9025
soc.culture.iranian: 40766
soc.culture.israel: 5151
soc.culture.italian: 28485
soc.culture.japan: 49678
```

```
soc.culture.jewish: 83844
soc.culture.jewish.holocaust: 8
soc.culture.korean: 32722
soc.culture.laos: 1306
soc.culture.latin-america: 22371
soc.culture.lebanon: 15986
soc.culture.maghreb: 719
soc.culture.magyar: 4805
soc.culture.malaysia: 17689
soc.culture.mexican: 20037
soc.culture.misc: 2940
soc.culture.mongolian: 175
soc.culture.native: 7462
soc.culture.nepal: 3479
soc.culture.netherlands: 19949
soc.culture.new-zealand: 15639
soc.culture.nordic: 33705
soc.culture.pakistan: 58989
soc.culture.palestine: 4974
soc.culture.peru: 1982
soc.culture.polish: 17380
soc.culture.portuguese: 9685
soc.culture.puerto-rico: 484
soc.culture.romanian: 7610
soc.culture.scientists: 7223
soc.culture.singapore: 11858
soc.culture.slovenia: 1
soc.culture.somalia:232
soc.culture.soviet: 45951
soc.culture.spain: 26341
soc.culture.sri-lanka: 7890
soc.culture.swiss: 1499
soc.culture.taiwan: 56103
soc.culture.tamil: 22019
soc.culture.thai: 20194
soc.culture.turkish: 64029
soc.culture.ukrainian: 3396
soc.culture.uruguay: 383
soc.culture.usa: 33842
soc.culture.venezuela: 13205
soc.culture.vietnamese: 64834
soc.culture.yugoslavia: 28943
soc.feminism: 9879
soc.history: 35838
soc.history.moderated: 1023
soc.history.war.misc: 357
soc.history.war.world-war-ii: 119
soc.human-nets: 1
soc.libraries.talk: 1843
soc.men: 79470
soc.misc: 3273
soc.politics: 139
soc.politics.arms-d: 76
soc.religion.bahai: 2204
soc.religion.christian: 33045
soc.religion.eastern: 7752
soc.religion.islam: 9516
soc.religion.quaker: 1979
soc.religion.shamanism: 543
soc.rights.human: 17775
k12.chat.elementary: 18036
k12.chat.junior: 33472
k12.chat.senior: 67106
```

```
k12.chat.teacher: 18393
k12.ed.art: 896
k12.ed.business: 1036
k12.ed.comp.literacy: 6100
k12.ed.health-pe: 1287
k12.ed.life-skills: 530
k12.ed.math: 5460
k12.ed.music: 3482
k12.ed.science: 6783
k12.ed.soc-studies: 2093
k12.ed.special: 1700
k12.ed.tag: 2117
k12.ed.tech: 3489
k12.lang.art: 2197
k12.lang.deutsch-eng: 5915
k12.lang.esp-eng: 4422
k12.lang.francais: 7120
k12.lang.russian: 2756
k12.library: 2353
k12.news: 411
k12.sys.channel0: 601
k12.sys.channel1: 677
k12.sys.channel10: 271
k12.sys.channel11: 1685
k12.sys.channel12: 875
k12.sys.channel2: 2093
k12.sys.channel3: 502
k12.sys.channel4: 341
k12.sys.channel5: 247
k12.sys.channel6: 368
k12.sys.channel7: 271
k12.sys.channel8: 280
k12.sys.channel9: 1476
k12.sys.projects: 1864
```

And then there is always something like alt.fan.monty-python for those times when you want a little break!

Libraries

Because of the education/research roots of the Internet, there are thousands of libraries worldwide available online. You can reach and search most major university library catalogs in North American using the Internet. In addition, a great many major library catalogs across Asia, South America, and Europe also are accessible. I have found this useful when hunting for a particular citation as I am writing, or when I want to locate a book that is particularly elusive. I then make use of inter-library loan, or UnCover2 to obtain the item.

Some libraries maintain access through telnet, others through Gopher and WWW. A few are first connected through alliances and then made available through the Internet. Locating a particular library can involve a Veronica search, the use of

Hytelnet or one of the large telnet sites, such as the Washington and Lee Law Library. Increasingly, access is through Gopher gateways that may link you to yet other sites.

Washington and Lee Law Library

Washington and Lee Law Library provides WWW and Mosaic access to libraries. In Mosaic, choose **O**pen URL... from the **F**ile menu, as shown in Figure 8.1, and then enter the address **http://honor.uc.wlu.edu:1020**. Using Lynx, press **G** for Go, enter the address, and then press Enter.

Figure 8.1. The Mosaic Open URL command.

CARL and UnCover

In the 1970s and 1980s, a number of libraries formed consortiums in order to provide access to services and materials. This happened before the Internet really "took off."

The *Colorado Alliance of Research Libraries* (CARL) offers access to a broad variety of databases, including online catalogs from academic and public libraries, ERIC, and a very useful index called *UnCover*. Uncover provides tables of contents, and some abstracts of journal articles. A commercial service available at many sites, including CARL, called *UnCover2* provides a unique service. In addition to making journal indices and tables of contents available, they will furnish the full text of the articles through Fax delivery within 24 hours. You can charge the fees to a credit card for this service which cover copyrights, faxing, and duplication. You can contact CARL by way of telnet to `pac.carl.org` with a login as **PAC**. In addition, CARL often is on the menu of numerous other libraries, such as the University of Maryland.

A Multitude of Other Libraries

There are hundreds of research organizations, and college and university libraries that have online catalogs and other services, including special collections,
databases, and unique materials. Texas Tech, for example, maintains Gopher linkages to large collections of images, and Michigan State University has sound archives available.

The number of libraries available on the Internet is truly staggering. Using
Lynx to connect to the Washington and Lee Law Library (`http://`
`honor.uc.wlu.edu:1020`), you can discover a huge listing of libraries. Following is
just a small sampling of the overall lists:

```
*  ..Restrict by Subject
   *  ..Restrict by Type (Telnet, Gopher, WWW)
   *  ..Sort: Date (for date coded entries) [1178 items]
   *  ..Sort: Geographic [1178 items]
   *  Aalborg University
      (Login: => at connected;pause 5;enter \r;at >;enter def;)
   *  Aarhus School of Business, Library
      (Login: => at user;enter MERKUR;)
   *  Aarhus University, Library
      (Login: => at login;enter rc9000;pause 2;enter: \033;at att;enter
      sol;pause 5;enter sol sol;)
   *  Aberdeen University, Library
      (Login: => at login;enter library;at vt100;enter 3;)
   *  Abilene Library Consortium
      (Login: => at user;enter alcpac;)
   *  Abstracts - Inst for Systems Research,Univ of Maryland,College
      Park
   *  Academia Sinica, Taiwan, Library
      (Login: => at login;enter library;at terminal;enter: v;)
   *  Acadia University, Library
      (Login: => at login;enter opac;)
   *  Access Colorado Library and Information Network (ACLIN)
      (Login: => at login;enter ac;at vt100;enter 1;)
   *  Ada Community Library, Idaho
      (Login: => at login;enter library;at vt100;enter: v;at
      confirm;enter: y;)
   *  Agnes Scott College, Library (OLLI)
      (Login: => note: no login script needed;)
   *  Agricultural Bibliographic Information System of the Netherlands
      (AGRALIN)
      (Login: => at agralin>;enter hello opac.bas;)
   *  Air Force Institute of Technology, Library
      (Login: => at username;enter AFITPAC;at password;enter LIBRARY;)
   *  Albert Einstein College of Medicine, Library
      (Login: => at connect;pause 4;enter ;)
   *  Albion College, Library
      (Login: => at login;enter library;)
   *  ALEPH (Automated Library Expandable Program - Hebrew University)
      (Login: => at username:;enter ALEPH;)
   *  Alfred University, Library
      (Login: => at username;enter FLORIS;at continue;enter ;)
   *  Allegeny College, Library (ALLECAT)
      (Login: => at login;enter library;)
- press space for more, use arrow keys to move, '?' for help, 'q' to quit
```

If you narrow your search to just education libraries, you will find this entry.

```
*  ..Sort: Date (for date coded entries) [13 items]
    *  ..Sort: Alphabetic [13 items]
    *  ..Sort: Geographic [13 items]
    *  Lyon School Learning Center (K-3) Glenview, IL, District 34
       (Login: => at login;enter library;at vt100;enter ;)
    *  Westbrook School Learning Center (K-3) Glenview, IL, District 34
       (Login: => at login;enter library;at vt100;enter ;)
    *  Ontario Institute for Studies in Education, Library
       (Login: => at login;enter eloise;)
    *  Pleasant Ridge School Learning Center (4-6) Glenview, IL, District
       34
       (Login: => at login;enter library;at vt100;enter ;)
    *  Georgia State University, Instructional Resource Center, Library
       (OLLI)
       (Login: => note: no login script needed;)
    *  Springman Jr. High School Learning Center (7-8) Glenview, IL,
       District 34
       (Login: => at login;enter library;at vt100;enter ;)
    *  Columbia University, Teachers College, Library (EDUCAT)
       (Login: => at login;enter library;)
    *  Institute of Education, Library (University of London)
       (Login: => at login;enter janet;at pass;enter ;at hostname;enter
       UK.AC.LON.CONSULL;at connect;pause 3;enter \r;at username:;enter
       LIBRARY;at vt100;pause 2;enter 1;)
    *  National Ping-Tung Teachers College, Library
       (Login: => at login;enter library;)
    *  Henking School Learning Center (K-3) Glenview, IL, District 34
       (Login: => at login;enter library;at vt100;enter ;)
    *  Colorado State Department of Education (CARL)
       (Login: => at choice;enter PAC;at line;enter 5;pause 2;enter
       ;pause 2;enter ;)
    *  Hoffman School Learning Center (4-6) Glenview, IL, District 34
       (Login: => at login;enter library;at vt100;enter ;)
    *  Glen Grove School Learning Center (4-6) Glenview, IL, District 34
       (Login: => at login;enter library;at vt100;enter ;)
    *  ..Text copy of links
```

You can search for other categories of libraries just as easily, and you also can use other search tools. The following list, for example, is a sampling of medical libraries in the United States found with the aid of Hytelnet:

```
United States Medical Libraries

<US376> Albert Einstein College of Medicine
<US011> Association of Operating Room Nurses
<US098> Audie L. Murphy Memorial Veterans' Administration Hospital
<US381> Cornell University Medical College
<US293> Creighton University Health Sciences Library
<US011> Denver Medical Library
<US145> Georgetown University Medical Center
<US214> HSLC HealthNET (Health Sciences Information Network)
<US408> Massachusetts College of Pharmacy
<US362> Medical College of Ohio
<US242> Medical College of Wisconsin
<US377> Montefiore Medical Center
<US299> National Institutes of Health
<US364> National Library of Medicine Locator
```

```
<US165> New York University, Ehrman Medical & Waldmann Dental Libraries
<US122> Northeastern Ohio Universities College of Medicine
<US302> Oregon Health Sciences University
<US011> Saint Joseph Hospital
<US011> Swedish Medical Center
<US429> Texas Health Science Libraries Consortium
<US257> Uniformed Services University of the Health Sciences
<US285> University of Alabama, Birmingham. Lister Hill Health Sciences
<US399> University of Arkansas Medical Sciences Library
<US011> University of Colorado Health Sciences Center
<US372> University of Maryland Health Sciences Library
<US168> University of Medicine and Dentistry of New Jersey
<US256> University of Miami Medical Library
<US224> University of Nebraska Medical Center
<US309> University of New Mexico - Medical Center Library
<US094> University of Tennessee at Memphis Health Science Library
<US099> University of Texas Health Center at Tyler
<US067> University of Texas Health Science Center-San Antonio
<US019> University of Texas Medical Branch at Galveston
<US162> University of Texas Southwestern Medical Center
<US189> University of Utah, Eccles Health Sciences Library
<US266> University of Virginia Health Sciences Library
<US200> Washington University-St Louis, Medical Library
```

You also can use Hytelnet to discover and make actual connections to University libraries. Again, amazingly enough, the following is just a sample of what is available:

```
Other United States Libraries

<US268> Abilene Christian University
<US348> Ada Community Library (Idaho)
<US126> Air Force Institute of Technology
<US236> Allegheny College
<US278> Alma College
<US341> Appalachian State University
<US305> Andrews University
<US138> Arizona State University
<US334> Armstrong State College
<US001> Auburn
<US320> Augsburg College
<US277> Augusta College
<US011> Auraria
<US432> Ball State University
<US127> Bates College
<US231> Baylor University
<US291> Beloit College
<US321> Bethel College
<US143> Boise State University
<US002> Boston University
<US128> Bowdoin College
<US077> Bowie State University
<US237> Bowling Green State University
<US406> Brandeis University
<US003> Brigham Young University
<US086> Brookhaven National Laboratory
<US004> Brown University
<US430> Brunswick College
<US260> Bryn Mawr College
```

```
<US013> Bucknell University
<US331> Butler University
<US005> Cal Poly State University
<US238> California Institute of Technology
<US174> California State University, Chico
<US110> California State University, Fresno
<US356> California State University - Fullerton
<US193> California State University, Hayward
<US006> California State University, Long Beach
<US239> California State University, Sacramento
<US254> California State University, San Marcos
<US294> Calvin College
<US247> Canisius College
<US164> Carleton College
<US007> Carnegie Mellon University
<US008> Case Western Reserve University
```

There are lists and guides to Internet accessible library resources. One called the *Internet Accessible Library Catalogs and Databases* compiled by Art St. George and Ron Larsen contains information on over a hundred library catalogs. It is available via FTP from `ariel.unm.edu`, in the `/library` directory, as the file `internet.library`. Another useful resource can be found at the University of Texas—Dallas Gopher `squirrel.utdallas.edu/Libraries.`, maintained as a collaborative effort by Billy Barron, Marie Christine Mahe, and Lou Rosenfeld. It also is accessible via FTP from `ftp.utdallas.edu` in the `/pub/staff/billy/libguide` subdirectory. For more information, get the file `libraries.intro`.

Electronic Journals

The Internet is becoming important in the publishing of scholarly work. The number of electronic scholarly journals is growing, offering refereed outlets for scholarship and research. Some of these are very similar to paper-based journals, with editors and referees. Some are more avant garde. Scholars serve as editors and referees for online journals, often receiving and critiquing articles using e-mail. Many paper-based journals now allow electronic submission using the Internet. In addition, opportunities for collaboration in writing articles at long distance is particularly and increasingly common.

In addition to scholarly journals, there are many other e-serials that can be of value in the academic setting. The CICNet Gopher provides an example of this—selecting it's top menu item, `Electronic Journals`, provides the following Gopher menu:

```
        Internet Gopher Information Client v2.0.15

                    Electronic Journals (via CICNet)

    1.  Read Me First!
```

```
—>  2.  A List of What's Here
    3.  Alphabetic List/
    4.  General Subject Headings/
    5.  About Electronic Publishing and E-Journals/
    6.  About the CICNet Electronic Journal Project/
    7.  Hypertext E-Journal Sampler/
    8.  Library of Congress/
    9.  Other Journal Archives/
    10. Thank You!  CICNet's Archive Volunteers
```

I chose #2 for a look at What's Here.

Here, it is possible to find out the name of the journal, its location, subject matter, how it is archived, and its Library of Congress number.

```
/* Last Updated: January 15, 1994
   Just starting to add URL's —pauls@cic.net */

%Title: AALL-GOV-LINE
%URL: gopher://gopher.cic.net:70/11/e-serials/alphabetic/a/aall-gov-line
%Descr: American Association of Law Libraries produces Gov-Line, a
        recorded telephone hotline that reports the latest news from
        DC and states.
%Info:  Ed pulled this out of GOVDOC-L
%LC:    AN
%Topic: Politics

%Title: AALL-LISP
%URL: gopher://gopher.cic.net:70/11/e-serials/alphabetic/a/aall-lisp
%Descr: American Association of Law Libraries Legal Information Service to
        the Public
%Topic: Legal

%Title: AARHMS
%URL: gopher://gopher.cic.net:70/11/e-serials/alphabetic/a/aarhms
%Descr: American Academy of Research Historians of Medieval Spain
%Info:  kufacts.cc.ukans.edu:/pub/history/Journals/aarhms
%Topic: History
%Archive: Mirror

%Title: ABLENET
%URL: gopher://gopher.cic.net:70/11/e-serials/alphabetic/a/ablenet
%Descr: Disabilities Newsletter
%Info:  handicap.shel.isc-br.com:/pub/nletter/able* (KA9Q)
%Holdings: V 1 # 2
%LC:    HV15513-3029
%Topic: Disabilities

%Title: Abyssinian Prince
%URL: gopher://gopher.cic.net:70/11/e-serials/alphabetic/a/abyssinian-prince
%Descr: PBEM Zine
%Topic: Email gaming 'zine

%Title: Academe This Week
%URL: gopher://chronicle.merit.edu:70/11/
%Descr: From the Chronicle of Higher Education
%Info:  chronicle.merit.edu via Gopher
%Topic: Education
```

```
%Title: ACM Newsletters
%URL: gopher://gopher.cic.net:70/11/e-serials/alphabetic/a/acm
%Descr: from Youngstown State University & Iowa?
%Info:  unix1.cc.ysu.edu:/pub/acm/newsletters
%Archive: Mirror
%Topic: Computer User Groups

%Title: ACQNET
%URL: gopher://gopher.cic.net:70/11/e-serials/alphabetic/a/acqnet
%Descr: Acquistions newsletter
%Info:  CRI@CORNELLC - editor
        dewey.lib.ncsu.edu:/pub/stacks/acq
%Archive: Mirror
%ISSN:  1057-5308
%LC:    Z689
%Topic: Library

%Title: Action Canada Dossier
%URL: gopher://gopher.cic.net:70/11/e-serials/alphabetic/a/action-canada-dossier
%Info:  csf.colorado.edu:/ipe/newsletters/action_canada_dossier
%Topic: Politics
%Archive: Mirror

%Title: ACTivist
%URL: gopher://gopher.cic.net:70/11/e-serials/alphabetic/a/activist
%Descr: Indigenous peoples in Canada fight low-level military flights
        over their lands.
%Info:  Posted to "alt.native", originally from Peacenet's
        "gen.newsletters", or contact them at +1 416 531 6154.
%Holdings: Vol 8#8-9, Jul-Sept 1992 check
%LC:    UG635.c2
%Topic: Military, Politics
```

As you can see, there is quite a range just on this first of numerous pages—Indigenous Peoples of Canada, Medieval Spain, and the Chronicle of Higher Education. Continuing on, I chose to look at the electronic journals found alphabetically under the letter E.

```
              Internet Gopher Information Client v2.0.15

                                 E

 —>  1.  E-Letter on Systems, Control, and Signal Processing/
     2.  EJournal/
     3.  Earth Journal/
     4.  East Asia Pacific Wireless Files/
     5.  East Timor Action Network (US)/
     6.  Eco Newsletter/
     7.  Economic History Newsletter/
     8.  Economic Research Reports/
     9.  EduCom Review/
     10. EduPage Newsletter/
     11. Education Policy Analysis Archives/
     12. Education Research and Perspectives/
     13. Education and Human Resources Reports (NSF)/
     14. Educational Uses of Industrial Technology News (EDUCOM)/
```

```
15. Effector Online/
16. Ego Project/
17. Eichstaett/
18. Electronic Antiquity - Communicating the Classics/
19. Electronic Journal of Analytic Philosophy/
20. Electronic Journal of Virtual Culture/
21. Electronic Journal of the Astronomical Society of the Atlantic/
22. Electronic Protocol/
23. Encyclopedia of Associations/
24. Energy Ideas/
25. Energy and Climate Information Exchange - Climate Digest/
26. Energy and Climate Information Exchange Newsletter/
27. Engineering Directorate Letters (NSF)/
28. Environment Link/
29. Environmental Resources Information Network/
30. Erlangen/
31. Eros Mailing List Digest/
32. Essen/
33. Estonian News/
34. Ethnomusicology Research Digest/
35. Euro Chart/
36. EuroNews/
37. European Counter Network/
38. European Go Centre and European Go Federation Newsletter/
39. Extreme Ultraviolet Astrophysics Center (EUVE)/
```

The preceding titles and subjects are quite varied—Ultraviolet Astrophysics, Climate, Economics, and Education. Because new titles are added almost every day, sites such as CICNet are worth repeat visits.

Electronic Texts

Increasingly, the Internet is becoming a repository for full text books and reports. To read *Oh, Pioneers*, I do not have to go to the library to check out a copy—I can download it to my computer and read it on-screen or print it out. In addition, I can download image files of the paintings of Georgia O'Keefe, for example. These full length books and other large documents often are called *electronic texts* on the Internet. There are several excellent sources of electronic text, chief among them are Project Gutenberg, and the Online Book Initiative at world.std.com. Both of these can be found on Gopher, FTP, and by way of telnet.

The Online Book Initiative is available using Gopher and FTP. Use anonymous FTP to `ftp.std.com`, and look in the `/obi` subdirectory, by way of Gopher (`gopher.std.com`), as in the following example. I have truncated the list to show just a sample of the authors represented in The Online Book Initiative sponsored by The World Software Tool & Die.

```
Internet Gopher Information Client v1.13

                     The Online Books

  —>  1.  Welcome to OBI.

      18. Arthur.Conan.Doyle/

      25. BookReviews/
      26. Booker.T.Washington/
      27. Boston/
      28. Bram.Stoker/

      34. Charles Dickens/
      35. Charles Hedrick/
      36. Charles Lutwidge Dodgson/
      37. Charles.Darwin/
      38. Christopher.Morley/
      39. Classics/

      57. Economics/
      58. Edgar.Allan.Poe/
      59. Edgar.Rice.Burroughs/
      60. Eduard.Douwes.Dekker/
      61. Edwin Abbott/
      62. Eleanor.H.Porter/
      63. Emily Bronte/
      64. Esperanto/
      65. Ethnologue/
      66. Ezra Pound/

      69. Fairy Tales/
      70. FoundingFathers/
      71. Francis.Bacon/

      74. Geoffrey.Chaucer/
      75. George Bush/
      76. Grimm/
      77. Gutenberg/
      78. H.H.Munro/

      82. Henry David Thoreau/
      83. HighTechReports/
      84. Hippocrates/
      85. Hiroshima Survivors/
      86. History/
      88. Horatio.Alger.Jr/
      89. Hugo Awards/

      95. JFK/

      101. Jnl Distance Ed/
      102. John Milton/
      103. John.Cleland/
      104. John.Donne/
      105. John.Greenleaf.Whittier/
      106. John.Henry.Newman/
      107. John.Keats/
      108. John.Stuart.Mill/
      109. Joseph Conrad/
```

```
110. Karl.Marx/
111. Katherine Mansfield/

114. Lewis Carroll/

118. Maps/
119. Mark.Twain/
120. Martin Luther King/
121. Mary.W.Shelley/
122. Mathematica/
123. Melville/

127. NIH/
128. NIST/
129. Nathaniel.Hawthorne/

141. Percy Bysshe Shelley/
142. Philip Agee/
143. Phone Dirs/

158. Roget/
159. Rudyard.Kipling/

161. Samuel.Clemens/
162. Security/
163. Shakespeare/
164. Sinclair.Lewis/
165. Soviet Archives/
166. Standards/
167. Star Trek Parodies/
168. Star Trek Stories/

173. Tennyson/
175. Thomas.More/
176. Thomas.Paine/
177. Titles.
178. Tommaso.Campanella/

195. Vatican/
196. Virgil/
198. Walt.Whitman/
199. Walter.Scott/
200. Weather Maps/
201. Wilfred Owen/
202. William Blake/
203. William Butler Yeats/
204. William.James/
205. William.Jefferson.Clinton/
206. William.Wordsworth/
207. Winston.Churchill/
209. World Factbook/
210. Xinu/

221. opinions.supreme-court/
```

One of the most famous of the full-text projects is called *Project Gutenberg*. This project is seeking to put as many texts as possible on the Internet. You can access these texts numerous ways. The following FTP sites, for example, host Project Gutenberg texts:

```
mrcnext.cso.uiuc.edu      /pub/etext

oes.orst.edu              /pub/almanac/etext
```

You also can receive these text via e-mail. Send a message of **send guide** *<filename>* to almanac@oes.orst.edu.

Following is an FTP listing of the electronic books newly placed in the archives from January through June, 1994:

```
<Opening ASCII mode data connection for INDEX200.GUT (4007 bytes).
Mon Year           Title/Author                     [filename.ext]  ##

Jun 1994 The Mayor of Casterbridge by Thomas Hardy      [mayrc10x.xxx] 143
Jun 1994 The $30,000 Bequest by Mark Twain/Samuel Clemens [beqst10x.xxx] 142
Jun 1994 Mansfield Park by Jane Austen                   [mansf10x.xxx] 141
Jun 1994 The Jungle by Upton Sinclair                    [jungl10x.xxx] 140
Jun 1994 The Lost World/Arthur Conan Doyle [Challenger #2] [lostw10x.xxx] 139
Jun 1994 Biography of George Sand by Rene Doumic         [sandb10x.xxx] 138
Jun 1994 Sara Crewe by Frances Hodgson Burnett [Burnett#1] [sarac10x.xxx] 137
Jun 1994 A Child's Garden of Verses/Robert Louis Stevenson [child10x.xxx] 136

May 1994 Les Miserables, by Victor Hugo [in English]     [lesms10x.xxx] 135
May 1994 Maria or the Wrongs of Woman, Mary Wollstonecraft [maria10x.xxx] 134
May 1994 The Damnation of Theron Ware, by Harold Frederic [dware10x.xxx] 133
May 1994 The Art of War, by Sun Tzu [English and footnotes][sunzu10x.xxx] 132
May 1994 The Art of War, by Sun Tzu [English w/o footnotes][suntx10x.xxx] 132
May 1994 The Pilgrim's Progress, by John Bunyan          [plgrm10x.xxx] 131
May 1994 Orthodoxy, by G. K. Chesterton                  [ortho10x.xxx] 130
May 1994 The Square Root of Two [to 5 million digits]     [2sqrt10a.xxx] 129
May 1994 The Arabian Nights, by Andrew Lang              [arabn10x.xxx] 128

Apr 1994 The Number "e" ["Natural Log" to 1 million places][ee710xxx.xxx] 127
Apr 1994 The Poison Belt by A. Conan Doyle [Challenger #1] [poisn10x.xxx] 126
Apr 1994 A Girl of the Limberlost/Gene Stratton Porter #2 [limbr10x.xxx] 125
Apr 1994 Deutercanonical Books of the Bible/Apocrypha    [apoc10x.xxx] 124
Apr 1994 At the Earth's Core, by Burroughs [Pellucidar #1][ecore10x.xxx] 123
Apr 1994 Return of the Native, by Thomas Hardy [Hardy #3] [nativ10x.xxx] 122
Apr 1994 Northanger Abbey, by Jane Austen  [Austen #2]    [nabby10x.xxx] 121
Apr 1994 Treasure Island, by Robert Louis Stevenson      [treas10x.xxx] 120

Mar 1994 A Tramp Abroad, by Mark Twain/Samuel Clemens     [tramp10x.xxx] 119
Mar 1994 Big Dummy's Guide To The Internet, by EFF        [bigd22xx.xxx] 118C
Mar 1994 Beethoven't Fifth Symphony [opus 67 in c-minor   [lvb5s10x.zip] 117C
Mar 1994 Motion Pictures of the Apollo 11 Lunar Landing   [landxxxx.zip] 116
Mar 1994 United States Census Figures Back To 1630        [uscen10b.xxx] 115
Mar 1994 Tenniel Illustrations for Alice in Wonderland/GIF [algif10x.zip] 114
Mar 1994 The Secret Garden, by Frances Hodgson Burnett    [gardn10x.xxx] 113
Mar 1994 Violists, by Richard McGowan                     [viols10x.xxx] 112C

Feb 1994 Freckles, by Gene Stratton Porter [Porter1]      [freck10x.xxx] 111
Feb 1994 Tess of the d'Urbervilles, Thomas Hardy [Hardy2] [tess10xx.xxx] 110
Feb 1994 Renasance and Other Poems by Edna St. Millay     [ednam10x.xxx] 109
Feb 1994 The.Return of Sherlock Holmes, by A. Conan Doyle [rholm10x.xxx] 108
Feb 1994 Far From the Madding Crowd, Thomas Hardy [Hardy1][crowd10a.xxx] 107
Feb 1994 Jungle Tales of Tarzan by Edgar Rice Burroughs   [tarz610x.xxx] 106
```

```
Feb 1994 Persuasion, by Jane Austen                     [persu10x.xxx] 105
Feb 1994 Franklin Delano Roosevelt's 1st Inaugural ["Fear"][fdr10xxx.xxx] 104

Jan 1994 Around the World in 80 Day by Jules Verne      [80day10x.xxx] 103
Jan 1994 Pudd'n'head Wilson by Mark Twain/Samuel Clemens [phead10x.xxx] 102
Jan 1994 Hacker Crackdown by Bruce Sterling             [hack10xx.xxx] 101C
Jan 1994 The Complete Works of William Shakespeare [LOF] [shaks10x.xxx] 100C
Jan 1994 Collected Articles of Frederick Douglass, a Slave [dugl210x.xxx]  99
Jan 1994 A Tale of Two Cities, by Charles Dickens [CD#1] [2city10x.xxx]  98
Jan 1994 Flatland, by Edwin A. Abbott [Math in Fiction] [flat10xx.xxx]  97
Jan 1994 The Monster Men, by Edgar Rice Burroughs       [monst10x.xxx]  96

<Transfer complete.
MRCNEXT.CSO.UIUC.EDU>
```

The fare here is varied—Thomas Hardy, Mark Twain, Jane Austin, Upton Sinclair, and Arthur Conan Doyle coexist with the square root of 2 (to 5 million places!), The U.S. Census back to 1630, and Motion Pictures of the Apollo 11 Moon Landing—yes, this is an actual "movie."

 Tip: Parents and high school students find the electronic texts especially useful in meeting term paper deadlines.

The Dartmouth University library offers a large collection of the works of Dante in electronic form. In addition, they provide a searchable database of the works of Shakespeare. Telnet to baker.dartmouth.edu, and type **select dante**.

The Center for Text and Technology, in their CPET project, maintains a catalog of electronic text archives. You can access this catalog by using telnet to guvax3.georgetown.edu, and then a username of CPET.

Discipline-Specific Information

You can access discipline- and subject-specific information on the Internet by using the search tools, such as Veronica, Archie, the WebQuery page of WebCrawler, and others. In addition, the University of Michigan maintains a Clearinghouse of Subject-Oriented Guides. You can find this item on many Gopher menus, and the Guide listing is broken down into Humanities, Social Sciences, Natural Sciences, and others. The opening screen shows the subject-oriented menu.

```
Internet Gopher Information Client v2.0.15

        The ClearingHouse of Subject Oriented Guides

  -> 1.  About the Clearinghouse (UMich)/
     2.  Search full texts of these Guides <?>
     3.  The Internet Resource Discovery Project (UMich)/
     4.  Helpful Information on using the Internet/
     5.  All Guides/
     6.  Guides on the Humanities/
     7.  Guides on the Sciences/
     8.  Guides on the Social Sciences/
     9.  Guides with coverage of Multiple Subjects/
     10. Clearinghouse Updates (last updated 6/6)  (UMich)
```

Then, the following is the first page of Guides to the Social Sciences:

```
Internet Gopher Information Client v2.0.15

                    Guides on the Social Sciences

  -> 1.  Adult/Distance Education; J. Ellsworth; 04/27/94
     2.  Anthro., Cross Cultural Studies, & Archaeology; G. Bell; v8; 03/94
     3.  Archaeology, Historic Preservation; P. Stott; v3.0; 06/10/94
     4.  Architecture, Building; J. Brown; 05/23/94
     5.  Archives; D. Anthony, N. Kayne; v1; 12/93  (UMich)
     6.  Bisexual; A. Hamilton; 06/94
     7.  Black/African; A. McGee; 01/94
     8.  Business, Economics; T. Austin, K. Tsang; 02/18/94  (UMich)
     9.  Business; C. Newton-Smith
     10. Business; L. Haas; v8; 03/94
     11. Canadian Government; A. Cannon; v1.1; 04/18/94
     12. Christian Resources; G. Bogart, J. Brubaker; v1.21; 06/10/94
     13. Communication Studies; P. Fehrmann; v8; 03/94
     14. Computer-Mediated Communication; J. December; v3.2; 01/22/94
     15. Diversity; L. Heise; 05/94  (UMich)
     16. East Europe; Z. Pasek; v4.0; 12/14/92  (UMich)
     17. Economics; B. Goffe; v6.0; 05/18/94
     18. Economics; L. Haas; v8; 03/94
     19. Education; D. Kovacs; v8; 03/94
     20. Education; vol 1 (LISTSERVs); J. Harris; v3; 04/25/94
     21. Education; vol 2 (telnets); J. Harris; v3; 04/25/94
     22. Education; vol 3 (FTP); J. Harris; v3; 04/25/94
     23. Education; vol 4 (infusion ideas); J. Harris; v2; 08/05/93
     24. Educators; (Usenet newsgroups); P. Smith; 01/93
     25. Educators; (e-mail lists); P. Smith; 08/29/93
     26. Employment Opportunities & Job Resources; M. Riley; v2; 04/11/94
     27. Futurology/Future Studies; A. Park, J. Miller; v8; 03/94
     28. Geography, Regional & Country Studies; G. Bell; v8; 03/94
     29. German History; K. McBride; 08/93  (UMich)
     30. Government Information; B. Gumprecht; v2; 02/26/94
     31. Higher Education; H. Weise; 04/93  (UMich)
     32. Human Resources & Industrial Psychology; L. Haas; v8; 03/94
     33. Information Retrieval & Information Systems; M. Kovacs; v8; 03/94
     34. International Trade & World Commerce; S. Herro; 03/11/94
     35. Journalism; J. Makulowich; v2.6; 09/20/93
     36. Journalism; P. Fehrmann; v8; 03/94
     37. K-12 School Libraries; R. Troselius; v1; 03/15/94
     38. Languages; D. Kovacs; v8; 03/94
```

```
39. Latin American Studies; G. Bell; v8; 03/94
40. Latin American Studies; M. Molloy; 04/28/94
41. Law, Criminology, Justice; L. Haas; v8; 03/94
42. Law; J. Milles; 05/17/94
```

Conferences and Calls for Papers and Participation

Calls for papers and conference announcements are common in both the discussion lists and on Usenet, offering opportunities for participation and publication. Conference announcements are posted on many lists. On Usenet, look for these not only in the topical groups, but also in the multi-subject group, news.announce.conference. These announcements come from all over the globe, which is valuable for extending your circle of contacts.

Calls for participation, such as the following, are more and more common:

```
Dear NET'ers: Last fall I informed you about a study tour being offered by
NIU to Italy. This tour will focus on the important archaeological sites in
Italy. It will provide opportunities to meet with faculty and to see current
excavations. Participants will visit a variety of educational programs in and
around Rome, Pompeii, and all of Tuscany. Current information on this tour for
faculty can be obtained from info@homer.cxix.edu.
```

These types of calls still come via snail mail (an Internet term for the postal system), but frequently are delayed in campus mail, and depend on paper-based mailing lists. Announcements through the Internet come in minutes, and are broadly distributed due to the economical nature of Internet distribution.

Syllabi

In addition to other information available on the Internet that is useful for scholarship are *course syllabi*. Increasingly, campus Gophers are carrying syllabi, course materials, and bibliographies useful in scholarly activity. As an example, you can find syllabi related to communications at comserve@vm.its.rpi.

A quick Gopher search for the word syllabus revealed some items such as the following:

```
12. Course Syllabus (Gerontology 523/623R-1)
13. Documentary Research in Chicano Studies: Syllabus
14. Course Syllabus
15. Syllabus
16. History 156b, Syllabus (History of Mexico)
17. History 156p: Syllabus for Proseminar in Mexican Revolution
18. History of Church in Latin America: H158L, Syllabus
19. 94-05-09 Syllabus 94: a higher education technology conference

37. syllabus:  intro to peace studies
39. Re: syllabus
40. Re: syllabus
41. Syllabus: Political Economy

45. Syllabus request on Comparative-Historical Methods

49. New Paradigms in IR Syllabus

78. SYLLABUS FOR TEACHING ADVANCED COURSE IN DEVIANCY

79. ENGR 1 [Staff, Syllabus, Info., Etc.]/
80. Syllabus, E.Chandler, Eng.1A, Spr /
```

Globalization

The very nature of the Internet is changing scholarship and research. Faculty are better able to work with other faculty worldwide. Corresponding with someone in Australia is as easy as corresponding with someone 20 miles away. Faculty often find that using the Internet for their research agendas has expanded their parochial horizons to all of North, Central, and South America, Africa, Europe, and the Pacific Rim. You can be in better touch with the literature, and current research in your field than ever before.

The Internet makes this globalization of teaching, research, and scholarship easy. The speed and reach of the Internet is amazing and this facilitates networking on a scale heretofor not possible.

From Here...

To learn more about the Internet and distance learning, continue on to Chapter 9. For tips on learning on your own, see Chapter 10.

PART

III

LIFELONG
LEARNING AND
SELF-STUDY

DISTANCE EDUCATION: LEARNING ACROSS SPACE AND TIME

"Would you tell me, please, which way I ought to go from here?"

"That depends a good deal on where you want to get to."

Lewis Carroll (Charles Lutwidge Dodgson)

What is Distance Education?

Distance Education involves the separation of people across geographical space. With the Internet, this often can mean separation across temporal space as well. This includes the separation of teacher from students, and the students from each other—an absence of a learning group or community.

In some cases, this separation is semi-permanent because the participants do meet face-to-face occasionally, but most of the educational activities occur while separated. In some cases, distance education and learning also is called *extended education and learning*.

Using technologies in support of distance education is not new, as is shown the following examples:

- Correspondence studies have been popular for more than 100 years across Europe, Africa, and North America.

- Over 40 years ago, instructional radio (both broadcast and two-way) began to be prevalent in Latin America and Australia, and in parts of North America.

- Educational TV in the 1960s bloomed in the United States, and now continues on both public and commercial channels.

- In 1963, Congress set aside funding and frequencies for Instructional Television Fixed Services (ITFS)—now in some places called ETV—and many of those frequencies are still in use.

- The delivery of educational programs via satellite has increased. Much of the educational programming has been shifting to *Ku* band since it can use a smaller dish antenna.

- Increasingly, two-way video is available through coaxial cable, or unconditioned telephone lines. Even *POTS* (what regular phone service is called in distance learning—Plain Old Telephone Service) is being used to support interactive video.

Now, the Internet has become one of the up-and-coming technologies for the delivery of distance education programs.

Varieties of Distance Education

Distance education can include courses, workshops, lectures, and seminars. In some cases, entire curricula and degrees are delivered at a distance, but more commonly, it involves the delivery of a discrete unit of the program—a course, a unit, or a lecture.

Distance Education covers a lot of ground—literally! Typically the following media, techniques, and technologies are currently used to deliver education at a distance:

- Audio cassettes
- Broadcast radio
- Broadcast TV
- Compressed video
- Computer-Aided-Instruction (CAI)
- Circuit riding teachers
- Correspondence (through regular mail)
- Interactive TV
- Independent programmed learning (computer or paper-based)
- Multimedia (CD-ROM)
- Satellite TV
- Short-wave radio
- Telephone
- Video cassettes
- And now, increasingly, the Internet

Most often distance education is delivered through a hybrid of these techniques—for example, television supported by print materials delivered through correspondence.

The Internet has been used very successfully in such hybrid situations. Increasingly, it is becoming a primary delivery vehicle for educational information and activities. The Internet may have the strongest potential for education of any of the previously mentioned technologies because it can incorporate images (still and moving), text, and sound, both as stored, searchable information and as realtime communications.

Following are some examples of distance education on the Internet:

- A recent discussion on the Educational Technology list (`edtech@msu.edu`) quickly identified more than 75 universities worldwide that were engaging in some type of online credit courses or degree programs. The New Jersey Institute of Technology (NJIT), for example, is providing a Bachelor of Arts Degree in Information Systems (BAIS) through "Access NJIT" the distance education program of NJIT. They combine online and video (VCR) technologies to deliver the degree.

■ James O'Donnell, a professor of Classics at the University of Pennsylvania has taken his Latin course out of the classroom—a course on Boethius's Consolation of Philosophy enrolled on campus and off-campus students. Designed for high-school Latin teachers, the course meets only online on the Internet using conferencing software, and uses a discussion mailing list. Readings are stored on a WWW server and via e-mail. Check out his homepage at `http://ccat.sas.upenn.edu/jod/jod.html`.

■ Tyler Jones at Willamette University has placed a series of Spanish lessons on their WWW server at `http://www.willamette.edu/~tjones/Spanish/lesson2.html`. The lessons cover vocabulary, pronunciation, and sound clips are planned for the lessons which can be used by a variety of students—high school and above. In addition, the WWW page provides a form for engaging in feedback with the instructor.

■ A special topics in Philosophy was taught at Valdosta State University by Ron Barnett conducted totally through the Internet. He established an electronic list called PHYCYBER to teach the class. In addition, he established the Virtual Library through the VSU Philosophy Gopher. Students were from Illinois, Texas, New York, North Carolina and "campus."

■ Recently created, The Virtual Online University, is beginning classes on the Internet in September, 1994. They are targeting traditional students who want online educational activities, and non-traditional students who have physical challenges, financial restrictions, or responsibilities that interfere with traditional educational experiences. It operates in a Virtual Education Environment using a MultiUser Object-Oriented environment (MOO). Telnet to `falcon.cit.cornell.edu 8888`, and when prompted, type **connect guest**.

■ Michigan's Cooperative Extension Service at Michigan State University (part of the USDA Extension Service at land grant universities) is offering courses throughout the state using Internet connections in county extension offices as their home base. Instructors from sites all over the state and beyond are deliver courses remotely.

In all cases, the teacher was at a distance from the students, and the students were at a distance from each other.

Characteristics of Distance Education on the Internet

Distance education using the Internet in general is different in many aspects from other means of instruction. Distance education using the Internet is characterized by the absence of audio and visual feed back, the absence of visual cues, and the nature of computer-mediated communication. (Chapter 7 has information on CMC and teaching.)

Distance Education on the Internet is characterized by the following:

High Speed   The backbone of the network can send the equivalent of a 20 volume set of encyclopedias in just seconds. Messages travel quickly—sometimes delivered within seconds.

Not Time Reliant   Messages can be composed, sent, and read at any convenient time. Teachers and learners can contact one another early in the day or after midnight, without being tied to fixed schedules.

Not Place Reliant   Messages and materials can be obtained and exchanged worldwide, and while traveling, at conferences, at home or at the office.

Synchronous Communication   Synchronous communications occur in realtime, where users are communicating at the same time, using IRC, MOOs, Talk, and so on. Courses with significant process content, such as counseling, will find these vehicles particularly useful.

Asynchronous Communication   Asynchronous communications are those which do not require each participant to be involved in communicating at the very same instant—the communication does not take place simultaneously. E-mail is a form of asynchronous communication—information does not flow in both directions simultaneously, as it does in a telephone conversation. Asynchronous methods make communication across time zones much easier.

Non-linear and Linear Learning   Learning can be structured by the teacher and/or learner, allowing for self-paced learning. The student can have great latitude in directing their own learning in a manner compatible with their learning styles. They can, for example, pursue information by reading documents in the traditional start-to-finish style, or by using the interactive hypertext based systems that enable newly discovered concepts to be thoroughly explored, before the student returns to the original document.

Being an active Internaut brings many benefits, such as opportunities to participate in research, offer and receive advice, and so on. This example demonstrates how the Internet is not time-reliant, and can use synchronous communication in support of education. This is an example of a distance education opportunity for a class to participate in a realtime discussion:

```
Date: Fri, 8 Jul 1994 15:51:47 EDT
From: "Andy Professor" <ap@opus.umsu.edu>
Reply to: EDTECH - Educational Technology <EDTECH@MSU.EDU>
To: Multiple recipients of list EDTECH <EDTECH@MSU.EDU>
Newsgroups: bit.listserv.edtech
Subject: Online Chat

Participants in our graduate course, "Microcomputer Applications for
School Administrators" will engage in an interactive chat today, using
Internet Relay Chat (IRC) on channel #7003. We invite any of you to join
us and/or participate should you desire.

We plan to begin chatting at 3:30 PM Central Time -- don't give up on us
if we're a minute or two late, as we have a guest speaker on network
wiring standards this afternoon, too.

To join us, just enter: irc at your system prompt, then when you get
on, enter: /join #7003  -- this will put you on channel #7003. As
soon as you get there, you might give yourself a new nickname, generally
your given name. To do this, enter: /nick (name) -- where (name) is
your nickname. For example, I will enter  /nick DrA  so my students
will know who I am.

Welcome one and all. Thanks for all your cordialities when working with these
neophytes on the network.

Andy Professor
```

As a primary distance education characteristic, the Internet has been, until recently, quite text-based. Information is transmitted in plain ASCII text, and often even graphs and drawings are presented using ASCII. This is an example of musical notation using just ASCII:

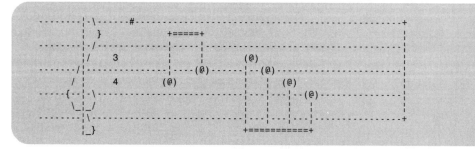

Much more sophisticated, high resolution graphics and color pictures can be sent using vector-based systems, such as PostScript (files ending in `.ps`) and with raster-based images (such as those with a filename extension of `.gif`, `.pcx`, or `.jpg`). "Movies" also are possible (filename extensions such as `.mmm`, `.mpg`, or `.fli`). Sound files also can be sent and stored on the Internet and played on appropriately equipped computers (for example, PCs with a "sound board"—look for filename extensions such as `.au`, `.vox`, or `.wav`). Each of these graphics and sound images requires the appropriate image viewer or sound player software to be installed (as determined by the filename extension) and for appropriate hardware to be installed on the computer.

With the advent of Mosaic, some of these characteristics of distance education on the Internet are changing. Mosaic, a user interface for WWW, makes an integrated presentation possible—it is the Internet equivalent of multimedia. Currently, Mosaic is the Rolls Royce of Internet interfaces, since it requires higher speed, more costly connections, and takes considerable bandwidth. Most educational institutions and students will find that Lynx is a useful WWW browser of increasing sophistication and flexibility to use in place of Mosaic.

For most instructors and students, distance education is a new context of interaction and feedback. "Old" styles of teaching and learning may not suffice, particularly when using the Internet.

Planning, Materials, and Methods for the Internet

Almost all facets of a course being taught using the Internet are affected by the nature of the medium: students, teacher, course materials, presentation, and evaluation. Distance education methods in general and the Internet methods specifically require careful, thorough, up-front planning concerning these aspects of teaching:

- *Community building*—Creating a virtual community of the students with the teacher

- *Forming intellectual opportunities*—Creating an atmosphere of learning, with challenges appropriate to the content and format

- *Fashioning contextual systems*—Distance learning, more than any other method, requires that a framework and context be created for all of the component material.

- *Supplying closure*—The need for closure in sessions, activities, and the course itself is important and critical to the completion of learning tasks.

> ### Conferencing
>
> I have used a computer conference with graduate students in a required research methods course. I planned the conference to include sections on statistics, design, evaluation—all the usual suspects. The sections were designed as places for me and the students to post reviews of relevant articles dealing with the subject.
>
> Now for the good part! The sections evolved from the postings of article critiques to places where very lively discussions took place about the articles, issues, and the critiques themselves.
>
> In addition, students began to create their own sections for discussion on degree procedures, assistantships, and so on, including one on good jokes they had heard.

The Teacher as Organizer

While all good educational settings and situations call for careful planning, using the Internet for distance education requires even greater organization and planning. The creation of material and preparation of text-based activities is crucial.

The necessary planning tasks include the following:

> *Up-front planning*—Significant time is needed in up-front planning of logistics, materials, support systems, and evaluation methods.
>
> *On-the-fly planning*—The Internet is built on thousands of computer systems, which will provide many opportunities to change directions due to changes in sites, technical glitches, Gophers, archived material, and more. This will necessitate considerable flexibility and on-the-fly planning.
>
> *Planning for serendipity*—With its considerable variety and vast storehouses of information, teaching with the Internet requires that the teacher go with the serendipitous resources, and to plan for these opportunities.

The teacher becomes an active agent for organization to a much higher degree than with traditional classroom methods.

> **Tip:** If you are using the Internet online in a demonstration, for example, be sure to have alternative routes and access to the Internet.

> Sometimes portions of the network will not respond for several minutes, or a favorite Gopher site has decided to reorganize and perform maintenance. Suddenly, you have to "vamp until ready" (improvise something until the problem is resolved). One of the best ways to continue with the curriculum is to create computer image files that emulate the screen to simulate sessions, or to capture screen images.

The curriculum to be taught using the Internet requires that teachers make the best use of their effective teaching skills. The unique character of teaching using the Internet means creating and/or adapting methods for student reinforcement and review, assessing the content for effective distance education methods, devising diversity in presentations, taking a look at the pace of the presentations and the course, and revising supplemental materials and methods.

Internet Course Design

Good course design for distance education using the Internet reflects good course design for any learning activity. The differences are in the emphasis placed on the steps involved, and the length of time that some of the steps take. Designing the distance education Internet course requires the following:

Identifying course goals—This is no different from any course goal setting activity.

Analyzing and organizing content—When working with content for Internet courses, the need is for isolating content that will present problems with delivery at a distance, and coming up with educational and organizational solutions.

Setting objectives—A traditional activity, keeping in mind student learning needs, CMC and the learning levels mentioned in Chapter 7

Designing of class sessions—This is a larger task than for traditional courses, because there is less room for improvisation.

Creating instructional materials—This is a multi-faceted large task in course design for the Internet. It involves designing materials particularly to reflect use and strengths of the Internet, producing materials for timely distribution, and pre-testing of all Internet tools and resource sites.

Creating an approach for support services—Who will provide on site assistance, what types of library material will be provided, and how can the Internet itself provide support services?

Designing a system for records management—In a distributed learning environment, record keeping systems may need revision because of the different methodologies.

Creating formative evaluation and feedback methods—This is similar to the need for on-going evaluation in a regular classroom.

Deciding upon summative evaluation methods—Again, this is similar to those created for traditional delivery systems.

> **Tip:** When you teach using the Internet, encourage students to be more proactive and responsive than in the traditional classroom, because of the "cool" nature of the Internet. Attempt to be more responsive yourself too.

Keeping Curriculum Goals on Top—Building in Success

Distance education creates some additional concerns for the faculty, primarily in the area of logistics. A common source of difficulty in these situations is that the logistics and technology overwhelm the educational goals, leaving faculty feeling out of control of the situation. Following are three key concepts to improve the chances that an Internet course will succeed:

- Faculty/Teacher ownership of course—While it seems obvious, faculty must control the course, and participate in key decisions regarding course delivery.
- Exercise caution that the process/technology does not dictate all outcomes and "watered-down" content.
- Appropriate support and assistance both on and off site is essential to overcome logistical/technological barriers.

Creating Variety in the Learning Situation

In distance education (as in traditional education), there is a high need to vary the learning activities. All too often, the courses and experiences become single track. Following are some of the most common ways of creating a variety of learning situations:

- Collaborative learning
- Demonstrations
- Didactic teaching

- Discovery
- Drill and practice
- Gaming
- Interactive/discussion
- Problem-solving
- Simulation
- Tutorial

The following sections discuss each of these methods and how they can be used with Internet distance education.

Collaborative Learning

As mentioned in Chapter 7, collaborative learning has the benefits of meeting a variety of learning style needs. Used in distance education, it is particularly helpful in breaking down the time and space barriers, creating class cohesion at a distance. Collaborative learning is supported most frequently by the use of computer conferences, e-mail, and Listservers. Computer conferencing systems are systems used on networks such as VAXNotes from the Digital Equipment Corporation or CoSy (short for Conferencing System) computer conferencing software from Softwords. Instructors post course materials for students to read and discuss. Students log on to follow the subject and participate in the discussions.

Demonstrations

Demonstrations often are difficult on the Internet, but not impossible. Demonstrations usually are accomplished on the Internet through the creation of scripts and menus, or through Lynx.

Didactic teaching

Using video this would be called "taking heads." This is the electronic equivalent of a stand-up lecture. A valuable, but overused technique in most situations.

Discovery

Discovery learning methods are particularly well suited to the Internet because of the availability of the tools of the Internet, such as Gopher, WWW, FTP, Veronica, Lynx, and Archie. Using the levels of learning found in Chapter 7, the discovery method can be especially useful.

Drill and Practice

Drill and practice methods are used most frequently on the Internet with programs available via telnet.

Gaming

Gaming is used on the Internet primarily through three tools: computer conferencing, WWW, and the MUDs/MOOs.

Interactive/Discussion

This is one of the most popular techniques for distance learning via the Internet. Group conferencing provides on-going information sharing, and can be controlled by the teacher or can be less moderated.

Using E-mail

E-mail can be used effectively for a variety of tasks, particularly where the opportunity to create a computer conference does not exist. E-mail has been used to broadcast information to students—about courses, schedules, events, speakers, and so on. Some institutions use Listservers for this, but anyone can create their own distribution list. I have one for advisees, one for each class I teach, and one for former students who want to keep in touch.

You also can use e-mail to provide academic advising and degree-planning advice as well. I have used e-mail to mentor former students as they move out into new professional experiences, and as an informal job-referral system.

Problem-Solving

Problem-solving exercises are quite popular in business and science curricula, and often depend on e-mail, computer conferencing, and Listservers, and extensive use of the Internet search tools.

Simulation

Like gaming, simulations most often are run through Lynx, computer conferencing, and the MUDs and MOOs.

Tutorial

Tutorials, both formal and informal, are most often carried out using e-mail because it is a private, flexible medium.

Tutorials

You can use computer conferencing effectively in a variety or ways, particularly through small group tutorials. As an example, you can use computer conferences to improve student writing. Asking students to post publicly a portion of an upcoming written assignment, and then asking each other student to post suggestions for revisions, makes for a lively discussion. Everyone has the role of posting and critiquing, and after the discussion, the revised piece is presented in class. The writing as revised is almost always an extraordinary improvement.

Many students find that the use of the computer conference eases the discomfort of the critique process—it can make it less personal and more professional.

An interesting way to enhance this activity even more is for the faculty member to post some of their own writing as a role model. In any case it is wise for the teacher to offer advice and criticism via e-mail privately.

Student Tip: Students can even arrange this type of critique/feedback on their own, without the teacher, if they want.

In addition, academic advising is carried out most frequently using e-mail, although course management/information can be provided through conferencing, Gophers, WWW, and a large variety of media.

Resources for Distance Education

There are a number of sites and resources of particular interest to distance educators. These resources include sources of ideas, teaching materials, research, and information on courses and curricula. A quick Veronica search for `distance AND education` reveals 11 pages of information—this is the first:

```
Internet Gopher Information Client v2.0.15

Search GopherSpace by Title word(s) : distance AND education

-->  1.  University's Distance Education Grant Proposal Funded by Bush
     2.  a distance education course in using Gopher
     3.  a distance education course in using Gopher
```

```
4.  a distance education course in using Gopher
5.  a distance education course in using Gopher
6.       DISTED:  Online Journal of Distance Education
7.  Online Database for Distance Education
8.  Online Database for Distance Education
9.  distance-education-chronicle
10. distance-education-chronicle
11. JEP Adaptation of the Method of Satellite Distance Educa..
12. Section 3.28: Online Database for Distance Education
13. Continuing Education Through Distance Learning for Rural Nurses
14. DISTANCE EDUCATION IN NURSING
15. Distance Education, Virginia Tech, and the Future
16. Ellsworth .Dr. E's Eclectic Compendium...Distance Education
17. *Free* Catalogue - Distance Education
18. ALA Program Announcement, Distance Education
19. SEEK POSITION IN INSTRUCTIONAL DESIGN, CBT, OR DIST EDUCATION
20. alt.education.distance/
21. Distance Education Conference to be Held
22. 3.28 Online Database for Distance Education
23. EJOUR> Welcome - Online Chronicle of Distance Education (fwd)
24. Online Database For Distance Education
25. Bibliography on Distance Ed, CAI, International Education, ...
26. Articles and Papers on Computer-Mediated Distance Education/
27. DEOSNEWS - The Distance Education Online Symposium/
28. Distance Education Courses (2k)
29. 6. Distance Education/
30. Going the Distance:  Distance Education Comes of Age
31. distance education
32. How to find Distance Education Courses
33. distance_education
34. online chronicle of distance education and communication
35. online chronicle of distance education and communication
36. Distance Education/
37. Distance Education/
38. Distance Education: Electronic Sources for Information

Press ? for Help, q to Quit, u to go up a menu          Page: 1/11
```

Lynx and WebCrawler/WebQuery can be used to find WWW-based distance education resources. A search for `distance` AND `education` finds hundreds of items, just the first screen of which is shown in Figure 9.1.

You can access these documents and images using both Lynx and Mosaic, but Lynx is quicker, cheaper, and takes less bandwidth.

Figure 9.1. The WebCrawler/WebQuery results in a search for distance education using Lynx.

The International Centre for Distance Learning Database

Based at the British Open University, the *International Centre for Distance Learning* (ICDL), has an online database of information on Distance Education. The database, funded by the British Government's Overseas Development Administration, is designed to provide an information service to the Commonwealth of Learning. The Commonwealth of Learning is organized to expand opportunities for students in Commonwealth countries through distance education.

The database is organized into three sections: Courses, Institutions, and Literature. You can access the database from the Internet using telnet. You need to be using a VT100 terminal.

Where to find it

Telnet   acsvax.open.uk

Username   icdl

Account Code Enter your country code here (USA, for example)

Password   AAA

You can reach the Open University via Gopher as well at `rowan.open.ac.uk` and WWW `http://hcrl.open.ac.uk/ou/ouhome.html`. The database now is free to all users, and also is available on CD-ROM.

The National Distance Learning Center

The National Distance Learning Center is a centralized electronic resource for information about distance learning programs and resources. The resources are for instructors, producers, and distributors. The NDLC contains listings of K-12, Higher Education, and Continuing Education courses as well as Teleconferences. They can be reached via telnet to `ndlc.occ.uky.edu` (`128.163.193.10`), with a login of `ndlc`.

Resources in Canada

There are a great number of distance education resources available in Canada. As examples, there are two very important sources of distance education information.

The *Technology And Distance Education Branch* (TDEB) of the Ministry of Education in British Columbia was established to support the goals of education by providing distance education and technology-based services and materials. Their goals are "to develop, communicate, and support a vision for distance education that will incorporate the effective use of a range of education technologies in the instructional design and delivery of distance learning to individual and home-based learners." You can reach their WWW homepage via `http://www.etc.bc.ca/edu.html`.

The *New Brunswick Distance Education Network*—TeleEducation NB—assists in the delivery of distance education courses in the province of New Brunswick, Canada. It is a network of community learning centers in New Brunswick, Canada. These electronic classrooms, "established in partnership with local communities, educational institutions, and industry are outfitted with specialized equipment both for receiving and delivering courses." In addition, they maintain information on distance education, located at `http://ollc.mta.ca/whatis.html`.

They also maintain a homepage called the *Distance Education Resources* located at `http://ollc.mta.ca/disted.html`.

Useful Gophers and WWW Sites with Distance Education Information

Here are some of the many Gophers that maintain distance education and learning resources.

The University of Minnesota, Department of Adult Education maintains a Gopher with a considerable number of adult/distance education resources. The URL is `gopher://aded.coled.umn.edu:70`.

The University of Utah Gopher also maintains an interesting collection of adult/distance education resources via their Gopher `gopher.cc.utah.edu:70`, in the submenu, `/Academic Organizations/Distance Learning`.

State University of New York, Buffalo Gopher at `adam.cc.sunysb.edu:70` has some useful information under the menus `/SBNEWS/Academic Services/Audio Visual Services/Distance Learning Project`.

On the University of Georgia located at `gopher.PeachNet.EDU:70` are some files relating to distance learning under the menus `/University System Information/ Office of Information Technology/Division of Academic Administration Systems/Distance Learning Sites`.

The Adult Education Discussion Network (AEDNET) list (see Chapter 7 for more information) is available on WWW, and features all AEDNET messages, and access to the electronic journal *New Horizons in Adult Education*, including an index and the current issue.

Using Lynx or Mosaic, connect to `http://alpha.acast.nova.edu/education/ aednet.html`.

> **Tip:** If you do not have your own WWW client, you can telnet to the University of Kansas at `ukanaix.cc.ukans.edu`, login as `www` and then press Enter to use VT100 terminal emulation. You then can use their Lynx program.

Useful Lists, Electronic Journals, and Usenet Newsgroups

There are a number of discussion lists, Usenet newsgroups, and electronic journals of interest to distance educators. *Dr. E's Eclectic Compendium of Electronic Resources of Adult/Distance Education* (maintained by this author) is a good guide to the Internet lists and journals. This guide is available via FTP from `ftp.std.com` in the /pub/je subdirectory as the file dre-list.txt. You also can find it via Gopher as a part of the Clearinghouse of Subject Oriented Guides maintained at the University of Michigan.

For learning more about distance education, engaging in discussion, and networking, the following are rewarding discussion lists:

ADLTED-L (Canadian Adult Education Network)

Where to find it

listserv@uregina1.bitnet

listserv@uregina1.uregina.ca

The Canadian Adult Continuing Education list is a world-wide discussion group concerned with a wide range of distance/adult education issues.

ASAT-EVA (Distance Education Evaluation Group)

Where to find it

listserv@unlvm.unl.edu

listserv@unlvm.bitnet

This is the AG-SAT Distance Education Evaluation Group. It is a broad, practical list sponsored by the Agricultural Satellite Corporation, addressing issues concerning the evaluation of all forms of distance learning and programs.

AUDIOGRAPHICS-L (Audiographics in Distance Education)

Where to find it

listserv@cln.etc.bc.ca

Audiographics-L is intended to provide a forum for the discussion of issues related to use of audiographics in the context of distance education. It supports the exchange of fact and opinion having to do with matters technical, methodological, developmental, and financial. Discussion is open to individuals and vendors.

CAUCE-L (Canadian Association for University Continuing Education)

Where to find it

```
listserv@uregina1.bitnet

listserv@max.cc.uregina.ca
```

The purpose of CAUCE-L is to provide an electronic forum where issues (broad, narrow, practical, theoretical, controversial, or mundane) related to university continuing education are discussed.

CREAD (Latin American & Caribbean Distance & Continuing Education)

Where to find it

```
listserv@yorkvm1.bitnet

listserv@vm1.yorku.ca
```

This is a digest list (messages are grouped together) of distance education information primarily focused on Latin America and the Caribbean.

DEOS-L (International Discussion Forum for Distance Learning)

Where to find it

```
listserv@psuvm.bitnet

listserv@psuvm.psu.edu
```

American Center for Study of Distance Education sponsors this large, diverse list. Currently there are 1,325 subscribers in 48 countries.

EDISTA (Educacion a Distancia)

Where to find it

```
listserv@usachvm1.bitnet
```

The University Distance Program (UNIDIS) at the University of Santiago sponsors Education at a Distance. (In English and Spanish.)

NLA (National Literacy Advocacy List)

Where to find it

`majordomo@world.std.com`

The National Literacy Advocacy Alliance-sponsored list is designed to provide information and discussion about adult literacy education and adult learners.

RESODLAA (Research SIG of the Open and Distance Learning Association of Australia)

Where to find it

`listserv@usq.edu.au`

This is a discussion list of the Open and Distance Learning Association of Australia's SIG on Research. Its purpose is to foster electronic discussion, symposia, and conferences on topical issues in distance education and open learning research.

TESLIT-L (Adult Education & Literacy Test Literature)

Where to find it

`listserv@cunyvm.bitnet`

`listserv@cunyvm.cuny.edu`

Adult Education and Literacy is a sublist of TESL-L, Teaching English as a second language. Discussions are primarily focused on issues of literacy and the teaching of English as a second language. Members also must be members of TESL-L.

VOCNET (Discussion Group for Vocational Education)

Where to find it

`listserv@ucbcmsa.bitnet`

`listserv@cmsa.berkeley.edu`

VOCNET is a discussion group focusing on vocational education managed by the Dissemination Program of the National Center for Research on Vocational Education.

In addition to the relevant discussion lists, there are several electronic journals related to distance education:

CATALYST (Community Colleges)

Where to find it

```
listserv@vtvm1.bitnet
listserv@vtvm1.cc.vt.edu
```

This is an electronic version of CATALYST, a refereed print journal for community college educators.

COLICDE (COL-ICDE Distance Education Research Bulletin)

Where to find it

```
colicde-request@unixg.ubc.ca
```

The Commonwealth of Learning (COL) and the International Council for Distance Education (ICDE) are establishing an electronic bulletin board for the dissemination of information about research in progress, or planned, in the field of distance education.

DEOSNEWS (The Distance Education Online Symposium)

Where to find it

```
listserv@psuvm.bitnet
listserv@psuvm.psu.edu
```

The American Center for the Study of Distance Education at The Pennsylvania State University organizes DEOS and publishes *The American Journal of Distance Education*.

DISTED (Online Chronicle of Distance Education and Communication)

Where to find it

`listserv@alpha.acast.nova.edu`

The Online Chronicle of Distance Education and Communication covers resources, articles, research findings, case studies, and announcements regarding distance education broadly defined.

EDPOLYAR Educational Policy Analysis Archive, refereed)

Where to find it

`listserv@asuacad.bitnet`

`listserv@asuvm.inre.asu.edu`

EDPOLYAR is an outgrowth of the EDPOLYAN scholarly discussion list. It publishes peer-reviewed articles of between 500 and 1,500 lines in length on all aspects of education policy analysis.

EDUPAGE (A News Update from EDUCOM)

Where to find it

`edupage@educom.edu`

A newsletter put out by EDUCOM summarizing information technology news. (You can subscribe by sending an e-mail message to `edupage@educom.edu` with your name, institutional affiliation, and e-mail address.)

EJCREC (Electronic Journal of Communications La Revue Electronique de Communication, refereed)

Where to find it

`comserve@rpitsvm.bitnet`

`comserve@vm.its.rpi.edu`

This is a quarterly, bilingual (English and French) journal for much of the communications field. (The sign up procedure is different for this journal: send this text as an e-mail message to Comserve: `join EJREC your_name`.)

EUITNEWS (Educational Uses of Information Technology)

Where to find it

`listserv@bitnic.educom.edu`

Educom's newsletter for the EUIT program, encompasses distance learning, self-paced instruction, CAI, video, and other information technologies for teaching and learning.

HORIZONS (New Horizons in Adult Education, refereed)

Where to find it

`listserv@alpha.acast.nova.edu`

New Horizons in Adult Education is transmitted to educators around the world via the AEDNET discussion list (mentioned previously). You can access a list of back issues by using the Listserv `index` command.

IPCT-J (Interpersonal Computing and Technology: An Electronic Journal for the 21st Century)

Where to find it

`listserv@guvm.bitnet`

`listserv@guvm.ccf.georgetown.edu`

This journal is an outgrowth of the IPCT-L discussion group. It is refereed, and covers a variety of communications, computing, and educational topics broadly.

JOE (The Journal of Extension)

Where to find it

`almanac@joe.uwex.edu`

The Journal of Extension is a peer-reviewed publication of the Cooperative Extension System. It covers all phases of Extension, including adult & distance education.

JTE-L (Journal of Technology Education, refereed)

Where to find it

```
listserv@vtvm1.cc.vt.edu
```

The Journal of Technology Education provides a forum for all topics relating to technology in education.

Pubs-IAT (Institute for Academic Technology Newsletter)

Where to find it

```
listserv@gibbs.oit.unc.edu
```

This newsletter shares information on publications, programs courses, and other activities of the Institute for Academic Technology.

TESL-EJ (Teaching English as a Second or Foreign Language: An Electronic Journal)

Where to find it

```
listserv@ucbcmsa.bitnet
```

```
listserv@cmsa.berkeley.edu
```

This is a journal focusing on ESL, EFL, and language acquisition, including teaching, learning, theory, and practice.

There are some Usenet newsgroups which discuss distance education and related topics. The alt.uu.* groups cover Usenet University. The alt.education.* groups are particularly good because they have very few superfluous postings, and the K12.ed.tech group is very active.

```
alt.education.disabled
alt.education.distance
alt.education.research
alt.uu.announce
```

```
alt.uu.future
alt.uu.lang.esperanto.misc
alt.uu.lang.misc
alt.uu.lang.russian.misc
alt.uu.misc.misc
alt.uu.tools
alt.uu.virtual-worlds.misc
k12.ed.tech
misc.education
misc.education.adult
misc.education.language.english
misc.education.multimedia
sci.edu
```

The Future of Distance Education

Distance education using the Internet is a substantial growth activity. The number of courses, programs, and teachers using the Internet is increasing rapidly, and that growth likely will continue. There are several maturing technologies that will contribute to this growth.

The development of the so-called "Information Superhighway" will affect the delivery of educational programs using the Internet. As connections improve and become more ubiquitous, access to the Internet will grow. In addition, the increased use of fiber optics and ISDN will promote greater and better use of the Internet for education because of their improved speed of data transfer. Community networks, such as the FreeNets, also will bring distance education opportunities to many more communities.

The expansion of Virtual Reality systems with their intuitive interfaces will contribute heavily to distance education on the Internet. This will include MUDs and MOOs (see Chapter 7), and technologies such as audiographics.

World Wide Web, with its hypertext/hypermedia also will contribute to a fuller online educational experience. WWW is accessible using Lynx and Mosaic. Lynx is a particularly useful tool for schools and universities because is requires no special Internet connections, it is easy on Net resources, and is not difficult to use. (See Appendix A for more information on how to use Lynx.)

From Here...

Continue to Chapter 10 for tips on learning more about the Internet on your own, and to find information on some interesting and useful Internet resources. Chapter 3 also contains several reference sources and solid information resources for ideas about the variety of learning available on the Internet for K-12.

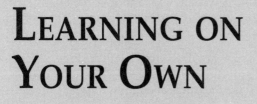

LEARNING ON YOUR OWN

Don't ever let school get in the way of your education.

Samuel Langhorne Clemens (Mark Twain)

The Internet is the largest educational enterprise ever invented—it is an education in itself!

While much of what we learn has come from formal educational situations—schools, courses, colleges, and so on, much more can come from our own self-planned learning activities. An inquiry can begin with a simple question: "I want to know more about cooking with less saturated oil," or "I am curious about what I can use to kill the weeds in my yard."

The Internet is bristling with information and resources—it is the biggest repository yet devised, providing access to ideas, information, resources, and people. It can be a challenge or bliss to work with the Internet on these types of projects.

A haphazard approach to the Internet probably will provide you with some information, but a planned, systematic use of the Internet will certainly yield more depth and breadth of information and resources. Following are some strategies for using the Internet to continue your own education and learning.

Getting Started on a Learning Project

One of the most common activities involved in learning on your own is the search for specific information. Parents, teachers, faculty, and students often want to discover information for professional and personal use. Suppose that you wanted more information on the Magna Carta, Antarctica, Teaching and Learning, Medieval Dress, Chemistry, and so on. Well, it's all out there. The mundane and the esoteric co-exist in cyberspace.

Following is one method that can prove useful for a self-planned learning inquiry:

1. Clarify or define your query—what is it that you want to find out? What is the question to be answered, or the specific information to be located?

2. State the question clearly, identifying keywords and related concepts.

3. Use all the tools in your Internet repertoire to gather information—cast a wide net, and follow your hunches in your search.

Tip: Use Appendix A as a quick course, or review of the basic Internet tools.

4. Evaluate the information you obtained in your first Internet search sessions. Organize it by concepts, look for patterns and relationships. Ask yourself what elements are missing and what keywords might help find them. Assess the value of the information you have gathered.

5. Create mental hooks or pegs to put the information on. If you don't know what cognitive mapping is, for example, it is hard to categorize and evaluate your information about cognitive mapping. At first it may not make any sense—it sounds like *blah, blah*—until you get your first peg on which to hang the information. If the subject matter is very new to you, study the partial information you have currently obtained. Even with a small incremental improvement in your understanding of the subject, you should be able to improve the accuracy and focus of your next session on the Internet.

6. Evaluate whether you have obtained the information you were seeking in both breadth and depth.

7. Recycle through these steps of searching, learning, and evaluating until you are satisfied with the results. Sometimes finding out what you are *not* looking for is a powerful piece of information.

This method is much easier in practice than it sounds. Clarify your goals in the search, specify some keywords, go out on the Net and search for data, evaluate your findings, and recycle as needed!

Strategies for Searching

Finding information that is useful requires an organized search strategy. While there are a number of ways to approach a search for information, the following steps outline a good strategy for performing a thorough search of cyberspace:

1. Write down your key words and related concepts—Internet searches can be both case-sensitive or insensitive, and they can work with or without wildcards, so your list may be quite long to start with.

2. Do a Veronica search of gopherspace and Gopher menus using your key words. (See Appendix A if you have forgotten how to use Veronica.)

3. Use Gopher to look at your search results and redefine your search (you were looking for brown bears—not the Chicago bears). Use Gopher bookmarks to create your own menus.

4. Use Archie to look for files that fit your search, and use FTP to fetch the results; refine your search if needed.

5. Search various subject-related guides (mentioned later in this chapter) for pointers, and use Gopher Jewels if need be.

6. Locate several of the "lists of lists" to find discussion lists and Usenet newsgroups related to your query.

7. Choose a few lists to join and newsgroups to read.

8. Read the discussion lists and newsgroup postings for a while to get a feel for the subject matter, depth, and signal to noise ratio, and then post some questions about your inquiry.

9. Use FAQ's from the discussion groups and Usenet newsgroups to answer common questions.

10. Perform a database search of appropriate discussion list archives.

11. Use World Wide Web, Lynx, or Mosaic to explore the WWW sites and resources that include documents, images, sound files, databases, and programs.

12. Use WAIS to search the WAIS indexed databases.

13. Create a network of cybercolleagues from the people you have met on the lists and newsgroups by exchanging e-mail with them.

14. Search remote library catalogs for resources.

 Tip: Because the resources available on the Internet change and increase rapidly, repeat the preceding steps at intervals.

Performing a thorough search can take a long time, but often, I do a Veronica search, burrow through gopherspace, and find most of what I need. Or, instead, an Archie search followed by FTP retrieval of files can be useful. Another good single source is WWW. Using one of the WWW browsers can be just the ticket. The long term rewards of working with the discussion lists and newsgroups, however, is critical to forming your own network of cybercolleagues.

Kidlink

Sometimes, the best way to start a search activity is with a question—there is a computer pen pal program for kids around the world. Where can I find information to pass along to my child?

As usual, I got out my trusty Gopher, and found the following:

```
Internet Gopher Information Client v2.0.15

            Search gopherspace (veronica) via SCS Nevada : kidlink

  --> 1.  Shelter Together Under the Sun.  Kidlink Project, Mar 12 - May 12
      2.  UMassK12, SpaceMet, Kidlink, and K12Net Informtion/
      3.  kidlink.people
      4.  KIDLINK (ends May 7, 1994)
      5.  Kidlink/
      6.  Kidlink/
      7.  Kidlink!
```

```
 8.  Kidlink gopher!
 9.  Kidlink again!
10.  KIDLINK: Global Networking For Youth 10-15/
11.  KIDPLAN KIDLINK Planning.
12.  KIDLINK
13.  KidLink IRC Client/Server/
14.  Kidlink kuvaus (english)
15.  kidlink.suomi_lyhyt
16.  What is Kidlink - Kids-95
17.  About Kidlink
18.  KIDLINK
19.  KIDLINK
20.  KIDLINK: KIDLINK Organization Listserver
21.  KIDLINK
22.  KidLink.../
23.  KidLink.../
24.  KIDLINK.../
25.  Portuguese KIDLink Coordination
26.  KIDLink Newsletter Distribution
27.  KIDFORUM KIDLink Coordination
28.  KIDLEADR KIDLink Coordination
29.  KIDLINK Project List
30.  (Education) Portuguese KIDLink Coordination
31.  (Kids) KIDLink Newsletter Distribution
32.  (KIDFORUM) KIDFORUM KIDLink Coordination
33.  (KIDLEADR) KIDLEADR KIDLink Coordination
34.  (KIDLINK) KIDLINK Project List
35.  (KIDPLAN2) KIDPLAN2 Kidlink Work Group
36.  (KIDPROJ) Special KIDLink Projects
37.  (KINDEX) KINDEX - KidLink Subject Summaries
38.  KIDPLAN2 Kidlink Work Group
39.  Special KIDLink Projects
40.  KINDEX - KidLink Subject Summaries
41.  Kidlink Project: International keypals & discussions
42.  Kidlink Project: International keypals & discussions

Press ? for Help, q to Quit, u to go up a menu                 Page: 1/5
```

Looking at several of these, I quickly located the information on Kidlink, its projects, and newsletter. I then decided to look up discussion lists and Usenet newsgroups on this, and while I did not find Kidlink, I found the following:

```
K12
--
K12Net is a collection of conferences devoted to K-12 educational
curriculum, language exchanges with native speakers, and
classroom-to-classroom projects designed by teachers. The
conferences are privately distributed among FidoNet-compatible
electronic bulletin board systems in Africa, Asia, Australia,
Europe, and North America, as well as available from uunet.uu.net
as Usenet newsgroups in the hierarchy k12.*

Classroom-to-classroom projects are featured in the K12 "Channels"
which are periodically reassigned based on usage and appropriate
project length. They comprise the k12.sys hierarchy.
```

```
Forums for casual conversation among students are divided by grade
level in the k12.chat hierarchy; there also is an area for teachers to
exchange general ideas about using telecommunications in education.

k12.ed.art        Arts & crafts curricula in K-12 education.
k12.ed.business Business education curricula in grades K-12.
k12.ed.comp.literacy    Teaching computer literacy in grades K-12.
k12.ed.health-pe        Health and Physical Education curricula in grades K-12.
k12.ed.life-skills      Home Economics, career education, and school counseling.
k12.ed.math       Mathematics curriculum in K-12 education.
k12.ed.music      Music and Performing Arts curriculum in K-12 education.
k12.ed.science    Science curriculum in K-12 education.
k12.ed.soc-studies       Social Studies and History curriculum in K-12 education.
k12.ed.special    Educating students with handicaps and/or special needs.
k12.ed.tag        K-12 education for gifted and talented students.
k12.ed.tech       Industrial arts & vocational education in grades K-12.
k12.library       Implementing info technologies in school libraries.
k12.lang.art      The art of teaching language skills in grades K-12.
k12.lang.deutsch-eng    Bilingual German/English practice with native speakers.
k12.lang.esp-eng        Bilingual Spanish/English practice with native speakers.
k12.lang.francais       French practice with native speakers.
k12.lang.russian        Bilingual Russian/English practice with native speakers.
k12.sys.projects        Discussion of potential projects.
k12.sys.channel0        Current projects.
k12.sys.channel1        Current projects.
k12.sys.channel2        Current projects.
k12.sys.channel3        Current projects.
k12.sys.channel4        Current projects.
k12.sys.channel5        Current projects.
k12.sys.channel6        Current projects.
k12.sys.channel7        Current projects.
k12.sys.channel8        Current projects.
k12.sys.channel9        Current projects.
k12.sys.channel10       Current projects.
k12.sys.channel11       Current projects.
k12.sys.channel12       Current projects.
k12.chat.elementary     Casual conversation for elementary students, grades K-5.
k12.chat.junior Casual conversation for students in grades 6-8.
k12.chat.senior Casual conversation for high school students.
k12.chat.teacher        Casual conversation for teachers of grades K-12.
```

Because the Gopher findings and the Usenet groups were so productive, I did not pursue an Archie or WWW search this time.

Cyberspace Colleagues

Many of us want to keep up-to-date in a particular area such as distance learning or learning styles, and one of the best ways to do this is to create your own network of cybercolleagues and experts. These are individuals you have found that are willing to help you, collaborate, or discuss issues and ideas with you.

These individuals often can be found through their postings on the discussion lists and Usenet. You can create and maintain your network by reaching out with good information yourself, both through postings and private e-mail—this is the notion of giving back to the network.

Additionally, cultivate your personal network by sending out interesting information to your own small mailing list.

Health Care Policy

I am interested in learning more about President Clinton's Health plan, and want to find out more about it. How can I find out about this on the Internet?

One good place to start is with a Veronica search for `clinton AND health`. Following are the results:

```
                    Internet Gopher Information Client v2.0.15

        Search gopherspace (veronica) via U.Texas, Dallas: clinton AND health

  --> 1.  How to get press releases on the Clinton Health Plan
      2.  AMA Synopsis of Clinton Health System Proposal (9/13/93)
      3.  120493 Clinton on Rural Health Care (Dec. 3)
      4.  Clinton's Health Care Reform Nothing But Snake Oil, Critic Says
      5.  93-08-23-18: Clinton and managed health care
      6.  93-12-02-23: HEALTH CARE: Single-Payer vs. Clinton's Insurance-Corp..
      7.  93-12-30-03: Health Care: Clinton would cut low-income care
      8.  93-10-18-18: Clinton Health Plan: What Every Worker Should KNow
      9.  94-03-20-18: HEALTH: The Clinton Plan: Hazardous to Our Health?
     10.  94-03-20-18: HEALTH: The Clinton Plan: Hazardous to Our Health?
     11.  Koop backs Clinton on health
     12.  OSU mixed on Clinton health plan
     13.  Clinton takes health pitch west
     14.  Clinton's health care plan
     15.  Clinton will compromise for health care
     16.  Clinton focuses on health and welfare
     17.  Clinton Health Care Press Release
     18.     Clinton Health Care Plan/
     19.  Clinton Economic Effects of Health Care Reform
     20.  H. Clinton: Health Care Townhall 9/17/93
     21.  B. Clinton & Others: Health Care Rally Remarks 9/23/93
     22.  Clinton Health Care Rally - 10/14/92
     23.  [Clinton Health Plan-Full] (1k) <HQX>
     24.  HEALTH CARE: Single-Payer vs. Clinton's Insurance-Corp-Bailout?
     25.  Clinton health plan
     26.  Clinton's Health Plan and Graduate Students
     27.  UCI-Study Says Clinton's Health Plan Ideas Tried and Rejected From ..
     28.  clinton at small business heroes health care event
     29.  clinton on health
     30.  clinton to health letter writers
     31.  clinton's remarks at womens health event 05-06-94
     32.  disability references in the clinton's health security report
```

```
33. hillary clinton health plan January 31, 1994
34. essential clinton: health care
35. clinton/gore on affordable, quality health care
36. clinton: little rock - national health care reform (8/3/92)
37. CLINTON_HEALTH_CARE_REFORM.hqx <HQX>
38. Clinton-Health-Plan  [12Oct93, 6kb]
39. LIF-Critique-of-Clinton-Health-Plan  [18Oct93, 38kb]
40. Clinton Health Plan/
41. Clinton's Health Plan
42. Clinton's health care package includes universal coverage; impacts ..

Press ? for Help, q to Quit, u to go up a menu              Page: 1/3
```

Now, finding that I have three screens of information, I continue.

```
43. SJSU reacts to Clinton health plan
44. Clinton's address to congress re: health
45. CLINTON_&_HEALTH_CARE
46. CLINTON_&_HEALTH_CARE
47. CLINTON_&_HEALTH_CARE
48. CLINTON_&_HEALTH_CARE
49. Hillary Clinton:  First Lady Promotes Health Plan
50. Health Security Report: Clinton Address to Congress
51. Health Security Report: Clinton Letter to American People
52. Health Security Report: Clinton Letter to Foley, Mitchell
53. Health Security Report: Clinton Address to Congress
54. Health Security Report: Clinton Letter to American People
55. Health Security Report: Clinton Letter to Foley, Mitchell
56. Health Security Report: Clinton Address to Congress
57. Health Security Report: Clinton Letter to American People
58. Health Security Report: Clinton Letter to Foley, Mitchell
59. Health Security Report: Clinton Address to Congress
60. Health Security Report: Clinton Letter to American People
61. Health Security Report: Clinton Letter to Foley, Mitchell
62. Health Security Report 1993: Clinton Administration         /
63. Health Security Report 1993: Clinton Administration/
64. Health Security Report 1993: Clinton Administration         /
65. Health Security Report 1993: Clinton Administration/
66.  Health Security Report: Clinton Address to Congress
67.  Health Security Report: Clinton Letter to American People
68.  Health Security Report: Clinton Letter to Foley, Mitchell
69.  Health Security Report 1993: Clinton Administration/
70. Mock election: Clinton is the Health-y choice
71. Hillary Clinton to visit U, talk on health care refor
72. <B%-2>Clinton talks<%0> health care
73. 1993 CLINTON HEALTH-CARE PLAN:  PRIORITIZES PREVENTIVE CARE
74. Costs of Clinton Health Care
75. 050694-Clinton_on_Women_Health         [11May94,  10Kb]
76. 040594-Clinton_Discussion_on_Health_Care [ 8Apr94,  32Kb]
77. 040894-Clinton_at_Health_Care_Reform_Ral [12Apr94,  25Kb]
78. 032394-Clinton_at_Health_Care_Providers_ [24Mar94,  17Kb]
79. 022494-Clinton-Health_Care_Task_Force   [ 1Mar94,   4Kb]
80. Clinton Health Plan Analysis (Text/ASCII)
81. How to Get the Clinton Health Plan via the Internet
82. The Clinton Health Care Reform Plan (Big File!)
83. Clinton Health Plan Analysis (WordPerfect) <PC Bin>
```

```
 84. Clinton's health care reform package (TJU)/
 85. HSP - President Clinton's Address on Health Security
 86. 10-27-1993 The Health Plan: Foreword -- Hillary Rodham Clinton
 87. National Health Security Plan, Clinton (9/93)/
 88. Public Interest - Clinton Health Report/
 89. New Net for Financing Clinton's Health Plan (fwd)
 90. clinton_health_reform.txt
 91. clinton_health_reform_book.txt
 92. clinton_health_reform.txt
 93. clinton_health_care_plan/
 94. clinton_health_care_plan/
 95. Clinton Health Plan Info
 96. PRESIDENT CLINTON HEALTH CARE REFORM DOCUMENTS
 97. Sec'y of Agriculture on Clinton Health Plan
 98. Health-Security-Act   Released Text of the Clinton health care pro../
 99. Health-Security-Act   Released Text of the Clinton health care pro../
100. Clinton's Health Care Plan Summary
101. Clinton's Health Care Plan Summary
102. Clinton Health plan now available
103. Health policy Clinton Administration
104. Replies received on Clinton Health Policy
105. Clinton's Health Care Plan Summary
106. Clinton Administration Health Policy Document
107. Clinton health care policy
108. Re: Clinton Administration Health Policy Document
109. Clinton Administration Health Policy Document
110. Re: Clinton Health Policy (long)
111. CLinton's health plan
112. Clinton Health Care proposal
113. Re: Clinton Health Care proposal
114. Clinton Health Plan
```

Exploring all 114 menu items would take quite some time but should provide
an immense amount of information. I continued this search with an Archie
search conducted through the same Gopher site that reveals:

```
Archie: search anonymous FTP archives: clinton health

--> 1.  swdsrv.edvz.univie.ac.at:..mac/game/clinton-11.hqx May 05 1993 229760
    2.  swdsrv.edvz.univie.ac.at:...s/clinton-issues-hc.hqx Aug 08 1992 663090
    3.  plaza.aarnet.edu.au:..info-mac/game/clinton-11.hqx May 05 1993 229760
    4.  sunb.ocs.mq.edu.au:..home/ifarqhar/documents/Clinton Oct 20 1993 1248
    5.  cs.dal.ca:/comp.archives/alt.politics.clinton/ Feb 17 1994 512/
    6.  nic.switch.ch:..irror/info-mac/game/clinton-11.hqx May 05 1993 229760
    7.  nic.switch.ch:..mac/info/nms/clinton-issues-hc.hqx Aug 08 1992 663090
    8.  wiretap.spies.com:/.cap/Clinton Apr 01 1994 29
    9.  wiretap.spies.com:/Clinton/ Jul 01 1993 512/
   10.  world.std.com:/obi/USElection/President/Clinton/ Jan 31 1993 2048/
   11.  world.std.com:..ais-sources.old/clinton-speechess.src Mar 15 1994 361
   12.  world.std.com:..di/wais-sources/clinton-speechess.src Mar 15 1994 361
   13.  world.std.com:..ais-sources.old/clinton-speechess.src Aug 31 1992 361
   14.  world.std.com:..b5/wais-sources/clinton-speechess.src Aug 31 1992 361
   15.  world.std.com:..FF/Policy/Access_govt_info/Clinton/ Feb 20 1994 8192/
   16.  world.std.com:..lications/CuD/Papers/clinton-sgi.gz Mar 01 1993 14477
   17.  athene.uni-paderborn.de:..auto/alt.politics.clinton/ Feb 16 1994 512/
```

```
18. info2.rus.uni-stuttgart.de:..o/alt.politics.clinton/ Feb 15 1994 512/
19. helios.cc.gatech.edu:..incoming/ImpeachClinton.readme Aug 04 1993 596
20. helios.cc.gatech.edu:..ncoming/ImpeachClinton.tar.Z Aug 04 1993 26232
21. gum.isi.edu:..wais/wais-sources/clinton-speechess.src Aug 31 1992 361
22. venera.isi.edu:..s/wais-sources/clinton-speechess.src Aug 31 1992 361
23. mintaka.lcs.mit.edu:..eports/clinton.hi-tech.speech Feb 25 1993 40784
24. kekule.osc.edu:..n/us_visas/ClintonGoreOnImmigration Dec 02 1993 6846
25. uceng.uc.edu:..EFF/Policy/Access_govt_info/Clinton/ Feb 19 1994 8192/
26. uceng.uc.edu:..blications/CuD/Papers/clinton-sgi.gz Feb 28 1993 14477
27. mrcnext.cso.uiuc.edu:..nfo-mac/game/clinton-11.hqx May 05 1993 229760
28. mrcnext.cso.uiuc.edu:..o/nms/clinton-issues-hc.hqx Aug 08 1992 663090
29. mimsy.cs.umd.edu:..us_visas/ClintonGoreOnImmigration Nov 13 1993 6846
30. grasp1.univ-lyon1.fr:..oups/alt/alt.politics.clinton May 08 1994 2504
31. grasp1.univ-lyon1.fr:..ups/alt/alt.president.clinton May 08 1994 2025
32. cnuce-arch.cnr.it:..info/nms/clinton-issues-hc.hqx Aug 08 1992 663090
33. cnuce-arch.cnr.it:..info/nms/clinton-issues-hc.hqx Aug 08 1992 663090
34. isfs.kuis.kyoto-u.ac.jp:..-mac/game/clinton-11.hqx May 05 1993 229760
35. akiu.gw.tohoku.ac.jp:..nfo-mac/game/clinton-11.hqx May 05 1993 229760
36. akiu.gw.tohoku.ac.jp:..o/nms/clinton-issues-hc.hqx Aug 08 1992 663090
37. metten.fenk.wau.nl:..mac/info-mac/game/clinton-11.hqx Jan 01 1970 114
38. metten.fenk.wau.nl:..c/info/nms/clinton-issues-hc.hqx Jan 01 1970 114
39. ftp.eff.org:/pub/CAF/civics/clinton-appointees May 04 1994 5879
40. ftp.eff.org:/pub/CAF/civics/clinton.press.pointer May 04 1994 1387
41. ftp.eff.org:/pub/CAF/civics/zzz/clinton-appointees.d May 04 1994 83
42. ftp.eff.org:../CAF/civics/zzz/clinton.press.pointer.d May 04 1994 120

Press ? for Help, q to Quit, u to go up a menu                    Page: 1/3
```

This Archie search obtained two more pages of file; therefore, well over 200 files and Gopher items were found in just a few minutes. Following the Gopher menu items to their submenus, and using Usenet and mailing list groups, probably would provide many hundreds more files and resources.

Online Educational Activities

Increasingly, there are courses, both credit and non-credit available online, and a few colleges are even offering degrees online. The number of online workshops that are useful and free is increasing. The net-happenings list announces these regularly.

Courses and Workshops

A number of colleges and universities are starting to offer credit-bearing courses using the Internet. The University of Wisconsin, for example, recently offered a Foundations of Rehabilitation course at the undergraduate and graduate level in which exams were given using floppy disks with the answers to be returned via e-mail to the instructor. Class discussion took place on a Listserv. The University of Phoenix offers complete degree curricula online.

Richard Smith and Jim Gerland offered an online course called "Navigating the Internet: Let's Go Gopherin'." It was an Internet workshop about all facets of using Gopher. They were surprised at the turnout.

```
Subject: Welcome to Let's Go Gopherin'

 NAVIGATING THE INTERNET: LET'S GO GOPHERIN'

 Richard J. Smith and Jim Gerland

 WELCOME

 Welcome!  This is the third Navigating the Internet workshop.  The first,
in August of 1992, attracted 864 persons from over 20 countries, the second
had 15,000+ participants from over 50 countries. As of 2pm on
Monday October 18, 1993 "Let's Go Gopherin'" has 16,111 participants
from over 50 countries.

 The first workshop was somewhat frantic because I did not expect that many
people, and I administered it rather crudely. (I mailed the lessons to the 864
people from my personal mail facility using an alias.) I suspect 864 would
constitute a large introductory class at a major university.  The  second
workshop was more like teaching a good size university.
```

Workshops such as these are offered from time to time, and usually constitute a good investment of time—you can drop in and out at will, picking up only the parts that you want.

The Global Network Academy

The *Global Network Academy* (GNA) is non-profit corporation whose long-term goal is to create a complete online accredited university. Their short term goals are to offer courses, put out a newsletter, and provide an umbrella for a range of Internet based educational initiatives.

GNA has started offering experimental courses on the Internet. Their target audience is any individual who is interested in the exchange of ideas through the Internet. In the future, they plan to offer both free and tuition courses.

One of the best ways to learn about GNA is to get their FAQ, available via FTP from `rtfm.mit.edu` in the subdirectory `/pub/usenet/news.answers` as the file `globewide-network-academy-faq`. Using a WWW browser, you can obtain information from `http://uu-gna.mit.edu:8001/uu-gna/`.

Related to GNA are the Usenet newsgroups dealing with Usenet University. These also are good places to get information for your own learning projects. Usenet University is a series of newsgroups dedicated to independent learning. Following are the current groups:

```
alt.uu.announce
alt.uu.comp.misc
alt.uu.future
alt.uu.lang.esperanto.misc
alt.uu.lang.misc
alt.uu.lang.russian.misc
alt.uu.math.misc
alt.uu.misc.misc
alt.uu.tools
alt.uu.virtual-worlds.misc
```

Lists, Newsletters, and Newsgroups that Assist in Personal Learning Projects

Keeping up-to-date in a particular area is supported by using the distribution and discussion lists and groups. There are over 9,000 subject-oriented discussion lists and Usenet newsgroups. Many that are education related are discussed elsewhere in this book and in Appendix C.

There are some distribution lists (meaning that they only distribute notices and information as opposed to serve as discussion lists) that will assist you in keeping up with the network, what is new with Gophers, announcements of new lists, and other items concerning the entire network.

The Scout Report, for example, is a weekly compendium of interesting Internet highlights, and it always has subject-oriented information. Here is their opening announcement.

```
                    The Scout Report
           A Weekly Summary of Internet Highlights


   The Scout Report is a weekly publication offered by InterNIC Information
Services to the Internet community as a fast, convenient way to stay informed
about network activities. Its purpose is to combine in one place the
highlights of new resource announcements and other news which occurred on the
Internet during the previous week.

The Scout Report is provided in multiple formats -- electronic mail, gopher,
and World Wide Web. The gopher and World Wide Web versions of the Report
include links to all listed resources. The Report is released every Friday.
Complete access instructions are included below this week's Report.
```

As an example of their education related information, the following is an announcement about the CoSN Gopher:

```
Gopher:
------

1) Coalition for School Networking (CoSN) gopher now holds the file:
"Distance Learning Projects in the US K-12" which was compiled by the
U.S. Department of Education, Office of Educational Research and Improvement
(OERI).

gopher:   cosn.org
choose:   Resources on the Network/Network Resources for Education/Online &
          Distance Education
```

Here are a few more items for keeping up with the network and its resources.

- For keeping up to date, you can't beat a distribution list called *The InterNIC Net-Happenings*. It issues notices, updates, announcements, and information on new Internet resources that are very useful. The moderator, Gleason Sackman, provides daily updates that are categorized by the type of item—newsletter, Gopher, FTP, Internet service, consulting, and so on. To subscribe, send a message to `majordomo@is.internic.net` with the message `subscribe net-happenings`.

- *E-D-U-P-A-G-E* is a electronic newsletter that covers a broad range of Internet subjects. Sponsored by Educom, it focuses generally on information technology. To subscribe to `edupage` send an e-mail request to `listproc@educom.edu`. The archives are available by FTP from `educom.edu`.

- *Network-News* is an electronic newsletter that provides regular updates on the resources of the Internet. It is available as a subscription to `nnews` from `listserv@ndsuvm1.bitnet` or `listserv@vm1.nodak.edu`. It is archived, which means that you can search and access the back issues via FTP from `vm1.nodak.edu` in the `/nnews` directory.

- *Usenet Groups* are some Usenet newsgroups that may prove useful in keeping up with network news items and resources.

  ```
  news.announce.conferences

  news.announce.important

  news.announce.newsgroups

  news.announce.newusers

  clari.news.education

  clari.news.education.higher

  alt.uu.tools
  ```

Finding Useful Lists to Use for Your Learning Projects

Surprisingly, no master "List of Lists" exists for the Internet, nor is there one single place to get all the information on lists. You will have to work with several sources.

- Arno Wouters has created a document called "How to Find an Interesting Mailing List." To get a copy of this, send e-mail to listserv@vm1.nodak.edu or to listserv@ndsuvm1.bitnet with a message of get new-list wouters.

- You can FTP to rtfm.mit.edu, and find the files part1, part2, part3, part4, part5, part6, part7, and so on through part14 located in the pub/usenet/news.answers/mail/mailing-lists subdirectory, which contain detailed listings of interest groups.

- *The Internet Dog-Eared Pages* Gopher entry is key-word searchable list maintained on the Gopher at calypso-2.oit.unc.edu. You also could search for dog-eared using Veronica to locate it at other Gopher sites.

- Marty Hoag has compiled a guide called *Some Lists of Lists* which also is useful in hunting down the elusive lists. This can be obtained by sending the e-mail message get listsof lists to listserv@vm1.nodak.edu.

- There is an annotated list of lists available via FTP from sri.com in the subdirectory /netinfo. With the filename interest-groups. It also can be obtained using e-mail. Send e-mail to mail-server@sri.com with the message sendinterest-groups.

> **Tip:** This "list of lists" is a file that currently is almost 1Mb. They send you the file broken into 14 parts, but be sure that your mailer and system can handle this much mail all at once.

- An extensive guide to scholarly academic lists, organized by subject, has been created by Diane Kovacs and her colleagues. To get an index of the subject files and the Hypercard stacks, send the e-mail message get acadlist index to listserv@kentvm.bitnet or listserv@kentvm.kent.edu. These guides also are available from the Clearinghouse of Content Oriented Guides at the University of Michigan, and via FTP to ksuvxa.kent.edu, in the subdirectory /library, as file acadlist.index.

- You can obtain a very large file containing a global list of BITNET lists by sending an e-mail message to listserv@bitnic.educom.edu (or listserv@bitnic.bitnet), with a blank subject line and the following in the body of the message list global.

- In addition to "serious" lists, there are hundreds of discussion lists on almost every facet of modern life. These use the same protocols and syntax as the other discussion lists. The lists cover art, personal matters, politics, health matters, humor, hobbies, and just about everything in between and beyond.

■ If you really are into keeping up with lists as they are formed, you might want to subscribe to a distribution list called *new-list*. You may subscribe to new-list@ndsuvm1.bitnet or new-list@vm1.nodak.edu using a standard Listserv subscription, or to interest-groups-request@nisc.sri.com.

These resources can help you maintain your edge by providing information not only on what is new, but by making you aware of the thousands of fascinating information trails available to you.

Hobbies

What if you wanted to find out more about a hobby, such as gardening. Does the Internet have that kind of information?

It sure does. A very quick Veronica search finds items such as the following:

```
articles on topics such as "Interpreting Garden Catalogs," and "Roses for your
Garden." There are some more heavy hitting items, such as "Cell-Wall-Bound
Invertase (Or Beta-Fructosidase)" and "Transposase Tam3--Garden Snapdragon."

links to information on lawn chemical disposal, and directions for locating the
Essex County cooperative Extension Office in New Jersey.
```

As usual, there are many entries—12 pages worth using *garden* and *gardening* alone as search words. Looking around on the WWW, you can locate another set of information. For example, at http://leviathan.tamu.edu:70/1s/mg, you will see an entry for the Master Gardener:

```
                    Master Gardener Information

       * Full text search of Master Gardener Menus
       * Introduction to Master Gardener files
       * Fruits and Nuts
       * Flowering Plants, Annual and Perennial
       * Ornamental Trees and Shrubs
       * Turf Grasses
       * Vegetables
```

The key to Internet information is the use of the various search tools such ass Veronica, Archie, and WebQuery.

Using FAQs in Self-Planned Learning Projects

A very useful practice associated with a variety of activities on the Internet had evolved. A great many of the discussion lists and Usenet newsgroups maintain documents that are called *Frequently Asked Questions* or FAQs (rhymes with Max). In addition, there are FAQs about Internet tools, such as Gopher, WWW, or FTP, on subjects such as Advertising on the Internet, Copyrights, Ice Skating, FAX on the Internet, and so on.

FAQs normally are configured as a series of common questions and their answers. The questions are those that a newcomer might have about the group and the subject.

These documents provide a good starting place. Often, they help avoid repeated recurring discussions of the same old subjects. These documents usually evolve and change over time. There are now at least 900 FAQs maintained at a variety of sites, most notably at the FTP archives at `rtfm.mit.edu`. These also are available by mail, by sending e-mail to `mail-server@rtfm.mit.edu`, with a message of just the word `help`. Many Gophers offer access to these as well.

As an example of a FAQ, this is the first page of a FAQ about FTP.

```
Subject: Anonymous FTP: Frequently Asked Questions (FAQ) List
Date: 18 Jan 1994 00:00:52 -0500
Summary: This document gives answers to some Frequently Asked Questions
         about Anonymous FTP
Keywords: FTP, File Transfer Protocol, FAQ, Anonymous FTP, FTP Sites, Sitelist

Archive-name: ftp-list/faq
Last-Modified: 12-Jan-94
Version: 2.4.4


                        Anonymous FTP
             Frequently Asked Questions (FAQ) List


Suggestions for changes and comments are always welcome.

** Updated News:
Tom Czarnik has stopped maintaining this list.
The last version he released was 2.4.2 of 29-Apr-93.
Starting with version 2.4.3 this FAQ and the Anonymous FTP
site list are maintained by Perry Rovers (Perry.Rovers@kub.nl)


Copyright 1994, Perry Rovers -- Text may be quoted without permission,
however please advise me of the target publication. Free distribution.

[Start Of File]
=====================================================================
```

```
I keep a directory of Internet sites accepting Anonymous FTP and mail
retrieval of their files.

Topics are shown below and with their respective answers.

Format: (Q#) for a question and (A#) for the answer.

        (1)  What is and how do I use the FTP program?
        (2)  What types of FTP information are available?
        (3)  What is the most current version?
        (4)  Retrieving the listings via email.
        (5)  Using FTP without direct Internet access.
        (6)  Getting help when you have problems with a site.
        (7)  Getting a site listed or changes made.
        (8)  What is Archie and how does it relate to the list?
        (9)  Using Gopher to access archives.
```

Following this brief listing of the questions, the FAQ proceeds to answer each of the questions in turn.

FAQ documents often are posted at regular intervals on lists or newsgroups as a way of helping newcomers, and reminding others of the focus of that group and the "rules of engagement."

Useful Guides and Tools for Learning On Your Own

The independent learner can find numerous guides and tools online that are of use in pursuing their own learning projects—be it learning more about the Internet itself and its tools, or about subjects such as education, taxes, the federal government, the human genome project, underwater archeology, humor, and on and on. There are guides, programs, lists, and navigation programs available via Gopher, FTP, and WWW. Here is a list of some of the best.

- Clearinghouse for Subject-Oriented Internet Resource Guides
- December's Guides
- Gopher Jewels
- Nettools: The Guide to Network Resources Tools
- Network Knowledge for the Neophyte
- NYSERNet's New User's Guide to Useful and Unique Resources on the Internet
- The Online World
- SURAnet—Information Available on the Internet: A Guide to Selected Sources
- Yanoff's Special Internet Connections

Clearinghouse for Subject-Oriented Internet Resource Guides

Based at the University of Michigan, The Clearinghouse for Subject-Oriented Internet Resource Guides is a collection of resource lists organized by subject. The guides are available via FTP and Gopher. Unlike many other guides, these guides are not organized by tool—Gopher, FTP sites, and so on—instead, they each focus on a theme.

Currently, the guides are in ASCII text format. The Clearinghouse intends to support other formats, such as PostScript, HTML, or others in the future. Access to these guides is available via anonymous FTP, Gopher, and World Wide Web/ Mosaic. From within Gopher, a WAIS index of the full text of these guides enables all documents to be searched for particular words.

Where to find it

Gopher

Site	`gopher.lib.umich.edu`
Menu	`What's New and Featured Resources`
Menu	`Clearinghouse...`

Anonymous FTP

Site	`una.hh.lib.umich.edu`
Subdirectory	`/inetdirsstacks`

HTML

`http://http2.sils.umich.edu/~lou/chhome.html`

`http://www.lib.umich.edu/chhome.html`

These guides contain information about resources from Gophers, anonymous FTP sites, telnet sites, e-mail lists, Usenet newsgroups, papers, conference announcements, and more. In some cases, there are multiple guides for a given subject. A dynamic site, this one is worth repeat visits.

December's Guides

John December has complied two documents that are detailed listings of resources and tools. *Information Sources: the Internet and Computer-Mediated-Communication* outlines access information and pointers to a huge range of information sources including the cognitive, communication, psychological, social, and technical aspects of the nets. The guide covers the information in seven sections:

- How to Use this document
- The Internet and Services
- Information Services/Electronic Publications
- Societies and Organizations
- Newsgroups
- Selected Bibliography
- Description of Items

As an example of its depth and breadth, the section on The Internet and Services covers such topics as New User Introduction and Motivation, Comprehensive Guides, Exploring, Training, Information Repositories, Document Services, Sources of Internet, Network and Related information, Services and Tools, Commercial Services, Free-Nets, Directories, and more. This is a very comprehensive, detailed, and useful guide to resources.

December's other guide, *The Internet Tools Summary* focuses specifically on Internet tools and how to access them. It outlines the tools for network information retrieval and computer-mediated communication. Under the listings about Internet Tools, for example, you can find information on not only the usual suspects such as Archie, telnet, FTP, E-mail, Gopher, and so on, but also on the more unusual tools such as Alex, Astra, Cello, Compass, Moo Gopher, and other services. This guide is organized as follows:

- Network Information Retrieval Tools
- Computer-Mediated Communication Forums
- References
- Protocols/Standards
- Action Notation
- Description of Items

These two guides are widely available:

Where to find it

Anonymous FTP

Site	`ftp.rpi.edu`
Subdirectory	`/pub/communications`
Files	`internet-cmc.txt`
	`internet-tools.txt`

HTML

```
http://www.rpi.edu/Internet/Guides/decemj/internet-
cmc.html
http://www.rpi.edu/Internet/Guides/decemj/internet-
tools.html
```

December has provided the guides in a variety of formats, including LaTeX, PostScript, text, .dvi and .dat.

Tip: Keep a current hard copy of both of these guides handy while you are online. It is a quick way to have the exact address of major Internet tools and resources, which can save you time.

Gopher Jewels

Gopher Jewels is a list of interesting Gophers created by David Riggins. It is organized by subject—the Gopher access tree is organized in the following way:

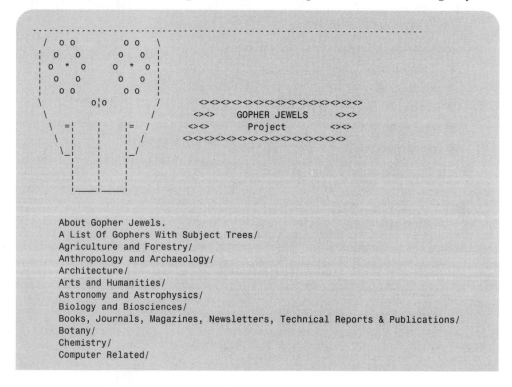

```
About Gopher Jewels.
A List Of Gophers With Subject Trees/
Agriculture and Forestry/
Anthropology and Archaeology/
Architecture/
Arts and Humanities/
Astronomy and Astrophysics/
Biology and Biosciences/
Books, Journals, Magazines, Newsletters, Technical Reports & Publications/
Botany/
Chemistry/
Computer Related/
```

```
Economics and Business/
Education and Research (Includes K-12)/
Employment Opportunities and Resume Postings/
Engineering/
Environment/
Federal Agency and Related Gopher Sites/
Fun Stuff & Multimedia/
General Reference Resources/
Geography/
Geology and Oceanography/
Grants/
History/
Internet Cyberspace Related/
Language/
Legal or Law Related/
Library Information and Catalogs/
List of Lists Resources Identified From A Veronica Search/
Math Sciences/
Medical Related/
Military/
Miscellaneous Items/
Patents and Copy Rights/
Photonics/
Physics/
Political and Government/
Products and Services - Store Fronts/
Religion and Philosophy/
Search Internet Resources by Type (WAIS, Gopher, Phone, Other)/
Social Science/
Weather/
```

The menu listings each lead to more specific Gopher access, and are updated frequently. Gopher Jewels is available on the Gopher at USC `cwis.usc.edu port 70` in the `Other Gophers and Information Resources` menu. In addition, it now is available through HTTP `http://galaxy.einet.net/gopher/gopher.html` (searchable form), or `http://galaxy.einet.net/GJ/index.html` (traditional hypertext structure).

Nettools: The Guide to Network Resource Tools

Produced by the staff at EARN, *Nettools* is a superior guide to Internet resources. This guide is divided into several sections covering all of the primary tools of the Internet.

- Exploring the Network—Gopher, Veronica, WWW
- Searching Databases—WAIS, ASTRA
- Finding Network Resources—Archie, WHOIS, Netserv
- Getting files—TRICKLE, BITFTP
- Networked Interest Groups
- Other Tools of Interest

Nettools has a distinctly European "look and feel" because of its origins in Switzerland. It provides many practical tips and hints. It is available by e-mail and via FTP.

■ E-mail from `listserv@earncc.bitnet` in both plain text and in Postscript format—send an e-mail message to the Listserv with the following in the body of the message:

GET NETTOOLS PS (PostScript format)

GET NETTOOLS TXT (Plain text format)

■ FTP from `naic.nasa.gov` in the `/files/general_info` subdirectory as either `earn-resource-tool-guide-v3.ps` or as `earn-resource-tool-guide-v3.txt`. Remember that when you get there, the version number may have changed.

Network Knowledge for the Neophyte

Network Knowledge for the Neophyte by Martin Raish is aptly subtitled *Stuff you need to know in order to navigate the electronic village.* It is full of helpful tips, hints, and information on topics such as e-mail, remote login, Internet tools, and FTP. It has a good set of appendices covering Network Guides—books, and FTP documents, and other good "*stuff.*" While it is designed to accompany a workshop as a training manual, it can hold its own as a free-standing guide. It is available by FTP from `hydra.uwo.ca` in the `/libsoft` subdirectory as `Network_Knowledge_for_the_Neophyte.txt`.

NYSERNet's New User's Guide to Useful and Unique Resources on the Internet

NYSERNet, the New York State Education and Research Network, provides a *New User's Guide* that is very useful. Designed for the new user, it can help all users learn about the Internet and its tools. While the guide is written primarily for educators, it has broad general coverage as well.

The New User's Guide is organized with sections on

■ Library Catalogs

■ Databases

■ Electronic Discussion Groups/Forums

■ Directories

■ Information Resources

- FTP Archives
- Fee-Based Information Services
- Software/Freeware
- BBS
- Miscellaneous

You can obtain the guide via FTP to `nysernet.org`, and the Guide is in the `/pub/ guides` subdirectory. Look for the current file by version.

The Online World

A shareware guide by Odd de Presno, *The Online World*, is an electronic guide of some 280 pages. It explores selected applications and services including commercial online service providers, such as CompuServe, AOL, and so on, and information on a large number of specific resources. The guide can be obtained currently in three languages: English, German, and Norwegian.

The guide is organized into three very broad sections:

- An Online World—The value of information, structure and content, using online services
- Applications—Hobbies, home, health, education, work, using the networks to manage projects
- Working Smarter—Practical tips

The Online World covers a lot of ground, and contains a useful index. To get information on how to obtain the latest version of the guide, send e-mail to `listserv@vm1.nodak.edu` with the message `get tow master`. The use of this guide requires a small payment to the author—the details are included with the guide, but it can be reviewed for free in keeping with its shareware identity.

SURAnet—Information Available on the Internet: A Guide to Selected Sources

From SURAnet, *Information Available on the Internet: A Guide to Selected Sources* provides good overviews of the Internet, directory services, and information services. The Contents include the following:

- Using the Internet
- Directory Services
- Information Resources—Including library catalogs and resources organized by topic/subject

- Networking Topics
- Supercomputer Centers
- Miscellaneous Information Sources
- Using Anonymous FTP

You can obtain the guide via FTP to `ftp.sura.net`, and the file is located in the `pub/nic` subdirectory. The file changes name each month, but it can be identified by the month and year.

Yanoff's Special Internet Connections

Scott Yanoff maintains a list called *Special Internet Connections* that is very handy. Updated twice a month, it is especially helpful because of the dynamic nature of the Internet environment. Yanoff includes a large variety of information, and *Special Internet Connections* should be considered a mainstay on your virtual reference shelf.

The listing is organized into the following sections:

- Agriculture
- Aviation
- Computers
- Economics/Business
- Education/Teaching/Learning
- FTP
- Games/Recreational/Fun/Chat
- Geophysical/Geographical/Geological
- Gopher
- Law
- Libraries
- Medical/Health/Biology/Genetics
- Music
- News
- Politics/Government
- Religion/Bible
- Science/Math/Statistics
- Services
- Software
- Space/Astronomy

- Sports
- Travel
- User Lookup Services/Whois
- Weather/Atmospheric/Oceanic

Yanoff's list is both very useful and quite entertaining—do you want to find out how to finger a soda machine in Australia to discover how many cold Cokes it contains, get information on amateur (ham) radio operators, find out where to play chess online, participate in a stock market simulation, check out the tablature and chords for the guitar, look at Nielson TV ratings, get NFL scores, or find subway routes of major French cities in French or English? If so, Yanoff's list is for you.

> **Tip:** Download a fresh copy of Yanoff's list every six weeks or so, to keep up-to-date. It is invaluable to have a print out handy while you are online.

This list is available via FTP from `csd4.csd.uwm.edu` in the `/pub` subdirectory as `inet.services.txt`, or finger Yanoff at `yanoff@csd4.csd.uwm.edu`. The html version of this list for WWW and Mosaic is `http://www.uwm.edu/Mirror/inet.services.html`.

Useful Programs and Sites for Digging

There are some programs—online and offline—that are useful in learning more on your own about the Internet and for locating information using the Internet. In addition, there are some unusual sites that offer more that the normal Gopher, telnet, or WWW services that are worth using frequently. The following sections discuss some of the best.

Hytelnet

Hytelnet by Peter Scott provides a user-friendly interface for telnet access to Internet information. It contains descriptive information, address, login, and other information about telnet accessible libraries, BBSes, Free-Nets, Gophers, databases, archives, and so on. The interface works a bit like the WWW/Lynx text-based browsers in that information is presented in a hypertext format in which the document, including the opening screen, has words you can highlight linked to other documents.

You can use Hytelnet online, so that you can make direct connections when you want, and as a TSR on your personal computer, to provide this information for making connections. Online, after you log on to Hytelnet, hunt for something of interest, move the cursor to the item, and use the right arrow to select it. Using the menu at the bottom of the screen, you can choose items and make actual connections.

Online, Hytelnet is interactively available via telnet at any one of the following sites:

Where to find it

Columbia Law School

Address	`lawnet.law.columbia.edu`
Login	`lawnet`

El Paso Community College

Address	`laguna.epcc.edu`
Login	`library`

Manchester Computing Centre

Address	`info.mcc.ac.uk`
Login	`hytelnet`

Oxford University

Address	`rls.ox.ac.uk`
Login	`hytelnet`

University of Adelaide

Address	`library.adelaide.edu.au`
Login	`access`

University of Arizona

Address	`info.ccit.arizona.edu`
Login	`hytelnet`

University of CA, San Diego

Address	`infopath.ucsd.edu`
Login	`infopath`

University of Saskatchewan

    Address   `access.usask.ca`

    Login   `hytelnet`

University of Denver

    Address   `du.edu`

    Login   `atdu`

Hytelnet also is available to be installed on DOS, Macintosh, UNIX, and VMS systems. Do an Archie search to find current versions of this software.

InfoPop for Windows

InfoPop for Windows is a program that runs as a Windows Help file so that you can use it while off- or online. It provides help on numerous topics, including the Internet, Gopher, FTP, Telnet, Archie, and more. In addition, it supplies some information on popular resources such as ERIC.

The contents include the following:

- About InfoPop
- What is the Internet?
- BBS Systems on the Internet
- FTP
- Getting an Internet Connection
- Internet Tools
- Library Catalogs
- Library-Oriented Lists
- Miscellaneous Internet Destinations
- RFC Documents
- Telnet
- WHOIS
- Bitnet
- Campus Wide Information Systems
- CompuServe
- Glossary

When you click on the subject, a new page appears, with specific connection and login information. You can obtain this free software from the GMUtant OnLine BBS (703) 993-2219, 9600 v.32), and from several of the software repositories on the Internet as `ipwin.zip`.

Merit's Cruise

Merit's Cruise of the Internet is a tutorial covering a variety of aspects of the Internet. This is an offline tutorial running under Windows, covering a bit about the Internet, e-mail, FTP, telnet, Gopher, WAIS, Archie, and some resources by subject.

It is available via FTP in both Macintosh and DOS format. Go to `nic.merit.edu` and look at the `/internet/resources/cruise.mac` or `/internet/resources/cruise.dos` subdirectories. You will find a number of files, but in each case, there is a README file that is useful.subdirectory. You can obtain instructions for the Cruise over the Net by sending e-mail to `nic-info@nic.merit.edu` with either `get merit.cruise2.mac.readme` or `get merit.cruise2.win.readme` as the text body.

Peripatetic, Eclectic Gopher—PEG

The University of California at Irvine provides us with *PEG* (the Peripatetic, Eclectic Gopher), designed to demonstrate the encyclopedic, diverse nature of the Internet. This is an unusually comprehensive Gopher, that is very user-friendly for both the novice and experienced Internet surfer. Here is its opening menu:

```
          Internet Gopher Information Client v2.0.15

University of California - Irvine, PEG, Peripatetic, Eclectic Gopher

  -->  1.  About PEG, a Peripatetic, Eclectic GOPHER
       2.  Biology/
       3.  Electronic Journals/
       4.  Exemplars/
       5.  Favorite Bookmarks/
       6.  GOPHERS/
       7.  Humanities/
       8.  INTERNET ASSISTANCE/
       9.  Irvine Weather and world events/
      10.  LIBRARIES/
      11.  MATHEMATICS/
      12.  MEDICINE/
      13.  PHILOSOPHY/
      14.  POLITICS and GOVERNMENT/
      15.  Physics/
      16.  VIRTUAL REFERENCE DESK/
      17.  VIRTUAL REFERENCE DESK  UCI SPECIFIC/
      18.  WOMEN'S STUDIES and RESOURCES/
```

Following is PEGs quick overview of purpose:

```
About PEG, a Peripatetic, Eclectic GOPHER (1k)
+-----------------------------------------------------------+

Welcome to PEG, a Peripatetic, Eclectic Gopher.

PEG was created to demonstrate the utility and the versatility of a gopher server
in providing improved access to needed information distributed throughout the
network.  PEG was designed to assist both the network novice as well as the network
expert.

Resources throughout the Internet are encyclopedic in nature. One of PEG's goals is
to ferret out exemplary resources.  In a few instances, comprehensive coverage has
been the aim, e.g, "United States Government Gophers/".  These selective menu
offerings highlight something of the burgeoning riches of the extended network.
```

One of my favorite places to look on PEG for interesting information is under #5 `Favorite Bookmarks`. There are a great number of very useful and unusual pointers on this menu. (I "virtually" drop in regularly to see what is here.)

```
Internet Gopher Information Client v2.0.15

                  Favorite Bookmarks

 --> 1.       NOTA BENE   Please Read FIRST
     2.       Search High-level Gopher Menus Using Jughead at W&L U. <?>
     3.       New Gophers/
     4.    United States GOVERNMENT Gophers/
     5.    California Gophers GALORE!/
     6.    INTERNET ASSISTANCE/
     7.  5,000,000+ journal articles (via CARL UnCover)/
     8.  ANTPAC UCI Library's online catalog  N.B. UCI access only <TEL>
     9.  Big Ugly Smiley
    10.  Biology: Biodiversity & Biological Collections (Harvard Univ)/
    11.  CAUSE Services/
    12.  Chronicle of Higher Education gopher/
    13.  Coalition for Networked Information/
    14.  Current Tables of Contents Library Science Journals/
    15.  Curtin University of Technology, Western Australia/
    16.  Directory of Academic Electronic Forums <?>
    17.  EDUCOM/
    18.  Electronic Newsstand (tm)/
    19.  Electronic Reference Books/
    20.  Franklin's Home Gopher/
    21.  GOPHER NEWSNet/
    22.  GOPHERS/
    23.  GOPHERS  NETWORK GOPHERS/
    24.  GOPHERS  USA/
    25.  GOPHERS  United States Library Gophers/
    26.  Gopher-Jewels (Riggins)/
    27.  HYTELNET (Login to Sites via Telnet via W&L U)/
    28.  Information Organization - by Subject  (Library of Congress)/
    29.  InterNIC: Internet Network Information Center/
```

```
30. Internet Hunt/
31. Internet file server (ftp) sites ARCHIE/
32. Kevin's World (a personal gopher)/
33. LAW: Cornell Law School/
34. LIBRARIES/
35. LIBRARIES  California Libraries Hytelnet/
36. LIBRARIES  United States Libraries Hytelnet/
37. Library Catalogs:  United States (Hytelnet Yale U)/
38. Library of Congress MARVEL Information System/
39. MEDICINE: CancerNet Information/
40. MEDICINE: National Institutes of Health (NIH) Gopher/
41. Merit Network gopher/
42. Michigan State University Gopher/
43. North Carolina State University Library gopher/
44. O'Reilly & Associates (publisher)/
45. O'Reilly Publishing <?>
46. POETRY Search a full text database of poetry <?>
47. RECIPES Search database of recipes <?>
48. RiceInfo (Rice University CWIS) Gopher/
49. SONG LYRICS Search a database of song lyrics <?>
50. Search "The World" Using Veronica/
51. Subject Tree (EUROGopher)/
52. Substring search of archive sites on the internet/
53. Sunsite gopher/
54. Texas A&M Gophers/
55. The WELLgopher - The Whole Earth 'Lectronic Link's Gopherspace/
56. U California - Santa Cruz, InfoSlug System/
57. UCI Campus Directory (Phone Book) <CSO>
58. UCI MAIN Gopher/
59. University of Southern California Gopher/
60. WAIS Everything/
```

Tip: Explore the `RiceInfo` item, Franklin's Home Gopher, and Kevin's World for many more useful (and fun) pointers.

Washington and Lee Law Library

The Washington and Lee Law Library maintains one of the largest compendiums of interesting databases, archives, Archie, Telnet and Gopher connections on the Net. Don't be fooled by its name—while it certainly maintains useful law related information, it has both breadth and depth in a huge number of subjects. You can reach it several ways.

Where to find it

Gopher	`netlink.wlu.edu 1020`
Telnet	`liberty.uc.wlu.edu`
Login	`lawlib`
http	`//honor.uc.wlu.edu:1020`
http	`//netlink.wlu.edu:1020`

This immense site provides many hours of browsing pleasure—check in often, because it is always being updated. On my last virtual visit, its menu listed approximately 3,000 different resources and services including Archie, Gopher, WWW, Lynx, and resources such as indexes, databases, and libraries. The menu program is easy to understand and use and includes a search feature.

World Wide Web

Browsing *World Wide Web* (WWW) using Lynx, Mosaic or any other web program to cruise the Internet can be quite educational. There are thousands of "home pages" available at numerous sites. These home pages provide links to other documents, images, sound files, databases, and more. Frequently, there are explanatory files about WWW, the site, and resources which themselves can serve as tutorials. Following the links can take you to sites around the world on any topic, providing a powerful search and learn activity. An example is shown in Figure 10.1 below, showing Mosaic displaying a World Wide Web guide.

WorldWindow

WorldWindow at Washington University Libraries in St. Louis is another large, multi-faceted site for the lifelong learner to explore. With an easy to understand menu, it provides all the usual Internet tools including WWW, Gopher, and Archie. It is an excellent place to begin a search for more information. Telnet to `library.wustl.edu`, and log in by pressing Enter to confirm use of a standard terminal type and then press Enter again to confirm guest status.

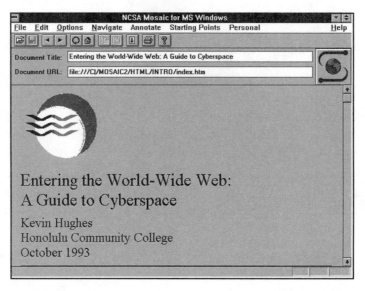

Figure 10.1. "World Wide Web: A Guide to Cyberspace" shown running under Mosaic for Microsoft Windows.

From Here...

Recommendations: To start with, get Yanoff, December, and Nettools, plus the Merit Cruise of the Internet if you are a very new user. Because new guides appear frequently, use Gopher, Veronica, Archie, and Hytelnet to search for and retrieve them. Next, head for Washington and Lee or PEG for an awe-inspiring cybervisit.

INTERNET 101:
A QUICK GUIDE
TO THE INTERNET
AND ITS TOOLS

It is not worth while to go around the world to count the cats in Zanzibar.

Henry David Thoreau

But on the Internet, you probably *can* count the cats in Zanzibar in just minutes, nevertheless.

Internet 101 is a quick course for those who

- Have never used the Internet before.
- Have learned how to use only a few of the Internet tools and want to expand.
- Need a quick review lesson.
- Think that the Internet is "just a large e-mail system with some games and stuff."

This course highlights the most useful Internet features and systems, and the most powerful commands and concepts.

Note: This course does *not* present a thorough, in depth, examination of any of the Internet tools or systems. For that, there are any number of highly-recommended Internet books available.

At this point in Internet history, no single Internet tool or system can provide access to all the Internet's resources (several are making great strides in that direction), so it is more productive at first to learn the most important features of many of the tools rather than to specialize in just one or two. After you have used the Internet for a while, you may find it worthwhile to study some of the tools and systems in greater depth.

Internet 101: Course Outline

- Brief History and Explanation of the Nature of the Internet
- How to Gain Access to the Internet
- The Internet Tools:

  Telnet

  E-Mail

  FTP

  Gopher

  Discussion Groups

  Usenet News

  World Wide Web

History and Nature of the Internet

A *computer network* is a group of computers connected together in some way so that they can send information back and forth among themselves. They may be connected by wires, phone lines, fiber optics, satellite links, or any combination of these.

Networks usually are set up so that groups or organizations that share some common goals (such as universities, schools, companies, and government agencies) can communicate better and make use of each other's computer systems and data.

Currently, approximately 25,000 of these networks are voluntarily connected together in a huge *network of networks* called the *Internet*.

The Problem of Standards

In the past, computer networks had difficulty communicating with other networks because so many different types of systems were used and because the networks often used idiosyncratic standards that were devised on the spot to solve a particular network's unique needs and problems.

This problem was solved substantially by the results of U.S. Defense Department research on networking in the 1970s. That research yielded a new system for sending data through networks. This system sent small groups of data that included addressing information about where that data was to go on the network (these groups of data with addressing information are called "packets"). These new techniques became a standard (in computer terms, a "protocol") known as *TCP/IP* (Transmission Control Protocol/Internet Protocol) which became the standard for the Internet.

In the 1980s, the National Science Foundation (NSF) set up a high-capacity data transfer backbone network based on TCP/IP, which became the core of the Internet (NFSnet). With this common protocol, networking grew rapidly within research companies, universities, and government-funded agencies.

The TCP/IP standard also encouraged the growth of other networks and internetworking, outside of the Internet. These networks often were set up to transfer data for commercial and other purposes that were not allowed by the NSFnet.

As Internet guidelines evolved, these outside networks were allowed to connect to the Internet, provided that the Internet's acceptable use policies were followed. These commercial networks then became easy access points for individuals via modems and personal computers, without institutional affiliations, to connect to the Internet.

This history is worth being aware of because it helps explain why the Internet has the unique blend of policies, rules, and customs, by which Internet users must currently abide.

The Internet Today

Today, the Internet is made up of approximately 25,000 networks which have over 2,000,000 host computers connected to them and which are accessible by approximately 30 million people world-wide.

The Internet is growing at a phenomenal rate of approximately 10 percent per *month*, and is expected to have 100 million people online by 1998! (See Figure A.1. for a display of the Internet's recent growth.)

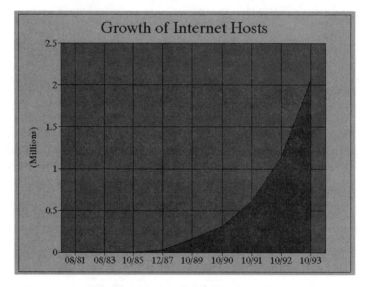

Figure A.1. Recent growth in the number of networks connected to the Internet.

As mentioned earlier, the Internet has evolved from a network only for research and higher education institutions. This is reflected in the number of networks that have registered their Internet address under various categories. Figure A.2 shows the most used categories (referred to as "domains" in the Internet addressing scheme).

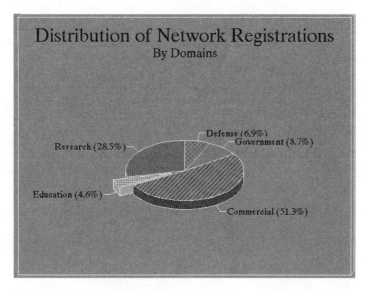

Figure A.2. Internet-connected networks by primary usage categories.

All 50 states in the United States have networks connected to the Internet, ranging from four in North Dakota to 3,107 in California.

Over 70 countries are connected to the Internet. While most of the networks are in the United States, other countries such as Canada, France, Germany, Japan, and the United Kingdom, each have over 1,000 connected networks. Those countries checking in with just one network (Cameroon, Fiji, Ghana, Kazakhstan, Kenya, Latvia, Nicaragua, Peru, and the Virgin Islands) provide an interesting look at the extent of worldwide Internet interconnectedness. (Antarctica isn't in this list—it already has two networks!)

Despite this worldwide coverage, the "lingua-franca" of the Internet is English. Local network activities often are in the area's native language, but it also is common for systems worldwide to use English in discussions, stored text, and system navigation activities, such as accessing databases.

While the instructions on using the Internet tools, presented later in this course, cover only the most important features, there are too many details to adequately absorb just by reading them. Practicing with the tools is critical to understanding them and in remembering how to use them. Therefore, the next obvious step is to obtain access to the Internet.

Access

The commonly used phrases "get on the Internet," "sign up for the Internet," and "get connected to the Internet" are all a bit misleading and do create some confusion.

To use the Internet, an individual needs to find an Internet *access provider* and get an account with the provider.

The access provider may be a non-profit organization or institution, such as a university or government agency, or the Internet access provider may be a for-profit company or organization.

The *access method* may be via your personal computer (with communications software and a modem) through standard telephone lines, or via terminals wired directly to an institution's host computer (this is common at universities and large companies).

Free Accounts

The first step in getting access to the Internet is to find out whether you have a free account available to you. Universities often have accounts available to faculty, staff, students, and even some alumni and others in the community. Some K-12 schools provide access for students and teachers, and some states offer teachers special access as well.

In an increasing number of cities and towns, libraries, city governments, non-profit community groups, and computer clubs are offering Internet access. Some, usually limited, access is available through community dial-up Bulletin Board Systems, such as the very successful "Free-Nets." Many companies also have access to the Internet available for employees. Ask around, look around, and contact the computer system staff of any institution or organization to which you belong.

Commercial Providers

If your search for free access doesn't turn up anything in a few days, go ahead and get an account at one of the dial-up Internet access providers. If you later find a free account, you easily can drop the pay account and switch to the free access.

Note: There always are at least two minor problems when switching access providers. First, you'll need to send your correspondents

> your new Internet address; and second, you may need to learn a few
> new computer commands because each system is a little bit differ-
> ent.

Access to the Internet for individuals has gone from unavailable, to thousands of
dollars per month, to the current situation in which accounts are available for as
little as $5 per month, with many providers from which to choose.

If you are fortunate enough to live in an area in which one of these providers is
within your local calling area, that $5 a month may be all you pay. If that isn't the
case, when considering which provider to select, consider the cost of phone rates
to various locations.

> **Tip:** If you will need to call long distance to connect with an Inter-
> net access provider, ask the provider whether you can connect to
> their service through one of several independent networks, such as
> Tymnet or CompuServe's network (not the CompuServe online
> service).

Services to Look For

In selecting an Internet access service provider, look for the following services:

- E-mail
- Telnet
- FTP
- Archie
- Gopher
- Lynx
- Usenet news
- SLIP or PPP

E-Mail and Telnet

E-mail and *telnet* are absolute must-have services. Almost all services provide e-
mail, but some charge for each message sent and/or received. Select a service with

no message charges, if possible—it is not unusual for those who use the Internet regularly to send and receive 100 messages per day.

Also, some providers limit the size of e-mail messages to, for example, 32K (32 thousand characters). You can work around this limitation, but it could make it much harder to receive a large document or message from another sender.

One additional feature to look for is a *MIME compliant* mail program. No, MIME is not some form of French pantomime—MIME-compliant mail programs enable you to send and receive binary files, such as word processor files and software, as part of an e-mail message (your correspondent also needs to be using a MIME-compliant mail program, such as Pine and Eudora.

Telnet is the basic tool that allows you access to all the other tools on the Internet, even if your access provider has not installed the software for these other tools on their computer.

Other Services

Following are other basic services that you should ask about or look for in the access provider's advertising:

FTP	Allows access throughout the world to millions of computer files and computers
Archie	Helps you locate those FTPable files
Gopher	A menu-based file and service search and retrieval system
Lynx	A text-based access tool to the World Wide Web hypertext system
Usenet News	The provider should offer a newsreader and access to Usenet newsgroups
SLIP or PPP	These services allow you to use Mosaic and other TCP/IP-compliant software directly on your own computer. These types of services usually are more expensive.

Hardware Requirements and Considerations

Despite the high-tech and massive nature of the Internet, its use of standard protocols means that literally hundreds of different types of computers and modems are suitable for the Internet.

As with many things, you will encounter trade-offs that require you to make decisions about where you want to strike the balance between time saved and money spent. The following sections discuss several things to consider when making these decisions.

Computers

Two absolute requirements for a personal computer to be used for dial-up access to the Internet are that it must have a modem (internal or external), and that the computer must have some sort of communications software. These are not big obstacles—almost all personal computers built in the last dozen years meet these requirements.

Other computer features are a matter of convenience, and a matter of what particular Internet activities on which you will be expending most of your effort:

Monitor	A standard monochrome monitor will work fine with much of the text-based tools and resources on the Internet, but with the increasing use of menu screens that use several types of highlights, bolding, and so on, these screens are becoming harder to read, and some information is lost. A color VGA monitor is much easier to read, and also allows for switching to a 50 line screen rather than the usual 25 lines. This particularly is useful for scanning long menus and lists, which are common on the Internet.
Hard Drive	If you've been using a computer for more than a few months, you probably are aware that no hard drive is ever large enough—what seemed like a warehouse when you bought it becomes a closet that you have to keep cleaning out. The bad news is that you will see so many useful files, software programs, and so on, on the Internet, that you will find downloading a couple megabytes of files per day is very easy. Buy the largest hard drive that you can comfortably afford—and get an extra box of floppy disks.
Computer model and speed	A fast computer speed is always nice to have, but even an old XT can comfortably keep up with a state of the art 14,400 bits per second (bps) modem during online Internet sessions. By today's standards, however, the XT will seem painfully slow when reading, transferring, or processing any files

or programs you've downloaded. This is another case of finding a comfortable balance between time spent and money spent. The more you use the Internet, the more you'll appreciate a faster machine.

Modems

Modems are devices that convert computer signals into sounds that can be sent over normal telephone lines and that can convert back into computer signals sounds it "hears" on the phone.

The purchase of a modem is again, of course, another place to consider the trade-offs between time and money, but in the case of modems, the trade-offs are extreme! Consider this: A file that takes a 14,400 bps modem using its best compression systems and using one of the faster transfer protocols 4 minutes to transfer would take a 2400 bps modem 1 hour and 36 minutes!

Even if you've got that hour and a half to spare watching the download, think of the differences in connect time charges from your access provider between 4 minutes and 1 hour and 36 minutes. And even worse, if you need to call long distance, imagine the extra charges. The 14,400 bps modems sell from discount dealers for around $100 and the 2400 bps modems sell for around $50. As you can see, the "savings" for the 2400 bps modem could quickly disappear to the phone company and your access provider.

Tip: Have your own modem?—that 300 bps modem in the back of the closet? Walk over to the closet, pick up the modem, place the modem in the wastebasket—that file that took the 14,400 bps modem 4 minutes to transfer to you will take that 300 bps modem 12 hours and 48 minutes! That would make for an impressive phone bill, wouldn't it?

Besides speed, the other main decision you need to make when purchasing a modem is whether to get an *internal* or *external* modem. This usually is not a particularly important decision, although it is one you will need to make.

Internal modems have the advantage of costing less, and requiring somewhat fewer cables and clutter. External modems have the advantage of being moved from computer to computer more easily, even when the computers are of different makes and models. (Internal modems sometimes are specifically designed for particular models or lines of computers.) Also, external modems usually have several lights on the front that can help when deducing some of the problems that may occur when establishing connections with a remote computer.

Software Requirements and Considerations

There are thousands of *communications programs* available from commercial, shareware, and freeware sources. Each of these have their own unique commands, features, and appearance. To successfully operate any one of these, you will need to resort to reading the on-disk or printed documentation for that program. There are, however, some elements relevant to the Internet, common to all communications software.

Communications software that you run on your own personal computer handles the details of operating the modem and transferring data to and from your access provider's computer. You can configure most programs in dozens of ways so as to communicate with various types of modems and remote computer systems.

One category of these configurations involves *terminal emulation*. When your software is configured to emulate a particular type of terminal, it acts as if it were that type of terminal, both in terms of how it displays incoming data and how it sends data to other computers. These emulation modes are based on specific models of terminal manufactured by various computer companies.

The Internet has minimal requirements for terminal emulators. The de facto standard terminal emulation on the Internet has come to be *VT100*. If at all possible, get a program that can be set to VT100. You can, however, use several other terminal types, such as ANSI or VT52, and even the so-called "dumb terminal." With these other terminal emulations, however, you may not receive all the display codes, such as those that clear the screen, move the cursor, change colors, and so on.

Another factor to consider when selecting a communications program is its selection of *file transfer protocols*. These protocols are standardized ways of uploading or downloading files between your computer and a remote computer.

Zmodem and Kermit are two of the most popular downloading protocols used on the Internet. Xmodem and Ymodem also are used, but not as often. If you are buying new software, be sure to get at least Zmodem and Kermit. If you already have some software that has one of these four, go ahead and see if it is supported on the Internet sites you visit. All the transfer protocols work quite well, it's just a matter of your computer and the remote computer using the same protocol. Kermit is rugged and stable, but usually slower depending on the version of

Kermit you are using. Zmodem is fast and enables you to recover from a break in the download—you know, when you pick up the phone accidentally while down-loading.

Most direct dial-up access providers want your communications parameters set to "8 bits, no parity, 1 stop bit." Consult the documentation for your communications software to learn how to change these settings. If you dial into one of the data communications networks to connect to your access provider, however, you may need to use "7 bits, even parity, 1 stop bit"—ask your access provider.

Internet Access Providers

The largest and most up-to-date lists of Internet access service providers are stored at several sites on the Internet.

The *NixPub* list of publicly accessible UNIX sites lists service providers who have at least some available Internet access. This list is available via FTP at `vfl.paramax.com` in the `pub/pubnet` directory as the file `nixpub.long`. (If the previous sentence appeared to be nonsense, don't worry, the use of FTP will be covered later in this course.)

The *Public Dialup Internet Access List* (PDIAL) is another excellent list of access providers whose services are available via normal telephone lines. This list is available via e-mail by sending a message to `info-deli-server@netcom.com`. On the subject line of the message, just type **send pdial**, and then leave the body of the message blank. (E-mail also will be covered later in this course.)

This is sort of a "catch-22", isn't it? The lists of access providers is on the Internet and you need some access provider to get on the Internet. To take care of this problem, several access providers are reviewed here and several others are listed with their phone numbers. Just select one of these providers and consider that they may be just your temporary address. After you get a little experience on the Internet, you will be in a much better position to select an access provider that meets your needs.

The World Software Tool & Die

The *World* provides dial up access to the Internet, with modem speeds up to 14,400 bps and supporting the compression and error checking protocols v.32, v.32bis, v.42, v.42bis and MNP5.

Internet tools offered include e-mail, telnet, FTP, Gopher, Lynx (World Wide Web), WAIS, Usenet news, and Internet Relay Chat (IRC).

It also provides other services such as the *Online Book Initiative*, with full text files of books, and ClariNet News Service which provides text-searchable recent news articles.

World also offers some options to become an Internet information provider by enabling customers to create and manage their own discussion lists and to offer files on Gopher and in an FTP archive. Contact them at (617)739-0202 (voice phone), or via e-mail at `staff@world.std.com`.

Delphi

Delphi offers dial-up access to the Internet, with an emphasis on new users. It provides a menu-oriented system for use with normal PC communications software, such as most BBSs do, and they also have available Delphi's custom personal computer communications software.

Delphi offers Internet tools, such as e-mail, telnet, FTP, Gopher, Hytelnet, WAIS, World Wide Web, Usenet News, and Internet Relay Chat. It also maintains its own conferences, database services, and reference materials.

The system generally is easy to use for the newcomer, but, because some things are done in ways unique to Delphi, you will need to relearn some procedures if you change to a site with the normal UNIX operating system appearance. You can contact Delphi at `walthowe@delphi.com`, or phone them at 1-800-695-4005.

Table A.1. Other Internet Access Providers for Individuals

Access Provider	Voice Phone Number
ANS CO+RE	(914)789-5300
CERFnet	(800)876-2373
Global Enterprise Services	(800)35-TIGER
PSINet	(800)82PSI82

CICNet

If you are interested in getting your entire K-12 or higher education organization, school, or institution connected to the Internet, contact the non-profit organization *CICNet* at 1-313-998-6521. They have information about educational networks through their Gopher `gopher.cic.net` and also provide networking services to a large part of the Midwest.

Telnet—Connecting to Other Computers

The first of the Internet tools to be discussed in Internet 101 is *telnet*. The telnet system enables you to command your Internet access provider's host computer to connect to another computer on the Internet, and to use that remote computer much as if you were connected to it directly. This enables you to log on to remote computers and use telnet Internet tools, files, databases, BBSs, and other services.

Therefore, with telnet, even if your access provider only has telnet and e-mail, you will be able to log onto remote computers and use Gopher, Veronica, World Wide Web, Archie, and so on. Even if your access provider does have these tools, you often will find improved or better supported versions of these tools at remote sites.

For telnet to work, both your access provider's computer and the remote computer must have the telnet software installed and configured. The administrators of the remote computer site decide which portions of their system to allow access to, and whether their system will be password-protected or open to the public.

The Basic Telnet Session

Telnet is not hard to learn or to use. Here is what you'll need to know to get started. To make a Telnet connection you need the following information:

- The address of the telnet site
- The login procedure

This information is available from many sources:

- References throughout this book
- Discussion group postings and archives
- Hytelnet
- Many guides and resource lists, as mentioned particularly in Chapters 3 and 10
- Subject categorized guides such as those available online from University of Michigan

In the typical online telnet session (following), the address is `liberty.uc.wlu.edu` and the response to the login prompt is `lawlib`.

To get started, dial up and log on to your Internet access provider's computer and go to the main system command prompt (usually a character such as $, %, or >).

(With the exception of a few sites using menus, you will be automatically at the system's command prompt after any opening announcements and/or a welcome screen.)

In this example, the command prompt used by my Internet access provider is world%. To initiate the telnet session, type **telnet**, followed by a space and then the remote computer's address, as in the following:

```
world% telnet liberty.uc.wlu.edu
```

Telnet will respond with the following line. (The numbers represent the same site address as the alphabetic address that was entered.)

```
Trying 137.113.10.35...
```

If the computers connect successfully, the following lines will appear, showing to which site you now are connected and what the escape character is.

Note: The use of the escape character is discussed later in this appendix.

```
Connected to liberty.uc.wlu.edu.
Escape character is '^]'.

HP-UX liberty A.09.01 A 9000/720 (ttyv2)

login: lawlib
```

When the login prompt appears, follow the directions that were listed with the telnet site's address. In some cases, the procedure is as simple as just pressing the Enter key one time; in other cases, you might need to respond to the login prompt with one word and respond to a password prompt with another word.

From this point on, telnet is invisible to you—any announcements, menus, BBSs, or other services you see are based on the software and data at that remote computer site. The commands and features normally available at your access provider's site are unavailable until you complete the telnet session.

The following example shows Liberty, a service provided to the Internet community by Washington and Lee University. While it is provided by the law library, it gives access to just about every category of information. In this case, the remote site presents a welcome/information screen and then the top menu:

```
Please wait...checking for disk quotas
```

```
  #       #    #####  ######  #####    #####   #   #
  #       #    #   #  #       #   #    #   #    #   #
  #       #    #####  #####   #   #    #   #     # #
  #       #    #   #  #       #####    #          #
  #       #    #   #  #       #   #    #          #
  ######  #    #####  ######  #   #    #          #

          Welcome to Washington & Lee University

               University Computing

               HP 9000/720

          LIBERTY.UC.WLU.EDU




          WASHINGTON & LEE UNIVERSITY
               LAW LIBRARY

               NETLINK


Press ? for Help, q to QuitReceiving Directory...Connecting...Retrieving Directory
...-Internet Gopher Information Client 2.0 pl10Root gopher server: honor.uc.wlu.edu
--> 1.  Search:<?>
2.  Menu:  Subject/
3.  Menu:  Type (Telnet, Gopher, WWW, WAIS)/
4.  Menu:  Geographic/
```

```
5.  Recent Additions (date coded entries)/
6.[Netlink Server - This Item for Help].
7.[Netlink Server - Please Leave Comment or Error Report]/
8.
9.--< Other Major Internet Services >--
10. High-Level Search of Gopher Menus (no field searching) <?>
11. Veronica Search of Gopher Menus/
12. WWW (World Wide Web Browser) <HTML>
13. USENET Newsreaders/
14. WAIS/
15. BITNET Mailing Lists/Listservs Archive Searches/
16. Archie FTP Site Searches/
17. Clearinghouse of Subject-Oriented Internet Resource Guides (Umich)/
18. Netfind Email Address Searches/

Press ? for Help, q to QuitPage:
```

Most telnet sites provide some way to end the telnet session, such as a menu item (Exit or Quit), or prompts that tell you which letter to type to end a session. In this particular example, at the bottom of the screen, it says q to Quit. In most cases, you will be returned to your access provider's prompt (in this case world%). If you see the prompt telnet>, however, just type **quit** and your access provider's prompt will reappear. Following is the telnet response to press **q** while at Liberty:

```
logout
Connection closed by foreign host.

world%
```

That's it! That is all you need to know for the typical telnet session!

Additional Telnet Features

The following sections discuss some additional commands and features of telnet that will be used less often, but can be very helpful.

Invoking Telnet Command Prompt

To use the telnet program's commands while connected to a remote computer, you need to signal telnet that you want the telnet command prompt. You do this by using telnet's *escape character*.

> **Note:** While the escape character is referred to here in the singular, you send it by holding down the Ctrl key and then pressing a second key.

Telnet escape characters can vary from site to site, so telnet announces its escape character each time it connects to a remote site, as was seen in the preceding session.

```
Connected to liberty.uc.wlu.edu.
Escape character is '^]'.
```

In this case, you enter the escape character by pressing and holding down the Ctrl key (that's what is meant by the up-arrow or caret (^) and then pressing the right bracket key (])). This will cause the telnet prompt to be displayed:

```
telnet>
```

This is the prompt you will need in order to use several of the telnet commands mentioned below. After each command executes, you will return to the online session with the remote computer. If you want to execute another telnet command, use the escape character again.

Viewing the Telnet Command Summary

Telnet provides a command list with brief explanations that can help you remember the commands, and enable you to become in the future a more advanced user of telnet. To display the following list (during a telnet session), use the escape character (^]) to get the `telnet>` prompt, press **?**, and then press Enter. The following command summary will be displayed.

```
telnet> ?
```

You can abbreviate commands. Commands are listed in table A.2. Where noted, typing the command followed by a space, a question mark, and a press of the Enter key will cause a list of options for that command to be displayed.

Table A.2. Telnet Commands

Command	Description
close	Close current connection
logout	Forcibly logout remote user and close the connection

Command	Description
display	Display operating parameters
mode	Try to enter line or character mode (mode ? for more)
open	Connect to a site
quit	Exit telnet
send	Transmit special characters (send ? for more)
set	Set operating parameters (set ? for more)
unset	Unset operating parameters (unset ? for more)
status	Print status information
toggle	Toggle operating parameters (toggle ? for more)
slc	Change state of special characters (slc ? for more)
z	Suspend telnet
!	Invoke a subshell
environ	Change environment variables ('environ ?' for more)
?	Show help information

Most access providers will have full telnet instruction manuals available online. These usually are best for the advanced user or the brave.

Viewing a Telnet Status Report

Occasionally, due to problems with your personal computer software, Internet data transfers, or with the software on the remote computer, you may have some question as to whether you actually are still connected with a remote computer and, if so, to which one? To determine the current situation, use the escape character to get the telnet> prompt, type **status**, and then press Enter.

Are you still connected?

While connected to the Liberty site shown in the telnet session example, the status report was as follows:

```
telnet> status
Connected to liberty.uc.wlu.edu.
Operating in single character mode
Catching signals locally
```

```
Remote character echo
Escape character is '^]'.
```

If, somehow, you weren't currently connected to a remote computer, but were still in the telnet program the status report would look like this

```
telnet> status
No connection.
Escape character is '^]'.
```

Closing a Telnet Session

Occasionally, you will encounter a remote computer that doesn't seem to have provided a way to exit its system, or you get yourself in a bind with the service or software at the remote site. Telnet provides a way out—which beats PLOKTA (Pressing Lots Of Keys To Abort).

First, use the telnet escape character, type the **close** command, and then press Enter. Telnet then will disconnect you from the remote computer and leave you at the telnet command prompt where you can use any of the telnet commands.

```
telnet> close
```

Telnet's response

```
Connection closed.
telnet>
```

Connecting to a Remote Site While at the Telnet Prompt

If you have disconnected from a site by using the close command, or you have typed telnet at your access provider's command prompt and, therefore, are back at the telnet> prompt, you can connect to another site without leaving the telnet program. Just type **open**, press the space bar, and then type the site's address.

```
telnet> open liberty.uc.wlu.edu
```

From this point on, the telnet session will be identical to one started from the access provider's prompt (world% telnet liberty.uc.wlu.edu, for example).

Quitting a Telnet Session

At any time that you are at the `telnet>` prompt or can get to it with the telnet escape character, whether connected to a remote computer or not, you can end the session immediately and return to your access provider's main command prompt. At the `telnet>` prompt, just type **quit** and press Enter. This is what it will look like.

```
telnet> quit
world%
```

Address Variations

In addition to the most commonly used address format, which is made up of groups of letters separated by dots (such as `liberty.uc.wlu.edu`) there is another system made up of just groups of numbers separated by dots (as in `137.113.10.35`). Each site has both addresses and either one can be used by telnet. Both of the following commands would connect to the Liberty site in the same way:

```
world% telnet liberty.uc.wlu.edu
```

or

```
world% telnet 137.113.10.35
```

Another variation in telnet addresses is the *port number*. If you see an address such as `liberty.uc.wlu.edu 734`, follow the address with a space and then the port number, as in the following:

```
world% telnet liberty.uc.wlu.edu 734
```

Other than that addition, nothing else about the telnet session will be different. If you see a port number listed with a telnet site's address, it must be used.

> **Note:** The Liberty site does not really use a port number, this is just an example.

Error Reports

There are several error reports that you will see quite commonly. One report, `Unknown host`, can appear if you make a mistake typing the address or your source for the address has misspelled some portion of the address. (You know, when your fingers are running ahead of your brain.) Here, the Liberty site's address was typed in with xx, where it should read uc. Following is the response:

```
world% telnet liberty.xx.wlu.edu
liberty.xx.wlu.edu: Unknown host
world%
```

Occasionally, Unknown host will be reported because the host is genuinely no longer available, or has been renamed.

Another reply you often will encounter is connection refused. Don't take it personally—this response usually is sent because the remote site temporarily is too busy to take any more logins. Just wait a while and try again. If you experience a great deal of difficulty checking onto a site, try to use the site when it won't be at peak load (usually outside of business hours in its time zone).

Occasionally connection refused may be reported due to technical or other problems with data links between the sites.

Eventually, you will have a connection to a remote site lock up and it will not allow you to leave or it won't even accept the telnet escape character. If you just hang up, you may still be accruing connect charges on your access provider's account. Ask your access provider beforehand how to deal with these lockups.

E-Mail: Communicating to the Far Reaches of the World

Electronic mail (e-mail) is the most widespread Internet service. It reaches areas of the world with no other Internet access. It also is the only form of communication available between the Internet and some of the large commercial online services and message handling networks.

In addition to its obvious use for sending and receiving messages from individual correspondents, e-mail is the basis for many other Internet activities. There are, for example, over 4,000 discussion groups that use automated systems to receive an e-mail message from one person and then automatically send that message to everyone else on the list. Also, you can use e-mail to get files from FTP sites, find resource through Gopher, and get information from databases. With all of these potential uses, it is not unusual for one who has been on the Internet for a while to send and receive 50, 100, or more messages per day.

How to Send and Receive E-Mail

There are dozens of mail programs in use at various access provider's sites. Two popular mail programs, for example, are *Pine* and *Elm*. It is typical for each site to have two or more different mail handling programs installed.

Each program has its own unique commands, screen appearance, and features. Because of these differences, you will need to read some of the online documentation on the mailer you choose (mailers run the range from cranky and cryptic, to self-explanatory and intuitive). There are, however, some concepts, common characteristics, and background that will be discussed in this appendix that can put e-mail in perspective.

Internet Addresses

To send and receive e-mail, you will need an Internet address. Its structure is different from a normal postal address but shares some characteristics.

A normal postal address for an individual might be

> Judy Brown
>
> 444 Lummistick Road
>
> East Lansing, Michigan

The postal address consists of an individual's name placed before a location name. In this case, the person *Judy Brown* is at the location 444 Lummistick Road, East Lansing, Michigan. In a similar manner, the Internet address consists of placing the individual's name (or other individual identifier) before the Internet access provider's Internet site address.

For example, if Judy had an account at the access provider World Software Tool & Die whose site address is `world.std.com`, she might choose for her address `jbrown@world.std.com` or `judybrown@world.std.com`. If you change access providers, your address will change (just as it would if you moved to a new house). If Judy selected the access provider Delphi, her address might be `judybrown@delphi.com`. If you have more than one account at one or more providers, you can have as many addresses as you want (or can afford).

There are some limits to your individual name that appears before the @ sign. Some access providers assign the name and don't provide the opportunity to choose one. Also, you may be limited in the number of letters you can use (often 11). Additionally, there can be no spaces and only a few punctuation marks and symbols can be used. Many systems, for example, permit you to use the underline or dash, but none of them permit you to choose the at sign (@) as part of you username because it is used for addressing conventions by the system.

During your first online session, you usually will have a chance to tell the access provider your name choice, or find out what the assigned one will be. Often, schools and universities assign user names, and sometimes, they are very cryptic—as in dk848f.

Sending Messages

The specific commands you will need to use and keys you will need to press will vary from program to program, but the following procedures are commonly carried out in order to send and e-mail message:

1. Start the mail program by typing its name (such as **pine**, **elm**, or **mail**).

2. When prompted, type the correspondent's e-mail address (or use the up- and down-arrow keys to move the highlighted cursor to the address line and then type it). Some mail programs contain an "address book" in which you can store e-mail addresses. These addresses then can be automatically inserted in the address field of the message by selecting the address from a list or by typing an easily-remembered short name for the correspondent on the address line and having the mail program fill it in.

3. At the cc: prompt or line, type the e-mail address of any other person you want to receive your message. (Somehow the notion of a cc: or carbon copy seems a little odd doesn't it?)

4. At the subject prompt or line, type in as descriptive as possible an explanation of the message.

> **Note:** Many people get 50 or messages per day, so even someone who knows you and is especially interested in your message may overlook a short cryptic subject.

Subject lines up to half a line long are common, but if they are longer, they may be truncated down to fit the needs of the mail program.

5. Move to the text field. (You sometimes can do by pressing the down-arrow key or Tab key, or just by pressing Enter after you complete the last line of the header.)

6. Type your message. If at all possible, select a mailer with *full screen editing* (that is, a mailer that enables you to move the cursor anywhere onscreen to make additions, deletions, and corrections). There are still some mail programs that require you to type the message and then go into an editing mode in which you can perform user-unfriendly procedures, such as call for lines you want to edit by their line number.

7. Insert a file. Some mail programs enable you to insert a text file you have uploaded or written online with the editor. This might be the entire message that you've written before you started the mail program, or some quoted materials or other paragraphs that you don't want to have to enter in messages repeatedly.

8. Before you finish, you may want to insert a *sig* (signature) file at the bottom of your message. Some mail programs enable you to insert a previously written short file at the end of your messages. These sig files usually are four to five lines long and contain any information about yourself that you want others to know, such as your phone number, fax number, institutional affiliation, professional position, and so on. Many sigs also include humorous or philosophical sayings, and small graphics drawings made with normal keyboard characters. A sig over five lines long is likely to procure complaints (flames) from others—especially those who pay based on the size and number of the e-mail messages they receive, or those who have slow links or modems.

9. When you are satisfied that the message is complete and correct, you need to signal the mail program to send the message. Depending on the particular program, you do this by holding down the Ctrl key and pressing a letter key, such as Z or X.

10. When you've completed the preceding step, most programs give a confirmation that the message has been sent. You can expect the message to arrive at your correspondent's access provider's site anywhere from a few seconds to a few minutes.

Note: Occasionally, if the Internet is particularly busy, or portions of it are not working, delivery may take an number of hours. If, for some reason, the message cannot be delivered, it will be "bounced" back to you. The two most common reasons for bounced message are incorrect addresses and temporary technical problems at the correspondent's site.

Check the address on the returned copy and be sure that you originally received the correct address. If everything seems in order, send it again. If you still are experiencing problems, talk with your access provider's system postmaster or send a message explaining your problem to postmaster@(fill in the name of your correspondents site after the @ sign—without their name or @ sign).

Receiving Messages

Most access providers have installed a system that will notify you if you have received new e-mail since your last log on. If your system doesn't provide this, you will need to start a mail program to see if new mail has been received.

Typically, mail programs display a list of your new mail messages that shows the subject, sender, and date of the message. For each message you will have several options:

- Read the message (onscreen)
- Turn the message into a file that you then can download from your home directory on the access provider's computer.
- Reply to the message

  This is a dependable way to send message back to its originator. It takes care of addressing the message and usually inserts Re: in front of the subject line. Be careful when using this feature with messages that come from a discussion group. Some mailers will mail it back to the discussion group at large, and some will mail it back just to the original individual who posted the message (it's that "read-the-manual" thing again).

- Forward a message

  If you receive a message that you want someone else to see, you can forward the entire message on to them.

Interpreting Message Headers

Message headers (the addressing a routing information above the body of the message) are often 20 to 30 lines long. In day-to-day activities, you won't need to understand all of the header, but there is some very useful information in it, so here's an example (actually one that's much easier to read than average) of the information you can get from the header.

```
From ellswort@tenet.edu Sun Jul 10 08:08:08 1994
Date: Fri, 8 Jul 1994 19:27:10 -0500 (CDT)
From: "J. Ellsworth" <ellswort@tenet.edu>
To: matt <oakridge@world.std.com>
Subject: WWW> FAQ Index via WWW search (fwd)


---------- Forwarded message ----------
Date: Fri, 8 Jul 1994 13:46:50 -0500 (CDT)
From: Gleason Sackman <sackman@plains.nodak.edu>
To: net-happenings <net-happenings@is.internic.net>
Subject: WWW> FAQ Index via WWW search (fwd)
```

```
---------- Forwarded message ----------
From: lcm@intac.com (Lawrence C. Mc Abee)
Newsgroups: comp.infosystems.www.providers
Subject: ANNOUNCEMENT: FAQ/manual pages WWW search available.
Date: 8 Jul 1994 17:29:40 GMT

For those interested, I have put up a FAQ index at:

    http://www.intac.com/FAQ.HTML.

and a SUNOS manual page (pages in HTML format) index at:

    http://www.intac.com/MainHelp.HTML

There are about 15Megs of FAQs, a good selection.

    Comments welcome at lcm@inatc.com.


        Mac.

--
Lawrence C. Mc Abee.(Silek@IRC)     INTAC Access Corp.
lcm@intac.com                       Operations Assistant.
         *** PGP 2.6 Key Available on request ***
```

Starting from the bottom of the header note, the first sender of this message is listed in the bottom-most `From:` line (in this case `lcm@intac.com`). There can sometimes be three to five "From:" fields, especially in forwarded mail as this is.

The most recent recipient usually is at the top, in this case, `<ellswort@tenet.edu>`. The date fields, and subject fields can be equally as numerous. Usually, the most recent are at the top and proceed chronologically to the oldest at the bottom. From looking at the bottom date, you can see it originated `8 Jul 1994 17:29:40 GMT` and was forwarded on to our business address (`<oakridge@world.std.com>`) on `Fri, 8 Jul 1994 19:27:10 -0500 (CDT)`.

Other headers vary substantially from this one in appearance and require unknown forces to read. One common element to be aware of, however, is that when responding to the message, if there is a `Reply to:` line, use the address in that line, not the address in the `From:` line.

Sending and Receiving Binary Files

To this point, all the e-mail messages that have been discussed have been *ASCII* (7-bit) messages, that is, messages made of letters, numbers, some punctuation marks, and a few control codes, such as line-feed and carriage return. Many files, however, are *binary* (8-bit) files, such as graphics files, software, data files from spreadsheets, an so on, that are not normally transferable through the Internet's mail system.

You can use the program *UUENCODE* to first convert a binary file to ASCII and then when the ASCII file is received by your correspondent as an e-mail message, you can use UUDECODE to convert in back into a binary file.

Recently, however, many access provider's have been converting to MIME-compliant mail programs. If both the sender and receiver have MIME-compliant mail programs, binary files can be "attached" to a message when it is sent and detached into a normal binary file at the receiving end. Pine, used often on UNIX systems, is MIME compliant, and to attach a file, use the Attchmnt field. When received, the recipient can **V**iew and **S**ave the file.

Gopher: A Search and Retrieval System

The *Gopher* system presents a uniform menu-based interface for many types of Internet tools, databases, and services. All Gopher sessions start by displaying the "top menu" for that particular Gopher client. The top menu features some items of local interest but almost always has a menu item that will take you to "all the Gophers in the world," and therefore, all of the resources available to those Gophers as well.

Menus often lead to other menus, and those menus lead still to others. Other menu items include text files that can be read, and binary files that can be downloaded, such as pictures, audio files, software, format specific files from word processors, databases, spreadsheets and CAD programs, formatted text, such as PostScript files, automatic connections to telnet sites, keyword database searches, and more.

Gopher is well thought-out and developed as a system, and because of its popularity, it has been linked to a substantial portion of the Internet's tools and resources sites.

It is an excellent first place to look when you start to explore the Internet due to the ease with which one can learn to use it. It also is an excellent place to look when you start to explore a new subject because the interactive nature of the searching fast branching to broader subject categories or fast focusing in from an originally broad category. And, because there is much very up to date and sophisticated data available, it will continue to help even in advanced research.

The Gopher system is based on a client and server system: the Gopher servers are installed on just a few computer systems and they provide information they collect and process to Gopher client software which is installed on many computers throughout the Internet.

A Typical Gopher Session

The following example is a light-weight Gopher session that would take about two minutes. Don't think you've seen it all though, the real power of Gopher is in the "additional features" discussed in the next section.

To start Gopher, type **gopher** and then press Enter.

```
world% gopher
```

Gopher will respond with your access provider's top Gopher menu.

```
      Internet Gopher Information Client v1.13Root gopher server: gopher.std.com
 1.   Information About The World Public Access UNIX/
 2.   The World's ClariNews AP OnLine & Reuters Newswire Index/
 3.   OBI The Online Book Initiative/
 4.   Internet and USENET Phone Books/
 5.   Shops on The World/
 6.   Commercial Services via the Internet/
 7.   Book Sellers/
 8.   Bulletin Boards via the Internet/
 9.   Consultants/
10.   FTP/
11.   Government Information/
12.   Internet Information and Resources/
13.   Libraries/
14.   Membership and Professional Associations/
15.   Metropolitan and Community News/
16.   News and Weather/
17.   Non-Profit Organizations /
18.   Other Gopher and Information Servers/
19.   Periodicals, Magazines, and Journals/
20.   Selected Archives, Mailing Lists, USENET Newsgroups, etc/
21.   University of Minnesota Gopher Server/
Press ? for Help, q to Quit, u to go up a mePage: 1/1
```

On this menu, item #3 looks interesting (OBI The Online Book Initiative). The up- and down-arrow key on your keyboard will move the pointer which is left of the numbers up and down the menu. Because the pointer was on item number 1, two presses of the down arrow positions the pointer to access the Online Book Initiative. To get to this next menu press the right arrow (the forward slash (/) at the end of the line indicates that this item is a menu). At the bottom of the screen this message will be displayed for a second or two.

```
Receiving Directory...         Connecting...
Retrieving Directory../
```

Then the new menu is displayed.

```
        Internet Gopher Information Client v1.13
OBI The Online Book Initiative
1.   About The Online Book Initiative.
2.   The OBI FAQ.
3.   About The OBI Mailing Lists.
4.   The Online Books/

Press ? for Help, q to Quit, u to go up a mePage: 1/1
```

Item number 1 looks like a good place to start. It is a file—the period at the end of the menu line indicates this. By pressing the right arrow (or pressing Enter) the file is displayed.

```
Receiving Information..¦
The Online Book Initiative Mailing List

The Online Book Initiative is being formed to make available freely
redistributable collections of information. There exists huge
collections of books, conference proceedings, reference material,
catalogues, etc. which can be freely shared. Some of it is in
machine-readable form, much of it isn't.

The purpose of the Online Book Initiative is to create a publicly
accessible repository for this information, a net-worker's library.

(A more complete description and original announcement
 is available under the sub-topic 'help obi' purpose.)

To bring people together in this effort two mailing lists have been
formed:

obi@world.std.comGeneral discussion
obi-announce@world.std.comAnnouncements-only

To be added to either mailing list send to:

obi-request@world.std.com

and specify which list you would like to be on (announce or
discussion.) If you don't specify I will put you on the discussion
list (all announcements will appear on the discussion list, you don't
need to be on both.)

Press <RETURN> to continue, <m> to mail, <s> to save, or <p> to print:
```

At the end of the file, Gopher gives the user several options for what to do with this file. If you press the m key (but don't press the Enter key!), the mail dialog box appears with a prompt requesting the e-mail address of the individual to which you want to send this file. You can mail it to yourself or to someone else. Just type the address and press Enter.

```
+-----------------------------------------------------------+
¦ ¦
¦ ¦
¦ Mail current document to: oakridge@world.std.com        ¦
¦ ¦
¦ ¦
¦ [Cancel ^G] [Accept - Enter]        ¦
¦ ¦
¦ ¦
+-----------------------------------------------------------+
```

During the mailing process, Mailing File.. will appear at the bottom of the screen. Depending on the file size and the amount of Internet activity, this can take from less than a second to several minutes.

After the mailing is complete you are returned to the menu from which you most recently came.

```
     Internet Gopher Information Client v1.13OBI The Online Book Initiative
1.   About The Online Book Initiative.
2.   The OBI FAQ.
 --> 3.   About The OBI Mailing Lists.
4.   The Online Books/

Press ? for Help, q to Quit, u to go up a mePage: 1/1
```

To end the Gopher session, just press **q**, and then respond to the Really quit (y/ n) ? prompt by pressing **y**. Gopher then will return you to your access provider's main prompt.

Additional Gopher Features

The preceding example session above shows the basic structure of an online Gopher session, but there is more on the Internet than one-page text files, so after you've tried a practice session similar to the preceding one, start experimenting with the additional Gopher features discussed in the following sections.

Downloading Binary Files

Binary files can't be used directly by Gopher, nor mailed, saved, or printed by the methods that are available for text files. Gopher does, however, have a system for directly downloading a file to your personal computer.

The following menu displays some menu items that are text files about Mars and some picture files of Mars. To download item number 8, a picture of the Viking Lander in the GIF image format, use the down arrow to move the pointer down to number 8.

```
Internet Gopher Information Client v2.0.15Images of Mars

1.   About_Images_of_Mars.txt
2.   EPB_File_ReadMe.txt
3.   GIF_SnapShots_ReadMe.txt
4.   HyperCard_Player.sea.hqx <HQX>
5.   Images_of_Mars_ReadMe.txt
6.   Images_of_Mars_v1.1.4.sea.hqx <HQX>
7.   Images_of_Mars_v1.1.5.sea.hqx <HQX>
8.   Viking_Lander.GIF <Picture>
9.   _Mars_GIF_Snapshots.sea.hqx <HQX>

Press ? for Help, q to Quit, u to go up a menu     Page: 1/1
```

Now type an uppercase **D** and a modem protocol dialog box will appear on the same screen as the menu. Select the modem protocol you have set up your software to accept. (Either type the number left of the protocol and press Enter or move the pointer down and press Enter.)

```
+----------Viking_Lander.GIF----------+
|                                     |
|  --1. Zmodem                        |
|    2. Ymodem                        |
|    3. Xmodem-1K                     |
|    4. Xmodem-CRC                    |
|    5. Kermit                        |
|    6. Text                          |
|                                     |
|  Choose a download method (1-6):    |
|  [Help: ?]  [Cancel: ^G]            |
+-------------------------------------+
```

At the bottom of the screen the `Receiving file...` status report appears. It may remain there half a second, or even 5 minutes if the Internet is busy. The screen then will clear and `Start your download now...` prompt will appear.

Check your communication software's manual or help files before you go online to find out what procedures to use to initiate a download on your personal computer. If you are too slow, the Gopher sending program may "time out" before you get your receive mode running. It isn't unusual, however, to see one or lines of miscellaneous characters writing to the screen before the download protocol is up and running. Don't worry about the missed lines, they aren't data, they are just the signals that the protocol uses to establish a connection. Look at the following example:

```
rz
**_B00000000000000
è
```

When the download is finished, Gopher gives a report similar to this:

```
Download Complete. 141312 total bytes, 1358 bytes/sec
Press <RETURN> to continue
```

The picture file now is stored in your personal computer's download directory, and after you press Enter, the previous Gopher menu is reappears.

Other Ways to Download Text Files

You also can download text files directly to your computer by positioning the pointer at the appropriate menu item and pressing **D** (uppercase). By taking a quick look at the first or second screen of the file, you can decide whether you want the file, and then download it for more leisurely reading at a later time.

Another approach to getting a text file is to use the save option which is available when you finish reading a text file:

```
Press <RETURN> to continue, <m> to mail, <s> to save, or <p> to print:_
```

When you press **s**, a dialog box will appear with the proposed name for the file which will be transferred to your home directory on your Internet access provider's computer. If the name what you want, just press the Enter key to start the transfer. If you want to rename the file, press and hold down the Ctrl key and press **u** to clear the line. Now type in the filename you want and then press Enter (alternatively, you can use the Backspace or Delete keys to delete a character at a time the proposed name).

```
+----------------------------------------------------------+
|7                                                         |
| Save in file:    About-the-College-of-Education          |
|                                                          |
| [Cancel ^G] [Accept - Enter]                             |
||                                                         |
+----------------------------------------------------------+
```

During the transfer process (rarely over a few seconds) the `Saving File...` prompt appears.

Bookmarks

In a normal Gopher session, you may wander through dozens of menus, and then find a resource that is exactly what you want! But you may think, "Hmmm, how did I get here and where am I now?". Gopher has a solution for this problem called *Bookmarks*.

When you find yourself in a valuable directory, you can move the pointer to menu items and press the *a* key. These items now are saved in your bookmark file and you will develop a custom, personal Gopher menu that you can call up not only in the current Gopher session, but in future ones as well. If you are already in the menu you want to save, and then use an uppercase **A** to save the Bookmark.

Gopher responds with a proposed name for this bookmark item. If you agree with the name, just press Enter. If you want a new name for this item, hold down the Ctrl key and press **u**. Now you can type in your own description of this item.

```
+---------------------Education (Includes K-12)------------+
¦ ¦
¦ Name for this bookmark:                                  ¦
¦ ¦
¦ Education (Includes K-12)                                ¦
¦ ¦
¦ [Help: ^-]  [Cancel: ^G]¦
+------------------------------------------- -------------+
```

After the bookmark is saved, you may want to confirm it by viewing your current custom Bookmark menu. To view the menu, press **v** and the Bookmark menu will appear.

```
                   Bookmarks
 1.  Gopher Jewels (Gophers by Category)/
 2.  State of Texas Information/
 3.  Veronica/
 4.  Jughead/
 5.  WAIS/
 6.  Hytelnet Log-Ons
 7.  Archie/
 8.  UseNet News/
 9.  UseNet News -- Search/
10.  Chronicle of Higher Education/
11.  Art and Images at Texas Tech/
12.  Simtel Mirror at Oakland/
13.  Arizona State University Gopher -- Education/
14.  All the Gopher Servers in World/
15.  Education (Includes K-12)/
```

If you no longer need one of these menu items move the pointer to it and press **d**.

Warning: There is no confirmation prompt—press **d** while in the Bookmark menu and that menu item is gone.)

To get back to the menu you were viewing before you looked at the Bookmark menu, use the left arrow key or press **u**.

Bookmarks save a great deal of time and ensure that you can return to valuable Internet resources again.

Gopher Commands Summary

While in a Gopher session you can get a help file pressing **?** (question mark). This file is an excellent reminder of Gopher's features and because Gopher clients vary from site to site, this file is especially good for keeping up with each one's idiosyncrasies.

```
                    Quick Gopher Help
                    .................
Moving around Gopherspace
.......................
Use the arrow keys or vi/emacs equivalent to move around.
Right, Return .......:  "Enter"/Display current item.
Left, u ............:  "Exit" current item/Go up a level.
Down ...............:  Move to next line.
Up .................:  Move to previous line.
>, +, Pgdwn, Space ..:  View next page.
<, -, Pgup, b .......:  View previous page.
0-9 ................:  Go to a specific line.
m ..................:  Go back to the main menu.
Bookmarks
.........
a : Add current item to the bookmark list.
A : Add current directory/search to bookmark list.
v : View bookmark list.
d : Delete a bookmark/directory entry.
Other commands
..............
q : Quit with prompt.
Q : Quit unconditionally.
s : Save current item to a file.
S : Save current menu listing to a file.
D : Download a file.
r : goto root menu of current item.
R : goto root menu of current menu.
= : Display technical information about current item.
^ : Display technical information about current directory.
o : Open a new gopher server.
O : Change options.
/ : Search for an item in the menu.
n : Find next search item.
g : "Gripe" via email to administrator of current item.
!, $ : Shell Escape (Unix) or Spawn subprocess (VMS).
Gopher objects:
```

```
Item tag    Type     Description
------------------------------------------------
(none)        0      file To Exit: Ctrl-Z ¦ Find a Keyword: Find key ¦ To
Scroll: Prev/Next Screen
/             1      directory
<)            s      sound file
<Picture>     I,g    image file
<Movie>       ;      movie file
<HQX>         4      BinHexed Macintosh file
<Bin>         9      binary file
<PC Bin>      5      DOS binary file
<CSO>         2      CSO (ph/qi) phone-book server
<TEL>         8      telnet connection
<3270>        T      telnet connection (IBM 3270 emulation)
<MIME>        M      Multi-purpose Internet Mail Extensions file
<HTML>        h      HyperText Markup Language file
<?>           7      index-search item
<??>        (none)   ASK form
The Gopher development team hopes that you find this software useful.
If you find what you think is a bug, please report it to us by sending
e-mail to "gopher@boombox.micro.umn.edu."
```

Veronica—A Search Tool for Gopher

With thousands of Gopher menus available on the Internet, it would be a massive task to perform a site-by-site, menu-by-menu search for all the information available on any particular topic. The Internet search tool called *Veronica* dramatically simplifies this task by maintaining a database of all Gopher menu items at all Gopher servers in its database that it "knows" about. This database itself is accessed through a Gopher menu item, and the results of the database search are presented as a custom Gopher menu that you can use just as any other Gopher menu.

A Typical Veronica Session

Most top Gopher menu's will have a menu item, such as Other Gopher and Information Servers/; select this item and you usually will see a Gopher menu item with the word veronica in it. Select that item to display a menu such as the following:

> **Note:** If you can't find Veronica on any of the Gophers that you regularly use, point your Gopher to gopher.micro.umn.edu.

```
     Internet Gopher Information Client v1.131.  How to Compose Veronica Queries -
June 23, 1994.
2.   FAQ:Frequently-Asked Questions about veronica  (1994-07-29).
3.   About veronica:  Documents, Software./
4.   .5.  Experimental veronica query interface: chooses server for you!/
--> 6.   Search GopherSpace by Title word(s) (via NYSERNet) <?>
7.   Search GopherSpace by Title word(s) (via University of Pisa) <?>
8.   Search GopherSpace by Title word(s) (via U. of Manitoba) <?>
9.   Search GopherSpace by Title word(s) (via SUNET) <?>
10.  Search GopherSpace by Title word(s) (via University of Koeln) <?>
11.  Search GopherSpace by Title word(s) (via UNINETT/U. of Bergen) <?>
12.  Find ONLY DIRECTORIES by Title word(s) (via NYSERNet) <?>
13.  Find ONLY DIRECTORIES by Title word(s) (via University of Pisa) <?>
14.  Find ONLY DIRECTORIES by Title word(s) (via U. of Manitoba) <?>
15.  Find ONLY DIRECTORIES by Title word(s) (via SUNET) <?>
16.  Find ONLY DIRECTORIES by Title word(s) (via University of Koeln.. <?>
17.  Find ONLY DIRECTORIES by Title word(s) (via UNINETT... of Bergen) <?>
Press ? for Help, q to Quit, u to go up a  Page: 1/1
```

Select from this menu one of the `Search GopherSpace by Title word(s)` menu items. Choosing the site nearest to you generally is best, but with experimentation you can determine which sites respond more quickly at what times of the day. Also, if a site responds with `Too many connections` or seems to not respond at all or malfunction, just switch to another one of the Veronica server sites listed and repeat the search.

Now for the actual search. When you select one of the preceding menu items, the following screen will appear. The cursor will be blinking, ready for you to type in a word for which to search Gopher menu titles. In this case, Gopher menu items containing the word `education` will be searched for:

```
+--------Search GopherSpace by Title word(s) (via NYSERNet)--------+
¦                                          ¦
¦  Words to search for education           ¦
¦                                          ¦
¦  [Cancel ^G] [Accept - Enter]            ¦
¦                                          ¦
+----------------------------------------------------------+
```

The search will start, and usually will be finished in less than a minute. You will see the following, with a spinning symbol in the right corner of your screen:

```
Searching Text...    Connecting... Searching..\
```

The result of the search is a custom Gopher menu made up of menu items from Gophers around the world.

```
     Internet Gopher Information Client v1.13 Search GopherSpace by Title word(s)
(via NYSERNet): education
 --> 1.  "Adult Education" redefined (Thu, 01 Nov 90..ley.EDU (Keith Bostic)).
2.  "Adult Education" redefined (Thu, 01 Nov 90..ley.EDU (Keith Bostic)).
3.  "Adult Education" redefined (Thu, 01 Nov 90..ley.EDU (Keith Bostic)).
4.  "Adult Education" redefined (Thu, 01 Nov 90..ley.EDU (Keith Bostic)).
5.  Continuing Education.
6.  About the FIS Continuing Education Program.
7.  What's new in public education?.
8.  Continuing Education.
9.  About the FIS Continuing Education Program.
10. What's new in public education?.
11. The FIS Continuing Education Program/
12. The FIS Continuing Education Program/
13. Improving Undergraduate Education.
14. education.log.
15. education.1st.
16. education.sas.
17. Education tables (K)/
18. Assessment of Multimedia in Education - bibliography.
19. Assessment of Multimedia in Education - bibliography.
20. the Internet - a Higher Education Communications Revolution.
21. the Internet - a Higher Education Communications Revolution.
22. Science Education.
23.    Native Education Policy Unit.
24.    SOC225Y   Sociology of Education (formerly SOC31152L, 2...
25Field Education Complainants vs. Emmanuel College Respondents.
26. Preparatory Education.
27. HEALTH EDUCATION.
28. Victoria University and Theological Education.
29. The Toronto Institute for Pastoral Education.
30. Ontario Institute for Studies in Education (OISE).
3ECO338HEconomics of Education  26L.
32. Faculty of Education Library.
33. Continuing Education for Ministers.
34. Undergraduate Education.
35. Requirements for the Master of Religious Education Degree.
36. Clinical Pastoral Education.
37Emmanuel College Complainants vs. Field Education Site Respon...
38. Graduate Education.
39.Master of Religious Education.
40. Master of Religious Education Curriculum Requirements.
41.    St. Andrew's Education Fund.
42. R.W.B Jackson Library (Ontario Institute for Studies in Education...
43.    Native Education Policy Unit.
Press ? for Help, q to Quit, u to go up a  Page: 1/5
```

Most Veronica searches are set to deliver 200 menu items. At the end of the list of 200 items Veronica displays an item indicating how many more menu items containing your searched for word are available:

```
201. ** There are 16319 more items matching the query "education" avail...
```

If you want more or fewer items displayed, type **-m(*number*)** before the word(s) for which you want to search. If you want all 16,519 education menu items, for example, enter the following search (and get some coffee for the wait):

```
+----Find ONLY DIRECTORIES by Title word(s) (via NYSERNet)------+
:                                                              :
: Words to search for -m16519 education                        :
:                                                              :
: [Cancel ^G] [Accept - Enter]                                 :
:                                                              :
+-------------------------------------------------------------+
```

After you complete exploring the results of a Veronica search, you can do another search just by pressing the back arrow (or any of the other normal Gopher commands for going back up one level in the menus).

Complex Searches

Complex searches are available to more accurately define (and reduce the size of) the search results menu items list. To do this, you can use the logic terms AND, OR, NOT, and parentheses ( ) with multiple words. The following example is a search for education and science:

```
+------Search GopherSpace by Title word(s) (via NYSERNet)-----------+
:                                                         :
: Words to search for education and science               :
:                                                         :
: [Cancel ^G] [Accept - Enter]                            :
:                                                         :
+--------------------------------------------------------+
```

This search narrowed the list down from 16,519 to 389 menu items that contain both science and education in their titles.

Following are examples of other searches you can make:

```
(education and science) not physics
education not science
(education and k-12) or (education and k12) or (education and primary)
```

Most Veronica servers have menu items with detailed documents explaining complex searches, and FAQ files answering many general questions about how to use Veronica.

FTP: Transferring Files

The *File Transfer Protocol* (FTP) system traditionally has been the primary method used to get copies of files stored on other computers on the Internet, and to send files from your access provider's computer to a remote computer. It gives you access to literally millions of files which are stored on computers worldwide.

A substantial portion of these FTP transfers are done with *anonymous FTP*. An Internet site that offers some of its files free, and open to the general public without secret password protection, is an anonymous FTP site.

The Basic FTP Session

To get a copy of a specific file via FTP, you will need three pieces of information.

- The address of the FTP site
- The directory in which the file is stored
- The exact name of the file

Many references are made throughout this book about files stored at FTP sites. Other sources of FTP file information include discussion group postings and archives (including FAQ files) and many of the general and subject oriented Internet resource guides available via the Internet.

To start an FTP session, dial up and logon to your Internet access provider's computer.

If you are unsure whether your access provider offers FTP, just type **ftp** at the computer system's main prompt. If the response is a new prompt that looks like this: ftp>, then you probably have access to FTP sites. Type **quit** to return to your access provider's main prompt.

In this example, a copy of a file called archpres:stott will be retrieved from the /inetdirsstacks directory of the una.hh.lib.umich.edu site. (This is the University of Michigan's archive of subject-oriented Internet resource guides.)

In order to download this file, a connection needs to be established between your access provider's computer and the remote site. To do this, at the access provider's main prompt type **ftp**, press the spacebar, and then enter address of the site, as in the following example.

```
world% ftp una.hh.lib.umich.edu
```

If FTP succeeds in connecting with the remote site, it will give a report on the connection an then prompt for Name:. At this name prompt, type **anonymous** and press Enter.

```
Connected to una.hh.lib.umich.edu.
220 una.hh.lib.umich.edu FTP server (ULTRIX Version 4.1 Sun May 16 10:23:46 EDT
1993) ready.
Name (una.hh.lib.umich.edu:oakridge): anonymous
```

Now you will receive a `Password:` prompt. In response to this prompt, type your full e-mail address (such as `jbrown@delphi.com` or `oakridge@world.std.com`). Because the FTP software considers this a password, it will not echo it back to your computer. In other words, the line will not display the letters you are typing. After you enter your address, press Enter.

```
331 Guest login ok, send ident as password.
Password:
```

When the `ftp>` prompt appears, type **cd**, press the spacebar, enter the directory name(s), and then press Enter. (In this example the desired file is in a subdirectory only one level away from the initial directory.) If the directory you have listed contains multiple levels of subdirectories, you can jump to the directory you want in one step by typing the subdirectories, separated by forward slashes (/), such as **/pub/software/dos/utilities**.

```
230 Guest login ok, access restrictions apply.
ftp> cd inetdirsstacks
```

After the `command successful` report, at the `ftp>` prompt type **get**, press the spacebar, and then enter the filename.

> **Note:** With FTP, filenames almost are always case sensitive. Therefore, `archpres:stott`, `ArchPres:Stott`, and `archpress:Stott` would all be considered different file names.

```
250 CWD command successful.
ftp> get archpres:stott
```

FTP now reports on which file is being sent, its size, and so on. This transfer may take less than a second, or several minutes, depending on the size of the file and how busy the Internet is. When the file transfer is finished, FTP will report that and provide an `ftp>` prompt again. A copy of the file you just requested now is stored in your home directory of your access provider's computer.

```
200 PORT command successful.
150 Opening data connection for archpres:stott (192.74.137.5,3049) (41985 bytes).
226 Transfer complete.
42866 bytes received in 0.91 seconds (46 Kbytes/s)
ftp>
```

To disconnect from the remote computer and return to your access provider's main prompt, type **quit** and press Enter.

```
ftp> quit
221 Goodbye.
world%
```

You can do a directory listing (1s with UNIX systems) to confirm that the file you requested is there. You now can download the file to your personal computer, or if it is a text file, you can read it using one of your access providers editors or viewers.

Additional FTP Features

While the preceding FTP session example is typical of most sessions, FTP offers several other features and variations on commands that can make FTP easier and more effective.

Renaming Files

Often, files at FTP sites will have filenames too long for use with some computer systems. DOS, for example, cleverly allows no more than eight characters in the main part of the name and no more than three in the extension (to the right of the dot).

As you can see in the example session, the file requested has 14 characters and no dot. Most software receiving this type of file during a download would just take the first 8 characters as the filename. You can, however, change the file name at the time you get it—both to get the filename into the proper format and to give it a name that has more meaning to you. To do this, type the **get** command, press the spacebar, and enter the filename as usual, then add an additional space and the name you want for the file. The file will be renamed and send to you in one step.

```
ftp> get archpres:stott archlist.txt
200 PORT command successful.
```

```
150 Opening data connection for archpres:stott (192.74.137.5,2542) (41985 bytes).
226 Transfer complete.
42866 bytes received in 0.92 seconds (45 Kbytes/s)
ftp>
```

At some FTP sites, you will be prompted for a name each time you request a file. On those sites, if you are satisfied with the file's current name, don't enter in a new name, just press Enter and the file will retain its original name.

Transferring Binary Files

The file that was transferred in the preceding example session was a plain ASCII text file. This type of file can be transferred by FTP in its ASCII mode or its binary mode. Binary files, however, must be transferred with FTP in binary mode. Many FTP sites have binary mode as their default mode; however, just to be sure, before you transfer any file that might be binary, you can set FTP to binary mode. To do this, type **binary** at any ftp> prompt and press Enter.

```
ftp> binary
200 Type set to I.
ftp>
```

FTP uses the term *image* for this binary mode, so the report back from FTP is Type set to I.

A filename's extension (the letters or numbers to the right of the period) often offers clues to whether a file is binary or ASCII. ASCII files often have either no extension or extensions such as .doc, .txt, .uu, .asc, .bsc, or .hqx.

Binary files often have extensions, such as .arc, .arj, .bin, .com, .exe, .gif, .jpg, .pcx, .sit, .tar, .z, .zip, or any of the filename extensions used by spreadsheet programs, word processing programs, CAD, and other programs that produce formatted files.

Viewing the Directory

While you are connected to an FTP site you can look at the list of files and subdirectories in the directory you are currently at. At any ftp> prompt, type **dir** and press Enter. (In some cases you will have to type ls to list the directory.)

```
ftp> dir
200 PORT command successful.
150 Opening data connection for /bin/ls (192.74.137.5,2173) (0 bytes).
```

```
total 198
-rwxr-xr-x  1 0      10         780 Jul 11 07:26 .cache
-rw-r--r--  1 214    10           1 Dec 21  1993 .links
drwxrwxr-x  7 200    10         512 Jun 15  1993 .oldstuff
drwxrwxr-x  2 23464  10         512 Jun 30 14:45 .tempgopher
drwxrwxr-x  4 200    10         512 Jul  8  1993 aboutgopher
drwxrwxr-x  6 200    10         512 Jun 22 15:34 aboutulib
drwxr-xr-x  3 517    10        1024 May  3 11:55 bin
drwxrwxr-x  9 200    10         512 Jun 24 15:44 census
drwxrwxr-x  2 200    10         512 Oct 22  1993 contents
-rw-r--r--  1 0      10      159744 Jul  2 07:16 core
drwxr-xr-x  2 23464  10         512 Jun 30 09:36 diss
drwxrwxr-x 29 517    10        1024 Jun 15 14:32 ebb
dr-xrwxr-x  2 200    10         512 Sep  9  1992 etc
drwxr-xr-x 10 520    10         512 Jun 30 09:24 genref
drwxrwxr-x  5 200    10         512 Jun 30 09:23 gophers
drwxrwxr-x 15 214    10         512 Jun 30 11:57 gsp
drwxrwxr-x 12 200    10         512 Jun 30 09:24 humanities
drwxrwxr-x 11 214    10        2048 Jun 30 09:22 inetdirs
drwxrwxr-x  4 214    10        4096 Jun 30 09:28 inetdirsstacks
drwxrwxr-x  4 200    10         512 Oct  8  1993 news
drwxrwxr-x  6 200    10         512 Jan 21 15:04 newstuff
drwxrwxr-x  8 214    10         512 Jun 30 11:59 orms
drwxrwxr-x  5 200    10         512 Mar  9 21:48 science
drwxrwxr-x 11 200    10         512 Jun 30 09:23 socsci
drwxrwxr-x  4 214    10         512 Jun 30 09:22 toc
drwxr-xr-x  3 0      10         512 Jun 30 09:39 usr
drwxrwxr-x  2 200    10         512 Jun 30  1993 yalelibs
226 Transfer complete.
ftp>
```

Some of the information worth noting are the following directory lists:

- If the character at the beginning of a line is a - (dash), that line represents a file that you probably will be able to download. If the character at the beginning of the line is a d, that line represents another subdirectory that probably will have another list of files and subdirectories.
- The word(s) at the end of the line are the file and directory names.
- The three columns to the left of the names represent the creation dates (or date and time) of each file or subdirectory.
- The column to the left of the dates list the size of each file in bytes.

Reading an FTP File Online

Most subdirectories at FTP sites have files with names such as README or INDEX. These files often provide descriptions of each file in that subdirectory, and/or provide some background and perspective on what the files are and why they are there. FTP provides a way for reading those files, or any other ASCII file while still in an FTP session. This is much more efficient than leaving FTP, reading the file on your access provider's computer, and then reconnecting and going back to the same directory. Remember though, you cannot view a binary file.

To read a file, type the **get** command, press the spacebar, and then type the filename in same manner as if you were going to perform a normal file transfer. Now add one space and type ¦**more**, and then press Enter (the character before the word more is a broken vertical line call a *pipe*).

FTP fills your screen and then stops scrolling. After you read the display, press the spacebar to display another screen of information from the file. You know you are not at the end of the document is --more-- appears at the bottom of the screen. At many sites, pressing **b** (not followed with Enter) will move you back up in the document.

```
ftp> get .README-FOR-FTP ¦more
200 PORT command successful.
150 Opening data connection for .README-FOR-FTP (192.74.137.5,2364) (10739 bytes).

.README-FOR-FTP lists guides and filenames found in the
Clearinghouse for Subject-Oriented Internet Resource
Guides. Each of these files is located in the directory
inetdirsstacks on una.hh.lib.umich.edu


Academic Computing Training & User Support; M. Kovacs; v8; 03/94
    filename: acadcomp:kovacsm

Adult/Distance Education; J. Ellsworth; 4/27/94
    filename: disted:ellsworth

Aerospace Engineering; C. Poterala, D. Dalquist; v2; 3/15/94  (UMich)
    filename: aerospace:potsiedalq

Agriculture, Veterinary Science & Zoology; L. Haas; v8; 03/94
    filename: agvetzoo:haas

Agriculture; W. Drew; v2; 10/14/93
    filename: agri:drew

Animals; K. Boschert; v3.0; 06/01/94
    filename: animals:boschert

Anthropology, Cross Cultural Studies, & Archaeology; G. Bell; v8; 03/94
    filename: anthro:bell

Aquatic Biology; B. Brown; 05/18/94
    filename: aquabio:brown

Archaeology, Historic Preservation; P. Stott; v3.0; 06/10/94
    filename: archpres:stott
```

```
Architecture, Building; J. Brown; 05/23/94
   filename: archi:brown

Archives; D. Anthony, N. Kayne; v1; 12/93  (UMich)
   filename: archives:kaynthony

Art & Architecture; K. Robinson; v8; 03/94
   filename: artarch:robinson

Art. Intelligence, Expert Sys., Virtual Reality; M. Kovacs; v8; 03/94
   filename: csaiesvr:kovacsm

Astronomy; A. Park, J. Miller; v8; 03/94
--More--
   filename: astron:parkmiller
```

Moving from One Directory to Another

If you are not sure which directory you are in at an FTP site, type **pwd** at the `ftp>` prompt and the list of directories from the top public directory down to your current directory will appear.

To move from directory to directory at an FTP site, use one of these variations of the `cd` command:

```
Going down--

cd (subdirectory)/(lower subdirectory)/(still lower subdirectory)

For example cd /pub/education/university

Going up--

cd ..    (This will move you up one level in the directory tree.)

cd ../.. (This will move you up two levels in the directory tree.)

cd ../../.. (Three levels, and so on.)
```

Status

To get an FTP status report, at an `ftp>` prompt type **status** and press Enter. This shows the current settings of FTP's changeable parameters. Each FTP site selects is own defaults for these, but often you can change the settings. For more information on each of these parameters, see the following help section.

Generally, the most useful elements of this report are the indications of whether you are connected to an FTP site and, if so, which one it is, and whether FTP is in the binary mode.

```
ftp> status
Connected to una.hh.lib.umich.edu.
No proxy connection.
Mode: stream; Type: binary; Form: non-print; Structure: file
Verbose: on; Bell: off; Prompting: on; Globbing: on
Store unique: off; Receive unique: off
Case: off; CR stripping: on
Ntrans: off
Nmap: off
Hash mark printing: off; Use of PORT cmds: on
ftp>
```

Help

On many systems, you can display a help file by typing `help` or `?` and pressing Enter. This provides a good reminder of the available commands. To display a one-line description of each item type **help**, press the spacebar, and then enter the item shown on the commands list, such as `help binary`, or `help status`.

```
ftp> help
Commands may be abbreviated.  Commands are:

!           debug         mget        pwd         status
$           dir           mkdir       quit        struct
account     disconnect    mls         quote       system
append      form          mode        recvs       unique
ascii       get           modtime     reget       tenex
bell        glob          mput        rstatus     trace
binary      hash          newer       rhelp       type
bye         help          nmap        rename      user
case        idle          nlist       reset       umask
cd          image         ntrans      restart     verbose
cdup        lcd           open        rmdir       ?
chmod       ls            prompt      runique
close       macdef        proxy       send
cr          mdelete       sendport    site
delete      mdir          put         size
     ftp>
```

Determining Where Retrieved Files Are When the FTP Session Ends

If you didn't change to another directory on your access provider's computer before you started an FTP session, you can be assured that the files you are downloading will land in your home directory and will be displayed in that directory by typing the system's file list command (such as `ls` or `dir`).

If you moved among directories before starting FTP, you might want to check which directory you are currently using on your access provider's computer so that you will know where to find the newly downloaded files. You can do this from within an FTP session by typing **lcd** at the ftp> prompt and then pressing Enter. FTP then will display the directory to which it will download files.

```
ftp> lcd
Local directory now /home/foyer/oakridge
```

If by chance lcd does not work for you, try ldir—some systems vary in their use of these commands.

Downloading Batches of Files

Rather than typing individually the names of each file you want, you sometimes can use the mget command to save time. In the following excerpt from an FTP directory, note that there are three chemistry-related files. A chemist might want them all.

```
-rw-rw-r--  1 214      10       14574 Apr  4 21:08 astron:parkmiller
-rw-rw-r--  1 214      10       14328 Apr  4 21:08 bio:langendorfer
-rw-rw-r--  1 214      10       74206 May  4 13:22 biodivers:gordon
-rw-rw-r--  1 214      10       70602 Jun  6 19:29 bisexual:hamilton
-rw-rw-r--  1 214      10       72613 Jan  8  1994 blackafrican:mcgee
-rw-rw-r--  1 214      10       12350 Apr  4 21:08 bothort:langendorfer
-rw-rw-r--  1 214      10       44962 Jan 26 18:37 buddhism:ciolek
-rw-rw-r--  1 214      10       20367 Apr  4 21:08 business:haas
-rw-r--r--  1 214      10        7404 Oct 14  1993 business:newton-smith
-rw-rw-r--  1 214      10       25977 May  3 17:10 canada:cannon
-rw-rw-r--  1 214      10       17260 Apr  4 21:08 chem:parkmiller
-rw-rw-r--  1 214      10        4891 Feb  4 20:14 chemistry:andcol
-rw-rw-r--  1 214      10       42908 Jun 10 23:01 chemistry:wiggins
-rw-rw-r--  1 214      10       47691 Jun 10 22:58 christian:bogbru
-rw-rw-r--  1 214      10      152040 Jan 27 14:05 cmc:december
-rw-rw-r--  1 214      10       11130 Apr  4 21:08 commun:fehrmann
-rw-rw-r--  1 214      10       29551 Apr  4 21:08 compdisc:kovacsm
```

To download all three files using one command, type **mget**, press the spacebar, and then type the number of letters needed to include only the group you want and not exclude any files you want, followed with * (an asterisk, which is a wildcard character).

In this case, for example, **ch*** would have downloaded all three chemistry files, but it also would have the file below it (christian:bogbru). By adding just one more letter (che instead of ch) the chemistry files can be made a separate group.

```
ftp> mget che*
```

FTP's response to this command is to ask separately whether you want each file of this group downloaded. In the following example, the first two files were accepted for downloading by pressing **y** and the third one was rejected by pressing **n**.

```
mget chem:parkmiller? y
200 PORT command successful.
150 Opening data connection for chem:parkmiller (192.74.137.5,2863) (17260 bytes).
226 Transfer complete.
17260 bytes received in 0.51 seconds (33 Kbytes/s)
mget chemistry:andcol? y
200 PORT command successful.
150 Opening data connection for chemistry:andcol (192.74.137.5,2876) (4891 bytes).
226 Transfer complete.
4891 bytes received in 0.26 seconds (19 Kbytes/s)
mget chemistry:wiggins? n
ftp>
```

Mget also can save time getting individual files by enabling you to type just enough characters to the point where no other file in the list has an equivalent beginning. In the preceding example, you could enter mget chem:* to download the file chem:parkmiller.

Sending a File to a Remote Computer

You occasionally might want to send a file to and FTP site. Uploaded files usually are only accepted in one or two subdirectories. These directories often have a name such as incoming. To send a file, use FTP just as you would normally to get connected to a site to move to the subdirectory to which you will be uploading the file. Now, rather than using the get command, type the **put** command, press the spacebar, and then enter the name of the file on your access provider's computer that you want to upload.

If you have a group of files to upload, you can use the mput command in the same manner that you use mget.

Finishing an FTP Session

You can stop an FTP session anytime the ftp> prompt is available. Type **quit** or **bye** and press Enter. FTP is very polite and will say Goodbye to you and return you to your access provider's main prompt.

```
ftp> quit
221 Goodbye.
world%
```

Emergency Bail-out

If, for some reason, you cannot get FTP to respond to commands, you can leave FTP and return to your access provider's prompt by pressing and holding down Ctrl and then pressing **c**.

Private FTP

Many access providers will set up for you FTP sites that are password protected. Then, only you, and those to whom you give the password, will have access to the site. The commands and procedures work in same manner as anonymous FTP, with the exception of the password prompt that will be looking for a particular password, not for an e-mail address.

Discussion Lists

The e-mail discussion lists on the Internet began with the development of *BITNET*, for the educational-research community of the Internet to exchange information and ideas freely and quickly, built on topic areas. These e-mail based distribution groups now number in excess of 3,500, and cover almost any subject you can imagine—and a few you can't imagine.

These discussion lists have been compared to all types of things: faculty lounge discussions, meetings at the water cooler, conference presentations, and conversations. Every list has a look and feel of its own—how frequently people post, how formal their postings are, how long they are, how much flaming is tolerated, and other style issues.

The discussion lists can focus on virtually any topic and can be useful for getting help or cooperation on a project, obtaining up-to-date information, networking with colleagues, running down a resource, and more.

Lists may or may not be moderated. Unmoderated lists post all messages exactly as they come in, with no interference. On moderated lists, the moderator most likely screens postings for long, off-topic, or offensive postings. Open enrollment lists will accept any subscribers, while a closed list is for members of particular organizations, or who meet certain criteria.

When you join a list, you usually will receive back a couple of very useful messages that you should save. One message is your welcome aboard message with information on the lists, its purpose, any special features and rules, and often, the commands needed for unsubscribing and setting up your mail options. Another short message may arrive confirming your subscription details, including the account you used to subscribe. Save these messages! You will be glad that you did.

After you subscribe to a list, it is a good idea to read the messages before posting—get an idea of the tone and form of the group first. High traffic lists can generate 30 or more messages a day, so joining several these will jam your mailbox perhaps more quickly than you would like.

The List Versus the Listserver

The distinction between the *Listserver software* and the *list* itself is critical. The Listserver software is the clerical robot that handles the details of subscriptions; the list is the subscribers who make up the discussion. These two "entities" have different e-mail addresses. To send a message to the clerical software, address the e-mail as follows, where `address` is replaced by the actual site:

- `listserv@address`
- `listproc@address`
- `majordomo@address`
- `list-request@address` (where `list` is replaced by the name of the list)
- `mailserv@address`

To subscribe to the list *aednet*, for example, you would send an e-mail message, such as the following:

```
To: listserv@alpha.acast.nova.edu

with the subject blank, and a message of:

subscribe aednet Yourfirstname Yourlastname
```

My subscription would read `subscribe aednet Jill Ellsworth`.

To send a message to the entire group of people who are members of a list, you address it to the list name itself. For example, once I joined `aednet` (in the preceding example), I would use the following address: `aednet@alpha.acast.nova.edu`, and I *would* include a subject to help everyone know what I was talking about.

Using Listservers

There are several pieces of software used to manage the discussion lists—Listserv (sometimes also called BITNET Listserv), Listproc, a UNIX-based ListProcessor,

Majordomo, and Mailserv. You also may encounter Mailbase from the UK as well.

Each of these pieces of software responds to a set of commands to make them work. Nicely, the commands for subscribing (getting on) to a list and unsubscribing (or getting off) from a list are the same for all of these programs. They all take the form of `subscribe listname Yourfirstname Yourlastname,` except `majordomo` which just uses `subscribe listname`. They all take the form `unsubscribe listname`.

Each of these Listservers also support other commands for managing your mail options, obtaining information regarding subscribers, setting up your mail delivery options, and working with archived files related to the list.

Many lists allow its members to get a list of the current membership of the list. Following are the commands for that procedure, where `listname` is replaced by the actual name of the list:

```
listserv        review listname f=mail

listproc        recipients listname

majordomo       who listname

mailserv        send/list listname
```

Some lists archive all their messages into a database for retrieval and review. Normally, all postings are maintained, and various of the listservers have commands for working with those archives. To obtain a list of archive files, for example, use the following command for all Listservers:

`index listname`

Using Caution

Just a quick bit of advice. As you learn to use the lists and become more comfortable with the commands, it can be easy to use your mailer's **R**eply command rather too quickly.

Most mailers use the Reply feature to send your message out to the entire list, as opposed to the person who sent it to the list originally. On every list I have ever joined, someone inevitably sends a message to the whole list that actually was meant for one person. Imagine, if you will, a nice chatty letter to a friend or spouse appearing in thousands of e-mail boxes. Or worse yet a *catty* note about what a jerk Bob is....

Usenet Newsgroups

Usenet is an interesting phenomenon—people who describe it often use very different words to do so, almost like the blind men describing the elephant—what you say all depends on which groups you read.

Usenet is a worldwide distribution of discussions called *newsgroups*. No one entity "owns" Usenet—it is a self-regulating network of newsgroups, with rules for creating and maintaining groups. *News feeds* are paid for by sites.

Usenet involves groups of people reading and posting public messages (sometimes called articles), that are organized by subject category. `alt.education.distance`, for example, is a group for discussions and issues of interest to distance educators.

The Usenet messages are organized into more than 4,000 thousand topics. You read and post (contribute) at your local Usenet site, and that site distributes the postings to other sites.

The groups names are always lowercase, separated by periods (said "dot") such as, `misc.education`, `rec.reading`, `sci.education`, or for fun, `alt.fan.monty-python`. The topics are organized hierarchically—going from the general level to the more specific level, as is the following:

```
rec

rec.sports

rec.sports.baseball
```

Following is a quick overview of the Usenet naming scheme:

comp	Covers virtually all computer-related topics, including software, hardware, and systems
misc	Items that do not fit elsewhere
news	News of the Internet and networks
rec	Hobby, arts, and recreation
sci	For all the sciences, relating to research or application
soc	For social issues and culture
talk	Debate-oriented, unusual topics, and long discussions

Outside of the regular Usenet hierarchies, are many less regulated topics, relating to locations, cities, businesses, countries, or even universities, such as `tx.jobs` or `austin.forsale`.

To access Usenet, you need one of two things—the capability to telnet to another site enabling guest use of their newsreader, or a local system that runs a newsreader. *Newsreaders* are software that allows for thread tracking, and kill files to sort out what you *don't* want to read. Popular news readers are *tin, rn, nn,* and *trn.*

One of the best ways to approach Usenet is to begin reading some groups of interest to see how it works. Many newsgroups have a *FAQ* (Frequently Asked Questions) document chocked full of useful information about the newsgroup and its operation.

Following is an example of how my tin menu looked one day as I was reading groups.

```
Group Selection (13)                        h=help

 1  clari.nb.windows            Windows and Windows NT
 2  alt.books.technical         Technical Books
 3  clari.nb.general            Newsbytes general computer news
 4  clari.news.education        Primary and secondary education
 5  clari.news.education.higher Colleges and universities
 6  alt.education.distance      Distance Education
 7  list.hyperedu               Hypermedia in Education
 8  list.novae-projects         K-12 projects
 9  alt.education.research       Educational Research
10  clari.nb.education          Computers in education
11  clari.nb.online             Online services, the Internet, BBS
12  biz.comp.services           Business Computer Services
13  misc.education.adult        Adult Education


<n>=set current to n, TAB=next unread, /=search pattern, c)atchup,
g)oto, j=line down, k=line up, h)elp, m)ove, q)uit,
r=toggle all/unread, s)ubscribe, S)ub pattern, u)nsubscribe,
U)nsub pattern, y)ank in/out
```

Most newsreaders have some similar commands, such as the following *tin Newsreader Commands—Newsgroup Reading*, to assist you in managing your newsgroup reading:

G	Go to a particular group
TAB	Move to the next unread article
H	Help
Q	Quit reading
C	Set the group to `all seen`
s	Subscribe to this group
u	Unsubscribe to this group
/	Search for *string*

While reading articles in virtually all newsreaders, there are commands for managing the read and posting of messages. Each reader has different commands, but as an example, using the `tin` reader, the following are useful for keeping and managing messages:

f	Post a follow-up message
m	Mail an article to yourself or another person
r	Send a message to the person who posted the article
s	Save the message or thread to a file
w	To create a new posting

World Wide Web (WWW)

World Wide Web (WWW) was started at the European Laboratory for Particle Physics, in a project designed to use the Internet for hypertext. World Wide Web (WWW or W3) is a system of linking documents by way of hypertext and hypermedia. To use the Web, you must use what is called a *browser*, such as Lynx, Mosaic, or Cello.

Hypertext provides a way to move from link-to-link, or item-to-item. A link might be a document, an image, or a site through specially marked documents. The user can open other documents or items by clicking or using the arrow keys to move around. Hypermedia is a mixture of text, images, sound files, and so on.

HyperText Markup Language (HTML) is the format needed for documents to be placed on the Web for use with Lynx and Mosaic. The information on the links are embedded in HTML documents. Using Lynx (a text-based browsers) some of the links appear as numbers in brackets (`[4]`), and image links appear as `[IMAGE]`, while in Mosaic, these will appear as buttons or icons and actual images.

There currently are two browsers that are most often used to access the Web: *Lynx* and *Mosaic*. Both are capable of making use of the Internet hypertext transfer protocols: HyperText Transfer Protocol (HTTP).

When using a graphical interface for the Web, such as Mosaic, you can access the WWW functions with a mouse, clicking on items to view or retrieve. In line mode, as with Lynx (text only), the selection of items is done with the arrows on the keypad, moving down, up, left, and right to follow the links.

If you do not have a WWW browser on your system, you can use Lynx as a guest at one the following sites.

Where to find it

Telnet (and login as www)

> ukanaix.cc.ukans.edu (USA)
>
> fatty.law.cornell.edu (USA)
>
> www.njit.edu (USA)
>
> vms.huji.ac.il (Israel (dual language))
>
> info.cern.ch (Switzerland (CERN))

Like so many topics on the Net, there is a FAQ on WWW.

Where to find it

FTP	rtfm.mit.edu
Directory	/pub/usenet/news.answers/www
File	faq

This FAQ is maintained very regularly, and so has the latest information on WWW.

> **Tip:** When you are connected to rtfm.mit.edu (MIT), don't call for a directory by using dir or ls to look at the subdirectory /usenet—it is a *very* long listing, and you will sit through many, many screens.)

Lynx

Perhaps the most useful WWW browser is *Lynx*. It the lowest common denominator. You only need a machine capable of VT100 emulation, monochrome monitor, and low-end Internet access to make use of it. From the University of Kansas, it gives a user-friendly interface for hypertext WWW.

There are some useful keys to be aware of when using Lynx. The arrow keys navigate up and down on the current pages, while the right arrow follows a link to a new page. The left arrow returns you to the previous link, and the spacebar will move you to the next page. Figure A.3 Shows the WWW Homepage using Lynx.

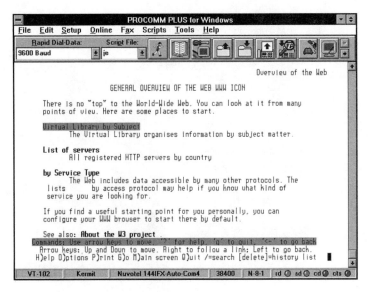

Figure A.3. The WWW Homepage as shown on Lynx.

Following are some other Lynx commands:

?	Help
P	Print, save or mail a file
O	Set up your options
G	Go to prompt for entering your own URLs
M	Return to the main screen
/	Search for a string
Q	Quit Lynx
D	Download an image or file

Mosaic

The other common browser for WWW is *Mosaic*. A high-end colorful interface, Mosaic for Windows requires a direct connection to the Internet or a special dial-up connection such as SLIP, a VGA monitor, and Microsoft Windows 3.1. Unlike Lynx, you cannot run Mosaic by telnetting to another location. Figure A.4 shows the opening page of Mosaic for Windows, with its graphical interface, mouse capabilities, and pull-down menus. Mosaic is available in versions for Windows, UNIX, and Macintosh, with other platforms and versions under development.

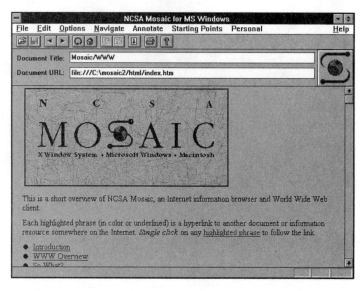

Figure A.4. The Mosaic Homepage.

Mosaic is a World Wide Web browser that is dynamic and makes full use of the capabilities of documents prepared using HyperText Markup Language (HTML). HyperText Markup Language embeds information in documents about formatting, style, color, and linkages to inline images and sounds using special files.

Connections made with Mosaic permit full media interaction (although a bit slowly), offering an Internet equivalent to multimedia on desktop computers. The Windows version features the usual Windows-style pull-down menus.

Mosaic is a rather new browser, but look for it to become more popular as new versions emerge. For schools, Lynx is the preferred browser at this time because of its low-end access requirements and it is easier on Internet resources.

And in Summation, Class....

Having learned about the basic tools of the Internet, it is time to try out those news skills. Your homework tonight is to get out there on the Net.

Class dismissed!

The ERIC System

ERIC (Educational Resources Information Center) is a nationwide information network that provides access to education literature. The ERIC system consists of 16 Clearinghouses, 6 Adjunct Clearinghouses, and system support components that include the ERIC Processing and Reference Facility, ACCESS ERIC, and the ERIC Document Reproduction Service (EDRS).

ERIC collects a large range of materials including papers, conference proceedings, literature reviews, and curriculum materials from researchers, practitioners, educational associations and institutions, and federal, state, and local agencies.

These materials, along with articles from more than 800 different journals, are indexed and abstracted for entry into the ERIC database. The ERIC database now contains almost 800,000 records of documents and journal articles. The materials are maintained in hard copy and microfiche, but all the current indices and abstracts are online on the Internet. Selected materials, digests, and reports also are available online as full-text. There has been significant migration of materials to electronic format.

The information contained in ERIC is of use to teachers and researchers at all levels in the educational system, and to parents as well.

ERIC is available through numerous libraries on the Internet, but the best access on the Internet is through the ERIC Gopher at `ericicr.syr.edu`, as follows:

```
         Internet Gopher v0.6 Copyright 1991 Univ. of Minnesota
                           Root Directory

    --     1.  News and Information about ERIC and AskERIC/
           2.  Map of the Library/
           3.  Search AskERIC Menu Items> <?<
           4.  Frequently Asked Questions (FAQ's)/
           5.  AskERIC InfoGuides/
           6.  Lesson Plans/
           7.  Education Listservs Archives/
           8.  ERIC Clearinghouses/Components/
           9.  ERIC Digests File/
          10.  ERIC Bibliographic Database (RIE and CIJE)/
          11.  ERIC Full Text Prototype (Experimental)/
          12.  Bibliographies/
          13.  Other Education Resources/
          14.  Professional Organizations/
          15.  Education Conferences (Calendars and Announcements)/
          16.  Electronic Journals, Books, and Reference Tools/
          17.  Internet Guides and Directories/
          18.  Gophers and Library Catalogs/
```

At the University of Maryland, ERIC is available for any Internet user. The opening screen of the ERIC sector is as follows:

```
-------------------- ERIC ------------------------------------
           Educational Resources Information Center

ERIC is a national information system which provides access to all aspects of
education.  Resources in Education (RIE) offers access to current research find-
ings, unpublished manuscripts, books, and technical reports.  Current Index to
Journals in Education (CIJE) covers current periodical literature. Both indexing
sources use the controlled subject headings outlined in the ERIC Thesaurus.  These
files contain the records for the complete ERIC database.

              70.  ERIC Thesaurus
              71.  ERIC RIE
                   (Resources in Education
              72.  ERIC CIJE
                   (Current Index to Journals in Education)
              73.  ERIC Combined
                   (RIE and CIJE)


  Enter the number of your choice, and press the <RETURN> key:
```

You may choose to use the thesaurus to find search terms, and then to search just the ERIC document system, or to combine your search with the Current Index to Journals in Education (CIJE). I selected the ERIC Combined to get results from the database and from the journals.

```
SELECTED DATABASE:  ERIC Combined


 The ERIC Combined database offers access to Resources in Education (RIE) and
Current Index to Journals in Education (CIJE), which are both part of ERIC, a
national information system which indexes materials on all aspects of education.
This database offers access to generally  unpublished materials and current
periodical literature.  The ERIC  Thesaurus serves as the list of controlled
subject headings.
To start your search, type:
                 N    for  NAME search
                 W    for  WORD search
                 B    for  BROWSE title
                 NB   for  NAME browse
                 SB   for  SUBJECT browse
                 SW   for  SUBJECT WORD SEARCH
                 S    to   STOP
      There is also a quick search--type QS or QS2 for details


            SELECTED DATABASE:  ERIC Combined

ENTER  COMMAND (use  //EXIT  to return HOME)>>
```

I selected to search for items containing improving reading.

```
>improving reading

IMPROVING + READING   449 ITEMS   ERIC Combined

Result sets larger than 300 items will not be sorted.


You may make your search more specific  (and reduce
the size of the list)  by adding another word
to your search. The result will be items in
your current list that also contain the new
word. You may also choose to limit by ERIC
context.
```

Because the search resulted in 449 items, and I did not want to wade through all 449, I decided to go ahead and further restrict the search by adding the term elementary.

```
To ADD a new word, enter it below and press <RETURN>, or

Type <D>isplay and press <RETURN> to see the current list, or

     <L>imit by ERIC context

Type <Q>uit and press <RETURN> to begin a new search


NEW WORD(S): Elementary

  1 Sanchez Esther                          ERIC       06/93
     Improving Comprehension and Reading Vocabulary i ED363123

  2 Coakley Barbara Fair                     ERIC       1993
     Improving the Academic Achievement of Third and  ED356071

  3 Saykanic Donna M                         ERIC       1993
     Improving Library Resources in an Elementary Med ED365317

  4 Wolf Shelby                              ERIC       1993
     "Writing What You Read": A Guidebook for the Ass ED364584

  5 Kolstad Rosemarie                        ERIC       1993
     Improving the Teaching of Fractions.     See full record

  6 Kaminsky Debra E                         ERIC       1993
     Helping Elementary English as a Second Language  ED365110

  7 Crosby Judith C                          ERIC     12/01/92
     Menu Strategy for Improving School Behavior of S ED359676

 <RETURN> To Continue Display
Enter <Line number(s)> To Display Full Records
<P>revious For Previous Page OR <Q>uit For New Search
```

To look at an entry, enter the line number of the item, and you will see similar to the following:

```
-------------------------ERIC Combined--------------
ERIC Number:    ED339786
AUTHOR(s):      Herrick, Susan C.
                Epstein, Joyce L.
TITLE(s):       Improving School and Family Partnerships in Urban
                   Elementary Schools: Reading Activity Packets and School
                   Newsletters. Report No. 19.
ERIC Issue:     RIEAPR92
Date:           Aug 91
Description:    54p.
Pub. Type:      Reports - Research/Technical
                Tests, Questionnaires, Evaluation Instruments
Abstract: This publication includes two reports describing the
    development and beginning evaluations of two separate
    programs of the Baltimore (Maryland) School and Family
    Connections Project designed to increase parents'
    involvement in their children's learning in urban
    elementary schools. The first report, "Reactions of Parents
    and Teachers to Reading Activity Packets in the Primary
    Grades" (S. C. Herrick and J. L. Epstein), examines the
    involvement in their children's learning in urban
    elementary schools. The first report, "Reactions of Parents
    and Teachers to Reading Activity Packets in the Primary
    Grades" (S. C. Herrick and J. L. Epstein), examines the
    reactions of 158 parents and 7 teachers to the Teachers
    Getting Involved with Families program at Elmer A.
    Henderson Elementary School(Maryland), which developed
    reading activity packets to help parents assist their
    children in reading at home. The second report, "Reactions
    of Parents to School Newsletters in the Elementary Grades".
    (S. C. Herrick and J. L. Epstein), examines the reactions of
    parents (70 families) to the I Care Parent Newsletter
    program at Dr. Bernard Harris, Sr. Elementary
    School (Maryland), which created and distributed
    newsletters to parents to make them feel welcome at school,
    inform them about the curriculum and their children's
    progress, and stimulate parents and children to read
    together. Both programs were viewed as successful in
    reaching parents and involving them more actively in their
    children's learning. Both programs are being revised and
    extended and will be evaluated in the future for their
    effects on student learning.
    Statistical data are provided in two tables. Two appendices
    children's learning. Both programs are being revised and
    extended and will be evaluated in the future for their
    effects on student learning.
    Statistical data are provided in two tables. Two appendices
    to the first report contain the teacher interview form, the
    parents' survey, and responses. Four appendices to the
    second report contain the survey and parent responses.
    (SLD)
```

```
Geogr. source:   U.S.; Maryland
                 Available in paper copy and microfiche.
                 EDRS Price - MF01/PC03 Plus Postage.
Contract no.:    OERI-R117R90002
Major descript:  *Educational Improvement
                 *Elementary Schools
                 *Newsletters
                 *Parent Participation
                 *Reading Achievement
                 *Urban Schools
Minor descript:  Educationally Disadvantaged
                 Elementary School Students
                 Intermediate Grades
                 Parent Attitudes
                 Parent Education
                 Parent School Relationship
Contract no.:    OERI-R117R90002
Major descript:  *Educational Improvement
                 *Elementary Schools
                 *Newsletters
                 *Parent Participation
                 *Reading Achievement
                 *Urban Schools
Minor descript:  Educationally Disadvantaged
                 Elementary School Students
                 Intermediate Grades
                 Parent Attitudes
                 Parent Education
                 Parent School Relationship
                 Primary Education
                 Program Evaluation
                 Teacher Attitudes
Identifiers:     *Baltimore City Public Schools MD
Institution:     Center for Research on Effective Schooling for
                   Disadvantaged Students, Baltimore, MD.
Sponsor Agcy:    Office of Educational Research and Improvement (ED), Washington,
                 DC.
```

You also can order from EDRS reprints of ERIC documents, on microfiche or in paper copy (see *Support Services*).

Educational Resources Information Center (ERIC)

Dues	None
Publications	*Resources in Education*
	Current Index to Journals in Education (CIJE)
	ERIC (Educational Resources Information Center)
	Office of Educational Research and Improvement (OERI)

Where to find it

E-mail   `eric@inet.ed.gov`
Phone   202/219-2289
Fax   202/219-1817

U.S. Department of Education
555 New Jersey Avenue NW
Washington, DC 20208-5720

ERIC Clearinghouses

The 16 ERIC Clearinghouses are organized by subject areas. Each of the following listings include the full mailing address, telephone number(s), fax number, e-mail address, director's name, and a brief description of the topic areas covered by that Clearinghouse.

ERIC Clearinghouse on Adult, Career, and Vocational Education

This contains all levels of adult and continuing education from basic literacy training through professional skill upgrading. The focus is on factors contributing to the purposeful learning of adults in a variety of situations usually related to adult roles (such as occupation, family, leisure time, citizenship, organizational relationships, retirement, and so on). This also includes input from the Adjunct ERIC Clearinghouse on Consumer Education.

Where to find it

E-mail   `ericacve@magnus.acs.ohio-state.edu`
Phone   614/292-4353
           800/848-4815
Fax   614/292-1260

Ohio State University
Center on Education and Training for Employment
1900 Kenny Road
Columbus, Ohio 43210-1090

Susan Imel, Director

ERIC Clearinghouse on Assessment and Evaluation

All aspects of tests and other measurement devices. The design and methodology of research, measurement, and evaluation. The evaluation of programs and projects. The application of tests, measurement, and evaluation devices/instrumentation in education projects and programs.

Where to find it

E-mail   eric_ae@cua.edu
Phone   202/319-5120
Fax   202/319-6692

Catholic University of America
210 O'Boyle Hall
Washington, DC 20064-4035

Lawrence M. Rudner, Director

ERIC Clearinghouse for Community Colleges

This Clearinghouse covers development, administration, and evaluation of two-year public and private community and junior colleges, technical institutes, and two-year branch university campuses. It also addresses two-year college students, faculty, staff, curricula, programs, support services, libraries, and community services. There are linkages between two-year colleges and business/industrial/community organizations. This also includes articulation of two-year colleges with secondary and four-year post-secondary institutions.

Where to find it

E-mail   eeh3usc@mvs.oac.ucla.edu

Phone   310/825-3931
         800/832-8256
Fax   310/206-8095

University of California at Los Angeles (UCLA)
3051 Moore Hall
Los Angeles, California 90024-1521

Arthur M. Cohen, Director

ERIC Clearinghouse on Counseling and Student Services

Covers preparation, practice, and supervision of counselors at all educational levels and in all settings. Includes theoretical development of counseling and guidance, including the nature of relevant human characteristics. Addresses group process (counseling, therapy, dynamics) and case work. Also includes the use and results of personnel practices and procedures.

Where to find it

E-mail   ericcass@iris.uncg.edu
Phone   919/334-4114
          800/414-9769
Fax   919/334-4116

University of North Carolina at Greensboro
School of Education
Greensboro, North Carolina 27412-5001

Garry R. Walz, Director

ERIC Clearinghouse on Disabilities and Gifted Education

This Clearinghouse covers all aspects of the education and development of persons (of all ages) who have disabilities or who are gifted, including the delivery of all types of education-related services to these groups. It includes prevention, identification and assessment, intervention, and enrichment for these groups in both regular and special education settings.

Where to find it

E-mail   ericec@inet.ed.gov

Phone   703/264-9474

Fax   703/264-9494

Council for Exceptional Children (CEC)

1920 Association Drive

Reston, Virginia 22091-1589

Bruce Ramirez, Acting Director

ERIC Clearinghouse on Educational Management

Covers all aspects of the governance, leadership, administration, and structure of public and private educational organizations at the elementary and secondary levels, including the provision of physical facilities for their operation.

Where to find it

E-mail   ppiele@oregon.uoregon.edu

Phone   503/346-5043

                800/438-8841

Fax   503/346-2334

University of Oregon

1787 Agate Street

Eugene, Oregon 97403-5207

Philip K. Piele, Director

ERIC Clearinghouse on Elementary and Early Childhood Education

Includes all aspects of the physical, cognitive, social, educational, and cultural development of children, from birth through early adolescence. Among the topics covered are prenatal and infant development and care; parent education; home and school relationships; learning theory research and practice related to children's development; preparation of early childhood teachers and care givers; and educational programs and community services for children.

Where to find it

E-mail   ericeece@ux1.cso.uiuc.edu

Phone   217/333-1386

Fax   217/333-3767

University of Illinois

805 West Pennsylvania Avenue

Urbana, Illinois 61801-4897

Lilian G. Katz, Director

ERIC Clearinghouse on Higher Education

Covers all aspects of the conditions, programs, and problems at colleges and universities providing higher education (such as four-year degrees and beyond). This includes governance and management, planning, finance, inter-institutional arrangements, business or industry programs leading to a degree, institutional research at the college/university level, Federal programs, legal issues and legislation, professional education (such as medicine and law), and professional continuing education.

Where to find it

E-mail   eriche@inet.ed.gov

Phone   202/296-2597

Fax   202/296-8379

George Washington University

One Dupont Circle NW, Suite 630

Washington, DC 20036-1183

Jonathan D. Fife, Director

ERIC Clearinghouse on Information and Technology

Covers educational technology and library and information science at all academic levels and with all populations, including the preparation of professionals. Includes the media and devices of educational communication as they pertain to teaching and learning in both conventional and distance education settings. This Clearinghouse also includes the operation and management of libraries and information services. Addresses all aspects of information management and information technology related to education.

Where to find it

E-mail	eric@ericir.syr.edu
Phone	315/443-3640
	800/464-9107
Fax	315/443-5448

Center for Science and Technology 4-194

Syracuse University

Syracuse, New York 13244-4100

Michael B. Eisenberg, Director

Internet-based education question answering service

AskERIC

E-mail	AskERIC@ericir.syr.edu
Phone	315/443-9114
Fax	315/443-5448

ERIC Clearinghouse on Languages and Linguistics

Covers languages and language sciences. Embraces all aspects of second language instruction and learning in all commonly and uncommonly taught languages, including English as a second language. Covers bilingualism and bilingual education. Covers cultural education in the context of second language learning, including intercultural communication, study abroad, and international educational exchange. Addresses all areas of linguistics, including theoretical and applied linguistics, sociolinguistics, and psycholinguistics. Includes input from the Adjunct ERIC Clearinghouse on Literacy Education for Limited-English-Proficient Adults.

Where to find it

E-mail   jeannie@cal.org
Phone   202/429-9292
Fax   202/659-5641

Center for Applied Linguistics (CAL)
1118 22nd Street NW
Washington, DC 20037-0037

Charles Stansfield, Director

ERIC Clearinghouse on Reading, English, and Communication

Covers reading and writing, English (as a first language), and communications skills (verbal and nonverbal), kindergarten through college. Includes family or intergenerational literacy. Research and instructional development in reading, writing, speaking, and listening. Also includes identification, diagnosis, and remediation of reading problems, speech communication (including forensics), mass communication (including journalism), interpersonal and small group interaction, oral interpretation, rhetorical and communication theory, and theater/drama. Also covers preparation of instructional staff and related personnel in all the preceding areas.

Where to find it

E-mail   ericcs@ucs.indiana.edu
Phone   812/855-5847
          800/759-4723
Fax   812/855-4220

Indiana University
Smith Research Center, Suite 150
2805 East 10th Street
Bloomington, Indiana 47408-2698

Carl B. Smith, Director

ERIC Clearinghouse on Rural Education and Small Schools

Covers curriculum and instructional programs and research/evaluation efforts that address the education of students in rural schools or districts, small schools wherever located, and schools of districts wherever located that serve American Indian and Alaskan natives, Mexican Americans, and migrants, or that have programs related to outdoor education. Includes the cultural, ethnic, linguistic, economic, and social conditions that affect these educational institutions and groups. Provides preparation programs, including related services, that train education professionals to work in such contexts.

Where to find it

E-mail	u56d9@wvnvm.wvnet.edu
Phone	304/347-0465
	800/624-9120
Fax	304/347-0487

Appalachia Educational Laboratory (AEL)

1031 Quarrier Street, P.O. Box 1348

Charleston, West Virginia 25325-1348

Craig Howley, Director

ERIC Clearinghouse for Science, Mathematics, and Environmental Education

Covers science, mathematics, engineering/technology and environmental education at all levels. Also includes the following topics when focused on any of the above broad scope areas: applications of learning theory; curriculum and instructional materials; teachers and teacher education; educational programs and projects; research and evaluative studies; and applications of educational technology and media.

Where to find it

E-mail	ericse@osu.edu
Phone	614/292-6717
Fax	614/292-0263

Ohio State University

1929 Kenny Road

Columbus, Ohio 43210-1080

David L. Haury, Director

ERIC Clearinghouse for Social Studies/Social Science Education

Covers all aspects of social studies and social science education, including values education (and the social aspects of environmental education and sex education), comparative education, and cross-cultural studies in all subject areas (K-12). Includes ethnic heritage, gender equity, aging, and social bias/discrimination topics. Also covered are music, art, and architecture as related to the fine arts. Includes input from the Adjunct ERIC Clearinghouse for U.S.-Japan Studies.

Where to find it

E-mail   ericso@ucs.indiana.edu

Phone   812/855-3838

        800/266-3815

Fax   812/855-0455

Indiana University

Social Studies Development Center

2805 East 10th Street, Suite 120

Bloomington, Indiana 47408-2698

John Patrick, Director

ERIC Clearinghouse on Teaching and Teacher Education

Covers school personnel at all levels. Embraces teacher recruitment, selection, licensing, certification, training, preservice and inservice preparation, evaluation, retention, and retirement. Also covers the theory, philosophy, and practice of teaching. Includes organization, administration, finance, and legal issues relating to teacher education programs and institutions. Addresses all aspects of health, physical, recreation, and dance education.

Where to find it

E-mail   dstewart@inet.ed.gov

Phone   202/293-2450

Fax   202/457-8095

American Association of Colleges for Teacher Education (AACTE)

One Dupont Circle NW, Suite 610

Washington, DC 20036-1186

Mary E. Dilworth, Director

ERIC Clearinghouse on Urban Education

Covers the educational characteristics and experiences of the diverse racial, ethnic, social class, and linguistic populations in urban (and suburban) schools. Includes curriculum for and instruction of students from these populations and the organization of their schools. Embraces the relationship of urban schools to their communities. Also covers the social and economic conditions that affect the education of urban populations, with particular attention to factors that place urban students at risk educationally, and ways that public and private sector policies can improve these conditions.

Where to find it

E-mail   lry2@columbia.edu

Phone   212/678-3433

           800/601-4868

Fax   212/678-4048

Teachers College, Columbia University

Institute for Urban and Minority Education

Main Hall, Room 303, Box 40

525 West 120th Street

New York, New York 10027-9998

Erwin Flaxman, Director

Adjunct ERIC Clearinghouses

The six adjunct Clearinghouses provide more limited and specialized services and often have strong relationships for referral and dissemination to one or more of the primary ERIC Clearinghouses. Each listing includes the mailing address, telephone number(s), fax number, and e-mail address.

Adjunct ERIC Clearinghouse on Chapter 1 (Compensatory Education)

Where to find it

E-mail	prcinc@delphi.com
Phone	317/244-8160
	800/456-2380
Fax	317/244-7386

Chapter 1 Technical Assistance Center
PRC Inc.
2601 Fortune Circle East
One Park Fletcher Building, Suite 300-A
Indianapolis, Indiana 46241-2237

Adjunct ERIC Clearinghouse on Clinical Schools

Where to find it

E-mail	iabdalha@inet.ed.gov
Phone	202/293-2450
Fax	202/457-8095

American Association of Colleges for Teacher Education
One Dupont Circle NW, Suite 610
Washington, DC 20036-1186

Adjunct ERIC Clearinghouse on Consumer Education

Where to find it

E-mail   cse_bonner@emunix.emich.edu

Phone   313/487-2292

          800/336-6423

Fax   313/487-7153

National Institute for Consumer Education

207 Rackham Building, West Circle Drive

Eastern Michigan University

Ypsilanti, Michigan 48197-2237

Adjunct ERIC Clearinghouse for ESL Literacy Education

Where to find it

E-mail   cal@guvax.georgetown.edu

Phone   202/429-9292, Ext. 200

Fax   202/659-5641

National Clearinghouse for Literacy Education (NCLE)

Center for Applied Linguistics (CAL)

1118 22nd Street NW

Washington, DC 20037

Adjunct ERIC Clearinghouse for United States–Japan Studies

Where to find it

E-mail   eabrooks@ucs.indiana.edu

Phone   812/855-3838

Fax   812/855-0455

Indiana University
Social Studies Development Center
2805 East 10th Street, Suite 120
Bloomington, Indiana 47408-2698

Adjunct ERIC Clearinghouse on Law Related Education (LRE)

Where to find it

E-mail   ericso@ucs.indiana.edu
Phone   812/855-3838
Fax   812/855-0455

Indiana University
2805 East 10th Street, Suite 120
Bloomington, Indiana 47408-2698

Robert Leming, Co-Director

Support Services

The following support services are both within and outside of the ERIC System.
Document indexing, reproduction, preparation for publication, database development, document sales and delivery are provided in the following locations.

Article Reproduction Clearinghouses (non-ERIC)

Where to find it

University Microfilms International (UMI)

E-mail   No service
Phone   800/521-0600 x2786

Article Clearinghouse
300 North Zeeb Road

Ann Arbor, Michigan 48106

$12.50 per article with no length restrictions

Institute for Scientific Information (ISI)

Give complete citation, and account information, or your phone number so that you can be called for billing instructions. $10.25 for first 10 pages, $2.75 for each next 10.

Where to find it

E-mail   tga@isinet.com

Phone   800/523-1850, Ext. 1142

Genuine Article Service

3501 Market Street

Philadelphia, Pennsylvania 19104

ERIC Document Reproduction Service (EDRS)

Operates the document delivery arm of the ERIC system. Furnishes microfiche and/or paper copies of most ERIC documents. Address purchase orders to the following address. Fax order and delivery service available.

Where to find it

E-mail   edrs@gwuvm.gwu.edu

Phone   800/443-ERIC (3742)

             703/440-1400

Fax   703/440-1408

CBIS Federal Inc. (Cincinnati Bell Information Systems)

7420 Fullerton Road, Suite 110

Springfield, Virginia 22153-2852

Peter M. Dagutis, Director

ERIC Reference, Indexing, and Database Development

ERIC offers several reference, indexing and database development services of use to educators.

ERIC Processing and Reference Facility

A centralized information processing facility serving all components of the ERIC network, under policy direction of Central ERIC. Services provided include acquisitions, editing, receiving and dispatch, document control and analysis, lexicography, computer processing, file maintenance, and database management.

Receives and edits abstracts from 16 ERIC Clearinghouses for publication in Resources in Education (RIE); updates and maintains the Thesaurus of ERIC Descriptors.

Publications   *Resources in Education*

Source Directory

Report Number Index

Clearinghouse Number/ED Number Cross Reference

Title Index

ERIC Processing Manual

Several other listings and indexes

Where to find it

E-mail   ericfac@inet.ed.gov

Phone   301/258-5500

800/799-ERIC (3742)

Fax   301/948-3695

ARC Professional Services Group

Information Systems Group

1301 Piccard Drive, Suite 300

Rockville, Maryland 20850-4305

Ted Brandhorst, Director

ACCESS ERIC

This is a toll-free service that provides access to the information and services available through the ERIC system. Staff will answer questions as well as refer callers to education sources. ACCESS ERIC also produces several publications and reference and referral databases that provide information about both the ERIC system and current education-related issues and research.

Publications	*A Pocket Guide to ERIC*
	All About ERIC
	The ERIC Review
	The Conclusion Brochure Series
	Catalog of ERIC Clearinghouse Publications
	ERIC Calendar of Education-Related Conferences
	ERIC User's Interchange
	Directory of ERIC Information Service Centers
Databases	ERIC Digests Online (EDO)
	Education-Related Information Centers
	ERIC Information Service Providers
	ERIC Calendar of Education-Related Conferences

Where to find it

E-mail	acceric@inet.ed.gov
Phone	301/251-5506
	800/LET-ERIC (538-3742)
Fax	301/251-5767

Aspen Systems Corporation
1600 Research Boulevard
Rockville, Maryland 20850-3172

Beverly Swanson, ERIC Project Director

Thesaurus and CIJE (Current Index to Journals in Education) Publishing

Where to find it

E-mail   `arhjb@asuvm.inre.asu.edu`

Phone   602/265-2651

           800/279-ORYX (6799)

Fax   800/279-4663 or 602/265-6250

Oryx Press, Suite 700

4041 North Central Avenue at Indian School

Phoenix, Arizona 85012-3397

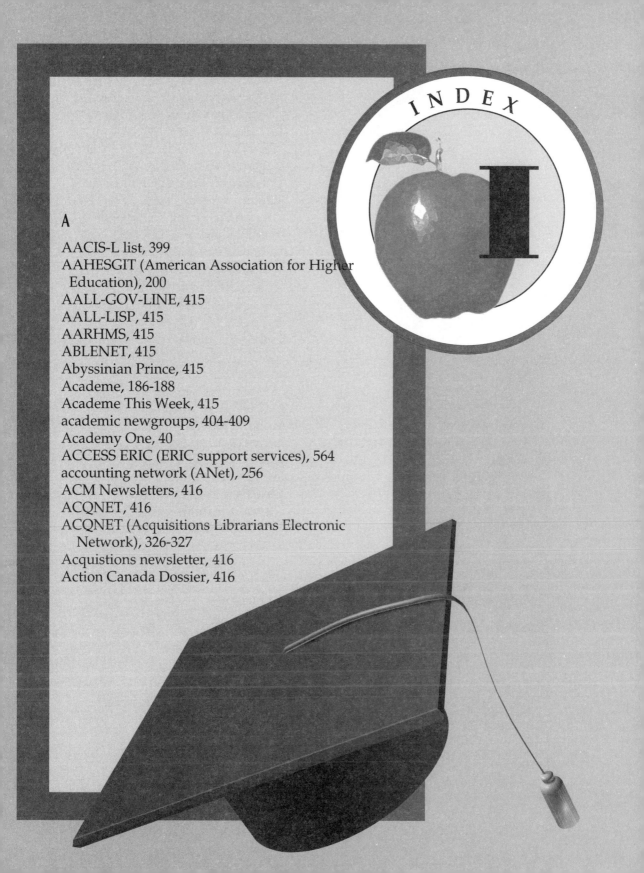

INDEX

A

M